SOCIAL DEMOCRACY
AND STATE FOUNDATION

Tobias Mörschel (Ed.)

SOCIAL DEMOCRACY AND STATE FOUNDATION

The emergence of a
new European state landscape
after the First World War

Bibliographical information of the German National Library

The German National Library catalogues this publication in the German National Bibliography; detailed bibliographic information can be found on the internet at: http://dnb.dnb.de.

ISBN 978-3-8012-0555-3

Copyright © 2019 by
Verlag J.H.W. Dietz Nachf. GmbH
Dreizehnmorgenweg 24, D-53175 Bonn, Germany

Cover design: Antje Haack | Lichten, Hamburg
Typesetting and infographics: Ralf Schnarrenberger, Hamburg
Map: Peter Palm, Berlin
Printing and processing: CPI books, Leck

All rights reserved
Printed in Germany 2019

Find us on the internet: www.dietz-verlag.de

Tobias Mörschel –
Social Democracy and State Foundation   11

An Introduction   11
Structure of the book   16

Mikko Majander –
Social Democracy and Nation-building in Finland   19

The Breakthrough   19
Independence   22
The Civil War   24
The Second Coming   25
Resilient Democracy   29
Legacy   32
Summary   33

Tõnu Ints / Kristjan Saharov –
The Inception of Social Democracy and Statehood in Estonia   35

Social Democracy prior to Independence   35
The Road to Independence   38
Building the New State   45
The Subsequent Role of the Social Democrats   51
A Look Back at the Achievements of the Social Democrats   57
Summary   59

Ivars Ījabs –
Latvian Statehood and Social Democracy   65

The New Agenda: Socialism and Latvian National Movement   67
Social Democracy and Statehood   77
Social Democracy and 18 November   85
The LSDSP and the Independent State   90
The Demise and Legacy of the LSDSP   98
Conclusion   101
Summary   104

Gintaras Mitrulevičius –
Social Democracy in the Formation of the Modern Lithuanian State   109

Introduction   109
Historical Context of Lithuanian Social Democracy and
  Ideological-Programmatic Assumptions and Political Aspirations   109
Role of the Social Democrats in the (Re)Construction of
  the Lithuanian State (1914–1919)   119
Social Democracy in the Consolidation
  of Lithuanian Statehood (1920–1922)   125
Summary   129

Anatol Sidarevič –
The Socialist Movement in Belarus and Belarusian Statehood   133

Introduction   133
BRH/BSH: First Programme – Hramada and
  other Socialist Parties in Belarus and Lithuania   136
Common Russian Revolutionary Movement: The Second Programme   139
Hramada's Cultural Formation and Nation Building   145
Shaping an Independent Belarusian-Lithuanian State   147
BSH in Eastern Belarus: The Party's Third Programme   149
October 1917–March 1918: Declaring the Belarusian People's Republic   152
Declaring Independence and the Break-Up of the BSH   155
Belarusian Communists and Bolsheviks:
  Birth and Death of the SSR of Belarus   158
Anton Łuckievič's Efforts, The Great Powers and Poland   161
Another SSRB: From Soviet Belarus to the Republic of Belarus   164
Summary   166

Yaroslav Hrytsak –
Ukrainian Social Democracy and the Ukrainian
Nation-State in 1917–1920   169

1899–1916: Genesis and Beginning of Ukrainian Social Democracy   169
1917: The Year of the Ukrainian Socialist Miracle   175
1918: In Opposition to a Conservative Regime   178

1919–1920: In a War of All against All 181
After 1921: Consequences and Challenges 184
Summary 188

Levan Lortkipanidze – Social Democracy and State Foundation: The Georgian Example 191

The Social Democratic Movement before Independence 191
The Social Democratic Party of Georgia in the First Republic 200
Social Democracy and Modern Georgia 208
Summary 210

Michał Syska – The Polish Socialist Party: Independence, Democracy, Social Justice 213

The Beginnings of the Polish Socialist
    Party (1892–1914) 213
Independence and the Role of the PPS 221
The Polish Socialist Party
    in the Independent State 227
Heritage 236
Conclusion 237
Summary 238

Oliver Rathkolb –The "Austrian" Revolution of 1918 and the Role of the Social Democratic Party of German-Austria 1918–1920 243

Starting Out Looking Backwards –
    Parliamentary Democracy in Austria 1918/19 243
Development of Social Democracy since 1888/1889 243
Parliamentary Revolution 1918 248
Social Policy and Early Forms of Consociational Democracy in Austria,
    1918–1920 253
Summary 259

Péter Csunderlink –Hungarian Social Democrats in a
Period of Revolutions and Counter-revolutions (1918–1921)   263

From Workers' Associations to a Popular Party One Million Strong –
   Hungarian Social Democracy from the Early Days until 1918   263
The Social Democrats in the 1918 Democratic Revolution   273
Attempts to Implement the Social Democratic
   Programme and to Build the "New Hungary"   278
From "Red Monster" to Government Party –
   The Social Democrats in Government and in the Elections   281
"Sister Party" or "Rival Party" –
   The Relationship of the Social Democrats to the Communists   284
Red Horizons – The MSZDP's Relations
   with Social Democratic Parties Abroad   286
What Can Be Learned from the Social Democrats during the
   Period of Revolutions and Counter-revolutions?   286
Summary   287

Martin Polášek –
Social Democracy and the Czechoslovak Republic, 1918–1938   289

Origin and Early Development of Social Democracy   289
The Birth of Czechoslovakia   290
Social Democratic Politics in the Czechoslovak Republic   294
Social Democrats on the International Scene   299
Social Democracy and Issues of Nationality   301
What Still Remains Alive?   306
Conclusion   308
Summary   308

Zuzana Poláčková –
The Role of Slovak Social Democracy in the Formation
of the First Czechoslovak Republic (ČSR)   311

The Rise of the Slovak Social Democratic Movement
   and the Nationality Issue   311
Slovak Social Democracy and Its Role in the Formation of the
   Czechoslovak State in 1918   319

Social Democracy and Building the New State   325
Conclusion   336
Summary   338

Ana Rajković / Tvrtko Jakovina –
A History of Unrealised Possibilities: Social Democracy and the Creation of the Kingdom of Serbs, Croats and Slovenes (1918–1921)   341

Why Don't Historians See Social Democracy?   341
The New States of 1918 and the Renewal of Workers' Parties   343
Social Democratic Ideas and the South Slavs until 1918   347
The Revival of the Workers' Movement and the Beginning of the Rift within the Social Democratic Parties   354
The Belgrade and Novi Sad Congresses – The Die Is Cast   359
The Joining of the *Centrumaši* and the Path towards Creating the SPJ   362
The Social Activities of the SPJ   365
The Social Democratic Legacy   367
Summary   368

Björgvin G. Sigurðsson –
Social Democracy and the Republic of Iceland   373

Introduction   373
A Nascent Labour Movement and Party   374
The "Fear Alliance"   376
A Sovereign Iceland   377
Negotiating the Union with Denmark   379
Social Democrats and Iceland's Social Model   380
Splits, Conflicts and Foreign Models of Social Democracy   382
Birth of the Republic and Divorce from Denmark   384
The SDP's Golden Age   385
A Century of Social Democracy   387
Summary   388

Authors   391

Europe after the Versailles Treaty 1919

SOCIAL DEMOCRACY AND STATE FOUNDATION

TOBIAS MÖRSCHEL

AN INTRODUCTION

It is hardly an exaggeration to say that the First World War was a key event in European history. Its end led to a reconfiguration of the map of Europe and a surge of democratisation across the board. The large multi-nation states disintegrated and many states in northern, central and eastern Europe won (nation) statehood for the first time or regained it, in some cases after centuries. Social democratic parties were among the principal driving forces of this Europe-wide democratisation of state and society, as well as state formation.

Even though in some cases the newly won sovereignty was short-lived or lasted only until the late 1930s or early 1940s, when the map of Europe was redrawn because of the Second World War, attaining statehood for these countries, sometimes for the first time, was a decisive event as regards both their historical and contemporary identity. Furthermore, it was a crucial reference point in the creation of a new European state order when the Cold War ended. Accordingly, centenary celebrations were held in many of these states in 2018.

The aim of the present volume is to highlight the contribution of social democratic parties to the emergence and formation of the new democratic nation states in the wake of the First World War. The countries within our remit range from Iceland to Georgia, encompassing Austria, Belarus, the Czech Republic, Estonia, Finland, Hungary, the Kingdom of Serbs, Croats and Slovenes, Latvia, Lithuania, Poland and Ukraine.

The principal questions that bind this enterprise together include the following. What are the role and significance of social democrats in the various state formation processes? What social democratic values and ideas managed to find their way into the constitutional orders of the new states? How successful was social democracy in elections and in government? What kind of exchange processes were there with social democratic parties from other countries? And finally, what is the legacy of that period?

Underpinning this book is the observation that, while in the countries presented in it the respective social democratic parties have made a crucial contribution to the founding of the new states their historical role and achievements are all but forgotten today. There are many reasons for this, often specific to the country concerned. Crucial, however, are the instability and discontinuity besetting states in eastern Europe. If one bisects the map of Europe along the 10° eastern latitude the state landscape (which is not the same thing as its forms of state) west of it has remained unchanged between 1900 and today.[1] The European map east of parallel 10° is another matter entirely. Over the same period it has changed repeatedly. The defeat of the German Empire in the First World War, the implosion of the multi-ethnic Austro-Hungarian monarchy and Russia's October revolution and the demise of the multi-ethnic Tsarist empire that came with it brought into being a unique political balance of power in central and eastern Europe, which enabled national freedom and independence movements in this geographical area to realise what they had been striving for since the late nineteenth century: the founding of independent nation states. Of course not all the states that emerged after the First World War were entirely new: some, such as Poland, Lithuania and Georgia, had vanished from the map over the centuries but could now be re-established. Others, such as Belarus, Estonia and Latvia, by contrast, had never previously existed as independent sovereign structures, while a third group, such as Austria, Hungary and Czechoslovakia, were compelled to establish new state structures and territorial borders after the Habsburg Monarchy had been blown apart after so many centuries.

Needless to say, this new (eastern) European state landscape did not simply fall into place after the end of the First World War. Territories and borders had to be defined and the newly founded states underwent a process of formation, establishment and stabilisation. Often this exacted a heavy price in blood. Many states had declared their independence even before the end of the First World War,[2] but the armistice of 11 November 1918 did not bring military violence to a close in eastern Europe, where the First World War in some instances transitioned seamlessly into cruel civil wars and wars between the newly founded states. The wrangling about the establishment of state sovereignty both internally and externally swept the states of eastern Europe into a vortex of (civil) war and violence into the early 1920s, which has largely been forgotten in central and western Europe.

Besides the often intensely violent domestic conflicts the communist Soviet Russia was a veritable hot spot for conflict due to its refusal to accept the independence of former Russian territories. Finland had already extracted itself successfully from the Tsarist empire in 1917, but the transition was much more difficult for Estonia and Latvia. For example, Soviet Russia recognised Estonia's sovereignty, in the Peace of Tartu of 2 February 1920, only after numerous military clashes. Just under six months later a peace agreement ended the war between Latvia and Soviet Russia and guaranteed the former's statehood and territorial integrity. War also prevailed between Soviet Russia and the reborn Poland, which was also fighting against Lithuania, Belarus and Ukraine. Only the Peace of Riga, concluded on 18 March 1921, ended the conflict with Soviet Russia. It procured Poland a considerable increase in territory and a defined eastern border, appropriating a little later on the annexed Lithuanian territory around Vilnius.

At the time of the Riga peace agreement, however, Belarus, Ukraine and Georgia had already lost their sovereignty once again and were integrated in Soviet Russia as socialist republics. Further bloody conflicts included the wars between Czechoslovakia and Hungary in 1918 and the Hungarian–Romanian war of 1919–1920. The new state landscape that emerged in central and eastern Europe in the wake of the First World War was fragile and extremely prone to conflict. Only 20 years later the map of Europe had been fundamentally transformed once again as a result of the Second World War. In common with Belarus, Georgia and Ukraine in the early 1920s now the Baltic states were permanently incorporated by the Soviet Union and Poland's territory shifted west after the end of the Second World War. What important sites of remembrance and reference points these state foundations of 1918 were for (historical) identity became evident at the latest after the peaceful revolutions in eastern Europe when those states that had been part of the Soviet Union were once again able to attain their independence.

The Baltic states were the first to regain their sovereignty, followed by Belarus, Georgia and Ukraine. In the 1990s all the states that had been newly founded after the First World War returned – even if sometimes with different borders – to the political map. Further changes occurred due to the peaceful separation of Czechoslovakia into the Czech and Slovak Republics, while the Kingdom of Serbs, Croats and Slovenes founded in 1918, which later formed the basis of Yugoslavia, split into a number of states after severe conflicts. Finland is something of a special case. In contrast to the states of central and eastern Europe in the 1930s and 1940s this young democracy did not transform itself into an authoritarian regime and was able to retain its state integrity and independence, even though Finland had to cede some territory to the Soviet Union in the wake of the winter war of 1939.

But the history of the countries we are concerned with here is much more than a tale of violence and conflict. Rather it is the history of an across-the-board surge of democratisation, accompanied by state foundations. In all these countries outdated structures were eliminated and systems of parliamentary government established. The modern era had arrived. The democratisation of state and society was the aim. Key actors in all the countries dealt with here were the local social democratic parties, which saw their task as providing answers to both the national and the social question.

The social democratic parties were founded mainly at the end of the nineteenth century or in the early twentieth century. In most of the countries we are interested in there were initially a number of social democratic or socialist parties and movements in competition with one another. Over the course of time mergers and amalgamations ensued, although there were also splits and fragmentations. In the multi-ethnic states there were often several social democratic parties oriented to a particular linguistic or ethnic "clientele". The German Social Democrats played an important role in many countries as a point of orientation for party programmes. The SPD's Erfurt Programme of 1891 met with particular international acclaim. Lassalle, Bebel and Bernstein were extremely popular in central and eastern Europe.

Even when social democracy aspired to be internationalist and the relationship between class and nation was often found to be contradictory and even antagonistic, in practice it was possible to establish some sort of coexistence and various forms of cooperation between social democrats, the nation state, parliamentary democracy and class consciousness in most central and eastern European countries. Social democracy was an integral part of national liberation movements and support from left-wing forces was decisive in establishing new statehood. The aim was not revolutionary upheaval but the peaceful establishment of independent democratic and parliamentary nation states. Anarchistic-revolutionary efforts or attempted communist coups were consistently resisted. The communist parties were regarded as opponents or enemies. In particular in the neighbouring states of Soviet Russia social democrats had to battle both domestic communists and the foreign Soviet threat. Hungary was something of a special case. There the social democrats and the communists formed a brief union, which formed the basis for the short-lived Hungarian "council republic" – the first one after Soviet ["Council"] Russia.

The central goal of social democratic parties was to establish parliamentary democracies in nation states. The idea was to improve living standards not through revolution but by means of gradual progress. A plethora of political and social reforms were instigated, achieving varying degrees of realisation in individual countries. But a number of things were common to social democrats in all countries:

- the establishment of general, equal, secret and free suffrage for men and women;
- implementation of the eight-hour day;
- strengthening of workers' rights;
- the establishment and expansion of social security systems (such as unemployment, sickness and pension insurance);
- comprehensive school and education reforms.

The social democrats saw themselves as representing the interests of the workers, even though in many, primarily agricultural eastern European countries industrialisation was still in its infancy. In eastern Europe in particular the peasantry were the social democrats' key constituency and their social plight was at least as urgent as that of the workers. In response, land reforms – far-reaching in some instances – were implemented with the expropriation of large holdings and redistribution to the peasants.

Social democratic parties did not accede to government in all countries but they did make key contributions to state foundation and state formation even so. The fact that by no means all issues could be addressed and demands met, or that most of these states were transformed into authoritarian regimes in the course of the 1930s – if they had managed to maintain state independence at all – takes nothing away from their historic achievements. Historical developments should be considered not only in terms of their end results, but also in terms of their origins.

STRUCTURE OF THE BOOK

The contributions to the present volume are arranged on the basis of geographical-political criteria. First we present the states that managed to detach themselves from the Russian empire at the end of the First World War. Finland opens the proceedings, having achieved its independence as early as 1917. Then follow the Baltic states Estonia, Latvia and Lithuania, as well as Belarus, Ukraine and Georgia. The volume then turns to the newly founded states in central Europe. The territory of the newly restored Poland had previously been divided up between the Russian Tsardom, Austria-Hungary and the German Empire. On the lands of the former KUK (*"kaiserlich und königlich"* or imperial and royal) monarchy emerged the Republics of Austria, Hungary and Czechoslovakia. The founding of Czechoslovakia is addressed in two contributions, first from the standpoint of Czech and then from that of Slovak social democracy. The new states were almost invariably constituted as parliamentary republics. An exception was the newly established Kingdom of Serbs, Croats and Slovenes, which emerged from former Habsburg territories and the Kingdom of Serbia. The volume concludes with a contribution on Iceland, which seems somewhat out of place geographically but was included here because this often neglected island state also managed to free itself, from Denmark, in 1918 and become a sovereign state.

The contributions gathered here are oriented towards a number of pivotal questions. First, the social democratic parties' historical circumstances are presented in terms of their foundation, membership development, party platforms and social policy goals. The main focus is on the role and influence of social democrats in state foundation and state formation processes. The aim is to clarify the extent to which social democratic policies and ideas found their way into the new states' constitutional orders. What key concerns could be satisfied and which ones not? Who were the outstanding social democratic actors of the time? Another point of interest is how successful social democratic parties were in elections, in their involvement in the parliamentary process and in government. A further focus is their relationship with communist parties, as well as their international relations and exchanges between social democratic parties. The contributions conclude with the question of historical context and an evaluation of the legacy of that period. The idea is to present, in a grand panorama, the multifarious paths, detours and some false trails, as well as the similarities and differences between the various state foundation processes 100 years ago and in that way to identify social democracy's historic role. The volume is also intended as a foundation for further comparative analyses.

This project would not have been possible without the help and commitment of many FES colleagues in the countries of northern, central and eastern Europe. Particular mention should be made of: Ülle Kesküla (Tallinn), Jolanta Steikūnaitė (Vilnius), Toms Zariņš (Riga), Marcel Röthig, Margarita Litvin and Maria Koval (Kyiv), Anne Seyfferth and Thomas Oellermann (Prague), Christian Krell and Meike Büscher (Stockholm), Felix Hett and Irina Seperteladze (Tiflis), Jan Engels and János Molnár (Budapest), Max Brändle and Blanka Smoljan (Zagreb), Bastian Sendhardt (Poland), Robert Žanony (Bratislava), Reinhard Krumm (Vienna) and Matthias Keil and Matthias Jobelius (Berlin). We would like to take this opportunity to sincerely thank them!

---

1   Unaffected by this are Germany's cessions of territory to Denmark, Belgium and in particular France after the First World War and the secession of the Republic of Ireland from the United Kingdom.

2   Finland 6.12.1917, Ukraine 22.1.1918, Lithuania 16.2.1918, Estonia 24.2.1918, Belarus 25.3.1918, Georgia 26.5.1918, Czechoslovakia 28.10.1918; them after the end of the war: Austria 12.11.1918, Hungary 16.11.1918 and Latvia 18.11.1918.

SOCIAL DEMOCRACY AND NATION-BUILDING IN FINLAND

MIKKO MAJANDER

THE BREAKTHROUGH

Finland is often described as a borderland between east and west, but it would perhaps be more correct to claim in relation to many phases of history that Russian and Scandinavian layers were present and exerted their effects simultaneously. Finland has not so much been between but a part of two hemispheres, east and west. Historical circumstances and balances of power have then affected which characteristics are emphasised, for example, high politics and the economy or deeper cultural features of the society.

The state institutions were established during the nineteenth century after Finland had become an autonomous Grand Duchy within the Russian Empire. Helsinki became the capital and the seat of a new central administration, the senate (that is, the government) and the parliament, which from the 1860s onwards convened on a regular basis. The state's own currency, the Finnish mark, was created, and the Finns even had a customs border to separate their finances from those of mother Russia. At the same time society continued to develop mainly along Scandinavian lines. Finnish lands had formed an integral part of the Swedish kingdom for 600 years, and the new Grand Duchy held on to its western cultural heritage and legal traditions – starting with the Lutheran church – even under the Russian Tsar. It has been argued that civil movements (from patriotic public education and the temperance movement to cooperatives and voluntary fire brigades) created the Finnish nation by mobilising the people, making them aware of their joint fortune and destiny.

The labour movement was part of that upheaval. Socialism entered Finland in its German form, first via Sweden, but soon the Finns were translating the classics and following current debates directly from Central Europe. While the Swedish labour leader Hjalmar Branting was present at the founding Finnish party conference in 1899, the famous Forssa programme of 1903 was virtually a straight copy of the Vienna programme of the Austrian socialists. The Finnish Social Democratic Party (SDP) became an active member of the Second International and adopted a Kautskyist view of socialism. The breakthrough to a real mass party was boosted in 1905 by the revolutionary turmoil that shook the autocratic political system of the Russian empire. In the autumn of that year, the SDP took

	Associations	Men	Women	%	Total
1899	64	8437	1009	10.7	9446
1900	69	7558	1607	17.5	9165
1901	31	4052	1963	33.6	5849*
1902	41	5498	1496	18.4	8151*
1903	66	10500	3013	22.3	13513
1904	99	12715	3895	23.4	16610
1905	177	30663	8575	18.9	45295*
1906	937	65017	18896	22.2	85027
1907	1156	63455	18873	22.9	82328
1908	1127	54438	16828	23.6	71266
1909	1217	43599	14694	25.2	58293
1910	1452	39853	12223	23.5	52076
1911	1490	37090	11316	23.4	48406
1912	1552	40149	11749	22.7	51798
1913	1584	40802	12280	23.1	53082
1914	1554	40874	10646	20.7	51520
1915	1528	40946	10857	21.0	51821
1916	1625	57919	14872	20.5	72691

Note: *Gender unknown: 1901: 734, 1902: 1155, 1905: 5060.

Tbl. 1: Membership of the SDP, 1899–1916

a leading role in organising a general strike that united the nation against foreign oppression. Red guards were formed for the first time to keep order.

The party membership surged to 85 000, which in relative terms made the SDP one of the strongest socialist parties in Europe. Although the total membership figures declined after the peak, the number of associations throughout the still very agrarian country continued to evince steady growth. Most of them also built a specific labour hall of their own in which, alongside political agitation, all kinds of cultural activities were conducted. Thus, the unusually rapid spread of social democracy reached not only the industrial workers but also the poor and the underdogs of an agrarian society.

The success of the national strike led to a radical reform of the Finnish parliament in 1906. The old-fashioned diet of four estates was replaced by a single-chamber parliament with 200 representatives. At a single stroke Finland became a forerunner of modern democracy. The members of parliament were elected by universal and secret ballot, which increased the size of the electorate about tenfold. Moreover, Finnish women were the first in Europe to be granted suffrage, and they were equally eligible to stand as candidates. There is no question that the labour movement was the main driver behind this reform. It was followed by the surprising results of the first general elections in 1907: the SDP won 37 per cent of the vote and 80 seats. Out of 19 elected women MPs, nine were social democrats. Even in the SDP women remained heavily underrepresented given that they formed over 20 per cent of the party's membership (see Table 1). Nevertheless, it is fair to claim that the labour movement has remained at the forefront of female emancipation and political participation in Finland ever since.

As Table 2 shows (see p. 22), the advance in general elections continued until 1916 when the SDP won an absolute majority on its own.

Despite the Social Democrats' parliamentary strength, the reformist approach did not yield great results. The Russian Tsar could still dissolve the Finnish parliament at will and refuse to verify proposed bills. The outbreak of the Great War in 1914 also brought Finland under martial law. Table 2 shows that total turnout in general elections declined, while socialist voters remained relatively active, thus increasing the SDP's proportional share of the vote.

Year	Seats	SDP %	Turnout %
1907	80	37.0	70.7
1908	83	38.4	64.4
1909	84	39.9	65.3
1910	86	40.0	60.1
1911	86	40.0	59.8
1913	90	43.1	51.1
1916	103	47.3	55.5
1917	92	44.8	69.2

Тbl. 2: Parliamentary elections in Finland, 1907-1917

INDEPENDENCE

The fall of the Tsar in March 1917 led to a national revival in Finland. A coalition government was formed with six social democrats and six centre-right senators, chaired by trade union leader Oskari Tokoi, who thus became, in practice, the first socialist prime minister in the world. The labour movement felt that its moment had finally arrived. Although no reliable figures are available, SDP membership surely rose to well over 100,000, while the trade unions and the re-established red guards experienced similar enthusiastic mobilisation. On the other hand, this meant that the party leadership lost its overriding authority within the movement, which now had several centres of power. The reformist senators as well as the socialist members of parliament were much more moderate than the unions and guards, which were tempted to take radical direct action.

The SDP attempted to combine the long-delayed reform policies with national liberation from Russian rule, while their non-socialist partners feared the spread of revolutionary sentiments. Mutual mistrust gained ground as unemployment increased in step with the collapsing Russian war economy, and shortages in food supplies led to local disturbances. With the help of the Russian provisional government, the centre-right parties forced yet another general election in October, in which the Social Democrats lost their majority in parliament. The socialist interpretation of this was that it was not just a setback but a counterrevolution. All through the summer society had become increasingly polarised on a class basis. The old tsarist law and order had collapsed, and a new one was sought by two hostile camps that had also acquired arms for their separate guards. Finland was trapped in a vicious circle that became more and more entangled with the deepening chaos in Russia as a whole and St Petersburg in particular.

The Grand Duchy of Finland had provided a relatively safe haven for Russian labour activists and other anarchists. In December 1905 the Bolsheviks even arranged a party congress in Tampere where Lenin and Stalin are said to have met for the very first time. On the other hand, St Petersburg was the city with the second biggest Finnish population, and some of the workers there were naturally engaged in local socialist activities and organisations. Yet it is curious how little the Finnish labour movement was affected by the Russian radicals or Bolsheviks before 1917. True, political refugees could be protected, as were smuggling routes for revolutionary goods and causes, but ideologically and pragmatically the SDP stood firmly on its Kautskyist principles. The Finnish comrades had barely heard of Lenin, much less read his treatises and theses. But in 1917 Finnish socialists were not immune to the spreading revolutionary spirit that, after all, their own agitation had also preached for two decades. The Bolsheviks were the only political group in Russia that promised support for the double objective of national and social liberation. The further the autumn proceeded, the more the SDP moderates lost the initiative and control. In November, after the Bolshevik coup in St Petersburg, the Finnish socialists largely followed suit: a general strike was declared and many terrorist acts were carried out against the "class enemy".

The last step to power remained untaken, however. But there was no return to reconciliation with the centre-right parties that rapidly formed a new senate with one overriding aim: to cut Finland loose from the sinking revolutionary Russia. Independence was declared and, on 6 December 1917, also confirmed by the parliament. The Social Democrats agreed in substance but suggested that Finland should proceed by negotiating with the new Bolshevik regime. In fact, this is exactly what the centre-right senate had to do. No Western country would recognise Finland's sovereignty before independence was formally granted by Russia. This was done on New Year's Eve by the Bolshevist people's commissariat and confirmed by a handshake between Lenin and P. E. Svinhufvud, the centre-right head of the senate. After that, international recognition started to pour in from 4 January 1918, starting with Sweden and France.

THE CIVIL WAR

National liberation was achieved, but the other part of the twofold objective, social revolution, seemed to slip further away. Svinhufvud's senate declared the white guards to be the government's official forces, and they started to disarm the passive Russian troops still garrisoned in Finland. At the same time, the red guards were not willing to give up their guns voluntarily, while the radicals and hotheads managed to get a majority within the leading nodes of the labour movement. Finland drifted into civil war. The SDP was hijacked by its own extremists. The Bolsheviks had conquered power in St Petersburg with relative ease, and it did not seem more difficult to achieve the same thing in Helsinki, when a state of revolution was declared on 27 January 1918 and strategic points were occupied. But Finland was soon divided not just into two political camps but two zones, as the reds controlled the more industrial south and the whites the rural northern territories of the country.

It is debatable how consciously revolutionary Finnish workers and poor people were in taking up arms. At least the collective sentiments were strong, and the labour movement remained remarkably united. This indicates two things. First, there were great injustices in society, enough to mobilise people to such a cause. On the other hand, past years and experiences had generated a common outlook: even when foolish acts were committed, it was better to commit them together. It required more courage to remain outside than to join in. Be that as it may, armed revolution was the gravest mistake in the history of the Finnish labour movement. The direct human cost of the three-month civil war with subsequent purges was close to 20,000 dead. Three-quarters of them were reds, not to speak of the 12,000 or so other victims who perished in the prison camps after the campaigns ended in total defeat.

Uprising against the legitimately formed government left lasting marks on Finnish political culture and consciousness. Such concepts as "fatherland" and "patriotism" were by definition identified with the victorious white side, which claimed to wage a war of freedom. The bourgeoisie has ever since been the "natural" bearers of the nation, even when Finland in later decades has often been led by centre-left governments. In a sense, labour has always represented a counter-culture. The wretched reds were branded agents of Bolshevist Russia, traitors who were ready to sell out the newly gained independence. This is an insulting and anachronistic interpretation, however, even if one accepts the view that in the longer run the "Socialist Workers' Republic of Finland" would probably have wound up as part of the Union of the Soviet Socialist Republics. But the USSR was not created until 1922. In January 1918 even Lenin was counting the days to see whether Bolshevik power would last longer than the ill-fated Paris Commune in 1871. It was not foreign Bolsheviks or local communists who staged the revolution in Finland and fought in the red ranks but rather members of the well-established Western-type labour movement that went astray. After the disastrous defeat, the split was inevitable. Thousands of reds fled to Soviet Russia, and the leading activists adapted to the new political realities. The Finnish Communist Party (SKP) was founded in August 1918 in Moscow. In Finland it remained an illegal underground organisation until the autumn of 1944. The abortive revolution held a heroic place in the history and self-understanding of the SKP. Their mistake was not in taking up the arms but in losing the civil war. The reason for the failure was evident: at the head there was no revolutionary party disciplined enough to lead the working class to victory. Finnish comrades had a lot to learn from Leninism and Bolshevik practices in that respect.

The Social Democrats drew almost the opposite conclusion, however: armed revolution had been a fatal exception to the gradualist tradition of the Finnish labour movement. The error was treated as some strange foreign element. The barbaric violence had been caused by eastern, even Asian influences in exceptional times. The rebirth of the SDP in the autumn of 1918 meant a firm return to the Western reformist mainstream through peaceful democratic means.

THE SECOND COMING

There were two things that made the rather rapid second coming of social democracy possible in Finland. First, a handful of reformist notables had rejected all forms of violence and refused to take any part in the armed revolution. After the inevitable disaster they were equally determined to condemn the extensive terror and inhuman prison camps with which the whites purged their red enemies. The most courageous and respected of these independent minded critics was Väinö Tanner, the director of the biggest cooperative enterprise in Finland and a former socialist senator. Tanner took the lead in re-establishing the SDP as a political force, and in due time he became the most prominent person in the history of Finnish social democracy. Second, the tide in international politics turned against the victorious whites, whose war effort had been aided by German troops. The bourgeois parties even hurried to elect a German prince as king of Finland before the Kaiserreich collapsed in November 1918. That no longer appeared to be such a brilliant idea after the Western democracies had won the Great War. Furthermore, in order to gain international recognition and respect, Finland had to change the punitive measures being taken against the labour movement into integrative ones. As a result, new general elections were held in March 1919, and labour was allowed – in principle, if not fully in practice – to participate on equal terms with the bourgeois parties. Amidst all the difficulties, past and present, the SDP suffered only a slight loss and remained by far the biggest party. A republican constitution was verified by the parliament, and a peace treaty was concluded with Soviet Russia in 1920.

Deep splits between the centre-right parties made it possible for the Social Democrats to gain influence. They supported centrist governments, while the social base of the new republic was strengthened by major legislation, from compulsory education to land reform, with the intention of healing the worst wounds of the civil war. At the local level, the Social Democrats played an essential role in many municipalities, although there were always limits on their actions. In the last resort, white hegemony was guaranteed by the civil guards, a nationwide armed mass organisation that exercised both official and unofficial power. Furthermore, democracy was not extended to the labour market. It was not until the Second World War that employers recognised trade unions as legitimate collective-bargaining bodies for workers' rights. On the left, the communists did their best to infiltrate the labour organisations, which led to further splits. In 1920 the radical faction broke away from the SDP and formed a new socialist workers' party that can be characterised as a front organisation for the illegal SKP. In general elections these "communist lists" scored 10–15 per cent of the vote before they were banned in 1930.

The social democrats held on to a clear majority among the working class, with about two-thirds of the combined labour vote, but the split hit the organisations hard. The majority of trade unions were controlled by left-wing radicals, and there were constant quarrels in the local associations and labour halls. The result of all this ferment was that in the 1920s the SDP lost half of its members to both competitors and passivity.

Year	SDP		"Communists"		Turnout
	Seats	%	Seats	%	%
1919	80	38.0	–	–	67.1
1922	53	25.1	27	14.8	58.5
1924	60	29.0	18	10.5	57.4
1927	60	28.3	20	12.1	55.8
1929	59	27.4	23	13.5	55.6

Tbl. 3: Parliamentary elections in Finland, 1919–1929

The national identity of the white republic was largely constructed in terms of the threat posed externally by Soviet Russia and internally by communism. The social democratic view tried to separate the two. Communism was indeed an existential threat to the SDP, but it had to be defeated in political battles and with progressive reforms, not by legislation and criminalisation. On the other hand, Finland had to seek peaceful relations with its eastern neighbour and abstain from any interventions in Russia's internal matters. The Social Democrats opposed the nationalist pipe dreams of a Greater Finland that the white activists nursed, with an eye on Karelian lands beyond the eastern border.

Relations with Sweden were not unproblematic either. There was an international dispute concerning the Åland Islands that the League of Nations solved in Finland's favour in 1921. Many nationalists also wanted to break the cultural and economic dominance that was traditionally represented by a Swedish-speaking minority in Finland. A young independent country had to prove in every way that it could stand on its own. The language quarrel was a minor question on the social-democratic task list. The SDP itself was a bilingual party and was actually allied with liberal Swedish-speaking

	Associations	Members
1919	1,124	67,022
1920	1,147	49,830
1921	1,105	37,541
1922	1,062	31,806
1923	1,133	27,750
1924	1,089	25,123
1925	1,188	27,268
1926	1,220	37,722
1927	1,286	34,905
1928	1,290	36,662
1929	1,293	33,930

Tbl. 4: Membership of the SDP, 1919–1929

circles in pushing through more important reforms. Neighbouring Sweden also provided increasingly appealing models as the Social Democrats there gained more power and influence. In 1928 Per Albin Hansson introduced the phrase "people's home" (*folkhem*) that sketched a middle way between capitalism and socialism. Four years later he started to turn the vision into practice as prime minister.

In domestic politics, the Finnish Social Democrats were always challenged on two fronts, from the right and the left. This balancing act reached its climax in December 1926, when Väinö Tanner formed a social-democratic minority government that ruled for a year, fairly average in those days. One of its wonders was Finland's first female member of the government, Miina Sillanpää, who served as the second minister of social affairs. For parliamentary democracy, it was a notable show of strength that only eight years after the bloody civil war the "reds" could reign by peaceful means. The experiment was not without consequences, however. In the late 1920s, right-wing radicalism reared its head, partly in the style of continental European models, partly as a reaction to communist and Soviet agitation. The Finnish activists felt that the white heritage of 1918 had been wasted by party politics and a soft parliamentary system. Determined leadership was needed in order to banish communism in its all forms. After that, it was only a short step to recognising that Social Democrats were actually Marxists as well ...

RESILIENT DEMOCRACY

Throughout the 1920s the SDP had been a staunch defender of civil and human rights. One of the main objects was to pardon the reds of 1918 from unreasonable punishment and to elevate labour from the rank of second-class citizenship. If the young nation wished to claim a place among civilised democracies, it had to live up to Western liberal standards. A great deal had been achieved in this regard before the rise of political terror challenged these endeavours. At the turn of the decade Finland's internal peace was yet again disturbed and its international reputation discredited. The summer of 1930 witnessed a violent patriotic movement that put Finnish democratic state institutions under heavy pressure. The bourgeois parties yielded in many respects. Anti-communist laws were forced through the parliament, and the 12 000-strong "March to Helsinki" was saluted by the leaders of the country.

On the darker side of this patriotic show of strength, some 250 "known communists" were captured and beaten at local level, and two or three of them murdered. Even a couple of left-wing MPs, the social-democratic speaker of the parliament as well as former liberal president of the republic K.J. Ståhlberg were attacked. Svinhufvud, the white hero from 1918, was first made the prime minister and then elected president in 1931. But the right-wing tide did not proceed further than that. The traditional bourgeois parties were not willing to sacrifice Finnish democracy to authoritarianism. The mobilising momentum was well past its peak when the patriotic front finally attempted a coup in early 1932. Even their own man, Svinhufvud, used his authority to disarm the rebels. With all its limitations, democracy in Finland endured this trial. True, communism was pushed underground, and the security police monitored the political scene closely and their suspicions were aroused by every hint of radicalism. On the other flank, the ballots in general elections showed that the active support for the "fascists" did not rise above 10 per cent of the vote.

Year	SDP		"Fascists"		Turnout
	Seats	%	Seats	%	%
1930	66	34.2	–	–	65.9
1933	78	37.3	14	–	62.2
1936	83	38.6	14	8.3	62.9
1939	85	39.8	8	6.7	66.6

Tbl. 5: Parliamentary elections in Finland, 1930-1939

Under "patriotic autocracy", social democracy would no doubt have been the next victim after communism. But the traditional trust in law as sacred weighed more heavily. Besides the left and progressives, many conservatives did not approve of lawless direct action that in 1918 had led to such devastating deeds on both sides. There had to be a better way.

One of the fascinating features of Finnish history is that in the 1930s the political system developed in the opposite direction from its counterparts in Central and Eastern Europe. Out of all the new independent states that saw the light of day in the aftermath of the Great War, Finland was the only one to remain a parliamentary democracy with free elections up to and even throughout the Second World War. Vigorous social democracy played a key element in this success. As Table 5 shows above, after the low point in 1930, the SDP strengthened its position in every general election, while the "fascists" kept losing ground. The organised and legitimate labour movement could credibly represent workers' interests and also affect political decision-making. The growing membership in the SDP in the late 1930s reflects this trend, as did, and even more so, all the men and women who joined the trade unions that were now firmly under social-democratic control.

The decisive moment came in the spring of 1937. Svinhufvud failed to be re-elected, and the new centrist president, Kyösti Kallio, formed a coalition government that brought the two mass parties, the Social Democrats and the Agrarians, together under a progressive prime minister, A.K. Cajander. Thus, for the first time, the dividing line from 1918 was crossed on the highest political level. This "red-soil" cooperation (in many different variations) remained the fundamental axis in Finnish politics for the next 50 years. De-

	SDP	SAK
1930	28701	–
1931	27434	19940
1932	25464	–
1933	24398	–
1934	25302	27160
1935	28243	33900
1936	29873	44500
1937	33989	64400
1938	37244	70300
1939	32897	68500

Tbl. 6: Membership of the SDP and the trade union central organisation SAK, 1930–1939

spite the dramatic twists and turns in high-level politics, culturally and in many other respects as well, Finnish society had all along been developing in the general Scandinavian manner. Finally it was mature enough to take its place as the fourth Nordic country in a political sense as well, and the first steps were taken in building the Finnish "*folkhem*".

From early on, the Social Democrats ked the way in establishing Nordic networks through their party and trade union contacts. Many later leaders in the respective countries had first met at youth conferences or other joint meetings. When it was Helsinki's turn to host the Nordic labour congress, in December 1935, Denmark, Norway and Sweden were all represented by social-democratic prime ministers. In security policy, however, "Nordism" and neutrality were not enough to save Finland from the two wars with the Soviet Union, though they did make the country strong enough to avert military occupation. Even hard-boiled communists fought the Red Army in the Winter War of 1939–1940. The SDP and Väinö Tanner in government guaranteed labour support for the war effort also in 1941–1944 when the Finns fought alongside Hitler's Wehrmacht against Stalin's troops. There was virtually no resistance movement in Finland.

No one could question the patriotism of Finnish social democracy any longer, it had been proven by bloodshed. But the times of trouble were not over. After the war, democracy was once more under threat when the reborn communists tried to direct Finland into the new Soviet bloc. The SDP became the staunchest defender of Nordic liberal democracy, while the Swedish labour movement provided both material and spiritual aid for their colleagues' battles for survival.

By the 1950s the existential threat in its crudest form was over. In the following decades, the Nordic – to a great extent social-democratic – model of the welfare state provided a road map for Finland, which rose to the top of the international rankings in almost every category, together with the Scandinavian countries.

LEGACY

It is true that the Finns achieved their dual objective of national and social liberation that the vanguard of early social democracy had dreamt about. It is an amazing success story for a country celebrating and commemorating the centenaries of both Independence and the Civil War. But the long twentieth century is over and no labour movement in any country can count on unwavering progress to prosperity and well-being. After decades of transformation towards a more just society, new economic, social and cultural inequalities are on the rise in Finland, as elsewhere.

The labour movement in all of its forms, from parliamentary parties and trade unions to political and social collectives, has been forced onto the defensive. In many respects social democracy is a victim of its own success. It defends its historical achievements and gets the blame if the public services and benefits do not function as well as they once did. The ultimate welfare state is currently something that lies in the past, not in the future.

The Social Democrats have to reconnect the underdogs of globalisation to a new positive and pragmatic vision that can be shared by the middle classes as well. In a good society, everybody needs a sense of belonging and a meaningful task. The legacy of the SDP lies in its ability to unite, both socially and politically: efficient governing coalitions have been formed around the party.

The new nationalists challenge this setting with their populist "anti-elitism", while the neoliberals try to remove all constraints on the market economy. Somewhere in between the Social Democrats need to overcome, as before, this fragmenting political landscape and become the bearer of the national narrative, in an integrating Europe, as well as in an ever-more globalised world.

SUMMARY

Social democracy entered Finland in its German form via Scandinavia at the turn of the twentieth century when Finland was an autonomous Grand Duchy within the Russian Empire. The breakthrough to a real mass movement in a still very agrarian country was boosted by the 1905 revolutionary turmoil that led to a radical democratic reform. The labour movement was the driving force in pushing through a unicameral parliament, elected by universal suffrage, including women. In the first elections in 1907 the Social Democratic Party won 37 per cent of the vote and 80 out of 200 seats. The reformist way forward was halted, however, by the autocratic Tsar, who could refuse to verify proposed bills and dissolve parliament at will.

The Russian revolution of March 1917 opened up opportunities to strive for the dual objective of national and social liberation. A new all-party coalition government was formed in Finland, and Oskari Tokoi became, in practice, the first socialist prime minister in the world.

National unity did not last. The bourgeoisie did not trust the socialists, who were radicalised by worsening living conditions and revolutionary Russian comrades. Military guards were formed and armed on both sides. Independence was declared in December 1917, but the nation was trapped in a vicious circle of internal hostilities. Finland drifted into civil war. After three months of bloody fighting the socialist revolution ended in a devastating defeat. Those reds who were exiled to Soviet Russia founded the Finnish Communist Party, which operated in Finland under the cover of front organisations and trade unions. The labour movement was split, the Social Democrats retaining approximately two-thirds of public support throughout the 1920s.

White hegemony prevailed, but alongside punitive measures against labour there were also integrative forces. Social democrats were needed to battle both domestic communism and the foreign Soviet threat. In 1926–1927

Väinö Tanner even led a social-democratic minority government that included the first woman, Miina Sillanpää, in a ministerial post. Tougher laws to ban communism were adopted in 1930, but otherwise Finnish democracy endured the challenges of right-wing radicalism. Thus, the political system developed in the opposite direction from its counterparts in Central and Eastern Europe. The dividing line from the Civil War was crossed in 1937 when the two mass parties, the Social Democrats and the Agrarians, formed a joint coalition government. Finland took its place as the fourth member in the Nordic family.

The "red-soil" cooperation and Nordic neutralism did not save Finland from the two wars with the Soviet Union, though they did make the country strong enough to avert military occupation. This made it possible for the Finns to follow the Scandinavian path after the Second World War instead of landing in the Soviet-led communist bloc. The Nordic (very social democratic) model of welfare state provided a road map for Finland, which has risen to the top of the international rankings in almost every category. The Finns achieved the dual objective of national and social liberation that the vanguard of early social democracy had dreamt about. The challenge remains how to carry the national success story into the ever-more globalised twenty-first century.

THE INCEPTION OF SOCIAL DEMOCRACY AND STATEHOOD IN ESTONIA

TÕNU INTS / KRISTJAN SAHAROV

SOCIAL DEMOCRACY PRIOR TO INDEPENDENCE

Beginnings of the Social Democratic Movement

Estonia has a complex and colourful history. After the German-Danish expansion in the thirteenth century, Estonia was also ruled by Sweden and Poland. Starting in 1710, Estonia and most of modern-day Latvia were part of the Russian Empire. The latter half of the nineteenth century saw a national and cultural awakening, although Estonia remained predominantly a peasant society.

Social democratic ideas reached Estonia in the late nineteenth century from Russia and Germany. The best known disseminator of these ideas was Mihkel Martna, originally a painter from Tartu. Martna's views proceeded mainly from German social democratic models. Different kinds of organisation were used to spread the ideas, many at first glance having no links with politics; in Tartu, for example, one such association was the Taara bicycling society. In Tallinn, activity revolved around the recently founded newspaper *Teataja*. Clearly, party-like organisations also emerged, mainly part of the Russian Social Democratic Labour Party (RSDLP). In 1903, a schism developed in the leadership of the RSDLP, resulting in two wings, the Bolsheviks and the Mensheviks, leading to ideological strife and organisational division.

In Estonia, the rift in the party was not particularly significant. The 1905 split into federalists and centrists was more important. Federalists envisioned the RSDLP as a federation of national parties, with Russia becoming a federal republic in future, with Estonia as one of its constituent states. The centralists considered the correct course to be to remain part of the RSDLP and preservation of the centralised party structure. The best known centralists were Aleksander Kesküla, Mihkel Martna, Hans Pöögelmann, Karl Ast and August Rei. The same year, federalists also formed, besides the RSDLP organisations, the Estonian Social Democratic Workers Unity (ESDWU), which raised the national question and brought up the issue of the special social and economic character of the Baltic states. The leading figures in this camp were the writer Eduard Vilde, Peeter Speek and Gottlieb Ast.

The first to start speaking openly about national-territorial autonomy for Estonia was Peeter Speek, in the newspaper *Uudised* (essentially the voice of the ESDWU): he expressed support for the federalisation of Russia and the granting of autonomous republic status to Estonia. RSDLP members accused the ESDWU of abandoning proletarian internationalism and harbouring extreme nationalist views. At the same time, it should be noted that there were no insurmountable differences between the two camps and members were also known to "cross the aisle" on various positions. During the 1905 revolution, the ESDWU enjoyed broad support and brought thousands of participants to the social democratic popular movement. Central ideas in the ESDWU's published programme were Estonian autonomy, schooling, expropriation and distribution to farmers of manorial land, and protection of workers' rights.

Ideologically, the events of 1905 were a watershed in the development of Estonian society. They left an imprint on the Estonian self-conception that continues to the present. The greatest strain was put on relations between Baltic Germans and Estonians, and grievances were aired over historical injustices. The revolutionary demands centred on the question of land. The Baltic Germans had retained their feudal holdings, and over half of the country's agricultural land was controlled by their manors and the church. This led to a peasant revolt and burning of manors in late 1905 in northern Estonia, followed by retributions in which German manorial overlords played a key role. The punitive actions were conducted without due process: Estonian peasants were executed by firing squad and flogged. Estonians developed anti-German attitudes in the first half of the twentieth century.

The year 1905 represented a breakthrough in Estonian literature and art. The literary movement Noor-Eesti (Young Estonia) was closely connected with the social democratic cause. Two of its leading members, Friedebert Tuglas and Gustav Suits, took part in the activities of political parties. The activities of the members of Young Estonia played a key role in establishing a modern, European Estonian culture and national ideology.

Beginning of the Trade Union Movement

The revolutionary events also opened the way to the trade union movement. Estonia's first trade unions were in essence semi-legal organisations. Their legitimacy stemmed from a proclamation of 17 October 1905 under which the Russian Tsar granted, besides other liberties, freedom of association. The most active period for joining trade unions was 1907. For instance, in October that year there were 2,224 members in six trade unions in Tallinn, including 1,180 metal workers and 463 woodworkers. In subsequent years, however, membership declined substantially. The sudden decrease in members, seen throughout Russia at that time, was the result of a harsh crackdown and a general cooling of fervour: workers were deprived of assistance in bettering their situation and feared incurring their employers' disfavour.

Social Democrats and Emigration

During the reactionary period that followed the 1905 revolution, the Russian imperial government's fight against separatism and its campaign to ensure the unity of the empire became more determined than ever before. Left-wing parties were dealt a harsh blow by repressions, and in the twilight of Tsarist rule, they operated illegally. The ESDWU's activities in Estonia were essentially shut down. Many Estonian social democrats were forced to emigrate to Western Europe. While in exile, they developed close ties with Social Democrats in Germany and other countries, thanks to which they were able to familiarise themselves with European social democratic ideas and policymaking. For example, in September 1915, Mihkel Martna took part in a European socialists' conference held in Zimmerwald, Switzerland, where most of the 38 delegates, including Martna, denounced support for the war but stopped short of endorsing Lenin's position in favour of turning the war into a civil war against the bourgeoisie. These international contacts were of decisive importance for the future, when the Estonian state and the Social Democratic Party each sought recognition from the West.

THE ROAD TO INDEPENDENCE

Founding of Social Democratic Parties in 1917

The February 1917 Revolution in Russia activated broad swathes of society, engaging them in political discussions, and brought the question of political self-determination for Estonians back onto the agenda. Interest in political ideas grew, laying a suitable basis for the formation of numerous parties. It should be noted that all of the parties founded in 1917 in Estonia – both on the left (other than the Bolsheviks) and the right – were in favour of a federal Russia in which Estonia would have autonomy. Estonia's Bolsheviks remained part of the All Russian RSDLP, strengthened their positions in unions and controlled a major part of the organised labour movement in Estonia. In 1917, three parties with a social democratic orientation developed in Estonia: the Estonian Social Democratic Workers' Party, the Labour Party and the Socialist Revolutionary Party.

The Estonian Social Democratic Workers' Party

On 31 May 1917, the Estonian Mensheviks reinstated the Estonian Social Democratic Association (ESDA) in somewhat altered form. The revival of activity did not go smoothly, however. There were differences of opinion regarding whether the Estonian faction within the RSDLP should be renamed or whether the organisation should strike out on its own. In addition, there were different views on ideological orientation, whether the model should be the positions of the Russian or the German Social Democrats. August Rei, Otto Sternbeck, Villem Maasik, Aleksander Hellat, Mihkel Martna, Nikolai Köstner, Aleksander Oinas, Hans Martna and Karl Ast proved to be the most active politicians in the party. At first, the ESDA elected not to cut ties with the Menshevik wing of the RSDLP but it did part company with the Bolsheviks. At the congress of 8–10 October, a new name was adopted, the Estonian Social Democratic Workers' Party (ESDWP). The party's programmatic basis was the Russian Menshevik programme adopted in 1903, with some modifications and additions. The Congress passed a decision on Estonian autonomy and called for the right of self-determination of peoples. Power sharing between federal states and central government was envisioned as follows: the legislative and executive branches would be vested in the federal states, while the central authority would be responsible for national defence, foreign policy, labour protection and public transport. The ESDWP embarked on securing democracy in Russia and they were prepared to work with the "progressive" part of the bourgeoisie to this end. The party newspaper *Sotsiaaldemokraat* emphasised in September 1917 that "socialists must not alienate the bourgeoisie in the name of saving democracy". Mihkel Martna noted that "the proletariat must support the bourgeoisie in matters of independence, in particular if it needed to be driven through in government circles, because the bourgeois layers of society are standing on a democratic-revolutionary platform when it comes to the autonomy question". There was a conviction that the time was not ripe for revolution in Russia, and thus democracy had to be defended against attacks that could potentially come from the monarchists or Bolsheviks. The latter were heavily criticised by the party, branded leftist extremists and counter-revolutionaries who were against federalisation and the establishment of an Estonian state. It could be said that the ESDWP were typical reformist social democrats.

The Estonian Labour Party

In April 1917, the Estonian Radical Socialist Party was founded. Its members and supporters were democratic radicals who sympathised with a socialist vision of society and "socialists who interacted with democratic radicals to carry out their basic programme". At the party's founding congress, support was expressed for people engaged in both intellectual and physical work and value was conferred on labour. Ideologically, the party's views were a fusion of ideas from Russian Trudoviks, Russian National Socialists, German revolutionists and the French radical socialists, adapted to Estonian conditions. As its immediate goal, the party committed itself to fighting for political freedoms and democratic rule, and socialism was set as a distant ultimate ideal. At the congress held from 30 September to 2 October 1917, the party's name was changed to the Estonian Labour Party, which was intended to better convey the nature of the organisation. The best known leaders were Jüri Vilms, Otto Strandman and Ants Piip. The name change did not result in any serious policy changes; only agrarian issues received more attention, especially the expropriation of all manorial lands (for the benefit of the Estonian state), with only farmland to remain untouched, although the federal state would have a pre-emptive right to purchase farmland. As regards other policies, one goal was to establish an Estonian democratic republic that would be part of the Russian federal republic. The Estonian Parliament was envisioned as having two chambers, with the upper house including representatives of other republics. The official language of administration would have been Estonian, with the caveat that all local peoples would have an opportunity to conduct official business in their respective native languages as well. A majority of the party congress supported the founding of a neutral Estonian state, although others also backed, variously, a Finnish-Estonian union, a Nordic union and a Baltic union. The Labour Party members criticised the Bolsheviks and Kadets (Constitutional Democratic Party encompassing constitutional monarchists and right-wing republicans) for their opposition to a federal Russia. The Bolsheviks were considered to be a regressive "red" force and their inclination towards a violent coup d'état was considered particularly dangerous. The party publication *Uus Päevaleht* wrote that "regardless of who will hold the majority in the Estonian Constituent Assembly, it will be the outcome of democratic elections and the will of the people, which gives the Assembly complete power and independence to organise the destiny of the Estonian land and people".

The Estonian Socialist Revolutionary Party

In September 1917, Tartu hosted the congress of the Estonian departments of the Russian Socialists-Revolutionaries party (the SRs) and a separate organisation, the Estonian Socialist Revolutionary Party (ESRP), was established there. The leading figures of this party would include Hans Kruus, later a renowned historian and pioneer of the Estonian nationalist view of history, and the writers Jaan Kärner and Gustav Suits. The main slogan of the Socialists-Revolutionaries was "Land and Freedom!" In essence, this meant supplanting Tsarist rule with a democratic republic and the distribution of manorial lands to the peasantry. The participants in the founding congress expressed unanimity that Russia must become a federal republic and Estonia one of its federal states. Cultural autonomy was sought for Estonians throughout Russia. This radical programme was introduced by Hans Kruus at the second congress of the ESRP and later in the newspaper *Töö Lipp*: it held the view that land controlled by the *Ritter*, private manors, churches and major landowners had to be expropriated, commercial circulation separated, the right of selling, purchasing, mortgaging and renting land abolished, and land made available to everyone. The Estonian SRs focused mainly on issues related to the peasantry. No compensation was to be made for expropriated land (except in the case of smallholders); Kruus' rationale for this was that it would be fair recompense for historical injustices, conquest and oppression. He said the large land owners and manor lords had received their fair due in the form of rental payments on leased farms, several times over.

Balance of Power in the Provincial Assembly

On the road to Estonian autonomy, the first victory was the decision of the Russian Provincial Government regarding the formation of a single autonomous Estonian governorate. The Provincial Assembly (also known as the Land Diet and by other names) – formed through indirect elections held on many levels – became the governorate's self-governing body. Starting from September 1917, the Provincial Assembly had 62 deputies. Five of them were held by the Bolsheviks, and the rest were divided more or less evenly between the bourgeois and socialist blocs. The ESRP had eight seats, the Mensheviks had nine and the Labour Party had 11 seats. The election of most of the Provincial Assembly deputies took place in May 1917, and by the autumn, popular sentiment had changed greatly. The political preferences of the era are best illustrated by the Constituent Assembly election results (elections were held in November and December of the same year). At that time, the Bolsheviks were at peak influence in Estonia, where their level of support (40.4 per cent) was even higher than the average in Russia. The Estonian SRs received 5.8 per cent, the Russian SRs 1.1 per cent, the Mensheviks 3 per cent and the Labour Party 21 per cent of the votes and the remainder was distributed between bourgeois parties.

From Autonomy to Independence

As in the case of other Eastern European countries and Finland, the geopolitical status quo that had taken shape in the First World War played a determining role in Estonian independence. Russia was domestically exhausted by the war, which precipitated the 1917 February Revolution and the collapse of the government. Although the Russian Provisional Government pledged the allies that it would continue participating in the war, Russia was no longer an equal adversary for Germany. In early September, the

Germans captured Riga and in October the western Estonian islands, which were an important part of the Peter the Great Naval Fortress, which protected the capital St Petersburg (Petrograd). The fate of Estonia and the Baltics, as well as Finland had become an international question. These events had a strong influence on sentiment in Estonia's political circles and future prospects. Still no Estonian party proposed the idea, either before or immediately after the October Revolution in St Petersburg and Tallinn, to break away from Russia and establish independent statehood. True, the question of Estonia's future status had been discussed for the first time at a closed session of the Provincial Assembly in August at the behest of Jaan Tõnisson, but no clear political goals were set. Gustav Suits, a member of the central committee of the ESRP, was the first Estonian politician who started propagating the idea of Estonian independence more widely, and doing so in quite an unusual way. He estimated that the German occupation of Estonia would last two months and saw two possibilities in the future: a German revolution or a Finnish-Estonian Union. In October 1917, speaking before the Helsinki Social Democratic Student Association, he argued that union with Finland was preferable to federation with Russia because the countries divided naturally by the Gulf of Finland should not intervene in each other's legislative or legal procedures and thus it would be better to establish a two-member national association, not a federal state. No Estonian party supported Suits' idea for the time being.

Although the Military Revolutionary Committee and the Executive Committee of the Council of Working People and Military of Estonia became the central power centres after the October Revolution, and they repressed their political adversaries right from the beginning, the opposition still had a number of channels for operating legally. On 28 November 1917, the Provincial Assembly of the Estonian Governorate declared itself the supreme power in Estonia, but the question of statehood remained open; it was to be decided by the Constituent Assembly elected in a plebiscite. The Bolsheviks did not support the decision and declared the Provincial Assembly disbanded. Nevertheless, the Provisional Council's council of elders and the Provincial Assembly continued activities underground.

The SRs' Idea for an Estonian Labour Republic

In December 1917, the stance on Estonian independence changed – on one hand, Bolshevik power in Russia made it questionable whether an Estonian federal state could be created within a Russian federation, and second, the threat of German occupation became more real. Already on 10 December 1917, the Estonian Labour Party at its conference declared Estonian independence to be its goal. The SRs' third congress on 10–11 December continued to back an Estonian state within a federal Russia. In late December, the SRs' position changed, at the urging of Suits and Kruus, and the new goal was an "Estonian Labour Republic", which was an ideological compromise with the Bolsheviks but which would have still meant, in essence, an independent democratic Estonia. In their memorandum, the SRs turned to the Soviet Russian government and the Estonian Executive Committee of Soviets and sought that Estonia be declared an independent "Labour Republic". They also lobbied Stalin, at that time the Soviet government's Commissar of Nationalities, with the proposal in St Petersburg. Both the Estonian and the Petrograd Bolsheviks rejected the proposal, calling it ludicrous. Although power-sharing with the Bolsheviks was planned in the initial Labour Republic phase (until the Constituent Assembly convened on 15 February 1918), had the plan gone into effect, it would have still meant the establishment of a democratic Republic of Estonia, and the end of the dictatorship of the proletariat.

The Decision on Independence

On 31 December 1917, a meeting took place between the leaders of the Provincial Assembly, the Council of Elders, the Provincial Government and party representatives (the Bolsheviks excluded). Bearing in mind the approaching German forces, the participants unanimously voiced the need to declare Estonia's independence post-haste. The Estonian Social Democratic Workers' Party led by Mihkel Martna dropped their sceptical stance on independence, declaring their own support for the idea a few days later. The Bolsheviks, however, were against any form of independent Estonia and after severing cooperation with the SRs and the Bolsheviks, there was a clear rift between the Bolsheviks and the other parties. Euphoric over the successful October Revolution, the top Bolsheviks in Estonia, led by Viktor Kingissepp, Jaan Anvelt and Hans Pöögelmann, had begun entertaining hopes of a possible world revolution and were in many ways more radical than their Russian comrades. Estonian independence did not fit into their worldview in any shape or form. Although the Bolsheviks had disbanded the Provincial Assembly, they supported going ahead with the elections to the Estonian Constituent Assembly. An obvious role model was the Bolsheviks' positions on the All Russian Constituent Assembly, but they also consented to holding elections in Russia, which they hoped to win. The election results were a grave disappointment to the Bolsheviks, who failed to garner a majority. To express their dissatisfaction over the results, the Russian Constituent Assembly was disbanded by force when it convened on 3 January 1918.

The elections to the Estonian Constituent Assembly were held in most places on 21–22 January 1918 according to the Julian calendar, yet in places where preparations for the elections were not completed in time they were postponed until 27–28 January. The election results to that point showed that the Bolsheviks would not garner a majority in Estonia, either. The Bolsheviks received 37.1 per cent of votes in the Constituent Assembly elections. Suddenly, the influence of the Labour Party led by Jüri Vilms had grown; 29.8 per cent of voters supported them (an increase of 8.8 per cent). The share of votes cast for bourgeois parties stayed more or less the same. To some extent, the SRs lost support (receiving 4.5 per cent), as did the Mensheviks (they garnered only 1.7 per cent). Thus, over 60 per cent of voters voted for parties who supported Estonian independence. On 28 January, the Executive Committee of Soviets of Estonia declared a state of siege. The main reason for resorting to this measure was probably the fact that the elections to the Estonian Constituent Assembly had not gone as the Bolsheviks had hoped and they faced the prospect of losing legitimate power. The establishment of the state of siege meant a cessation of practically all political activities.

On 10 February according to the Gregorian calendar, at the Brest-Litovsk peace talks, Germany presented the Soviet delegation with an ultimatum: the areas of Russia that had been captured by the Germans thus far would remain under German control. The Soviet delegation did not accept these conditions and exited the talks, announcing that they would not continue fighting. In fact, the old Russian army had lost all fighting capacity by that time and when the German forces started advancing on 18 February, they met no noteworthy resistance. The old Russian army, solitary Red Army units and the Soviet government started quickly pulling out of Estonia in the face of the oncoming German forces. Estonian political parties and politicians decided to take advantage of the power vacuum and declare independence. To do this, a Salvation Committee with special powers was formed of representatives of the largest parties on 19 February. Full national power was vested in the Salvation Committee, whose members were Konstantin Päts, and Labour Party members Konstantin Konik and Jüri Vilms.

A declaration of independence was drafted, in which Estonia was described as an independent democratic republic for the first time. A Provisional Government was formed from members of the parties, and it took office on 24-25 February 1918 in Tallinn. This was a broad-based coalition government led by Konstantin Päts, and besides his right-of-centre Rural League and the Estonian Democratic Party, it included Labour Party members (Jüri Vilms, Juhan Kukk, Ferdinand Peterson) and a social democrat (Villem Maasik). The newly formed cabinet declared Estonia neutral in the conflict between Russia and Germany. The German occupation forces did not recognise the Republic of Estonia or its government but treated Estonia as an area they had temporarily captured from Russia. At the same time, the Baltic Duchy was founded by the Baltic Germans, which in its final phase would have meant the creation of a vassal state loyal to Germany. Under certain conditions it would have been a serious alternative to the Republic of Estonia, but the step foundered in connection with the outbreak of revolution in Germany.

BUILDING THE NEW STATE

The Estonian Provisional Government Takes Action

At the outset of the occupation, the German military forces were circumspect about further action, taking a wait-and-see approach, but after a while, Estonian politicians and public figures faced a crackdown and imprisonment. It is likely that Labour Party leader and minister in the Provisional Government Jüri Vilms also fell victim to German military forces while in Finland. The Bolsheviks, who had evacuated from Estonia, became concentrated in the Estonian departments of the Russian Communist Party (Bolsheviks). At the seventh congress of the Bolshevik wing of the RSDLP in

March 1918, the party's name was changed to the Russian Communist Party (RC(B)P) and the party started to be known as "the communists".

The defeat of Germany in the war and revolution ended the occupation in Estonia. On 11 November 1918, the Estonian Provisional Government resumed activity. There was a cabinet reshuffle the next day. The Provisional Government was in power, with minor changes, until the cabinet appointed by the Constituent Assembly on 8 May 1918. The Rural League, the Democratic Party, the ESRP and the Labour Party were all in the government coalition. Democratic Party representative Jaan Poska believed there was a definite need to include the social democrats in the cabinet, to consolidate the Estonian people during a difficult period. Years later, August Rei said that if the ESDWP had taken a passive, neutral stance on this question, the War of Independence would probably not have been fought. The Estonian Social Democrats and the Labour Party were among the first left-wing parties in Europe to form a unity government with right-wing parties. The precondition for participating in the coalition for the ESDWP was legislation establishing an eight-hour working day, which was also passed. The SRs, who were not in the government, nevertheless supported it and clearly opposed the Bolsheviks' plan to reinstate Soviet rule. The domestic political situation was nevertheless very complicated in November 1918. From 8 to 12 November, there was a general strike targeted against the German occupation forces. The strike was a significant means of applying pressure and helped to revive the Provisional Government's activities. At the same time the pro-communist Tallinn Council of Workers' Deputies also resumed activity. The council declared that the objective of the Estonian working people was to extend a fraternal hand to the Soviet working people, in the fight against a common enemy, and for the Estonian Soviet republic. The Bolsheviks hoped that a similar coup to 1917 would take place, but the situation had changed and most of the Russian workers, soldiers and sailors who had supported them had left Estonia. Among Estonian workers, pro–Estonian independence views had become stronger. The Bolsheviks agitated significantly against the Estonian government and planned an armed uprising. As a result, the government closed the newspaper *Kommunist* and in mid-December banned the Bolshevik organisations completely. The Bolsheviks continue operating illegally, but their influence dwindled quickly.

The Unrecognised Government of the Commune of the Working People of Estonia

Upon hearing of the German revolution, the Soviet Russian government annulled the Treaty of Brest-Litovsk on 13 November 1918 and launched a "holy war" to establish a Soviet Europe. The communists among peoples around the periphery of Russia were pledged all manner of support and "independent" Soviet governments. In late November, the Red forces invaded Narva, where a Soviet government was proclaimed with their support, called the Commune of the Working People of Estonia. It is hard to assess exactly what was meant by the name. The idea of a "commune" was fairly broad in Russia at that time; it could mean a cooperative of manor sharecroppers running a manor they had requisitioned or an administrative authority with a very extensive territory. In its rhetoric, the commune styled itself a shadow government opposing the "bourgeois" Provisional Government operating from Tallinn and the propagandists saw the Soviet war on Estonia as a class struggle and civil war. In its essence, the Commune of Working People represented Soviet Russian civilian rule in the rear of the Red Army and their activity was largely under military command and control. In terms of domestic policy, Estonia's Bolsheviks were even more radical than their Russian confederates. With their reign of terror and their decision that Estonian manors were to be retained and transformed into agricultural communes that farms had to join, the Bolsheviks had alienated many people. The activity of the Commune was thus destined to fail.

The Political Situation in the Run-up to the Constituent Assembly Elections

Although by the beginning of 1919, the Republic of Estonia's national army had driven the Red Army out of nearly all of Estonia, the war dragged on and the domestic situation was still complicated. Estonia's own national authority and self-rule had only recently been formed and were weak. Many civilian functions were performed by the military and this created serious tensions. A number of disagreements between the coalition parties occurred. The social democrats criticised the Provisional Government for following a Rural League-oriented domestic policy, excessive intimidation and summary executions due to fears of a military coup. Besides the ESDWP, the SRs and some Labour Party members also criticised the government. The upcoming Constituent Assembly elections also added tensions. Naturally, holding an election during a war was a tall order for a nascent country, but it managed the task well.

The electoral programmes of all three social democratically-oriented parties were similar. In day-to-day politics, criticism was levelled at the curbs on democracy imposed due to the wartime conditions and the activities of the ruling party in the Provisional Government, the Rural League; there were also demands to achieve peace with Russia as quickly as possible. Long-range goals in both the Labour Party and the social democrats' programmes included nationalisation of manorial lands and their distribution to farms. An eight-hour working day and a minimum wage, a labour code and freedom to strike were sought to protect workers' rights. The Labour Party set the following as their general goal: "A government of and by the people on the broadest footing, so that no individual privileged groups in society could rule over the others." The ideal was a completely parliamentary republic with no president.

The criticism levelled at the government by the SRs was even harsher. In the case of long-term goals, unlike Labour and the Social Democrats the SRs felt that a better and more equitable social order – socialism – could be achieved not via evolutionary, parliamentary means, but through revolution. The SRs did not distance themselves from the ideal of a nation-state either, however, and they recalled the idea of the Labour Republic proposed the previous year. The right-wing parties were more reserved on the matter of land reform and sought compromises with the Baltic Germans both prior to elections and during the discussions on the Land Act in the Constituent Assembly. Their objections had both an economic rationale – the fact that small farms are less efficient – and ideological and political arguments: that the land of manorial lords was also private property, which should be inviolable. The rightist parties felt that Estonians needed the support of the Baltic Germans and Germany proper. On the matter of statehood, the parties already had a relatively high level of consensus by this time. The Bolsheviks decided to boycott the elections and continued to engage in agitation among workers and trade unions against an independent Estonian state.

The Social Democrats Enter the International Arena

At the international level, a symbolic event for the Estonian social democratic movement was the acceptance of the Estonian Social Democratic

Workers' Party as a member of the Second International. Estonia's representative was Mihkel Martna, who submitted resolutions in support of Estonia's self-determination and neutrality, but most of the congress did not wish to treat Estonia separately from other emerging independent countries. At a conference held in Amsterdam in late 1919, Martna emphasised the Estonian people's desire to establish an independent country, while living in peace with Russia and resolving economic issues. Now, in a resolution adopted unanimously, Estonia's right to independence was declared, something that was not done at the main conference in Bern. At the conference held in Lucerne in August 1919, Martna noted that Estonia was fighting a defensive war against Russia. At the conference, support was also expressed for the right of Estonia, Latvia, Lithuania, Ukraine and the people of the Caucasus to national independence.

The Social Democrats in the Constituent Assembly

The elections to the Constituent Assembly were held on 5–7 April 1919, and the social democratic parties in Estonia (Labour, ESDWP and the ESRP) received a total of 78 seats and an absolute majority. A contributing factor to the success of the parties was the demands for radical land reform and the goal of signing a peace treaty with Russia quickly. The elections were a disappointment for the Bolsheviks – the workers had voted social democratic. On 23 April 1919, the newly convened Constituent Assembly elected Social Democrat August Rei as their chairman. On 8 May 1919, the Labour Party's Otto Strandman formed the new cabinet, which included Labour, the social democrats and the People's Party. The SRs were left out of the government. On 19 May, the Constituent Assembly adopted a declaration on the sovereignty of Estonia, which was aimed mainly at the international community and which reaffirmed Estonia's desire to secede from Russia and continue as an independent democratic republic. The first major decision made by the Constituent Assembly was the Land Reform Act passed on 10 October 1919, which was pushed through by the Social Democrats and Labour Party.

The discussions on the Land Act in the Constituent Assembly began in the summer, when the Landeswehr war was at its height. This fact added ideological weight to the discussion. Anti-German positions were heard in the Constituent Assembly and they also resonated among soldiers at the front near Cesis, Latvia. It should be noted that the land issue also came up on the Estonian–Soviet front, in encounters between Estonian national forces and Red Army soldiers of Estonian origin. Getting land and the "socialist" government in Tallinn were often among the reasons that Estonians defected from the Red Army to the Estonian national side. At the start of the discussion on the Land Act, Prime Minister Otto Strandman said: "Future generations will assess the work of the Constituent Assembly based on how well it met the real-life demands of the Estonian people." Estonian land reform was one of the most radical in Europe at that time and it fully aligned with popular expectations. The greatest accomplishment of the cabinet was stabilising Estonia's international's position, which started even before independence was declared through the work of foreign delegations, in which the Labour Party and social democrats played an important part. Although Western countries supported Estonia economically and militarily, relations with the First World War allies were not all plain sailing.

The leaders of most Western European countries took a tentative position, waiting to see how the Russian Civil War would be resolved, hoping that a non-Bolshevik government would come to power after the war, one with which the possible secession of border states from Russia could be resolved together. As a result, Estonia's bid for peace with Soviet Russia did not get the immediate blessing of allied countries. The Estonian government nevertheless managed to achieve its goal and signed the Tartu Peace Treaty with Russia on 2 February 1920, under which the Soviet government recognised Estonian independence completely. On 13 February the Constituent Assembly ratified the peace treaty with Soviet Russia. This treaty also paved the way for the recognition of the Republic of Estonia by the West.

On 7 May, the Constituent Assembly passed the Public Elementary Schools Act, which provided for compulsory, free and secular sixth-form education in Estonian as the first tier of the education system. To begin with, four grades of compulsory education were implemented. On 15 June, the Constituent Assembly adopted the Estonian Constitution, which above all was the work of the social democrats and the Labour Party – this would underpin life in Estonia for the next 14 years. The supreme power was vested in the people and they exercised their power in parliamentary elections, referendums and popular initiatives. The 100-seat unicameral Riigikogu was the representative assembly. The prime minister, who bore the title of *riigivanem* (state elder) served as head of state. The institution of president was not established at this time. August Rei noted that the "Republic of Estonia must be completely democratic from the roof to the foundation. The entire power must be in the hands of the people. The supreme power in the state must lie with the assemblymen or parliament who are elected by the entire people. Voting must be universal and uniform, direct, secret and proportional." For its time, the Estonian Constitution was one of the most democratic in the world. Embodying social democratic values, the Constitution was one of the first to provide for women's suffrage. In the general sense as well, men and women were equal under public law. In addition, ethnic minorities were granted cultural autonomy. The Constitution permitted minorities to establish autonomous institutions to safeguard their cultural interests. People enjoyed the right to a school education in Estonian and the right to decide on their ethnic affiliation. In regions in which minorities made up a majority, they were granted the right to use their native language as the official tongue in local government. Citizens of German, Russian and Swedish origin had the right to use their native language in written communications with the central government institutions. At the proposal of the social democrats, separation of church and state was also set forth in the Constitution.

In early 1920, three ESDWP members were in Jaan Tõnisson's coalition government, which was the third government since the Republic of Estonia was founded. On 2 July of the same year, the ESDWP announced that the social democrats were leaving the government. The reason, they said, was that the socialists could govern the country with bourgeois parties only in extraordinary conditions – if the people had to protect the state in a life-or-death matter. Going into opposition, the ESDWP hoped to expand its base and enjoy success in the next parliamentary elections.

THE SUBSEQUENT ROLE OF THE SOCIAL DEMOCRATS

The First Years of Independence

In general, the ESDWP and the Labour Party can be considered the social democratic parties in Estonia in the first half of the 1920. The SRs merged with the aggressive left-wingers who had split from the ESDWP to form the Estonian Independent Socialist Workers' Party, whose positions were similar to those of the communists. The first Riigikogu elections were held from 27 to 29 November 1920 and the Labour Party received 22 out of 100 seats, the ESDWP 18 seats. Otto Strandman of the Labour Party was elected speaker of the Riigikogu. In a speech delivered on 4 January 1921, the newly elected speaker said that the Riigikogu faced difficult tasks, the critical years were not yet over and that Estonia's economy was in a difficult situation. In July 1922, a new socialist-oriented party was formed, the Independent Socialist Workers' Party (ISTP). The working class did not warm to the party, however, and its influence remained slight. After some time, the ISTP began moving closer to the ESDWP.

	1919	1920	1923	1926	1929	1932
Left-wing parties						
Extreme left		5	10	6	6	5
SRs/ independent socialists	7	11	5			
Social Democrats/ Socialist Workers' Party	41	18	15	24	25	22
Labour Party	30	22	12	13	10	
Centrist parties						
People's Party	25	10	8	8	9	
Settlers			4	14	14	
National Centre Party						23
Right-wingers						
Christian People's Party	5	7	8	5	4	
Rural League/ Farmers' Assemblies	8	21	23	23	24	
United Farmers' Party						42
Other		1	8	2	3	
Ethnic minorities	4	5	7	5	5	8
Seats in the Constituent Assembly and Riigikogu, total	120	100	100	100	100	100

Tbl. 1: Seats in the Constituent Assembly and Riigikogu following elections in 1919–1932

In the second elections to the Riigikogu held on 5–7 May 1923, the Labour Party got 12 seats out of 100, the ESDWP, 15. In 1923, Estonia was hit by an industrial and financial crisis. Many companies went bankrupt and many households experienced difficulties. In May 1924, the Labour Party's Otto Strandman became the finance minister and began restructuring Estonian economic policy with the aim of reducing government spending, stabilising the exchange rate of the Estonian mark, reining in lending by the Bank of Estonia, raising tariffs, reducing imports and increasing exports. On all these items, he succeeded, although he also faced much radical opposition in both political and economic circles. As a part of monetary reform, Otto Strandman proposed introducing the *kroon* (crown) as the national currency, modelled after Scandinavia.

In 1923, changes took place in the international social democratic movement. A new International uniting socialist organisations was created, known officially as the Socialist Workers' International. Estonia's ESDWP joined up. The organisation was led in the interim by an executive committee in which parties were given seats based on their size. Until 1928, Estonia was represented together with Latvian colleagues; after that, it was granted an independent seat on the executive committee, which was filled by August Rei and Mihkel Martna.

The Attempted Communist Coup of 1924

The following year, 1924, was of particular importance. There was an unsuccessful communist coup. Defying the communists' expectations, however, it did not meet broader resonance or support among workers and led to a ban on the communists. The Estonian Working People's Party had already been shut down (essentially a front for the communists). The failed communist putsch brought to an end the communist tendency that had dominated in the trade union movement since 1918. The Central Council of Estonian Trade Unions, which united Estonian trade unions, later the Estonian General Confederation of Workers' Unions, had come largely under communist influence and their activity was based on the principles of the Profintern, an organisation that united communist trade unions. For the following few years, the operating principle of free trade unions and a social democratic mindset began to dominate the movement.

The coup attempt was strongly denounced by the social democrats. As a result, the social democrats and independent socialists were brought closer together. In April 1925, a merger congress was held. The name of the merged party was the Estonian Socialist Workers' Party (ESWP) and it had 4,200 members. The congress gave its blessing to take part in the "wall-to-wall" government of Jüri Jaakson. August Rei became the party's chairman. The coalition government formed on 16 December 1924 included the social democrats Karl Johannes Virma, who became roads minister, and minister without portfolio Karl Ast.

The August Rei Government

In the elections to the Riigikogu held from 5 to 17 May 1926, the ESWP won 24 out of 100 seats, and the Estonian Labour Party, 12. The ESWP leadership became more committed to the idea that socialists should not wait for an extraordinary situation to join the governing coalition but rather could do so if the opportunity presented itself. In 1928, during the latest in a succession of government crises, the speaker of the Riigikogu proposed that ESWP chairman August Rei form a new government. The party's Riigikogu faction and the central committee gave their consent and on 4 December 1928, the Riigikogu confirmed the government. The cabinet had eight members, of whom three were socialists: state elder August Rei, minister of finance, trade and industry Aleksander Oinas and minister of labour, social welfare and education Leopold Johanson. The ESWP congress held at the end of the same year saw a few speakers who criticised the fact that the socialists had joined the coalition but most supported the step. The Rei government lasted seven months, and during that time it managed to increase social welfare funding somewhat, but due to opposition from other parties it did not prove possible to carry out fundamental reforms such as a health insurance act and a shop stewards act. The Rei government also initiated a plan for the construction of new railways. The elections to the fourth Riigikogu were held in 1929 and the ESWP no longer was a part of the next government formed in July.

Changes in the Estonian Political Landscape

In the 1920s–1930s, the Estonian social democrats' policies remained unchanged. The main focus lay on reforms to improve workers' social and economic situation, with a socialist society as a goal for the distant future. In terms of tactics, the ESWP became more flexible over the years; forming coalition governments with bourgeois parties was not a problem. The ESWP was the largest parliamentary party in Estonia from 1926 to 1932. The number of members had grown to 6,000 by summer 1931.

The Estonian trade union movement also experienced significant changes in the latter half of the 1920s. As mentioned earlier, a socialist mindset became predominant after the failure of the communist coup. A central organisation called the Estonian Confederation of Workers' Unions was formed in 1927 and it abided by free trade union principles. In 1928, the confederation became a member of the International Federation of Trade Unions. Independent trade unions – unions that sought to change society by democratic means – called themselves apolitical. Nevertheless, they were closely connected with social democrats and the more active members also belonged to political parties.

The elections to the Fifth Riigikogu were held from 21 to 23 May 1932. In the run-up to the elections, changes took place in the party landscape – the Labour Party, which had moved away from social democracy, merged with the People's Party, the Christian People's Party and the Homeowners' Association to form the National Centre Party.

Crisis of Democracy and the Occupation

The Great Depression that started in 1929 had a strong influence on politics around the world. Populist parties came to power in many European countries and parliamentary democracy was replaced with authoritarian regimes or even extremist dictatorships, as was the case in Germany. Estonia was not unscathed by this crisis, unfortunately. The crisis first manifested itself in the economy and the rapid fall in the value of the Estonian *kroon*.

Regrettably the parties were incapable of achieving sustainable political agreements in the Riigikogu. The right-wing parties demanded a constitutional amendment to create the institution of president, which they said would balance the less temperate decisions of the Riigikogu. Two referendums were held to change the Constitution, but both failed. Finally, a draft law introduced by the War of Independence veterans groups went through, setting forth the institution of strong state elder (president). The War of Independence participants movement had started out as a veterans' organisation but quickly took on the characteristics of a political party. It was a populist movement that had clear role models in Italy and Germany. The War of Independence veterans' groups were convinced that the only answer for Estonia was the elimination of the existing parties and an iron fist. The conflict between the veterans' groups and socialists proved particularly acute, culminating in street clashes and rallies. Early 1934 saw the start of an election campaign for new Riigikogu elections and the election of a state elder. It could be clearly be anticipated that the War of Independence veterans' groups would get a significant majority in the elections, as they had just done well in local elections to town councils. The constitutional amendments had already partially come into force and the state elder now had more power. This enabled the state elder Konstantin Päts to declare a state of emergency, imprison the leaders of the veterans' groups, halt the elections and not convene the Riigikogu again. At first, the other parties, including the socialists, accepted this step, and Karl Ast had the main role in achieving an understanding between the state elder and the socialists. Unfortunately, Päts reneged on the agreement to reinstate democracy and in 1935 all political parties were banned.

Before that, a major conflict took place within the ESWP. The main part of the ESWP was still fairly united in 1930 and 1931, but at the party's seventh congress in December 1932, a number of delegates of a local association expressed strong criticism regarding the policy of cooperation between the ESWP leadership and right-wing parties. From the standpoint of the party's leftist opposition wing, intensive work had to be undertaken to obstruct the veterans' groups and convince the workers to mount joint initiatives for the protection of democracy. The left-wing socialists did not rule out cooperation with the communist-orientated organisations, either. The right wing of the ESWP, however, was opposed to any contacts with communists. The standoff escalated at the party congress held in Tartu in February 1934. The outcome was that the leaders of the leftist wing led by Nigol Andresen were expelled from the party as they had started cooperation with underground communists and they had secret ties to the Soviet embassy. In 1940, after the Soviet occupation, the ministers in Johannes Vares' puppet government were drawn from their ranks. The Estonian trade union movement also underwent great changes after 1936. In that year, the leadership of the Estonian confederation of trade unions was forcibly replaced with temporary leaders more amenable to the government. The government-friendly

Estonian National Labour Union (ERT) also emerged alongside the confederation for this reason. In addition, the authoritarian Päts government began controlling the activity of the trade unions.

In 1938, Estonia was the only one of the three Baltic countries to take steps toward restoring democracy. Elections to the Chamber of Deputies (the lower house or Riigivolikogu) were held, consisting of the election of individuals in one-mandate election districts. At the elections, the only legally permitted political association, the Fatherland Union (Popular Front for the Implementation of the Constitution), received a majority. During the Soviet occupation starting in June 1940, social democrats in leading positions also fell victim to repressions, deportations and executions, along with other Estonian politicians and public figures.

During the Nazi occupation (1941–1944), the social democrats left in Estonia participated in the resistance movement, in a so-called search for a third way. They served in Otto Tief's government of September 1944 and its desperate attempt to restore Estonian independence in the interregnum between retreating Nazi forces and invading Soviet troops. The foreign minister in that government, August Rei, fulfilled the duties of head of government in exile after the death of Prime Minister Jüri Uluots. In the conditions of the newly consolidated Soviet occupation in 1944, political dissent was inconceivable and repressions against independence-era politicians continued. In 1945, socialists who had fled to Sweden formed the foreign wing of the Estonian Socialist Party under the leadership of Gustav Suits and Johannes Mihkelson. In the international arena, this organisation was an active advocate for Estonia's interests and played quite an important role in the reinstatement of social democracy in Estonia.

A LOOK BACK AT THE ACHIEVEMENTS OF THE SOCIAL DEMOCRATS

The social democratic movement in Estonia has been, from the very beginning, closely bound, besides politics, to the community, literature and art. Writers and scientists who have gravitated towards the social democratic ideology have played an important role in building Estonians' worldviews and their understanding of history. Eduard Vilde and his historical novels are a good example, as are Young Estonia members Suits and Tuglas with their European take on literature. Their works were quickly adopted as classics in Estonia.

Estonia may have been a predominantly agrarian society at the turn of the twentieth century, and politically a small ethnic fragment on the outskirts of the Russian Empire, but a decisive development took place during the first decade of the new century. The year 1905 was one of political awakening as a nation, and young social democrats played an important role. For the first time, women began to play an active role in the wider community, and they did it in social democratic ranks.

Estonian parties with a social democratic leaning were significant guides on the road from a province of the Russian Empire to autonomy, and from an autonomous governorate to an independent state. While the SRs were the first to float the idea of independence in the form of their Labour Republic, the practical steps toward declaring independence in February 1918 were taken by politicians mainly from the Estonian Labour Party, headed by Jüri Vilms.

Social democratic parties played a leading role in the Constituent Assembly after the 1919 elections. The foundation of an Estonian state and free society was laid at the assembly, and that foundation still has significance today. The Constituent Assembly passed land reforms that exerted substantial influence on Estonian society and hastened its development. Baltic German estates were requisitioned and redistributed among Estonian farms, creating a circle of small estate ownership. The move had such a deep impact that Soviet powers did not dare expropriate land from small farms immediately after the occupation of Estonia and approved the land for eternal use. The Soviets only ventured to establish collective farms after the war, from 1949. The 1919 land reform was certainly a model for the property and land reform bills of 1990–1991.

Education bills passed by the assembly adopted a multi-level approach to education. The same approach is in use in Estonia's education system today. The Estonian state took a distinctly secular path. The church was separated from the state and its position in the public domain quickly diminished. Religious studies became voluntary for students. Marriage registration also had to be done through the state apparatus.

The 1920 Constitution instituted a parliamentary republic and universal suffrage. The Constitution guaranteed equal rights to men and women and society took its first steps to implement them. The short-lived independence period prevented the full implementation of equal rights, falling short mostly in questions of inheritance and family relations. The Constitution begins with a chapter on basic citizens' rights, a chapter which has by and large been transposed to the current Estonian Constitution.

As viewed by conventional Estonian historiography, the role played by social democrats was modest. This is because serious historical works on the independence era were only written from the second half of the 1930s onwards, when Konstantin Päts was in power. The role of Päts and General Johan Laidoner in the founding of the state were highlighted. People tend to remember the last few years of independence more, a period in which political party activity was prohibited. In historical works during the Soviet era social democrats were either ignored or were portrayed as traitors of the working class. Evidence of the social democratic spirit did manage to survive, however, and the Soviet powers failed in their attempt to delete it from history. As the times changed, the restoration of social democracy in Estonia was possible. Social democratic policies and deeds of the past century served as a great example and inspiration for today's Social Democrats during the restoration of Estonian statehood.

SUMMARY

At the beginning of the twentieth century urban social democratic organisations were formed in Estonia, which belonged to the Russian Social Democratic Workers Party. The Russian Social Democratic Workers Party famously split into Bolsheviks and Mensheviks; in the case of Estonia there was a similar split into Federalists and Centralists. By 1917, however, Estonian social democrats had established some sort of coexistence between nationalism, parliamentary democracy and class consciousness. The Estonian political parties with a social democratic orientation played a decisive role in the development from province of the Russian empire to autonomous province to independent state.

By the end of 1917 the idea of Estonian autonomy among social democrats had developed into a strong conviction that Estonia should become an independent state. The first definite concept of Estonian independence was declared by the Estonian Socialist and Revolutionary Party in the memorandum on the Workers' Republic of Estonia. The first practical steps for announcing the republic in February 1918 were made by politicians of the Estonian Labour Party, with Jüri Vilms at the forefront. After the German occupation, on 11 November 1918 the Estonian Provisional Government was able to re-establish itself and the Estonian Socialist Workers' Party took part in it. In a difficult war situation it was important for the consolidation of the people.

The Estonian Constituent Assembly of 1919, in which social democratic parties played a leading role, laid the foundation for the Estonian state and society. Land reform was adopted; manorial lands belonging to Baltic Germans were expropriated and given to farms. Peace was concluded with Russia. The educational laws adopted by the Constituent Assembly introduced the principle of the comprehensive school, the church was separated from the state and its importance in public life declined rapidly.

The Estonian Constitution, which was adopted in 1920, was created primarily by social democrats and the Estonian Labour Party. The Constitution established a parliamentary republic and universal suffrage (in other words, including women). Among other things, the Constitution granted cultural autonomy to national minorities. In the 1920s and 1930s, the Estonian Social Democrats' platform remained unchanged; the main focus was on reforms to improve workers' social and economic situation. As the years went by, however, tactics became more flexible; it was no longer considered a problem to be in a coalition with right-wing parties. The Social Democrats made progress. From 1926 to 1932, the Estonian Social Democratic Workers' Party was the largest parliamentary group. Although in the second half of the 1930s the influence of the Social Democrats in Estonia was small, important steps were taken in terms of Estonian statehood.

Bibliography

Aava, Timo (2014): Mihkel Martna internatsionalismi ja rahvusluse vahel: sotsialismivoolude kohandumine Eestis 19. sajandi lõpus ja 20. sajandi alguses (Mihkel Martna between internationalism and nationalism: the adaptation of streams of socialism in the late nineteenth century and early twentieth century Estonia), Master's thesis, University of Tartu, Institute of History and Archaeology.

Aint, Jüri (2012): August Rei – Eesti riigimees, poliitik, diplomaat (August Rei – Estonian statesman, politician and diplomat), Tartu, National Archives.

Andresen, A. et al. (2010): Eesti ajalugu V, Pärisorjuse kaotamisest Vabadussõjani (Estonian History V. From emancipation to the War of Independence), Tartu, Ilmamaa.

Eesti Radikaal-Sotsialistlik Erakond (3 July 1917): Töö Lipp, p. 2.

Eesti Sotsiaaldemokraatlik Erakond: Riigi rajajate ja hoidjatena (The Estonian Social Democratic Party: framer and steward of the state): http://www.sotsid.ee/erakond/ajalugu/riigi-rajajate-ja-hoidjatena/ (retrieved July 2018).

Eesti Tööerakonna konverents (13 December 1917) Uus Päevaleht, p. 3.

ERR (2016): Ajavaod. Riigi mehed: Mihkel Martna: https://arhiiv.err.ee/vaata/ajavaod-riigi-mehed-mihkel-martna-204547 (retrieved July 2018).

ERR (2006): August Rei: https://arhiiv.err.ee/vaata/174429 (retrieved July 2018).

ERR (2008): Eesti lugu. EV- 90. Alma Ostra-Oinas: https://vikerraadio.err.ee/788067/eesti-lugu-ev-90-alma-ostra-oinas (retrieved July 2008).

Estonica (ND): Vähemusrahvused Eesti Vabariigis enne Teist maailmasõda (Ethnic minorities in Republic of Estonia before World War II) http://www.estonica.org/et/V%C3%A4hemusrahvused_Eesti_Vabariigis_enne_Teist_maailmas%C3%B5da/ (retrieved July 2018).

Graf, Mati (1993): Eesti rahvusriik. Ideed ja lahendused: ärkamisajast Eesti Vabariigi sünnini (The Estonian nation-state. Ideas and solutions from the national awakening to the inception of the Republic), Tallinn.

Graf, Mati (2000): Parteid Eesti Vabariigis 1918–1934 (Parties in the Republic of Estonia), Tallinn, TPÜ Press.

Hiio, Toomas (2008 [1924]): Aasta mässukatse Eestis koos eel- ja järellooga (The coup attempt of 1924 in Estonia with prologue and epilogue), in the collection Detsembrimäss/aprillimäss (December revolt/April riot), compiled by Pruuli, Tiit, Eetriüksus, p. 46.

Iher, Leili (2011): Gustav Suitsu jälil. Fakte ja mõtisklusi. (Seeking Gustav Suits. Facts and ruminations), Tallinn, Varrak.

Jansen, Ea. (2001): Eestlaste rahvuslik ärkamisaeg (Estonian national awakening), in the collection *Eesti identiteet ja iseseisvus* (Estonian identity and independence), compiled by Bertricau, A., Avita, p. 104.

Kaljuvee, Gertrud (2013): Eestimaa Töölisühingute Keskliidu kujunemine ja välissuhted 1927–1936 (Development and international relations of the Estonian Confederation of Workers' Associations), Master's thesis, University of Tartu, Institute of History and Archaeology.

Karjahärm, Toomas; Sirk, Väino (2001): Vaim ja võim: Eesti haritlaskond 1917-1940 (Power and spirit: the Estonian intellegentsia), Tallinn, Argo.

Kuuli, Olaf (1999): Sotsialistid ja kommunistid Eestis 1917-1991 (Socialists and communists in Estonia), Tallinn.

Kruus, Hans (2005): Sotsialistide-Revolutsionääride agraarprogramm ja maaolud Eestis (The SRs' agrarian programme and rural conditions in Estonia) [1917], in the collection *Eesti küsimus* (The Estonian question), compiled by Karjahärm, Toomas and Runnel, Hando, Avita, pp. 337–38.

Laaman, Eduard (1992): Eesti iseseisvuse sünd (Birth of Estonian independence), Tallinn, Faatum.

Kiik, Lembit (1995): Eesti Vabariigi ametiühingud. Ajalooline ülevaade (Trade unions in Rep. of Estonia. An historical survey), Tallinn, Estonian Confederation of Trade Unions.

Liim, A. et al. (1997): Eesti ajalugu elulugudes. 101 tähtsat eestlast (Estonian history in biography form. 101 important Estonians), Tallinn, Olion.

Mertelsmann, Olaf (2014): Mihkel Martna, sotsialist, publitsist ja Eesti patrioot (Martna: socialist, publicist, Estonian patriot), Sirp: http://www.sirp.ee/s1-artiklid/c9-sotsiaalia/mihkel-martna-sotsialist-publitsist-ja-eesti-patrioot/ (retrieved July 2018).

Pillak, Peep (2005): Riigimees Otto Strandman – 130 (130th anniversary of birth of statesman Otto Strandman), Eesti Päevaleht: http://epl.delfi.ee/news/kultuur/riigimees-otto-strandman-130?id=51025277 (retrieved in July 2018).

Postimees (1886–1944), no. 78, 21 March 1936, p. 5.

Reier, Teet (2015): August Rei: jurist, sotsiaaldemokraat, ajakirjanik, riigivanem, minister, diplomaat ja pagulane. (Rei: jurist, social democrat, journalist, state elder, minister, diplomat and émigré), Maaleht: http://maaleht.delfi.ee/news/eestielu/arhiiv/august-rei-jurist-sotsiaaldemokraat-ajakirjanik-riigivanem-minister-diplomaat-ja-pagulane?id=71663329 (retrieved in July 2018).

Reinart, Heili (2016): Alma Ostra – esimene naine Eesti Vabariigi kõrgetes ametites tülitses nooruses Postimehega (Alma Ostra – first woman in senior position in Rep. of Estonia had a row with Postimees in her youth): https://sobranna.postimees.ee/3911009/alma-ostra-esimene-naine-eesti-vabariigi-korgetes-ametites-tulitses-nooruses-postimehega (retrieved July 2018).

Riigikogu (ND): Asutav Kogu (Riigikogu: The Constituent Assembly): https://www.riigikogu.ee/tutvustus-ja-ajalugu/riigikogu-ajalugu/asutav-kogu/ (retrieved July 2018).

Riigikogu (ND): Eestimaa ajutine maanõukogu ehk maapäev (The Provincial Assembly or Land Diet): https://www.riigikogu.ee/tutvustus-ja-ajalugu/riigikogu-ajalugu/eestimaa-ajutine-maanoukogu-ehk-maapaev/ (retrieved July 2018).

Suits, Gustav (2002): Soome-Eesti unioon (Finland-Estonia union) [1917], in the collection Vabaduse väraval (At the gates of liberty), compiled by Olesk, Peeter and Runnel, Hando, Tartu, pp. 78–81.

Toomla, Rein (1999): Eesti erakonnad (Estonian parties), Tallinn, Estonian Encyclopaedia Press.

Valge, Jaak (2014): Punased I. (Reds I), Tallinn, Tallinn University Estonian Institute for Population Studies: National Archives.

Ministry of Foreign Affairs (2010): Mihkel Martna: https://vm.ee/et/mihkel-martna (retrieved July 2018).

LATVIAN STATEHOOD
AND SOCIAL DEMOCRACY

IVARS ĪJABS

Satirist Andrejs Skailis, one of the most pro-democratic Latvian writers of the past half-century, has the following recollections of his childhood in the Riga Grīziņkalns, a workers' neighbourhood, in around 1930:

> At a May Day celebration at some time in my beautiful youth I sat on my father's shoulder in Grīziņkalns, holding a little flag in each hand: one red, the other red, white and red. I already knew the meaning of these flags: the red one was for the workers, the red, white and red one for Latvians. We were a Latvian workers' family, so both flags were ours. It was very simple! In 1933, my father's friend Lasmanis, a 1905 revolutionary and fighter for Latvia's freedom, died and his coffin was draped with both flags, the red one and the red, white and red one. It looked very beautiful, so I was struck by a thought – if I were to die one day, which of course was not very likely, then my coffin, too, should be draped with both flags. Unfortunately now it cannot be done, such an act would lead to an unpleasant incident – after I was buried, the patriots resting nearby would throw me out of the cemetery, flags and all.[1]

It is said that every joke is a joke only in part. The relationship between the red, white and red flag of the Latvian state and the red flag of social democracy is not simple – even if the red flag is without the Soviet hammer and sickle in the upper corner. It was the social democrats who brought Latvians into the world of modern politics, yet they told them that it was not as important to be a Latvian as to be a worker. The social democrats were the first to mobilise Latvians politically in the revolution of 1905, but this revolution ended in bloodshed and the murder of innocent people. Latvian social democrats supported the foundation of the Republic of Latvia in 1918, but other Latvian social democrats from Russia immediately wanted to destroy the young country. Social democrats were instrumental in developing and guarding the 1922 Constitution of Latvia, which is still in effect. Nevertheless these same social democrats did not bat an eyelid when a dictator put a stop to the functioning of the Constitution in 1934 and more than one greeted the Soviet occupation of 1940 to their own misfortune.

In other words, the relationship between social democracy and the Latvian state has been complicated. The problem is that without an understanding of the historical role of social democracy the development of Latvian statehood cannot be understood. This chapter is a historical "essay" in which I have attempted to outline the relationship between Latvian social democracy and the Latvian state instead of attempting a comprehensive study of the subject matter. Much of what I say may be debatable. But it seems undeniable that, generally speaking, the study of Latvian social democracy has not been a priority since the renewal of independence, with the fundamental works by Aivars Stranga and Jānis Šiliņš outstanding exceptions. A good many opinions about the role of the Latvian Social Democratic Workers Party (LSDSP) in the history of Latvian statehood still seem to be based on memoirs. Given the aims of the memoirist at hand, it is not always objective. This can be said not only about the well-known biography of Pēteris Stučka by his fellow Bolshevik Pauls Dauge but, in equal measure, about the memoirs of Mensheviks, such as Fēlikss Cielēns, Brūno Kalniņš, Voldemārs Bastjānis and Klāra Kalniņa published in exile and the recently published memoirs of Klāvs Lorencs. For that reason, the field for research is still wide open, including study of the social democrats' texts themselves, to follow the interrelationship between the socialist and nationalist agendas. In this chapter, I will first (Section 1) describe the origins of Latvian social democracy at the end of the nineteenth century. Then, in Section 2, I will tackle in more detail the various approaches of social democrats to Latvian statehood and autonomy. In Section 3, I will discuss the role of social democrats in the founding of the state. The last (4) section will be dedicated to the activities of the LSDSP in the interwar period, from its decisive role during the Constitutional Assembly to the underground work under Ulmanis' dictatorship. Finally, I will present some overarching conclusions.

THE NEW AGENDA: SOCIALISM AND LATVIAN NATIONAL MOVEMENT

The LSDSP is the oldest political party in Latvia with roots in the nineteenth century. Up until 1917 when, after the February Revolution, Russia experienced a rapid rise in political activity, the LSDSP was in fact the only Latvian party with a mass membership that workers in a position to play a real political leadership role. The most striking evidence of this was the Revolution of 1905–1907, whose dramatic unfolding to a great extent took place under the leadership of the LSDSP. In founding the state in 1918, the Social Democrats were likewise an influential, albeit not always a positive factor. The relationship between the Social Democrats, the first Latvian mass political party, and the Latvian state has always been close and also complicated. It is impossible to discuss the political development of the Latvian state and the formation of its self-confidence without discussing the impact of social democracy. Nowadays, the red and the red, white and red flags symbolise two mutually exclusive systems of values for most of Latvians. This is understandable, given the experience of Soviet occupation and loss of statehood in 1940. But looking back at the past, one cannot help but notice the multifaceted relationship between the two flags – from opposition and conflict to closeness and overlapping.

Although the LSDSP was founded in 1904, the origins of the social democratic movement go back to the 1890s. At that time, rapid modernisation was taking place in the territory of Latvia, affecting not only the economy but also its culture. Owing to the New Latvians movement, which began in the 1860s and 1870s, a new generation of Latvian intelligentsia had appeared on the scene by the 1890s, which wanted to step out of the patriarchal and provincial framework put in place by the conservative Riga Latvian Society (Rīgas Latviešu biedrība (RLB)). In Latvian history, this movement from the 1890s has acquired the name "New Current" or simply "The New Ones". If, prior to their appearance, Latvian culture mainly busied itself with ethnographic, pseudo-ethnographic or sentimental matters, the New Current was interested in broader horizons of modern culture: realist literature and contemporary natural science, as well as social emancipation and the so-called "workers' question". The primary publication of the New Current was the newspaper *Dienas Lapa*, around which a good part of oppositional youth gathered. It was as participants in the New Current or the circle of *Dienas Lapa* that people who were destined to play an important role in the formation of Latvian social democracy met. During the newspaper's most important period, its editors were two Latvian lawyers who had studied at the University of St Petersburg: Pēteris Stučka and Jānis Pliekšāns (Rainis). It was they, and particularly Pliekšāns, who steered the newspaper in a leftist and democratic direction.

At that time, Latvian university and gymnasium students began to rally around *Dienas Lapa*, united by their belief in social progress, the irony of Heinrich Heine and a radically critical attitude toward the "official Latvianness" propagated by the RLB. The New Current was neither a political party nor even an organised group, but rather a relatively loose network of likeminded people and correspondents based in the Baltics and the metropolises of Russia and western Europe. Along with Pliekšāns and Stučka, the representatives of the most active generation of the New Current were Liepāja-based Janis Jansons-Brauns, Fricis Roziņš (Āzis) and Miķelis Valters; but the wider circle around *Dienas Lapa* also included Eduards Veidenbaums, Aspazija, Pauls and Aleksandrs Dauge, Kārlis Kasparsons, Antons Birkerts and many other people later important to Latvian culture.

The ideological profile of the New Current is sometimes termed "socialist". Without a doubt, socialism had an important place in the views of its members. It was socialism broadly understood: an interest in the workers question and its development in the industrialised West; concerns about the fate of Latvian workers both in the countryside and the urban centres; and moral indignation about the callousness and arrogance of the privileged classes. But socialism as Marxist social democracy was important but not dominant. Around 1893, the Latvian New Current first got in touch with German Social Democrats. In that year, Pliekšāns (Rainis) went to Germany where he met with August Bebel, listened to Karl Liebknecht and illegally brought home enough Social Democrat literature to begin to introduce social democracy to a wider Latvian audience. In the contacts between the New Current and German Social Democrats, a role was played also by the Latvian dentistry student Pauls Dauge who published the Erfurt Programme of the German Social Democratic Party in *Dienas Lapa*. It is an interesting historical curiosity, given that *Dienas Lapa* was a legal publication subject to censorship: apparently, the Tsar's censors at that time did not see anything revolutionary in Marxist propaganda.[2]

But it would be erroneous to think that all New Current associates were Marxists or even interested in Marxism. In contemporary society New Current gained popularity with two issues not directly related to Marxism: the emancipation of women and a critique of Latvian nationalism. The theme of women's emancipation appeared on the Latvian agenda in 1894, when Hermann Sudermann's play *Honour* and young Latvian poet Aspazija's play *Forfeited Rights* were staged. Dealing with the fate of women in a patriarchal, hypocritical society, both works of course caused a scandal in Latvian "good society". Second, the New Current openly – albeit not always justly – mocked the achievements of Latvian culture, including pseudo-nationalist romanticism in literature and the General Latvian Singing Festival held in 1895 by the RLB. According to Fricis Roziņš, it was not a real "people's celebration" but rather a meeting of Latvian intellectuals and commercially minded middle classes that had nothing to do with the genuine Latvian people. In this respect, the New Current was rather an expression of the modernisation and democratisation of Latvian public life that went far outside the framework of a single ideology.

At the same time, it was the New Current milieu that created conditions for the popularisation of Marxism, which gradually led to the establishment of groups that self-confidently identified themselves as social democrats. Thus Fricis Roziņš in his article "Broad Views" in *Dienas Lapa* in 1896 criticised another Latvian socialist, the internationally renowned statistician Kārlis Balodis, for straying from the Marxist world view. Marxist theory with its rigid, seemingly scientific causalities and universalist logic applied to the whole of human society apparently appealed to the young Latvian New Current participants, many of whom had been raised in a critically sceptical positivist atmosphere and were imbued with a socially critical spirit of protest. At the same time, it should be mentioned that other sources of inspiration, including Darwin, Nietzsche, Ibsen, the Russian

Narodniks and anarchists, coexisted with Marxism. To summarise, Latvian social democracy was born in the broad context of the modernisation of Latvian cultural life, in which the entire Latvian culture of the twentieth century is also rooted.

Within the New Current, illegal Marxist groups were formed, propagating political literature and organizing various activities: celebrating May Day, learning together and engaging in cultural activities among workers. Gradually, they began to establish contacts with similar groups in Moscow and St Petersburg. It was because of these latter groups that the New Current was destroyed in 1897: 130 New Current participants were incarcerated, with some spending as much as two years in prison within the framework of pre-trial investigation. The case was dismissed in 1899, but the most prominent members of the New Current, Pliekšāns, Stučka and Jansons-Brauns, were punished with deportation to central Russia, while Roziņš, Valters, Ernests Rolavs and others managed to flee abroad. From that moment until the end of the First World War, the activities of Latvian social democracy were geographically split; some activists were in the Baltics, while others were abroad and helped to bring illegal literature into Latvia, particularly from Great Britain and Switzerland. The social democrats who still lived in the Baltics were primarily busy with matters of practical organisation, recruiting workers and organising strikes, whereas the social democrats abroad could devote more time to theoretical work and debates about conceptual issues regarding social democracy. The first Latvian social democratic publications were also launched abroad. As early as 1898, the émigré Dāvids Bundža in Boston began to publish *Auseklis*; a year later, the newspaper *Latviešu Strādnieks* began publishing in London.

The Latvian social democrats had a variety of influences and role models in the West, above all in Germany. This was natural, not only because most of the New Current had an excellent command of German, but also because German social democracy and the SPD were the centre of attention of leftist democratic parties throughout Europe. Such figures as August Bebel, Karl Kautsky, Karl Liebknecht and others were not only symbols of the mobilisation of German workers under the leadership of the Social Democrats but also a political success: the SPD in Wilhelmine Germany had acquired notable political influence in spite of Bismarck's *Sozialistengesetz*, and its progress to power seemed inevitable. It was in this context that the SPD's Erfurt

Programme was drawn up in 1892, from which the Latvian social democrats drew liberally. Confidence in the imminent victory of the workers by democratic – that is, electoral – means, an inevitable collapse of capitalism in the near future, the achievement of a new social order by peaceful and democratic means, all these postulates of the Erfurt programme gained popularity as so-called "Second International Marxism". The Latvian social democrats, for whom the greatest intellectual authority was Karl Kautsky, were no exception.

At the same time it would be a mistake to deny the ties of Latvian social democrats with Russian social democrats and the Russian Social Democratic Workers Party (RSDRP), although the latter were also directly influenced by the Germans. Their collaboration was based on an obvious commonality of interests. Even if the German Social Democrats were right and capitalism was doomed, the Russian situation was radically different. Despite its police regime, Germany was a country under the rule of law and a more or less constitutional parliamentary monarchy, whereas Russia at the end of the nineteenth century was an autocracy without even an illusory representation of the people or state-guaranteed human rights and freedoms. Latvian and Russian social democrats alike were confined to the underground; in accordance with Marxist theory, it was at a different stage of development: while bourgeois democratic revolutions had already taken place in Western Europe, Russia was yet to experience one, whereby a parliament and protection of human rights would be established. Thus Russian and Latvian social democrats shared a common enemy: Tsarist autocracy. This is not to imply, however, that Latvian social democracy saw itself only as a part of Russian social democracy. Quite the opposite: according to contemporary observers, Latvian social democracy at the turn of the twentieth century was sceptical of the Russians' low level of organisation and lack of unity. At least until 1906, when the LSDSP and the RSDRP united in the revolutionary aftermath, relations between Russian and Latvian social democrats were symmetrical instead of hierarchical.

The path toward the establishment of the LSDSP in 1904 ran along two parallel tracks; one was located abroad, the other in Latvia. First, not long after the destruction of the New Current, the exiles who had escaped from Russia established the Western European Association of Latvian Social Democrats in London; because of its small size and weak organizational structure it had yet to be called a party. This group, which published *Latviešu Strādnieks*, was split in 1900 into "Londoners" (Roziņš, Fricis Vesmanis, Hermanis Punga) and "the Swiss" (Miķelis Valters, Emīls Skubiķis, Ernests Rolavs); the first were more orthodox Marxists, whereas the others interpreted social democracy more freely, synthesising it with the tradition of Russian Narodniks. The groups were in conflict both in terms of ideology (the national question; acceptability of terrorism; tasks of the socialist press) and with regard to purely practical matters, above all the ownership of the printing press set up by the Association in London. This caused the group led by Roziņš to be expelled from the Association in 1900 and later to launch their its publication, *Sociāldemokrāts*; the Swiss group retained the name of the Association but was forced to do without its own regular publication until 1903 when, with support from the United States, it participated in publishing the newspaper *Proletāriets*. The Association existed alongside the party as a competitive yet incomparably weaker organization, mostly made up of intellectuals and only weakly tied to the Latvian working class.

Parallel to the events in London and Zurich, workers in Latvia were mobilising and self-organising. An increasing number of former agricultural workers were coming to the urban centres Riga, Jelgava and Liepāja hoping to find work in factories; a workers' movement was launched in cities and towns, representing itself with increasing confidence in relations with factory owners and local authorities. Strikes and boycotts gradually became a normal part of industrial relations. Sometimes confrontations turned violent; the most striking incident was the so-called Riga mutiny in May 1899, during which the conflict between the owners of the Flax and Jute Factory and their female workers escalated into chaotic unrest in the entire city, lasting several days. The social democrats managed to take on the leadership role in the workers' movement, which was no easy task, as several socialist organizations were vying for influence among the workers. The most numerous was the Baltic Latvian Social Democratic Workers Organization (BLSDSO), represented abroad with the aforementioned London group with its publication *Sociāldemokrāts* and with Pēteris Stučka as an author from his exile in Russia. In Riga, however, RSDRP members were active, primarily among Russian workers, as was the Latvian Social Democratic Association, supported from Switzerland by Valters and Rolavs. Among Jewish workers and craftsmen, the Jewish Workers' Association or "Bund" was active.

There was no hostility among these organisations at this time: their borders were often vague and they were in contact through specific individuals. The social democratic organizations had varied international contacts as well. Thus Skubiķis and Rolavs in Switzerland helped Lenin to illegally get the newspaper *Iskra* across the German–Russian border in Courland. A fascinating case that has been little covered in the literature was the so-called Koenigsberg Conspiracy of 1904. In Koenigsberg in East Prussia, German citizens were put on trial for smuggling banned literature to Russia, despite the fact that none of the articles in question was banned in Germany. Latvian social democrats living abroad were involved in the case as witnesses and the German SPD (Karl Liebknecht, August Bebel and so on) used this widely publicised case to discredit both despotism in Russia and the upper echelons in Germany for aiding the Russian secret police in its fight against the social democrats.

In June 1904 the Latvian Social Democratic Workers Party was established, uniting various social democratic organisations. At the moment of founding the organisation had a membership of 2,500, most of whom were based in the largest Baltic industrial centres.[3] The nucleus of crystallisation was the BLSDSO, represented at the time by prominent Latvian social democrats Roziņš (Āzis), Jansons-Brauns and Jānis Ozols (Zars). Stučka, Vilis Dermanis and Jānis Luters (Bobis) also participated in the Congress. The so-called Courland Group, with Pauls and Klāra Kalniņš as the most senior members, also joined the party. In terms of the programme, the First Congress of the LSDSP discussed a document ideologically akin to the SPD's Erfurt Programme but also emphasising the need for political struggle against Russia's autocracy. In 1904, the main illegal newspaper of the LSDSP, *Cīņa*, began publishing. In contrast to the *Sociāldemokrāts* printed abroad it already possessed features of mass propaganda.

In 1905 the newly established LSDSP played a leading role. The outbreak of the revolution was the consequence of many coinciding factors, among them the protracted economic crisis, the failures of the Tsarist army in the Russo-Japanese War, as well as recklessness and criminal disregard resulting in shooting at a peaceful workers' demonstration in St Petersburg on 9 January. In Latvia, which was one of the most industrialised and highly educated regions of the Empire, these events resonated widely. Immediately after 9 January the LSDSP organised a general strike, which kept expanding.

On 13 January, the tsarist gendarmes shot at a workers' demonstration on the Daugava Embankment by the Iron Bridge, killing some 70 people, many of whom were members of the LSDSP. As the strikes spread, workers managed to win many economic benefits: a shorter working day, higher pay, inclusion of workers' representatives in enterprise management and so on. Gradually, the protest movement spread to the countryside: farmhands organised strikes and renters refused to pay rent to the local landlord. The government was also petitioned to improve the situation of farmers. The LSDSP was at the helm of these processes, working within the so-called Federal Committee together with local representatives of the Bund and the RSDRP. The membership of the LSDSP also grew rapidly: at the time of the Second LSDSP Congress in June 1905, the party counted some 10,000 members.[4]

A new turning point was 17 October 1905 when the famous Tsar's manifesto, which proclaimed a quasi-constitution, led to the kind of widespread political activity the Baltic public had never before seen. It involved a whole range of participants, from social democrats to monarchists and the aristocracy. But only the social democrats had wide support among the underprivileged classes and a notable mass organisation. One of the gains from the manifesto was the guarantee of freedom of expression and association, which was immediately put to the test as the social democrats published in the legal press and organised mass events. Their membership had grown to 15–18,000.[5] In these "days of freedom" in the autumn of 1905, a number of events crucial for Latvian democracy took place, to a great extent under LSDSP guidance and control. On 10–15 November, the Congress of Latvian Elementary School Teachers took place, while on 19–20 November it was the turn of the Congress of Municipality Delegates from Livonia and Courland (Vidzeme and Kurzeme). The latter had an important role in the development of Latvian democracy because it was based on newly elected democratic local government organisations, the so-called action committees, which were charged with the task of governing independently of the local administrations controlled by the Tsarist government and aristocratic landowners. It also provided experience of extensive, consolidated action: the Riga general strikes were the largest in the Russian Empire.

It would be a mistake to idealise the course of the revolution of 1905 and the role the LSDSP played in it. Robberies and murders often took place under the banner of social democracy; a large number of cultural treasures were destroyed. At the same time, just as in any other revolution, it provided Latvians with a valuable experience in freedom and self-confidence in organising their own lives. The revolution was suppressed in a lengthy and bloody reaction: as early as November 1905, there were attempts to introduce martial law in Livonia; the LSDSP responded by organising a general strike. In spite of internal opposition, the party resisted launching a united armed uprising, even when, in December 1905, such an uprising was already taking place in Moscow. As a result, there were scattered local armed clashes with Latvian revolutionaries on one side and the local German self-defence or *Selbstschutz* units and Tsarist forces on the other. The latter managed to suppress the unrest, which was followed by merciless revenge that took the form of so-called punitive expeditions: the burning of houses, arrests, torture, shooting suspects for "attempting to flee" and so on. The LSDSP lost a number of selfless and energetic members. Many escaped abroad or went underground. Under these conditions, in the summer of 1906, the party made the decision to join ranks with the RSDRP, becoming the Social Democracy of Latvia (LSD, Социалдемократия Латышского Края) as an autonomous unit inside it. This meant closer integration with the RSDRP, participating in its congresses and cooperating in agitation and propaganda. As is obvious from the very name, the LSD was a territorial organisation (while the LSDSP was national), and thus it had to collaborate with non-Latvian organisations active in Latvia. For instance, the Jewish Bund was active in Riga, as was the local chapter of the RSDRP, headed for some time by Maksim Litvinov, who later became the Soviet People's Commissar for Foreign Affairs during the Stalin era. At the same time, up until the First World War, the LSD retained a remarkable degree of autonomy: it had its own press organs and internal polemics with an agenda that was largely different from that of the RSDRP.

Participation in the RSDRP, however, brought into the Latvian milieu the antagonism between the Bolsheviks and the Mensheviks that had plagued Russian social democracy since 1903. Even though the LSD itself did not split until 1917, the ideological debate was often influenced by Russians. The doctrinal differences between the Bolsheviks and the Mensheviks are difficult to describe briefly. The Bolsheviks primarily supported a smaller but more consolidated and ideologically united party, while the Mensheviks preferred more pluralism and democracy within the party. Most of the

Mensheviks were for cooperation with bourgeois parties, including liberals, various petty bourgeois and peasant socialists (Socialists-Revolutionaries, anarchists and so on) and various ethnic parties, whereas the Bolsheviks considered such cooperation a threat to the interests of the proletariat and susceptible to covert bourgeois sabotage. As far as political struggle was concerned, there was another fundamental difference: while the Mensheviks generally supported a gradual struggle within legal boundaries, for example, in the parliament and legal associations, the Bolsheviks insisted on the need for armed proletarian revolution. After the revolution of 1905 the debate focused on the fate of the illegal party: the Mensheviks called for its liquidation, for under the conditions of "pseudo-constitutional monarchy" it would be better to make use of the opportunities inherent in legal struggle – for instance, in the Duma established by the Manifesto of 17 October – the legal press and the trade unions rather than constantly risk arrest and remain in conflict with the authorities. The Bolsheviks, on the other hand, called for preserving the illegal party as a fighting organisation for the coming revolution, which, in their view, was inevitable. The legal possibilities were to be used for agitation, but the core of the party was to remain illegal.

These differences were reflected among the Latvian social democrats. The LSD was successful in its legal activities: overall, the party did well in the Duma election. It did not participate in the very first election in spring 1906 because it was impossible for it to mobilise voters under the conditions of post-revolutionary terror. LSD member Jānis Ozols was elected to the second convocation of the Duma in early 1907 and submitted interpellations on torture and other activities of punitive expeditions in the Baltics. When the Second Duma was dissolved and voting rights substantially limited, social democrat Andrejs Priedkalns was elected to the third Duma. The illegal party in the meantime suffered several substantial attacks from the authorities, with resulting difficulties for its work. In 1907 and 1908, many Riga social democrats were arrested. In 1908 and 1909, the police arrested all of the participants in the LSD Riga conference; similar actions were undertaken in Liepāja and Ventspils. Several illegal printing presses were confiscated and the publishing of *Cīņa* was moved abroad. Party congresses, similarly to the RSDRP general congresses, were organised abroad as a result of repressions. In 1911 there was an attempt to organise a congress in Helsingfors (present-day Helsinki), but when the police caught on, the congress was held three years later, in 1914 in Brussels. In the meantime, several party members from intelligentsia circles took an active part in the polemics in the legal press, sometimes discussing political issues in a veiled way, including historical materialism and the role of Latvian intelligentsia.

The LSD spent the pre-war years under Menshevik leadership, which had no particular hopes of any resumed revolutionary unrest and called for the exploration of legal activities in associations, educating workers and other low key activities. Some party groups (for example, Riga IV, the so-called Alexander Gate district) were closer to the Bolsheviks, but up to the fourth congress of the LSD in April 1914, the Mensheviks dominated the central committee of the party. They were also the ones that expressed the LSD's condemnation of Lenin's purely Bolshevik Prague Conference of 1912 as illegitimate. The main points of contention between the Mensheviks and the Bolsheviks was the attitude towards the so-called "liquidators" – that is, those who wanted to limit the work of the illegal party and did not insist on organising a revolution – and conditions for reuniting the RSDRP. The LSD's fourth congress in June 1914, in which Lenin took part as a guest, was a turning point: the Bolshevik position took the upper hand, with the question of the relationship between the LSD and the Bolshevik and Menshevik factions of the RSDRP put to one side for the moment. The majority of Latvian social democrats decided to follow Lenin, while not agreeing to merge with the Bolshevik party. In conclusion, we can say that despite the plurality of opinions and the influence of the fundamentally split Russian party, the LSD managed to retain unity until 1917 when the war and the revolution in Russia gave rise to a completely novel situation.

SOCIAL DEMOCRACY AND STATEHOOD

To understand the relationship of Latvian social democrats to statehood generally and to a sovereign Latvian nation-state in particular it is necessary to touch briefly upon the theory of social democracy. Marxism views the political development of humankind from an economic aspect: how people live at a certain point in time is determined by the existing productive forces and their interaction with the relations of production, first of all, ownership relations. Statehood and politics are subject to the economy and in every society political power lies with the ruling class, those who control the means of production (land, factories and so on). Even Western European liberal, constitutional states of the nineteenth century first and foremost acted in the interests of the ruling class, namely the bourgeoisie: although formally it declared people to be free and equal, in reality the interests of the bourgeoisie prevailed. When the transition from a bourgeois regime to a socialist one eventually took place, the system would inevitably change as well. The bourgeois constitutional state based on private property would be replaced by a workers' republic, which, for the first time in history, would act not in the interests of the moneyed few but in those of the working majority: private property would be abolished, goods would be distributed justly and everyone's needs would be tended to, without discrimination. The political views of the social democrats do not make sense without taking into account progress. It was firmly believed that the existing political system would not last forever and sooner or later would be replaced by a more just one, in which democracy would no longer be merely formally political but also social.

The development of social democracy in the nineteenth century coincided with the emergence of various nationalist ideologies. The social democrats, however, viewed the future in international terms. The contradictions between nations caused by nationalist ideology, according to social democrats, was an instrument used by the bourgeoisie to subjugate the working class. It created an illusion about the seeming unity of interests between the bourgeoisie and the working class, but in reality the Polish proletariat, for example, had much more in common with the German proletariat than with the Polish bourgeoisie. Capitalism itself had become cosmopolitan: it flowed across borders, looking for new profits everywhere in the world. For that reason, all the self-conscious workers of all nations should unite in a common struggle against global capitalism (hence the famous slogan "Workers of the world, unite!"), instead of harbouring any illusions about national solidarity with their fellow countrymen in the bourgeoisie. As will be made clear below, practice inevitably amended this pure theory. Nationalism for the social democrats was inevitably bourgeois: the "national unity" propagated by bourgeois ideologues de facto worked for the benefit of the privileged classes.

At the same time, it was important that social democracy was international, instead of anti-national or cosmopolitan; in other words, that it did not deny the right of individual nations to retain their own language and culture. To preserve the latter, however, the isolated nation-state was supposedly not necessary. On the contrary, country borders were needed by the local bourgeoisie to be able to mercilessly exploit the internal market; when people lived in a free proletarian republic there would be no need for such separation and such republics would be able to enjoy being part of a free federal union. This train of thought requires a more detailed explanation. In today's Europe, we have accepted "*small is beautiful*" as a norm; in other words, that even small nation-states can be economically efficient and politically successful (sometimes forgetting that the success of these countries is actually guaranteed by their integration with international organisations, such as the EU). But at the end of the nineteenth century, when social democracy developed, the proliferation of small nation-states was considered a peculiarity, perhaps even a reactionary return to feudal fragmentation. Moreover, it was a view not limited to the social democrats. The expansion of capitalism fostered the development of large and increasingly integrated spaces: the British Empire was the most influential in the world, but even Europe itself saw the establishment of the German Empire and a united Italy in the second half of the 19th century. Social democrats, who saw the world in social and economic categories, did not feel that each ethnos should also have its own nation state. For that reason, a number of social democrats in, say, Germany or Great Britain were bona fide imperialists: they may have supported solidarity among the working people, yet the self-enclosure of these working people in their own national cubby holes seemed pointless. After all, the future promised the establishment of the global socialist federation.

At the same time, social democrats at the turn of the twentieth century had to acknowledge nationalism as an important factor in mobilisation, even among working people. Karl Marx had no sympathy for the movements of "national self-determination", but his most influential follower, Vladimir Ilyich Ulyanov-Lenin took this factor most seriously. With this in mind, the Russian social democrats at the very start included people's right to self-determination – including the right to separate from Russia – in their programme. In time, this right to self-determination was subject to many different interpretations, but it is important to view it in context. First of all, any means were deemed acceptable in the fight against Russian autocracy. If the national movement in, say, the forever restless Poland, weakened the Tsar's autocracy, then the social democrats would support it. The question arises of what was to be considered a "people", however. For Lenin, it was first and foremost the proletariat, not the nationalist bourgeoisie and intelligentsia. Peoples of course were not supposed to use their right to self-determination to establish a bourgeois republic. Rather it was in their interest to establish democratic proletarian republics, which would then have no desire to separate from other democratic proletarian republics, with which they shared a common goal, to develop a socialist society. In other words, the right to self-determination asserted by social democrats was to be understood only in the context of their programme and not as an unlimited right to separate.

The application of social democratic theories to the context of Latvia and the Latvians was of course specific. The New Current had, on one hand, arisen from the Latvian nationalist movement and saw itself as promoting its emancipatory ideals. The official Latvian nationalism, represented by the RLB had, according to the New Current, lost its social critical dimension and interest in the fates of unprivileged Latvians. It had become self-satisfied, conformist and bourgeois. On the other hand, the New Current shared with traditional Latvian nationalism convictions about the future of Latvians within Russia: the leaders of the national movement (Fricis Veinbergs, Aleksandrs Vēbers and so on) saw Latvia as an autonomous province in a liberalised empire, but gradually its participants began to consider transforming the empire into a socialist federation, although naturally dependent on developments in Europe, above all in Germany.

The first open polemics on the future of Latvians began in the London-based newspaper *Latviešu Strādnieks* in 1899, with Fricis Roziņš and Miķelis Valters, both born in Liepāja and both escapees from Russian prisons, weighing in. Miķelis Valters saw the budding Latvian social democratic movement as a continuation of the former Latvian national movement, wherein the proletariat had inherited the mission of liberating the Latvian people: "if previously its enemy was the German Lutheran minister, estate manager or Burgher, now it is the Latvian Burgher". Roziņš, on the other hand, was a strict internationalist, asserting that "a social democratic workers' movement is national in form, not in content".[6] Latvians were to fight their own national bourgeoisie but, as socialism was achieved, national differences would become meaningless.

This text from 1900 already shows the differences between the later "party-ists" (*partijnieki*) and "associationists" (*savienībnieki*); the former were strict internationalists, whereas the latter, particularly their main ideologue Valters, had a very broad understanding of social democracy and attempted to synthesise it with various other currents. In his article "Down with Autocracy! Down with Russia!" of 1903, published in the relatively little-known "associationist" journal *Proletāriets* Valters for the first time proposes the break up of Russia as the most efficient way of fighting against autocracy:

> "You need your self-respect and not only for yourself; you must fight for your personal freedom and it is for the benefit of all peoples living in Russia", we say to everyone. We have to say this to all the peoples of Russia: "establish your self-respect, recognise your personality, your essence, break out of Russia, foster divisionary trends in Russia, for it is for the benefit of all peoples and citizens or Russia; expand the corral of your freedom, try to be a master of your fate, learn self-organisation, self-government, self-judgment, be a lawmaker yourself".[7]

According to Valters, classic social democracy did not have a positive programme for national self-determination. It was to be found in the concept of republican self-organisation. After its founding, the LSDSP also tackled the national question. When, in June 1905, the first LSDSP programme was adopted, it demanded, when "a democratic republic of Russia is established, self-determination rights for all peoples that live within the borders of the current Russian state".[8] At the same time, this demand was not expanded on, given that the political demands of the congress focused on a radical democratisation of Russia, civic freedoms and the abolition of classes, as well as an eight-hour working day and insurance for workers, among other things. In general, the LSDSP recognised peoples' rights to self-determination while not seeing them as a means of separating Latvia from Russia. The "proletarian nationalism" of the "associationists" was suspected of having a petty bourgeois bent.

That is not to say that the LSDSP was not aware of its national peculiarity. After all, it was founded as a Latvian party and was not going to deny this. This becomes apparent when one reviews the discussions of 1904–1905 on the relationship between the LSDSP and the RSDRP: should it take the form of a union or a federation? Even the subsequent Latvian Bolsheviks – for example, Pēteris Stučka – supported a federative arrangement, similar to the one the Jewish Bund maintained with the RSDRP.[9] In other words, the LSDSP was taking shape as an internationalist party of ethnic Latvians.

Social demands were undeniably at the centre of the revolution of 1905. Several documents testify to demands for national cultural rights, however, for instance, to resume education in Latvian in elementary schools. The LSDSP social democrats also demanded broad autonomy for Latvia within Russia. The congress of municipality delegates – numbering about 1,000 people – that was convened on 19–20 November, met with the widest response.[10] At the congress local government reforms were discussed, given that it was only logical if in the future they led to the establishment of an autonomous Latvia, including Latgalia or "Vitebsk Latvia", whose delegates also took part in the congress. On the other hand, this autonomy project, although widely discussed, was never formulated or adopted; the expectations for the future were too optimistic.

During the revolution the Association, whose members were mostly from the intelligentsia, was also active, albeit on a smaller scale. Alongside Valters, Rolavs and Skubiķis, its membership (or at least strong supporters) in 1905 also included Jānis Akurāters, Jānis Poruks, Apsesdēls, Kārlis Dišlers, Kārlis Skalbe, Eduards Treimanis (Zvārgulis) and other well-known Latvian intellectuals. In terms of autonomy, the demands put forth by the LSS in December 1905 were more radical. On one hand, the Association called for the immediate convening of a Russian Constitutional Assembly to turn the empire into "a free people's democratic republic with direct legislation". On the other hand, de facto sovereignty was demanded for Latvia:

> 5. The entire land inhabited by Latvians – Courland, Southern Livonia and Inflantia [Latgalia] – should be united in a single self-governed region, Latvia, with full self-determination in the internal life of this region.
> 6. Self-determination rights should be conferred on the entire citizenship of Latvia, irrespective of gender, religion and ethnicity.

7. Latvia's self-determination rights should be expressed: a) in the autonomy of its legislation, that is, the work of its separate parliament and decision-making through all inhabitants of Latvia; b) in the autonomy of its executive actions or autonomy of governing and justice, that is, in electing authorities and oversight of institutions.[11]

Be that as it may, the revolution and the ensuing reaction fostered the current of centralism in Latvian social democracy. In 1906, the LSDSP joined the RSDRP and was territorially renamed "Latvian Social Democracy". The LSS also formally joined the Russian Socialists-Revolutionaries (or SRs), but the most prominent members had already abandoned the Association. The intellectuals returned to their peacetime professions and reflections while the radical terrorists continued their underground activities as part of the Russian social revolutionary fighters' organisations.[12]

Leftist Latvian politics resumed the national theme only on the brink of the Great War, when two Latvian intellectuals published their reflections in book form: the LSD Menshevik Marġers Skujenieks issued *The National Question in Latvia* (1914) and the "associationist" Miķelis Valters *The Democracy of Latvian Culture, Its Forces and Tasks* (1913). These works did not so much offer positive programmes as express dissatisfaction with the dominant a-national, internationalist current among the social democrats. Both were attempts to rehabilitate the national question in the eyes of Latvian democratic circles, freeing it both from the conformism of the Riga Latvian Society and from the national nihilism of the Bolsheviks. Skujenieks followed the then popular Austromarxist (Otto Bauer and Karl Renner) tradition: the proletariat should take on the development of the national language and culture because only through them could it hope to improve its situation. Culture should become the property of the unprivileged working class, preventing a monopoly of the upper classes and bourgeoisie over cultural development:

> If even now large numbers of workers are robbed of the chance to take advantage of cultural gains, an unmistakable trend is still obvious: the democratisation of culture and thus also the nation. While in the Middle Ages, culture was

an advantage of the clergy and, later, also of the aristocracy and later still the bourgeoisie joined these groups, now ever larger masses make use of culture. Modern capitalism is making great strides in bringing people to democratisation. When we regard a people as a process, then we can talk about it as a community united by a common culture. Workers are the main democratisers of the nation; the evolutionary-national politics of the working class, says O. Bauer, is no impediment to the development of the nation's character but rather an attempt to transform the people into a nation.[13]

Skujenieks activated the national question in the context of the reforms of the self-government of Baltic *gubernias*, in which once again an attempt was made to replace the regional assemblies with *zemstvos*. He argued for the autonomy of Latvia (including Latgalia), emphasising its Western European character and suggested that it develop democratically elected local government and expand Latvian language rights. National autonomy did not mean the disappearance of classes among Latvians; it meant opportunities for the lower classes – that is, workers – to develop and catch up with others. Skujenieks called this approach "an evolutionary national politics".

Miķelis Valters also talked about national autonomy as a precondition for cultural development, albeit without specifying what political institutions would be necessary to achieve this goal:

In other words, our various cultural institutions will be able to develop successfully only if they are based on the bloc of all Latvian cultural strata, beginning with the far left wing and ending with those liberals that have not clouded their minds to the extent that they fail to see that the *internal structure* of our people itself is a democratic bloc. [...] But a cultural movement that in our circumstances would want to be satisfied with everyday petty cultural questions would find itself on the wrong path. [...] Our cultural issues are much broader because they want to lay down the most indispensable forms as a foundation for cultural work as a whole.[14]

In any case, before the First World War, increasing interest in the problems of national autonomy was observed in Latvian leftist democratic circles and a desire to seek compromises between social emancipation and Latvian cultural autonomy. National culture, self-confidence and a feeling of togetherness were increasingly understood as a resource instead of an obstacle for achieving social goals, while at the same time disassociating from the "official" nationalism of the Riga Latvian Society.

The LSDSP had not achieved consensus regarding the issue of national autonomy. After the revolution of 1905, the internationalist trend was strong owing to the influence of Lenin and the Bolsheviks. At the same time, a substantial number of members believed that Latvian culture and autonomy were important. At that time, the public visibility of the Association had diminished and in the Party no one proposed any ideas about secession and the establishment of an independent Latvia. It should be borne in mind, however, that at the time such views were not common in the Latvian political sphere, whether among RLB-associated conservative monarchists with Fricis Veinbergs and Frīdrihs Grosvalds at the helm, or Latvian liberals rallying around Arveds Bergs and *Dzimtenes Vēstnesis*. From 1905, projects concerning Latvian autonomy became widely discussed under the influence of debates in the Russian Duma. Most active in this debate, however, were social democrats of various kinds – from the socialist revolutionary "associationists" to Mensheviks and Bolsheviks. It is a remarkable fact that many of the social democratic discussions took a negative tone, as attempts to combat "separatism" and "nationalism".

SOCIAL DEMOCRACY AND 18 NOVEMBER

The war that began in August 1914 saw the LSD with Bolshevik leadership. A few months before the beginning of the war, to a great extent following the internal conflicts of the Russian party, Lenin sympathisers Jānis Lencmanis, Roberts Eihe, Jānis Šilfs-Jaunzems and others had taken over the leadership of the central committee. As the war began, they of course supported Lenin's position on "turning the imperialist war into a civil war". That meant using the war to foster an armed rebellion. At the same time, Mensheviks such as Voldemārs Rikveilis, Pauls and Klāra Kalniņš, Fricis Menders and others still had great authority among the membership. The Mensheviks were not united in their attitude towards the war. Most of them followed the so-called Zimmerwald internationalist path; they did not support the war (including the forming of Latvian Riflemen battalions) and called for disarmament; a minority supported the Russian troops against the German aggressor (the so-called "*oborontsy*"). The war decimated the already diminished ranks of the LSD: the workers of many industrial enterprises were evacuated together with their factories to central Russia. Even before the February Revolution of 1917, a number of Mensheviks among the social democrats launched a discussion of different projects concerning Latvia's autonomy. The main worry not only of the left, but also the so-called bourgeois politicians was developments that might place Latvia under Germany; this scenario was not hard to imagine, given that Courland was already under German occupation.

When the Tsar had abdicated and chaos overtook the former power in Latvia, spontaneous attempts at self-organisation began in the part of Latvia unoccupied by the Germans. Workers' deputy councils were established in Riga and smaller towns, the United Executive Committee of Latvian Riflemen's Regiments (Iskolatstrel) and others; in many of them Mensheviks – for example, Pauls Kalniņš and Marģeris Skujenieks – were dominant. The Latvian Bolsheviks, on the other hand, were concentrated in Moscow where, after electing a new party central committee independent of the Mensheviks, they set put on the path to a final rupture. With the Bolsheviks gradually penetrating Latvia as well, the party held its congress in Riga in June 1917. The Bolshevik position predominated: instead of a gradual progression to a "bourgeois" democracy through the election to the Russian Constitutional Assembly, the approach should be "all power to the soviets" and an immediate socialist revolution. This was followed by lengthy spontaneous processes with elections at various levels: the LSD claimed victory in the election to the Riga City Council (electing the Menshevik Dr Pauls Kalniņš as chairman) and in the election to the Livonia regional council, in which it won the absolute majority (for the most part, Bolshevik). The Menshevik party gradually gained independence from the Bolshevik Central Committee. During this complicated period, the LSD was the dominant political choice of the majority of Latvians, and the lion's share of this support benefited the Latvian Bolsheviks. This was borne out by the elections to the Russian Constitutional Assembly that took place at the end of 1917, already after the Bolshevik coup: in Latvia, 72 per cent voted for the Bolsheviks, substantially more, on average, than in Russia. The Mensheviks remained marginalised.

At the same time, it was the Mensheviks among whom the idea of Latvian autonomy took hold. The main reason was the terror tactics adopted by the Bolsheviks, which had nothing in common with the understanding of democracy present in the tradition of democratic socialism. Menshevik Fēlikss Cielēns was active during this period; he saw autonomy (not yet independence) first and foremost as an opportunity to escape the German sphere of influence, which was a real threat, particularly after Riga fell to the Germans at the beginning of 1918. In order to gain support for such autonomy, Latvian Mensheviks got in contact with the German USPD (Independent Social Democratic Party) Reichstag deputies – for instance, Georg Ledebour and Hugo Haase – and at the same time sought, by splitting from Russia, which was now in the throes of civil war, to evade the clutches of Germany. Thus, in the summer of 1918, the LSD finally split: in May, the Bolsheviks expelled the Mensheviks from "their" LSD, which resulted in the latter establishing their own party in June under the historical name the LSDSP.

These Latvian Mensheviks played an important role on 18 November 1918. As an eyewitness to these events, Brūno Kalniņš later remembered: "the struggle for democracy and Latvia's independence set the social democrats against the Bolsheviks and gave rise to two parties, which later fought each other tooth and nail".[15] It would be erroneous to perceive the freshly re-established LSDSP as a nationalist organization, however. Its basic values were rather left-democratic: the establishment of a free, democratic and socially just system in Latvia's progression towards world socialism, sometime far in the future. In 1918 Latvia's independence seemed the best format for realising this programme, certainly better than German imperialism or the bloody terror of the Bolsheviks. For this reason, the LSDSP became fully involved in the founding of the Republic of Latvia. The Democratic Bloc (*Demokrātiskais bloks*) established in Riga in 1917 served as a platform for this initiative, uniting, alongside social democratic Mensheviks and the recently established Latvian Farmers' Union, other, smaller Latvian democratic parties: the social revolutionaries, radical democrats, national democrats and so on. The Democratic Bloc was founded in Riga shortly after the German invasion, and the Mensheviks, such as Dr Pauls Kalniņš, Marģers

Skujenieks and Fricis Menders, took leadership positions in it. This organisation consolidated Latvian democratic forces, which understood with increasing clarity that the only possibility for a free and democratic future was an autonomous, internationally recognised Latvia.

In its quest for international recognition of Latvian interests, the Democratic Bloc sometimes found itself in conflict with another organization founded in late 1917, representing the Latvian right-wing. This was the Latvian Interim National Council (LPNP), which was active in the unoccupied part of Livonia and Petrograd, and later in the German-occupied Valka. As opposed to the Democratic Bloc, the LPNP was not formed from parties but Latvian civic organisations. Nevertheless it represented a substantial number of Latvians scattered throughout Russia and considered itself the only representative of the Latvian people. The LSDSP did not participate in the LPNP, but maintained informal contact to it. The LPNP had in its ranks some outstanding bourgeois politicians (such as Arveds Bergs and Voldemārs Zamuēls), as well as some public intellectuals (for example, Jānis Akurāters and Kārlis Skalbe). A compromise between the LPNP and the Democratic Bloc was needed. The participation of socialists was a stumbling block for many right-wing politicians, however, making them look askance at founding the state on this basis: the LPNP majority did not want to collaborate with the socialists; even the group led by Andrievs Niedra of the Farmers Union, which was part of the Democratic Bloc, was categorically against such cooperation. The crucial role in establishing the Latvian state with the support of social democrats, who enjoyed popularity among the masses, was however played by two leaders of the Farmers Union, the former socialist and "associationist" Miķelis Valters and the head of the Provisional Government-in-making Kārlis Ulmanis.

The National Council, which was tasked with proclaiming Latvia's independence on 18 November 1918, was a pre-parliament formed by the parties, in which the LSDSP played an important role: in its various compositions, the party accounted for about one-third of the National Council membership and Marģers Skujenieks became vice chairman of the National Council. Of course, in participating in the founding of a "bourgeois" or liberal democratic state, the LSDSP did not cease to consider itself socialist. This is obvious from the opinion of the LSDSP fraction expressed by Dr Pauls Kalniņš at the state proclamation meeting of 18 November:

> The storms of world revolution have also given rise to the idea of a free and independent Latvia. Today, on 18 November 1918, the representatives of united Latvian democracy proclaim the founding of an independent Latvia. We, too, as representatives of the Latvian Social Democratic Workers Party, consider it necessary to foster the free Latvia developing into an independent state. The free and independent Latvia, however, is not our goal but only a means toward achieving our goals. Just as before, our foundation is the Socialist International. Its goal, and therefore our own goal, is a socialist republic in a union of free nations.[16]

This last phrase read out by Dr Kalniņš is often understood as proof of the "disloyalty" of social democrats, in the sense of their readiness to abandon the idea of Latvian independence in the name of socialist internationalism. At the same time, we should keep in mind that the goals of the social democrats were basically of a social and economic, not a cultural nature. The LSDSP was convinced that social justice and growth could be achieved in a democratic and independent Latvia. The transition to "a socialist republic in a union of free nations" was a very distant goal, when democratic and liberal Latvia would have the economic preconditions in place, instead of the results of an imminent coup as envisaged by the Bolsheviks. In this respect the LSDSP had bitter conflicts with the Latvian Bolsheviks, who had already begun to call themselves the Latvian Communist Party and were willing to establish a socialist order immediately.

In the struggle for statehood, most problematic was the withdrawal of the LSDSP from the National Council in January 1919, during the invasion from Russia by Pēteris Stučka's Bolsheviks. This historical episode is fraught with contention: formally, the party withdrew from the National Council in protest against the Ulmanis government's agreement with the German Freikorps, which now was supposed to fight for a democratic Latvia. Instead, the LSDSP called for a general mobilisation. It is more likely, however, that the party did not want to openly support fighting against their former colleagues, the Latvian Bolsheviks, because it would have had a negative effect on its reputation in the eyes of the workers and peasants who were still bolshevised to a great extent. There are no grounds for accusing the LSDSP of disloyalty to the Latvian state: the party never considered any kind of collaboration with Stučka, and its opposition to Bolshevik dictatorship was principled.

The LSDSP returned to the National Council after the so-called "Manteuffel putsch" on 16 April 1919, when the German army and the so-called Iron Division arrested Ulmanis' provisional government and established the pro-German Niedra/Vankin cabinet. LSDSP members at this time were in the first ranks of the defenders of democratic Latvia, participating in the War of Independence. The Party also actively rallied its membership to fight against Pavel Bermondt-Avalov's West Russian Volunteer Army, which tried to eliminate Ulmanis' government in Autumn 1919. Several of the LSDSP leaders were awarded the Order of Lāčplēsis.

THE LSDSP AND THE INDEPENDENT STATE

During the entire period of democracy in Latvia – from the Constitutional Assembly elected in 1920 to the dissolution of the fourth Saeima in May 1934 – the LSDSP had the largest faction in the parliament. It was a mass organisation: according to Brūno Kalniņš's data, in 1932 the LSDSP had 12,525 members, a considerable number, second only to Ulmanis' agrarian Latvian Farmers Union (LZS), whose membership is estimated to have been around 32,000–39,000.[17] The LSDSP electorate was varied: in the Constitutional Assembly the party won 38.7 per cent of the votes, and much of its electorate were supporters of radical agrarian reform, the landless peasantry; the majority, however, were workers in the urban centres and it was their interests that the programme of the party reflected. For various reasons, support for the party diminished during the period of democratic elections: in the first Saeima, elected in 1922, the party gained 31 seats, but in the fourth, elected in 1931, that number fell to 21. We will return to the reasons for this below. For now, it's important to remember that the LSDSP remained the largest parliamentary faction with a substantial and stable electorate.

The LSDSP had a significant impact on the constitutional structure of the newly established Republic of Latvia. Although the party did not have an absolute majority in the Constitutional Assembly, it strongly influenced the final version of the Constitution. First of all, social democrats fulfilled the main task of adopting an expressly democratic and parliamentary constitution. For its time, the Constitution really was outstandingly democratic. It provided not only for general, equal and direct elections by secret ballot and for both genders, but also for vesting power in a proportionally elected multi-party parliament. The issue of a directly elected president turned on a principle: the LZS, the Baltic Germans and others supported such an arrangement, whereas the LSDSP initially did not want a separate head of state, suggesting that the speaker of the Saeima should have the relevant ceremonial duties. The result was a compromise: a president elected by the parliament with relatively circumscribed powers. Regarding direct democracy and referenda, the LSDSP was split: most saw the danger of populism, whereas some supporters of a Swiss type of democracy, including Pliekšāns-Rainis and Kārlis Dzelzītis, wanted the option of people's legislation. The latter was included in the Constitution, although the prescribed conditions were set rather high. The so-called Second Part of the Constitution, which was to include a charter of basic rights, also gave rise to much discussion. The charter was not adopted, primarily because of the opposition of the social democrats: the majority of the Constitutional Assembly considered most of the social rights that this would have entailed excessive.

What were the main reasons for the LSDSP's inter-war popularity? First of all, the party membership included several very well known and loved politicians. Up until his death in 1929, the famous poet Rainis was a candidate on the LSDSP list; his wife, the poet Aspazija, was also elected to the Constitutional Assembly from the LSDSP. A number of other popular politicians, most of whom had been active before the war, also belonged to the party: Pauls Kalniņš, speaker of the Saeima from 1925; his son Brūno Kalniņš, who headed the active Workers' Sports Union, the later Workers' Sports and Guard (SSS), which also helped in maintaining public order; Marģers Skujenieks, a statistician with great intellectual authority (he left the party rather early on, however); and Fēlikss Cielēns, an expert on international affairs and a brilliant speaker. A popular, albeit controversial figure was the long-serving LSDSP faction leader Fricis Menders, who had a sharp mind and an equally sharp tongue. The party was fairly successful in exploiting its experiences in 1905, to which wide circles of Latvian society responded: several of the party's leaders, including Rainis, in fact had been very active in 1905. It is only fitting that in one of his speeches Menders even discussed the LSDSP's role in founding an independent Latvia as a kind of continuation of the Revolution of 1905.[18]

Alongside such personalities, the LSDSP also had a number of popular policies. The party held on to the Marxist rhetoric about the coming socialism and struggle to serve the interests of the proletariat, but its initial success was agrarian reform which, starting in 1920, was carried out on a large scale and was termed "Bolshevist" by its opponents, primarily aristocratic Baltic German landowners. Given the large number of landless people, immediate agrarian reform was absolutely necessary to ensure political stability in Latvia: the latifundia of the landed gentry could not be preserved. At the same time there were disagreements on how the agrarian reform should be implemented: the main point of contention was whether aristocratic landowners should be left with some of their land and whether they should be compensated for what was taken away. In contrast to the right-wing conservative LZS, the LSDSP argued against leaving some land with its existing owners and paying compensation and this position proved to be victorious. The amount of land to be left with its former owners was set at only 50 hectares and the compensation issue was put aside for later.

Agrarian reform is a good illustration of a distinctive feature of interwar social democracy: "social" justice was very closely to with "historical" justice, and the latter was carried out primarily against the Baltic German landed gentry. At its most radical moments, the LSDSP acquired features of ethnic chauvinism as the struggle against the legendary "Black Knights" took on an anti-German character, instead of concentrating on the privileges of the gentry. These ethno-political retributions were expressed in active support for "trying" the pro-German Andrievs Niedra[19] and the LSDSP-instigated referendum against conferring land acquisition privileges on the Baltic German Landeswehr for their contribution to fighting the Bolsheviks in 1919. In this respect, the LSDSP drew some of its legitimacy from the historical legacy of the anti-German sentiments that the First World War reinforced. The LSDSP was more radical in this regard than the "official" right-wing nationalist parties, Arved Bergs's Latvian National Association and others. At the same time, it would be wrong to call the LSDSP a nationalist party. It was the party who most often took a stance to protect the rights of national minorities; moreover, the Jewish Bund, led by Dr Noah Meisel in the Saeima, was an integral part of the party.

In terms of strategy, the LSDSP was most split over the issue of working in coalitions. Often there were disagreements between the orthodox "left" of the party and some prominent members who were on friendlier terms with the right-wing parties. The leader of the leftists was the aforementioned Dr Fricis Menders, who held to his strong conviction that social democrats should not enter governing coalitions with bourgeois parties unless they have a "determining influence". Menders also thought that a coalition with the right would make sense only if the main player among the bourgeois parties, the LZS, were part of it. Usually there was no such opportunity: of the 19 interwar Latvian governments (including three provisional governments), the LSDSP participated only in two. The first was the short-lived Jānis Pauļuks government (27 January 1923–27 June 1923), the second, the "leftist" and longer lasting government led by Marģers Skujenieks (19 December 1926–23 January 1928). Otherwise the LSDSP was in opposition.

This strategy of the social democrats provoked a rather heated debate in both the contemporary press and in memoirs and historiography. Most – for example, Brūno Kalniņš and Fēlikss Cielēns – criticised this tactic as wrong: after all, it is even possible that if the LSDSP had been part of the government, the coup d'état of 15 May might have been averted. Such assertions should be subjected to critical scrutiny, however. For the most part they originate with Menders' political opponents, who, as opposed to their faction leader, could later look for the guilty parties from safety beyond the borders of Sovietised Latvia. Menders was of course a doctrinaire politician, but his position was not without some logic. In his view, the very economic foundation of capitalism had to be first restored in Latvia after the devastating war and the evacuation of industry. That could not be done under the leadership of social democracy for it did not serve capital but defended the interests of workers. Referring to the traditional authority figure for the LSDSP, the German social democratic theoretician Karl Kautsky, Menders wrote about the differences between the tasks facing West European and East European social democrats:

> The life forces created by capitalism broke the semi-feudal system, destroyed absolutism and laid the groundwork for democracy, yet they also encountered an economy in ruins, which meant that there was no place to think about a transi-

> tion to socialism as analysed in Kautsky's later works [...] instead they had to figure out how to "start anew" – to restore "damned" capitalism, so that it would be possible at least to live and create a new material basis for economic development and the possibility of existence to the life force of socialism, the proletariat.[20]

In other words, the "bourgeois" revolution – the transition to liberal democracy – had taken place under circumstances in which the capitalist economy had to be built up anew. Even under such circumstances, the social democrats could become part of the government, but only for short periods and depending on the situation; in other words, it "wanted to remain truthful to itself, that is, to the workers and did not want to turn into a group of petty bourgeois under a socialist coat of paint".[21] The social democrats, who wanted a place in the government at any cost, were to be considered opportunists who had no place in Menders' strict construction of historical development.

Given that this position was that of the main theoretician and Saeima faction leader, we can draw some conclusions about the ideas shared by Latvian social democrats at least partly from Menders' words. The goal of the social democrats was democratic socialism and it was taken very seriously. It was not supposed to be achieved by armed uprising and dictatorship of the proletariat but by allowing the economic potential of capitalism to develop until a democratic transition to collective ownership of the means of production became possible. To achieve such a position, Latvia had a long road ahead of it, given that the country's economic potential had suffered substantial damage in the war. But this process should not take place under the leadership of social democrats; rather the bourgeois parties should undertake the task of rebuilding capitalism. In other words, social democratic politics required a certain level of economic development, which could only be reached in Latvia in the future. Otherwise, the social democrats could either build capitalism themselves (and thereby cease to be social democrats) or turn to "barracks socialism" and a total restriction of human liberties, as in Soviet Russia. Menders may be guilty of too doctrinaire an approach and getting carried away with Marxist scholasticism, but there is little reason to reproach him for being politically inconsistent. Like many other LSDSP members, he took the ideology of the party seriously. It is another issue that such consistency had practical political consequences. As early as 1921, the group of LSDSP deputies led by Marģers Skujenieks at the Constitutional Assembly threw its support behind the right-wing Meierovics government but then, by the time of the election of the first Saeima, broke off from the mainstream and founded their own, rather weak social democrat Menshevik (*Mazinieku*) party. Skujenieks, the popular leader of this party, continued his political career: from heading the 1926–1928 "leftist" government to becoming deputy prime minister in the authoritarian cabinet of Ulmanis. Another competitor of the LSDSP on the left were the Communists who, after the ban on their party was lifted, were represented as the "faction of workers and peasants" in the third and fourth Saeimas. This organisation was financed and controlled by the USSR, which accused the LSDSP of being insufficiently radical and even "social fascist".

Among the greatest achievements of the LSDSP in the parliamentary period, at the forefront were efforts to protect workers' rights with regard to insurance and safe working conditions, among other things. An important party policy was organising sickness insurance funds. The LSDSP suspected the right-wing coalitions of constantly attempting to curtail constitutionally secured democratic rights and of corruption. It was an important part of the party's activities to identify various conflicts of interest and wasteful use of public funds by rightist governments. At the same time, the LSDSP fostered an increase in the state's role in the economy: regulation by the state, nationalisation and state allotted benefits were considered a solution to many problems facing workers and peasants.

The LSDSP also did much to secure independent Latvia's international position. At the founding of the state, its representatives, including Fēlikss Cielēns, Fricis Menders and Ansis Buševics, participated in brokering peace with both Soviet Russia and Germany. The leading expert in foreign affairs was Cielēns, who was also deputy foreign minister under Zigfrīds Anna Meierovics in Pauļuks' cabinet and foreign minister in Skujenieks' government.

In general, the party's foreign policy orientation was toward a broad regional integration that would benefit a rebirth of industry and the situation of the workers. The relationship with Soviet Russia and later the USSR played a special role: the LSDSP supported a broad economic integration of Eastern Europe that would also involve Russia as Latvia's "natural" economic partner. Of course, such ideas might seem naïve, particularly because Russia would try to achieve political dominance in such an alliance. We should keep in mind, however, that the USSR of the 1920s, at least in the eyes of LSDSP theoreticians, was not the totalitarian superpower that it later became. In Russia this was the period of the so-called New Economic Policy (NEP), when it seemed that even the Bolshevik government was ready to make political concessions in pursuit of economic revival and welfare. At this time, owing to the LSDSP, Cielēns and Skujenieks' "leftist government", Latvia signed a sizeable trade agreement with the USSR, whose main objective was to stimulate Latvia's industry and renew the economic relations broken by war. The agreement, however, was only a partial success.

In general, throughout the interwar period, the LSDSP feared right-wing radicalism, various expressions of national conservative authoritarianism, rhetorically labelled "fascism", both inside and outside the country. The attitude toward communism was much more nuanced. The LSDSP did fight against the local communists or "leftist trade unionists", but ideologically they were much closer to the party than to the various right-wing nationalist forces and particularly the LZS. Regarding the USSR, the party long held on to the hope that the neighbouring superpower would gradually become more democratic and be interested in peaceful collaboration, ignoring the fact that developments in the Soviet empire were going in the opposite direction. Soviet authorities and Latvian social democrats shared similar goals, but their approaches to achieving them were diametrically opposed. To quote Menders once again:

> If they [the Bolsheviks], with fire and sword, were to install Soviet power after the Russian pattern in Latvia, social democracy will use propaganda and, within the limits of red dictatorship, will fight for the *minds of the workers* so that they would achieve an understanding – perhaps through many sacrifices – that the struggle of the proletariat for a life worthy of human beings must not, in the name of socialism, walk over the dead body of democracy, but instead proceed via a flourishing democratic system, which will give the proletariat the material foundation, strength and ability not only to take

and conquer power but also to hold on to it and transform society as a whole on the basis of socialism.[22]

Most surprising here is the illusion that "within the limits of red dictatorship" democratic socialists would have a chance to compete for "the minds of workers" as if the Bolsheviks would ever have tolerated any alternatives to their dogma.

But the LSDSP in fact took the competition for hearts and minds very seriously. The party worked with the public very intensively: it had much experience with propaganda from the time of the Tsar and Russian Civil War. Moreover, the need for propaganda far exceeded the tasks of the election cycle: activities to raise the awareness of the proletariat stemmed from party ideology, according to which social democrats could not and should not turn against the government of the country: on 18 November, an independent, democratic country had been established with general voting rights and broad civil liberties. Under these conditions, the party had to work on workers' minds to guide them to a new and more just system, while not giving in to populism on either the right, fascist side, or on the left, communist side.

The party had its daily press: the best known was the newspaper *Sociāldemokrāts*, later also *Dienas Lapa* and *Liepājas Avīze*, as well as weeklies published by the regional chapters in many urban centres of Latvia. The Women's Central Executive Council, led by Klāra Kalniņa, published the magazine *Darba Sieviete* ("The working woman"). The theoretical publication of the party was *Domas* ("Thoughts"), in which Menders, Cielēns and others published their theoretical articles. At the same time, the party's publishing efforts were not limited to periodicals: its publishing arm Nākotnes kultūra ("Culture of the Future") also issued brochures and books on a variety of issues topical for Latvia and elsewhere.

Alongside the territorial chapters or groups of the party, whose number reached 287 in 1932, it also had a number of subordinate units. Among those was the Social Democratic Youth Association, which in 1926 was transformed into Working Youth with a membership of 2,182 and the magazine *Darba Jaunatne* ("Working Youth"). The party also had some satellite organisations, which did not consist solely of party members but maintained a regular relationship with the party, including trade unions, abstinence societies and student organisations. The party was also substantially involved in the education system: it had its own teachers' section and its members took part in the work of the so-called Riga People's University, offering a wide range of public lectures on different social issues. The party specialised in various mass events: celebrating May Day, pre-election rallies at both local and national level, and sporting and commemorative events. In other words, just like many other interwar European social democratic parties, the LSDSP found it necessary to attract the support of the masses with a significant presence in various areas of public life, including culture, education, sporting activities and consumer cooperatives.

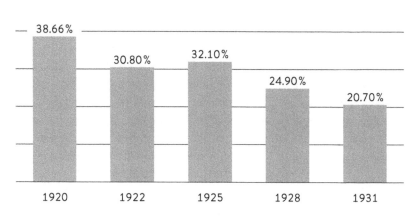

Fig. 1: LSDSP in elections to the Constitutional Assembly and the Saeima (% votes)
Source: Central Election Committee, www.cvk.lv

THE DEMISE AND LEGACY OF THE LSDSP

In the early 1930s, the economic situation in Latvia deteriorated under the impact of the world economic crisis. The democratic regime suffered attacks from both the communists and the fascists. In 1934, then Prime Minister Kārlis Ulmanis dissolved the Saeima and established an authoritarian dictatorship, ostensibly to prevent a coup d'état planned by Latvian fascists. The LSDSP, with its paramilitary organisation the SSS, put up no resistance. The party was not even prepared for such a possibility because an armed struggle against the "bourgeois" government was not compatible with its ideological doctrine. According to historian Aivars Stranga, "Under such conditions of capitalist 'doom' [...] Menders and Latvian social democracy generally lived to see 15 May 1934: in their bourgeois flats and without as much as entertaining the thought of any other form of political struggle, except civic parliamentarianism".[23]

The social democrats were Ulmanis' political opponents; therefore it is hardly surprising that the LSDSP was most damaged by the coup. The most prominent members of the party were arrested and imprisoned in the well-known political prisoners' camp in Liepāja, usually spending several months there. Brūno Kalniņš estimated that about 2,000 party activists, both in Riga and elsewhere, were arrested. Ulmanis purged LSDSP members from all state institutions – ministries, schools and the army – all societies related to the party were dissolved and its press and publishing houses were liquidated. There was an odious "trial" of Dr Pauls Kalniņš, Brūno Kalniņš, Jūlijs Celms and Pēteris Ulpe in 1935–1936 ostensibly for the illegal possession of firearms and the LSDSP itself was banned.

At the same time, the coup of 15 May marked the beginning of the downfall of the LSDSP, from which it would never recover. After the coup, the party returned to the underground where, until the occupation of 1940, it functioned as the Latvian Social Democratic Workers and Peasants Party (LSSZP), with a membership of 200–300 and issuing illegal publications. At this time, fighting Ulmanis' dictatorship from the underground, the party developed closer ties with the communists and became more pro-Soviet. Only the Stalinist USSR was considered as a serious force able to oppose the growing influence of Hitler's Germany, at least until the signing of the Molotov–Ribbentrop Pact on 23 August 1939. The occupation by the Soviet Union in June 1940 gave rise to revanchist elation among some of party members: there was hope that the democratic Constitution would be restored. These illusions were soon disappointed: Kirhenšteins' government refused to register the renewed LSDSP. The reputation of the social democrats was seriously tarnished in 1940 by the fact that a number of prominent LSDSP members became bureaucrats in the openly pro-Soviet Kirhenšteins' government: Brūno Kalniņš became the political head of the Latvian army, Voldemārs Bastjānis headed a department at the Ministry of Finance and Klāvs Lorencs became the director of a bank. But it would be a mistake to claim that members of the LSDSP led the Sovietisation of Latvia or even had a considerable impact on it, even though Brūno Kalniņš' high position in the army caused many people to harbour illusions about the democratic character of the new regime. It should also be kept in mind that Latvian politicians from a variety of parties and movements seemed ready to collaborate with the Soviet power: Kirhenšteins himself was a member of the Progressive Union and minister of justice Juris Pabērzs a member of the Latgallian Progressive People's Union. Many social democrats did not support Latvia being incorporated into the USSR but, in their own opinion at least, tried to "save what could be saved". The most striking symbol of the democratic stance of the LSDSP was the behaviour of Dr Pauls Kalniņš. As chairman of the last democratic Saeima of the Republic of Latvia he did not accept any offers to collaborate. In that capacity, together with many left- and right-wing Latvian politicians in 1944 he signed the memorandum of the Latvian Central Council (LCP) on the restoration of the Latvian state. The LSDSP itself, long since driven underground by the Nazis, also issued a resolution demanding the restoration of democratic Latvia. With their participation in the LCP, the Latvian social democrats went full circle in cooperating with other Latvian democratic parties in the name of Latvian statehood: from the Democratic Bloc and National Council at the end of the First World War to cooperation with their former opponents in the LZP within the framework of the LCP.

The successive occupations by the two totalitarian superpowers decimated the ranks of the LSDSP: a number of prominent members were subjected to communist repression; for the Nazis, social democrats were among the main objects of their hatred. After the war, some LSDSP members, for example, Voldemārs Bastjānis and Klāra and Brūno Kalniņš managed to make it to the West; many of them, including Fēlikss Cielēns, gathered in Sweden. Here, the Swedish Latvian Social Democratic Club was active, representing the LSDSP abroad. Others, however, including Fricis Menders and Klāvs Lorencs, were deported and had to experience heavy repression under the Soviets. One of the tasks of the LSDSP membership abroad was to turn the attention of international social democratic organisations to the fates of Latvian social democrats in the "workers' paradise", the USSR. It was owing to such influence that repressions were softened against Fricis Menders, who was allowed to die in peace in 1971 – albeit exiled to a home for the disabled in Varakļāni as punishment for writing his (as yet unpublished) memoir *Thoughts, Works, Life*. The LSDSP resumed activities in Latvia during the so-called Third Awakening, in 1989: Brūno Kalniņš, then 90, lived to see it.

CONCLUSION

What can we conclude about the relationship between Latvian social democracy and the Latvian state established in 1918? First, social democracy was the first Latvian mass political movement which, starting in the 1890s, galvanised the political life of Latvians, inviting them to think, debate and make their own decisions. Until the rise of social democracy, Latvian political life was conducted under the control and tutelage of societies and pseudo-aristocratic "leaders of the people" who were loyal to the autocratic regime and in search of a mythological past. Social democracy brought modernity to Latvian political life: a demand for political participation, civil rights and freedoms and social justice. Of course, all these were adjusted to the conditions in the Baltics: the postcolonial relations with the Baltic Germans, the specific attitude toward the Russian Empire and the conformism of the Latvian middle class. Much in the activities of the social democrats was exaggerated, extreme and meaningless; much was borrowed, without thinking, from the Western European socialist tradition, attempting to press the reality of Latvia into "objective" schemes and clichés. But it should be remembered that Latvian social democrats had precious little in terms of national cultural traditions from which to draw, in addition to a practically non-existent tradition of Latvian national political thought. Most of the prominent turn-of-the-century social democrats (and not just them, but the Latvian intelligentsia as such) were first-generation intellectuals; their openness to various political ideas and distaste for Baltic provincialism were almost limitless.

The Latvian social democrats were internationalists: the most important items in their programme were to improve the lot of the working people and build a socially just society. By and large they were not anti-nationalist, however. They recognised the cultural needs of different peoples and understood that Latvians should organise their lives themselves. Of all the Latvian autonomy projects that were created by 1917, the lion's share of credit should go to the social democrats. In those too, the cultural needs of Latvians and the right to self-government played a prominent role. Of course, before 1917, the social democrats did not talk about Latvia as a sovereign nation-state. Even if such an idea had seemed politically feasible, their economically-oriented thinking would have made such a scenario absurd to the social democrats: they saw Latvia's economic future only within a federalised, republican Russia. Such an approach was also characteristic of the Young Latvians and the entire early Latvian nationalist tradition, with the difference that the latter saw the future reformed Russia as a monarchy instead of a republic.

The role of the LSDSP in establishing the Latvian state and its political life was unequivocally positive. Even those who opposed the LSDSP, including Kārlis Ulmanis, had to admit that the LSDSP joining the National Council platform brought the kind of mass support for the new state that no other Latvian political force could have hoped to attract. The support of the social democratic Mensheviks for the Republic of Latvia was decisive in persuading a large part of the proletariat and peasants to turn away from Bolshevism, particularly after the fiasco of the Stučka invasion. The activities of the social democrats in the Constitutional Assembly made the new regime decidedly democratic; it fully conformed to contemporary democratic idealism. It might be asked whether the chosen form of constitution was conducive to allow the new state to remain democratic even in economically and politically difficult times. But how can one reproach loyalty to democratic ideals if these ideals are betrayed by the realities of the time?

At the tactical level, the LSDSP took a series of problematic decisions. They include staying out of coalitions, getting carried away with extending the state's economic role and illusions about the likelihood of the USSR becoming more democratic. But such reproaches are relevant only if we evaluate the alternatives as they presented themselves to the participants in the process. One of the arguments in favour of not establishing coalitions was the need to control the radically left-leaning electorate (which was not insignificant) for fear that it might go over to the communists, a radically anti-democratic force, which really was an enemy of Latvian statehood. Were these worries justified? We are unlikely to find out unless we are ready to fully enter the area of "virtual history". The desire for more decisive involvement by the state in the economy was ideologically predetermined for the Latvian social democrats. It seemed to them that the influence of the party on the democratic political process should first and foremost be used to improve the situation of the working people and that it could only be done with the help of the state apparatus, by controlling, redistributing, regulating and subsidising. The fact that such an approach usually leads to mismanagement of funds, bureaucratisation and corruption did not seem more important than the common mission of social democracy. As far as the relationship with the "world's first country of workers and peasants", Soviet Russia or the USSR, the Latvian social democrats allowed illusions to replace their sense of reality. After all, their former party colleagues were in high positions in the Soviet state (although later they disappeared into Stalin's meat grinder one by one). The social democrats saw the main threat from a right-wing dictatorship; a totalitarian dictatorship by the left seemed morally more acceptable to them, if only a little. This tendency became ever stronger when Ulmanis' authoritarian government, with its political police, drove the social democrats underground, threw them in prison and kicked them out of work at state institutions. For that reason, occupation by the USSR seemed to many to bring positive change, however tragically mistaken such illusions might seem. Regarding the later collaboration by social democrats we have to admit that, apart from some scandalous instances, such as Brūno Kalniņš' few months in command of the army, it was nothing extraordinary compared to that of others. After all, when we think about the most infamous Latvian collaborators, the list is headed by people who had nothing in common with social democrats, such as Vilis Lācis and Vilhelms Munters. Collaboration was unfortunately party-colour blind; the opportunities to make a career under the new regime were taken by all kinds of people, and most of them came from the "bourgeois" circles loyal to Ulmanis' regime and not from the social democrats who were driven underground. The same can be said about Soviet period dissidents and critics of the Soviet regime: there were social democrats among them as well.

Latvian social democracy is one of the basic elements of Latvian political history and it is impossible to understand the creation and development of the Latvian state without considering its role. Yet the social democrats did not have eyes in the backs of their heads. They could not predict the turn of events and sometimes relied too much on theoretical dogma. They had their own, sometimes very strong illusions. In the political landscape of their time, however, they represented a leftist democratic movement that enjoyed much public support. If we try to toss out social democracy from

Latvian history, we are also turning our backs on democratic participation, civil rights, social justice and peaceful cooperation between countries within an integrated Europe – against ideals which, in a very Latvian way, warts and all, were defended by this historical party.

SUMMARY

The Latvian Social Democratic Workers' Party (LSDSP) was the main Latvian political movement before the First World War and its role in state-building has not previously been fully evaluated. Of course, relations between Social Democrats and independent nation-statehood have often been problematic, not only in Latvia but in most central and eastern European countries. Nationalists and socialists have opposed each other fiercely and relations between class and nation were often seen as contradictory and even antagonistic. In practice, however, there have been multiple overlaps and forms of cooperation; the support of Leftist forces for new statehood has often been crucial.

The Latvian socialist movement was born out of the split in the Latvian nationalist movement, when the energetic younger generation of intellectuals, such as Eduards Veidenbaums, Jānis Pliekšāns-Rainis, Pēteris Stučka, Aspazija and others, found themselves unwilling to remain within the conservative structures dominated by the Riga Latvian Society (RLB). The "New Current", as they called themselves, was not a Marxist party. It included many facets of European modernism of the time, including realism in literature, Darwinism in science various democratic, Leftist and feminist ideologies coming from both Western Europe and the main Russian cities of Moscow and St Petersburg. The "New Current" was crushed by the Tsarist authorities, however, and henceforth the underground movement became increasingly social democratic.

The LSDSP was established in 1904 as a social democratic party for Latvians; ideologically, it followed the German SPD and Karl Kautsky. In political terms, however, it joined forces with Russian Social Democrats, especially after the Revolution of 1905, when the party had its first experience in mass organizing. Despite the strong influence of Lenin, the LSDSP retained its independence and did not split into Bolsheviks and Mensheviks until 1917.

In that year, after the February Revolution in Russia, the Latvian Bolsheviks split off and prepared themselves for an armed insurrection in order to overthrow the Provisional Government. The Latvian Mensheviks, however, established an independent party and planned for a democratic, autonomous Latvia. Their support was decisive for the establishment of Latvian statehood in 1918; they were the only Latvian political force that enjoyed something like mass legitimacy.

The LSDSP, led by Fricis Menders and Pauls Kalniņš, played a prominent role in the first period of democracy. It helped to draft a democratic, parliamentary constitution (Satversme), adopted in 1922. The party also made an important contribution to the defence of workers' rights and social justice. Despite having the largest faction in all three inter-war convocations of the Latvian parliament (Saeima), however, the LSDSP did not join any ruling coalitions (except for two brief periods) and was mainly in opposition. Probably for this reason the party was unable to prevent the 1934 coup d'etat by the right-wing agrarian Kārlis Ulmanis. After the coup the party merged with the communists and went underground, only to re-emerge briefly after the Soviet occupation of 1940. Some Social Democrats collaborated with the Soviets. Many, including the leaders Menders and Kalniņš, joined with other democratic politicians and called for the restoration of democratic Latvian statehood. Many Social Democrats fought for the restoration of 1918 Latvia, both as severely repressed Soviet dissidents and as exiles living in the West.

1. Skailis, A., *Toreiz blusas lēca augstāk. Pirmskara puikas un palaidnības*, Riga, Likteņstāsti, 2001, p. 192.
2. Dauge, P. [P. D.], 1893, Sociāldemokrātu stāvoklis Vacija, *Dienas Lapa* 7: pp. 1–2.
3. Miške V. et al. *Latvijas Komunistiskās partijas vēstures apcerējumi. Latvijas KP CK Partijas vēstures institūts* – PSKP CK Marksisma-ļeņinisma institūta filiāle; (Vol. 3), Riga, Latvijas Valsts izdevniecība, 1961–1981, Vol. 3, p. 74.
4. *LKP 25 gadi. Rakstu un materiālu krājums. Kongresu, konferenču un CK svarīgākie lēmumi un rezolūcijas*, Moscow, Prometejs, 1929, p. 39.
5. LKP vēstures apcerējumi, *op. cit.*, Vol. 1, p. 118.
6. Valters, M. [M.W.], 1900, Iz latviešu sadzīves, *Latviešu Strādnieks*, No. 5, pp. 151–162; Roziņš, F. [A.], 1900, Tauta un tēzeme, *Latviešu Strādnieks*, No. 5 (April).
7. Valters, M., 1903, Patvaldību nost! Krieviju nost!, *Proletāriets, Politikas un Zinātnes laikraksts*, No. 11, pp. 65–67.
8. LKP 25 gadi. p. 41.
9. Stučka, P., 1904, Vienība vai federācija, *Sociāldemokrāts*, No. 24, pp. 1–24.
10. Sk. Longworth, J., 1959, *Latvian Congress of the Rural Delegates*, Northeast European Archives.
11. Latviešu sociāldemokrātu savienības pirmais vispārējais Kongress, noturēts Rīgā, 29. un 30. decembrī 1905. g. (brochure) Riga, 1905, p. 5.
12. See, for example, Pumpuriņš, T., 2005, Terora lielmeistars – Alberts Traubergs no Cēsīm, *Informācija, revolūcija, reakcija 1905.–2005. Starptautiskas konferences materiāli*. Riga, Latvijas Nacionālā bibliotēka, 2005, pp. 134–40.
13. Skujenieks, M., 1914, *Nacionālais jautājums Latvijā*, St Petersburg, A. Gulbis, 1914, p. 15.
14. Valters, M., 1913, *Latviešu kultūras demokrātija, viņas spēki un uzdevumi*, Riga, Valters un Rapa, pp. 22–25.
15. Kalniņš, B., *Latvijas sociāldemokrātijas 50 gadi*, Riga, 1993.
16. Meeting of the National Council, 18 November 1918, transcript.
17. Freivalds, O., *Latviešu politiskās partijas 60 gados*. Stockholm, Imanta, 1961, p. 108.
18. Menders, F. (1925) Divas revolūcijas. Revolūcijas piemiņas runa, turēta 26. janvārī 1925. gadā Valmierā, 1905. gada janvāra notikumu 20 gadu piemiņas dienā, Riga, Sociāldemokrāts.
19. See, for example, Kroders, A., *Prūšu un baronu sazvērestība pret Latvijas valsti 16 aprīlī 1919 Liepājā*, Riga, 1919.
20. Menders, F., Koalīcijas politika un sociāldemokrātija, Riga, *Sociāldemokrāts*, 1923, p. 19.
21. Ibid.
22. Menders, F., Partijas konference, *Sociāldemokrāts*, No. 15, 28 December 1918.
23. Stranga, op. cit. p. 19.

Bibliography

Bastjānis V. *Demokrātiskā Latvija: vērojumi un vērtējumi*. Stokholma: Emīls Ogriņš, 1966.

Brüggemann K. *Licht und Luft des Imperiums: Legitimations- und Repräsentationsstrategien russischer Herrschaft in den Ostseeprovinzen im 19. und frühen 20. Jahrhundert*. Wiesbaden: Harrassowitz, 2018.

Cielēns F. *Laikmetu maiņā: atmiņas un atziņas*. Lidingö: Memento, 1961–1964.

Dauge P. *P. Stučkas dzīve un darbs*. J. Vilka red. Rīga: Latvijas Valsts izd., 1958.

Ezergailis A. The Bolshevization of the Latvian Social Democratic Party. *Canadian Slavic Studies*, I, No. 2 (Summer, 1967), 238- 252.

Ezergailis A. *The Latvian Impact on the Bolshevik Revolution: The First Phase; September 1917 to April 1918*. Boulder, Colo.: East European Monographs, 1983.

Ijabs I. Break Out of Russia: Miķelis Valters and the National Issue in Early Latvian Socialism. *Journal of Baltic Studies*, 43:4, 2012, 437–458.

Ijabs I. The Nation of the Socialist Intelligentsia: The National Issue in the Political Thought of Early Latvian Socialism. *East Central Europe*, 2012, vol. 39, no. 2–3, 181–203.

Kalniņa K. *Liesmainie gadi: atmiņu vija*. Stokholma: LSDSP Ārzemju Komiteja, 1964.

Kalniņš B. *Latvijas sociāldemokrātijas piecdesmit gadi*. Stokholma: LSDSP Ārzemju Komiteja, 1956.

LKP 25 gadi. Rakstu un materiālu krājums. Kongresu, konferenču un CK svarīgākie lēmumi un rezolūcijas. Maskava: Prometejs: 1929, 39. lpp.

Miller A. and Berger S. (eds) *Nationalizing Empires*. Budapest: CEU Press, 2015.

Miller A. *The Romanov Empire and Nationalism: Essays in the Methodology of Historical Research*. Budapest: CEU Press, 2008.

Miške V. u. c. *Latvijas Komunistiskās partijas vēstures apcerējumi*. Latvijas KP CK Partijas vēstures institūts – PSKP CK Marksisma-ļeņinisma institūta filiāle. (3. sēj.). Rīga: Latvijas Valsts izdevniecība, 1961–1981.

Stranga A. *LSDSP un 1934. gada 15. maija valsts apvērsums: Demokrātijas likteņi Latvijā*. – Rīga: Autora izdev., 1998.

Šiliņš J. *Padomju Latvija 1918–1919*. Rīga: Vēstures izpētes un popularizēšanas biedrība, 2013.

SOCIAL DEMOCRACY IN THE FORMATION OF THE MODERN LITHUANIAN STATE

GINTARAS MITRULEVIČIUS

INTRODUCTION

The possibility of restoring (and creating a modern) Lithuanian state in 1918–1919 was determined by a number of external factors. They include the First World War, which led to the collapse of the old political system in Europe; the revolutions in Russia and Germany during the war and the collapse of their empires; the German defeat in the war; the coming of the Bolsheviks to power and the civil war in Russia; and the popularity of the right of nations to self-determination. Lithuania would not have become an independent state, however, if the Lithuanians themselves, including both individuals and groups with different worldviews and different political beliefs (and thus political parties), had not taken the opportunities that presented themselves and actively participated in building their country. One of the political parties that played a role was the Social Democratic Party of Lithuania, the LSDP. In this chapter we briefly present the role of this party in the formation of the Lithuanian state[1].

HISTORICAL CONTEXT OF LITHUANIAN SOCIAL DEMOCRACY AND IDEOLOGICAL-PROGRAMMATIC ASSUMPTIONS AND POLITICAL ASPIRATIONS

Although the establishment of the LSDP was announced in 1896, the Lithuanian social democratic movement had emerged a few years earlier. Its origins date back to 1893, when Vilnius residents Alfonsas Moravskis and

Andrius Domaševičius became leaders of the first Lithuanian social democratic groups. In 1895, a conference led to the establishment of the organisation called "Lithuanian Social Democracy". On 1 May 1896, at the 13th Social Democrat Meeting held in Vilnius, which was later recorded in history as the LSDP I Congress, it finally became a political party.

The emergence of the LSDP was influenced by similar factors to those that led to the formation of social democratic parties in other countries and by more local circumstances. It is well known that the emergence of social democracy in the second half of the nineteenth century was connected to the convergence of socialism and the workers' movement. As far as Lithuania is concerned, although socialism had already manifested itself, it was related mainly to the Russian "*Narodniks*", which developed into "Narodnaya Volya" ("people's will") socialism. From the beginning of the 1880, a number of partially "pro-Narodnaya Volya" and partially pro-Marxist socialist figures and interest groups were associated with the Polish revolutionary "Proletariat" party.

No independent socialist organisation had been formed that was native to Lithuania, however, and none of the aforementioned manifestations of socialism in Lithuania took root until the last decade of the nineteenth century. Socialism really developed only in the wake of the social democratic movement. But the emergence of the latter, too, required certain socio-economic prerequisites that were rapidly forming in Lithuania at the end of the nineteenth century.

In the second half of the nineteenth century, when serfdom was abolished, capitalist social-economic relationships began to develop more rapidly in tsarist Russia, and thus in Lithuania as well, which had been merged with Russia at the end of the eighteenth century. At the same time, the conditions for a workers' movement began to develop. This created favourable ground for the spreading of socialist ideas from Western European countries (often through Russia and Poland), where these ideas had already become very popular. At that time, an intelligentsia began to form in Lithuania, whose representatives often became distributors of socialist ideas among the workers.

The development of the aforementioned processes in Lithuania and throughout Russia was considerably delayed compared with Western European countries. As a result, Lithuania remained an agrarian country.

According to the Russian nationwide census of 1897, 73.3 per cent of the population of Lithuania belonged to the peasantry, while urban dwellers accounted for just 20 per cent. The slow development of industry, along with the slow growth of the working class and, in general, the urban population, meant that Lithuanian social democracy began to manifest itself only in the 1890s. At the end of the nineteenth century and in the first decades of the twentieth century, it still did not attain the same influence as in more industrialised countries.

The slow process of industrialisation and urbanisation was also influenced by the policy of national oppression pursued by the Russian Empire, which became even more onerous following the prohibition of the press (until 1904) in Latin script in Lithuania after the 1863 uprising. Nonetheless, the national revival and national movement that were partially a reaction to the oppression also served as one of the prerequisites for the emergence of Lithuanian social democracy.

It should also be noted with regard to the circumstances fostering the emergence and development of social democracy that the autocratic Russian political system did not allow political parties to operate legally. Although parties had been allowed to operate on a semi-legal basis since the end of 1905, the actions of the socialist parties were still severely restrained and persecuted.

Another important characteristic was the national composition of the population of Lithuania, especially in cities and in Vilnius in particular. When the LSDP was formed, the composition of the country's population was 58.3 per cent Lithuanians, 13.3 per cent Jews, 10.3 per cent Poles and 14.6 per cent Eastern Slavs (Russians, Belarusians and Ukrainians). As much as 93.3 per cent of all Lithuanians were still peasants, however. According to the Russian nationwide census of 1897, Lithuanians made up only 3.9 per cent of all urban dwellers. Additionally, 42.1 per cent of Lithuanian urban dwellers considered Yiddish to be their mother tongue, 24 per cent Polish and 21.5 per cent one of the Eastern Slavic languages, while only 7.8 per cent considered the Lithuanian language as their mother tongue.

Taking this into account, it is understandable why the first social democratic group in Lithuania is considered to be the group, international in its nature, founded in 1887 and headed by the famous Polish (later German) social democracy activist and Jewish socialist Leo Jogiches (Jan Tyszka). It is also understandable why the social democratic movement in Vilnius fragmented, at least to a large extent on a national basis, in the 1890s.

When Leo Jogiches emigrated in May 1890, the new social democratic organisation that continued the work of his group, unlike its predecessor, is referred to in the literature as a Jewish social democratic group in Vilnius. Indeed, Jews were the first among the Lithuanian people of different nationalities to establish social democratic organisations on a national basis. In 1897, in Vilnius, they founded a general trade union composed of Russian and Polish Jews called the Bund.

Since the beginning of the 1890s, besides the Jewish social democrats, small labour groups had operated in Vilnius that were also influenced by the Polish socialists, and from 1893, a unit of the Polish Socialist Party (PSP) that had been founded in 1892 in Paris began to emerge in Lithuania as well. The activities of the Jewish and Polish socialists served as an incentive for the emergence of the Lithuanian social democratic movement, and for the formation of the LSDP in 1895 and 1896.

In the second half of the 1890s, more socialist organisations were launched in Vilnius, including the Lithuanian Trade Union (LDS) founded in 1896 by Stanislavas Trusevičius, who left (or was forced to leave) the future LSDP. Members of the LDS together with members of Social Democracy of the Kingdom of Poland (SDKP), founded in 1893, and some of the ex-members of the LSDP founded Social Democracy of the Kingdom of Poland and Lithuania (SDKPiL) in 1900–1901, another party that operated in Lithuania under the same name until 1906. In that year, the SDKPiL merged with the Russian Social Democratic Labour Party (RSDLP) formed in 1898, and its members continued to function in Lithuania as members of the RSDLP. It should be noted that the RSDLP was one of the social democratic parties that operated in the territory of ethnic Lithuania (partially from the end of the nineteenth century and entirely from the beginning of the twentieth century) through the Bund, which became part of the RSDLP in 1898 (until 1903) and then again from 1906. The Belarusian Socialist Assembly (Belarusian Socialist Hramada) and the Russian Socialist Revolutionary Party, as well as several Socialist-Zionist Jewish parties, were still operating in Vilnius at the beginning of the twentieth century.

Among all the parties mentioned here, however, only the LSDP represented Lithuanian social democracy. As a matter of fact, there was one more organisation that fit this definition, the Social Democratic Labour Party of Lithuania (LSDDP), but it existed only very briefly. It was founded in 1905, but merged with the LSDP in the same year. The LSDP was also the only Lithuanian party to represent the Lithuanian socialist movement in general, before the members of the Lithuanian Democratic Party (LDP) became socialists-populists. Besides the aforementioned LSDDP, the LSDP was also the only socialist party in Lithuania (before the Democrats became socialists-populists) that was also a part of the national social and political movement. The Lithuanian social democrats who founded the LSDP were also the first Lithuanian proto - political group to emerge between the end of the nineteenth century and the beginning of the twentieth that developed into a political party. It was also the Lithuanian party that presented the first Lithuanian statehood restoration programme.

The programme adopted by the LSDP in 1896 is considered the first party manifesto. In its theoretical part, it describes the development of the Lithuanian economy after the abolition of serfdom based on a Marxist analysis of social development. The programme states that the formation of a socialist regime requires political freedom and that cooperation between different countries is necessary because the socialist order cannot be created in a single country. Friedrich Engels declared in a preface to the 1892 Polish edition of the *Communist Manifesto* that "a sincere international collaboration of the European nations is possible only if each of these nations is fully autonomous in its own house". Accordingly, the task of the LSDP is stipulated as "to hasten and organise the class struggle of the Lithuanian proletariat, both its economic and political constituents, [and] to indicate the final goals of this struggle and the gradual stages ...". The party programme goes on to say:

> In order to organise as soon as possible, and to prepare for the emergence of a socialist order necessary to ensure the greatest possible welfare and the widest possible political freedom in these times of doing one's duty, the Lithuanian Social Democratic Party, relying on the abovementioned grounds [the theoretical programme comprising the first three sections, *author's note*], formulates the following minimum programme: a self-governing democratic republic, consisting of Lithuania, Poland and other countries, based on a free federation[2].

Annex 4 of the programme indicates that by "other countries" the authors of the LSDP programme meant Latvia, Belarus and Ukraine. According to historians, such a composition of a "free federation" shows that the LSDP programme of 1896 is still referring to "the old noble notion of the Lithuanian state" and that the "Lithuanian statehood formula" stipulated in the LSDP programmes is evidently based on the "unified" tradition of the former statehood of the Grand Duchy of Lithuania.[3]

A. Moravskis, however, when commenting on the wording of the LSDP Programme of 1896 mentioned the Swiss example, which was popular among party members. According to Moravskis, "the Lithuanian social democrats depicted the future independent Republic of Lithuania, liberated from Russian oppression, as a federal democratic republic consisting of Lithuania, Poland and other territories with full autonomy".[4] Therefore, the wording of the first LSDP programme on the political future of Lithuania was determined by more than an allusion to the tradition of the Grand Duchy of Lithuania.

As far as the wording of the LSDP's main political position is concerned, it should also be noted that the opinions of the participants in the Congress of 1896 were scarcely unanimous. The minority included Felix Dzerzhinsky, who was then a member of this party but soon became a member of the SDKPiL, and later a Bolshevik activist. He spoke against Lithuania's goal of separating from Russia. In addition, in 1896 (before the congress), there had been disagreements between the leaders of the LSDP and S. Trusevičius and his followers, who also opposed the "separatism" of the former.

The historian Vytautas Merkys wrote that the LSDP programme of 1896 on the political future of Lithuania shows "a clearly defined task of the political liberation of Lithuania from the tsar's power", as well as "the demand of the Lithuanian nation for the right to sovereignty". According to another historian, Česlovas Laurinavičius, it also generally represents "the first programme on the restoration of the Lithuanian statehood".[5] Until that time, the entire Lithuanian national movement had considered the matter of a liberated Lithuania only occasionally and abstractly, if at all. It should be noted that one of the first people to write about the future "of a free Lithuania" and about the fact that "Lithuania wants to be politically independent" was one of the first Lithuanian socialists in the 1880s, Jonas Šliūpas.

It should be further noted that, when specifying the political credo in their commemorative speeches on 1 May 1894, A. Moravskis and A. Domaševičius called socialism a "future goal" and pointed to the demand for Lithuanian statehood as an immediate political aspiration. In another speech they also stated that the populations of some European states were smaller than that of Lithuania and that there were three million Lithuanians who could form a separate state. Because, according to A. Moravskis, the "local revolutionary forces were not sufficient to seek a completely independent and separate state of Lithuania" the founders of the LSDP favoured a "free federation", as mentioned in the 1896 programme.[6] From a modern understanding, this could have meant either something between a federation and a confederation, or maybe even a confederation rather than a federation.

Moreover, with respect to the 1896 LSDP programme, it should be mentioned that following the goal of forming an "independent democratic republic", the programme further describes the "foundations of the Constitution" for this future republic. In these foundations we can see a programme of radical democratic demands including: the sovereignty of the nation; a universal, democratic, proportional electoral system; equality of all citizens; freedom of speech, the press, assembly and organisation; universal, compulsory and free education; separation of church and state; free courts, with the principle of the choice of judges; abolition of the death penalty; replacement of the army with the *militsiya*; and utilising the international peace courts to resolve international conflicts. Also mentioned was the "equalisation of the remuneration of officials and deputies with payment for physical labour". The programme also formulates social requirements such as free health care, "free medicines and funerals", progressive taxation of profits and property, the abolition of all direct taxes and moreover "gradual limitation of the right to leave wealth to one's heirs".

Thereafter, demands for the "protection of the rights of economic workers" were laid down. These included: a shortened working day, "continuous rest for at least 36 hours per week for each worker", minimum wages and wage equalisation for men and women, the improvement of work health and safety, social protection, labour protection, labour inspections, labour exchanges, laws on a labour secretariat, recognition of the freedom to strike and labour movement rights, as well as the demand for the regulation and supervision of state economic processes. It ends with a goal typical of the social democrats of those times: "gradual confiscation of the land, means of production and communication to be managed by the community" (that is, the public, *author's note*), in other words, the gradual socialisation of the means of production[7].

The 1896 LSDP programme therefore provided not only for the separation from Russia and Lithuanian statehood, but also for a certain vision of the social and political nature of such a state, along with a clear and even radical programme for the consolidation of a democratic system. At first glance, the programme looks like an analysis of the development of a Marxist society and of the fight for social and national liberation.

According to the long-standing leader of the LSDP, Steponas Kairys, the theoretical justification of the 1896 LSDP programme was "purely Marxist, as was the case with the German or Austrian social democrats", which "clearly showed the complete orientation of the authors of the programme towards the West", where "the explanation for the changes in the Lithuanian economy and good examples of related activities were sought". The content of the basic programme was "based on the growing experience of the socialist movement in the West".[8]

Indeed, the 1896 LSDP programme drew on the Social Democratic Party of Germany's (SPD) Erfurt Programme of 1891, as well as the resolutions of the Second International Congress and the Polish Socialist Party's SDKP and PSP programmes. Thus, the text of the 1896 LSDP programme, as well as its sources testify to the idea expressed by historians that the LSDP was an "international party in nature". It should be noted that the establishment of the LSDP in 1896 was also related to the wish of the Lithuanian social democrats to be independently represented at the Second International Congress in London. It turned out, however, that the US Lithuanian Socialist J. Šliūpas, who was supposed to represent the LSDP, was absent from the Congress.

To conclude the discussion on the LSDP's 1896 programme, it should also be noted that apart from the wording of its main political demands and the related programme annexes, the remainder of the programme (the theoretical part and the part stipulating the specific political and economic demands) remained almost unchanged from the late nineteenth century until the beginning of the twentieth century, and throughout the First World War, as well as partially during the initial period of the Republic of Lithuania.

Nevertheless, the wording of the main political demands was later amended. The new version of the party programme adopted at the 1897 LSDP Congress was finalised following heated debates. It described Lithuania's political future as follows: "Voluntary federation of the regions with the self-government of the people passing laws and governing in the state, the krai, the province and the volost."[9] Although some interpretations have it that at the congress of 1897 the Lithuanian social democrats surrendered their goal of separating from Russia, in fact, the wording of the 1897 programme was somewhat obscure. For example, as Moravskis shows, the term "free federation" was supposed to be made up of nations that had separated from Russia.

This interpretation is also supported by the following demand raised in the social democrats' proclamations in 1898: "the demand for Lithuanian autonomy, based on the relations of a free federation with those of neighbouring nations, which will recognise Lithuania's autonomy". This demand was repeated at the 4th LSDP Congress held in May 1899.

It is important that the word "autonomy", which at that time was understood differently than in 1906–1907, should not be misinterpreted. Apparently, it was understood as explained in the resolutions of the 6th LSDP Congress of 1905:

> in the event of a misunderstanding of the word "autonomy", the congress explains that the political autonomy of Lithuania, as currently demanded, was understood as it is currently explained in our programme: the democratic Republic of Lithuania, willingly comprising the neighbouring nations and coordinated on the basis of a federation.[10]

Such explanations led to the conclusion that, if Lithuania were to join the federation on a voluntary basis, then it would first of all have to gain independence and only then, as was provided in the wording of 1898, would it have been able to choose its partners to establish a federation-based relationship.

The resolution of the 5th LSDP Congress of 1902 states that the LSDP shall recognise the right of every nation to decide its fate and shall "strive to create a democratic Lithuanian republic federated with neighbouring nations that are at the same level in terms of a social and political stature".[11]

Such a provision eliminated Russia from the future federation, as a rather underdeveloped region.

At the LSDP Conference of 1903, a number of ideals were again spoken of favourably: "full political freedom of the workers", "universal people's freedom" and "national Lithuanian freedom... which would provide for ... a democratic republic of Lithuania ... united with the equal republics of neighbouring nations". It should be noted that the latter phrase was not mentioned in the resolutions of the 1903 Conference in relation to "a free democratic republic".[12] In 1903 and 1904, however, the LSDP repeatedly spoke in favour of an "independent Lithuania", a "Lithuanian democratic republic" and "an independent Lithuania, a Lithuanian republic".[13] Notably, at that time, no other Lithuanian social nor political force had spoken out so radically for the political future of the Lithuanian national-social movement.

Thus, toward the end of a decade of LSDP activities, the emphasis on forming a "federation" in the party's programme began to weaken, while the aspiration for an independent democratic Lithuania grew stronger. According to a later affirmation by Vincas Kapsukas, the editorial office of the LSDP newspaper *Workers' Voice* "considered the demand for a federation to be a demand for independence" because "without independence, there cannot be, without coercion, any 'free will' in the merger of one land with another".[14]

Vincas Kapsukas and Zigmas Angarietis, former social democrats who then became communists, in common with communist historiography in general, criticised the LSDP's actions at the turn of the twentieth century due to its aspiration for Lithuania to secede from Russia and for Lithuanian statehood. They interpreted this "separatism" on the part of the LSDP as a "manifestation of reformism", "opportunism", "social patriotism" and "bourgeois nationalism ... among the members of the LSDP", as well as a demonstration of the "relationship of the LSDP with the petit bourgeoisie" or even the "bourgeois nature of the LSDP".[15] This was only the communist view, however. From the point of view of the social democrats themselves, or at least a considerable part of them, the aspiration for the independence of individual nations, or the pursuit of their statehood, did not stand in opposition to the aspirations of the proletariat.

According to various historians, in the wake of the "national revolution" that took place in Lithuania in 1905, the LSDP was the "most active" and "most influential" political force, as well as the most "influential organisation in Lithuania".[16] On the other hand, in the year of the revolution it was shown that the aspiration for a separate and independent Republic of Lithuania, at least in the wording of the goals of the programme, was not yet stable.

The defeat in the revolution was a hard blow to both the LSDP as an organisation and its activities and influence in society; it also shaped the party programme. At the 7th Congress of the LSDP held in 1907, the participants spoke in favour of declaring that the LSDP's political programme should aim at "forming a democratic republic and the political autonomy of Lithuania".[17] This meant that the LSDP favoured the autonomy of Lithuania as part of Russia.

According to S. Kairys, such a change in the LSDP's political programme in 1905 was determined by the collapse of the Russian revolution of that year, which

> undermined not only the struggle for freedom, but also the party programme, perhaps not so much due to the new situation, but rather due to the lack of confidence in the forces of democracy and not seeing the only way forward as unifying the efforts of the entire proletariat of the Russian empire.[18]

The LSDP continued to be guided by this provision concerning Lithuania's political future until the First World War.

ROLE OF THE SOCIAL DEMOCRATS IN THE (RE)CONSTRUCTION OF THE LITHUANIAN STATE (1914–1919)

The beginning of the First World War and the German occupation of Lithuania meant that the remaining Lithuanian social democrats, whose options as regards organisation and political activities conditions had been narrow even before the war, would have to amend their programme as regards the future of Lithuania. These amendments were made as soon as discussions about the Lithuania's political fate became relevant.

LSDP members predicted that the war would lead to changes in the political map of Europe. They rejected the programme of 1907 and very clearly and apparently somewhat earlier and more radically than the other Lithuanian political forces at that time, decided "to name an Independent Democratic Lithuania as the highest aspiration of the Party". The matter of relations with other countries remained open, although it was "aimed at becoming acquainted with their democracy in order to jointly fight to acquire freedom and to guarantee that freedom once acquired".[19]

Having established such a goal and in order to popularise it, but without being able to act publicly, the LSDP illegally disseminated its proclamations and occasionally illegal publications, in which it not only explicitly advocated an independent democratic Lithuania, but also emphasised the need for a democratic order in the future state, as well as indicating how it should be done. Given the current situation, the LSDP amended its position on cooperation with other political currents in Lithuania, although earlier, as well as at the beginning of the war, it had pursued cooperation only with other socialist parties. Therefore, the social democrats joined the joint social structures of various political currents in Lithuania, aimed at organising support for the victims of war, discussing political issues and representing Lithuanian affairs. In this way, they participated in the joint actions of representatives of various currents in order to improve the state of Lithuania. For example, in July 1916, Steponas Kairys, Antanas Smetona and Jurgis Šaulys attended the conference of the League of Nations Oppressed by Russia, at which, for the first time, an official demand was made on behalf of the Lithuanian representatives for the "completed undefined independence of Lithuania".[20]

Of course, the fact that the social democrats took part in these joint actions along with other political currents did not mean that their mutual disagreements had disappeared. Indeed, the social democrats coordinated with right-wing activities aimed at promoting Lithuania's "main political goals" abroad in order to obtain support from European and global democratic forces.[21]

The LSDP's relations with right-wing parties were once again aggravated in spring 1917; however, they did not completely break with them at that time, and in summer 1917 the social democrats supported the idea of creating a Council of Lithuania. Although they were in favour of a democratic election, they did not agree with the principle of co-option when choosing participants for the conference, which was proposed by the presidium for the summoning of the Lithuanian Organising Committee Conference. However, given the fact that the Germans would not allow elections to be organised, they suggested a "semi-co-option – semi-election" alternative, and encouraged not only Lithuanians to be "invited", but also other nationalities who "sympathise with Lithuania".[22]

The social democrats took part in the election of the participants in the Lithuanian Conference and actively participated in it (18–22 September 1917). When discussing the general political resolution of the conference on the future of Lithuania, they were firmly opposed to the establishment of any relations with Germany, and clearly expressed their strong support for the independence of Lithuania – although, due to German pressure, it was necessary to note in the resolution that Lithuania would enter into some kind of relationship with Germany. The LSDP representatives highlighted the significance of the Constituent Assembly of Lithuania (the "Seimas") to be elected democratically, which would have determined both the internal political order of Lithuania and its relations with its neighbours. They also concurred that the resolution on the future of Lithuania must also deal with national minorities, who should be granted cultural autonomy.

The social democrats supported the election of the Council of Lithuania. However, when the various representatives failed to agree on proportional representation, only two members of the LSDP and two left-wing representatives, S. Kairys and M. Biržiška, were initially elected. After some tensions between the left- and the right-wing parties, certain compromises were made by the latter. Thus, instead of two priests who had withdrawn from the Council of Lithuania, two left-wing politicians were elected: the democrat (socialist-populist) Jonas Vileišis and Stanislovas Narutavičius, who was close to towards the social democrats. In 24 September 1917, at the first meeting of the Council of Lithuania, S. Kairys was elected its first deputy chairman.

The left-wing quartet on the Council of Lithuania was the strongest opponent of German annexation plans in Lithuania. The left-wingers spoke clearly against the Council resolution of 11 December 1917 and declared not only the goal of secession from Russia and the restoration of an independent Lithuania, but also of a "firm, eternal alliance" with Germany, as was established under the four conventions. On 26 January 1918, S. Kairys, M. Biržiška, J. Vileišis and S. Narutavičius, after disagreeing with the policy of connivance with Germany that was accepted by the majority of the Council of Lithuania, withdrew from the Council under the leadership of A. Smetona, and agreed to return only when a majority of the Council accepted, in principle, their draft Declaration of the Independence of Lithuania. Thus, the role and contribution of the social democrats (and of the left-wing in general) in the final formulation and adoption of the Act of 16 February 1918 (as it was published) was quite significant.

Beginning in the middle of November 1917, the social democrats had started publishing the newspaper *Labour Voice* (*Darbo balsas*) which, despite censorship, made a clear statement on the creation of an independent and democratic Republic of Lithuania, while emphasising the need to ensure the rights of national minorities, as well as protesting against the undemocratic actions of right-wing political forces and against the desire of Polish landlords to annex Lithuania to Poland.

Speaking in favour of creating a democratic state of Lithuania, the left-wing quartet of the Council of Lithuania, following the adoption of the Act in 16 February 1918, suggested that the Council should convene a second Lithuanian conference as soon as possible and prepare for the elections to the Constituent Assembly, although under the circumstances of those times, this was unrealistic. Germany, recognising only the resolution of 11 December 1917, prevented Lithuania's declaration of independence and, until the very end of the war, stopped any actions by the Council of Lithuania aimed at restoring statehood. Therefore, the majority of the Council sought to find a way out of this situation and, in order to strengthen their position and to stabilise Lithuanian statehood in any form possible, they decided on 11 July 1918 to declare Lithuania a monarchy and to elect Prince Wilhelm von Urach, Count of Württemberg, as king. The social democrats (like the other left-wing parties) protested against this decision. They blamed the majority of the Council of Lithuania for breaching their authority and for usurping the rights of the Constituent Assembly, as they had not taken part in the work of the Council since 12 July 1918. Having withdrawn from the LSDP, in autumn 1918, M. Biržiška returned to work at the Council of Lithuania, which at that time was called the State Council of Lithuania (the "LVT"), as a private individual rather than as a representative of the social democrats.

From 1915 to 1918, Lithuanian social democracy had a presence not only in German-occupied Lithuania, but also further afield, in Scotland, the United States and Russia. Nonetheless, most of the Lithuanian social democrats who were active in the country during 1917–1918 surrendered to the ideological and political influence of Russian Bolshevism and became communists. (There is no room here to discuss the latter's ideological-political development and political assumptions regarding Lithuania's statehood.[23])

With the exception of certain positions of the Polish socialists who belonged for some time to the LSDP, in general, there were no significant differences between the ideological and political assumptions of the Lithuanian social democrats in Vilnius in the period 1915 to 1917. In 1918, however, a certain ideological and political differentiation influenced by Russian Bolshevism began to manifest itself in the Lithuanian Social Democratic Movement as well. As a result, in summer and autumn 1918, the Lithuanian-Belarusian Communist Party (LBKP) was created.[24] In autumn 1918, the Bolsheviks' LBKP, which was fully supported by Russia, was very active in Lithuania. It should be noted that Lithuanian social democrats who had remained faithful to social democracy were violently attacked at this time, through written and oral communist propaganda and agitation.

In the second half of 1918, the latter group criticised and negatively assessed Russian Bolshevism in the newspaper *Labour Voice*. During this period, these social democrats, without changing their principles, did not recognise the LVT. They demanded a new regional conference and the election of a new Council of Lithuania, which in turn should strive to organise democratic elections to the Constituent Assembly as soon as possible.

The social democrats did not recognise the formation of the First Provisional Government of Lithuania led by A. Voldemaras. Instead, they discussed the possibility of forming the Lithuanian government only from representatives of the socialist parties. Later, they joined negotiations with these parties on the formation of the Revolutionary Council of Lithuania as a provisional supreme authority. These negotiations were soon transformed into negotiations on the election of the Vilnius Council of Workers' Representatives (DAT), however, which was supposed to have the highest authority in Lithuania until the Congress of Representatives of the Lithuanian Councils of Workers and Peasants. In December 1918, most members of the LSDP's Vilnius organisation supported this idea, with A. Domaševičius at the forefront.

In December 1918, however, other LSDP members in Vilnius and in other cities of Lithuania (in Šiauliai, Rokiškis and Utena they played a major role in the organisation of democratic local municipalities) continued to speak out in favour of a new Lithuanian conference to elect a new LVT, or of a congress composed of delegates from the municipal councils to create a new provisional Lithuanian government. At the end of December 1918, some other prominent figures in the LSDP joined the Second Provisional Government of Lithuania formed by the leader of the Lithuanian Socialist-Populist Democrats (LSLDP), Mykolas Sleževičius, and they began working in the structure of the developing Lithuanian state authority. As a result, the branch of the LSDP that was headed by A. Domaševičius became detached. At that time, he did not recognise the government that had proclaimed itself the highest authority in Vilnius, which was led by V. Kapsukas and comprised only communists.[25]

The split in the social democrats was deepened at the beginning of 1919. Some members of the LSDP, such as S. Kairys, J. Paknys and others, actively participated in the restoration of Lithuanian statehood at that time. Meanwhile, in January 1919, the section of the LSDP led by A. Domaševičius, in contrast to the position it had declared in December 1918, recognised V. Kapsukas' communist government "brought" to Lithuania by the Bolshevik Red Army on behalf of the entire LSDP. The group collaborated with this government, and was finally named the Communist Party of Lithuania or LKP (creating the so-called "A. Domaševičius' LKP") and proposed that the LBKP should open negotiations on a merger. For various reasons, however, this did not happen and the new LKP gradually collapsed and disappeared.

Following these events, in 1919 the only group of social democrats continuing to act on behalf of the LSDP was the group led by J. Paknys and S. Kairys, who maintained a negative attitude towards Bolshevism and whose representatives were members of the second and fourth provisional Lithuanian governments, under the leadership of M. Sleževičius.

The social democrat ministers S. Kairys and J. Paknys, who were in the fourth provisional Lithuanian government that played an important role in the struggle for independence, were also sharply critical of the anti-democratic developments in the new state of Lithuania, and constantly demanded faster organisation of elections to the Constituent Assembly and the municipalities. Following the fall of the fourth provisional government in autumn 1919, the representatives of the LSDP refused to enter the fifth provisional government led by Ernestas Galvanauskas and sharply criticised its policies and those of the LVT.

In summer and autumn 1919, the social democrats began reorganising the party. On 3 October 1919, the LSDP was registered for legal activities in the Republic of Lithuania. At that time, a new version of the 1896 programme was adopted.

SOCIAL DEMOCRACY IN THE CONSOLIDATION OF LITHUANIAN STATEHOOD (1920-1922)

Despite the demands of the social democrats, in 1918–1919 there were no opportunities to convene elections to the Constituent Assembly. Therefore, these elections took place only on 14–16 April 1920 (notably, they did not take place in the Polish-occupied region of Vilnius). The elections were won by the most influential political force at that time, the former Christian Democratic Bloc (KDb), which received 317,300 votes (out of 682,291), and 59 (out of a possible 112) representatives in the Constituent Assembly. Second place was taken by the Peasant Populist Bloc (VLb), which received 155,600 votes and 29 representatives.

The LSDP, which was extremely weak in organisational terms, harassed by the government and fiercely attacked by the communist workers, received 87,051 or 13 per cent of the votes and 13 (12.5 per cent) representatives in the Constituent Assembly. In the circumstances, this was a success. By comparison, the Party of National Progress (TPP) led by A. Smetona, which had played an important role in the political life of Lithuanians in 1917–1919 received only 12,000 votes, and no representatives in the Constituent Assembly.

Among the social democrats elected to the Assembly, there were some well-known figures from the national liberation and socialist movements, including some who played a significant role in the history of Lithuania in the twentieth century (S. Kairys, Kipras Bielinis). Almost half of the members of the parliamentary group had been arrested and imprisoned in Tsarist Russia (and one of them in Bolshevik Russia).[26] The LSDP refused to enter the ruling coalition of the KDb and VLb, forming part of the opposition in parliament, despite the fact that the parties that had joined the VLb were its closest political associates in 1919. In their radical declaration about the new government, the social democrats declared that they would "not be in power" until they saw "the possibility of using it for matters of the working people". The LSDP parliamentary group also stated that it "came here to defend the concerns of the working people" and that "for that purpose, every occasion and every opportunity will be used".[27]

Both the declaration of the LSDP parliamentary group, and its position in the debate on the drafting of the provisional Constitution adopted on 10 June 1920, as well as of the permanent Constitution adopted on 1 August 1922, and the statements, inquiries and interpellations of its members show that the social democrats devoted a lot of attention to the radical democratisation of Lithuania. For example, in discussing the drafts of the constitutions, the social democrats spoke in favour of a radical parliamentary republic in which the Seimas expressed the "power and authority" of the sovereign and, at the same time, was the most important public authority, whose ministers could only be members of the Seimas. There would be no presidential authority at all, and all the functions provided for this authority would be carried out by the chairman of the Seimas. They justified their position against a presidential authority not only by the fact that this option was too expensive for Lithuania, but also because it was opposed to the "authority of Seimas as a sovereign government" and was even an "anti-democratic institution" opposed to democracy in general.

Apparently, at that time, the social democrats did not adequately assess the powers of the presidential authority provided for in the draft constitutions. In addition to the more general factors that will be mentioned later, the position of the LSDP at that time was determined by an extremely negative assessment of the Lithuanian experience in 1919. Moreover, the "spirit of the time" was determined by the collapses of undemocratic monarchies that took place in 1917–1918, as well as the democratic thrust of its radically "French" parliament. These factors, together with ideological traditions, underpinned other LSDP positions, such as their demand that elections to the Seimas and municipal councils would take place not every three years, but every two; that judges would be "elected and re-appointed by the people" and that all privileges, titles and orders be abolished.

The social democrats also defended and continued to develop their 1896 programme with new social and economic requirements, the nature of which shows their characteristic understanding of social and economic democracy and their attempt to implement it. Through this prism, the social democrats also considered the adoption of a Land Reform Bill, which was extremely important for Lithuania as an agrarian country. The LSDP parliamentary group led a real fight against anti-democratic developments, first of all, under the conditions and consequences of the war, including the arbitrary behaviour of military commanders, censorship, the repression of the workers' movement, the arrest of its leading figures and beatings of political prisoners. Its aim was to defend freedom of thought, the rule of law and the rights of the members of the Seimas as the nation's elected representatives. It was also in favour of separating church from state, politics and school; it supported the adoption of the Amnesty Law and the abolition of the death penalty; and it defended the rights of national minorities.

The social democrats from the KDb were accused of defending the communists, with suggestions that "Moscow was standing behind them and directing them". They strongly rejected such accusations, however. They criticised and condemned Russian Bolshevism for the events that took place in Lithuania during 1918 and 1919, as well as for the rejection of democracy and the anti-democratic methods applied in the creation of socialism, as well as for the repressions and terror in Russia and for the "occupation of socialist Georgia".[28] The LSDP also clearly criticised the LKP's actions as "very false and unacceptable tactics with regard to the workers", which was encouraging "artificial revolutions" and "pushing the workers' movement in erroneous directions", as well as contributing to the "depletion and division of labour forces" and "giving an opportunity" to the Lithuanian authorities to suppress and even "terrorise the Lithuanian workers' movement". The social democrats blamed the communists for "impudent demagogy", describing the "tactics of slander and lies that the communists followed in their press and agitation" against the LSDP. The social democrats described the communists as their enemies on the left, and as one document said, "the ideological struggle against the communists and against their tactics is becoming one of the most important tasks of the social democrats". The social democrats also emphasised, however, that they "fight with the communists ... only ideologically" and that they "fight against their views" in an attempt to "persuade the workers of Lithuania that the communists are wrong". Therefore, the LSDP did not support the government's approach to fighting the communists by "putting them in prison, with trials in military courts and the death penalty". According to the social democrats, "in Lithuania, if it wants to be a democratic country, everyone should be given the opportunity to present their views freely".[29]

In view of the relationship of the LKP with national statehood and with Soviet Russia, however, as well as its actions during those days, it can be argued that, by pursuing only an ideological struggle against the communists, the social democrats, or at least a considerable part of them, did not always adequately assess communist actions. Nonetheless, their position was consistent with their statement about unconditional "genuine" democracy.

Such a political attitude was determined by both the ideological-political traditions of socialism and by adherence to what, at that time, was one of rather radical, but not Bolshevik, and "left-socialist" Marxism. That is why, at the LSDP Conference held in 1921, when the Third International and the restored Second International parties were criticised, it decided to "support" the so-called Second and a Half International, created at the beginning of 1921. It was one of the social democratic parties who called themselves "the followers of revolutionary socialism" and who distanced themselves from both Bolshevism and, according to these "revolutionary socialists", from the "opportunists of the Second International". In 1922, however, when the Second and a Half International started to come closer to the Second International, a merger took place in 1923 into the Labour and Socialist International Parties, to whom the LSDP belonged from the beginning.

As we have seen, the social democrats played an important role in the Lithuanian national movement and, despite the subsequent split of the communists, in the process of the re(construction) of Lithuanian statehood. During the work of the Constituent Assembly, that is, during the period of the establishment of statehood, as has been briefly outlined, they put a lot of effort into making the Republic of Lithuania as democratic and as socially just as possible.

A similar political stance was maintained by the social democrats during the years of the First and Second Seimas (1923–1926), when they again became unanimous in their opposition to the ruling KDb (and in 1923–1924, also to the coalition of the KDb and the LVLS). In the second half of 1926, after the elections to the Third Seimas, the LSDP entered a coalition with the ruling majority of (democratic) left-wing parties, which strongly democratised the country's politics and sought to implement other elements of its programme. However, these processes were discontinued in 17 December 1926, due to the overthrow of the government. Following this and after the abolition of democracy, the political activities of the LSDP, like those of the other parties, were restricted and later completely banned. It is understandable that, during the years of the Soviet regime, legal activities on the part of the social democrats were out of the question. Lithuanian social democracy was able to express itself only in emigration.

As Lithuania celebrated 2018 the 100th anniversary of the creation of a modern state, today's Social Democrats, in remembering their historical "namesakes", could learn much about ideological consistency and strength, as well as political integrity, the unconditional defence of democracy and the resolve to defend the ideals of social democracy.

SUMMARY

The emergence and development of social democracy in Lithuania at the end of the nineteenth century and the beginning of the twentieth was influenced by the rise of social democratic movements in various countries, as well as the specific circumstances in Lithuania: the agrarian nature of the country, the delay in capitalist development, the diversity of the ethnic composition of the urban population, the presence of Lithuania in the autocratic Russian empire, the latter's policy of national oppression, as well as emerging processes of national regeneration and national movements .

The ideology and programme of the Lithuanian Social Democratic Party (LSDP), as representative of Lithuanian social democracy, at the turn of the twentieth century, were characterised, like those of many other social democratic parties at that time, by the primacy given to Marxism. For most of the period, however, national liberation was presented as a precondition for social liberation.

As a result, Lithuanian social democracy became an integral part of the Lithuanian national liberation movement, and in 1905, when the "national revolution" began in Lithuania, the LSDP was the most active "political" force in the ensuing events. The defeat of the revolution dealt a severe blow to the LSDP's organisation, operational capabilities, influence on society and programme, however, and from 1907 until the First World War, the LSDP advocated autonomy within the Russian Empire.

The beginning of the First World War and the German occupation of Lithuania meant that the social democrats' approach to the future of Lithuania had to be adapted. LSDP members, in anticipation of the possibility of war-driven changes in the political map of Europe, began to call for an independent democratic Republic of Lithuania established in a democratic way, and actively promoted it (including in its publication Labour's Voice in 1917–1918), including participation in joint action by various political currents focused on achieving national liberation.

Social Democrats Steponas Kairys and Mykolas Biržiška, elected together with two left-wing members of the Lithuanian Council, Jonas Vileišius and Stanislovas Narutavičius, were the main opponents of Lithuania's "strong and everlasting union" with Germany, proclaimed by a resolution of the Council of Lithuania on 11 December 1917 and established by four conventions. They were also, in essence, the main authors of the Lithuanian Independence Act, which was adopted on 16 February 1918. Protesting against the decision by the right-wing majority of the Lithuanian Council to proclaim Lithuania a monarchy and elect a king, the Social Democrats withdrew from the Council of Lithuania, arguing that it had exceeded its powers.

Although from 1917 to 1919 some Lithuanian Social Democrats, especially outside Lithuania, became communists, those who remained faithful to the ideological tradition of social democracy, during the creation of Lithuanian statehood in 1918, in the autumn of 1919 and then in the period of the establishment of statehood, from 1920 to 1922, constantly emphasised the necessity of a free democratic state in Lithuania, but also a democratic approach to creating such a state. They had no illusions about the ideology and political practices of the Russian Bolsheviks and entered the Lithuanian government to fight the Bolsheviks for Lithuania's independence. They also clearly opposed the aspirations of Polish land owners to annex Lithuania to Poland. In 1919, 1920, 1922 and in subsequent years, the Social Democrats protested unequivocally against undemocratic tendencies in the ideology and actions of right-wing political currents and strove hard to achieve the radical democratization of Lithuanian society and to make the Republic of Lithuania as democratic and socially just as possible.

1   In a monograph, the author of this text has analysed in detail the relationship between the social democrats and the process of creating the Lithuanian statehood. See Mitrulevičius G., *Lietuvos socialdemokratijos ideologinė-politinė raida 1914–1919 metais. Istoriografija, tarptautinis ir istorinis kontekstai, santykis su Lietuvos valstybingumo kūrimu.* Vilnius, 2017.
2   *Programas lietuviškos socialdemokratiškos partijos.* (Tilžė, 1896 : 8–9).
3   Merkys, V., *Knygnešių laikai. 1864–1904,* Vilnius (1994: 321); *Lietuvos Didžiosios Kunigaikštijos tradicija ir tautiniai naratyvai,* Vilnius (2009: 130).
4   Lietuvis, A. [Moravskis A.], *Lietuvos darbininkų judėjimo istorija sąryšy su Lietuvos valstybės atgimimo judėjimu. Pirmas dešimtmetis: 1892–1902 m. Įvadas,* Kaunas (1931: 30).
5   See Merkys, V., *Lietuvių nacionalinio išsivadavimo judėjimas [ligi 1904 m.],* Vilnius (1987: 246); Lietuvių atgimimo istorijos studijos, t. 4, Vilnius (1993: 439).
6   Lietuvis, A. [Moravskis A.], Lietuvos darbininkų judėjimo istorija sąryšy su Lietuvos valstybės atgimimo judėjimu. p. 30.
7   Programas lietuviškos socialdemokratiškos partijos. p. 9–12.
8   Kairys, S. *Lietuva budo,* New York (1957: 275).
9   Skyc program Litewskiej social-demokratycznej organizaciji//LMAB RS. F. 64–58. L. 5.
10 Kairys, S., *Lietuva budo.* pp. 342–43, 409.
11 Vilčinskas, J., *Lietuvos socialdemokratija kovoje dėl krašto nepriklausomybės. Istorinė apžvalga* (London 1985: 42).
12 Ibid., pp. 43, 46–47.
13 Mitrulevičius, G., *Lietuvos socialdemokratijos ideologinė-politinė raida 1914–1919 metai,* p. 238.
14 Ibid., pp. 238–39.
15 Ibid., pp. 88–138, 392–415.
16 Ibid., pp. 246–252.
17 Kairys, S., *Tau, Lietuva* (Boston, 1964: 226–29, 388).
18 Ibid. p. 410.
19 Ibid., pp. 248–49, 411.
20 *Lietuva vokiečių okupacijoje Pirmojo pasaulinio karo metais 1915–1918. Lietuvos nepriklausomos valstybės genezė,* Sud. E. Gimžauskas (Vilnius, 2006: 100–102).
21 Mitrulevičius, G., *Lietuvos socialdemokratijos ideologinė-politinė raida 1914–1919 metais,* pp. 291–302.
22 Apie socialdemokratų santykį su LT išrinkimu, jų darbą ir nuostatas LT, see ibid. 307–87.
23 See ibid., pp. 388–516.
24 In 1920 the LBKP split into the LKP and the BKP. For the development of the LBKP see ibid., pp. 517–548.
25 For information about the assumptions and the political position of the LSDP in the second half of 1918, see ibid., pp. 548–651.
26 For information about the performance of LSDP at the elections of the Constituent Assembly and the members of its parliamentary group, see *Socialdemokratai Lietuvos Respublikos Seimuose* (Vilnius, 2006: 65–66, 105–109, 111–124, 136–140, 145–146, 155–156, 161–178, 184–194).
27 Ibid., pp. 67–68, 677–682. For more information, see Mitrulevičius, G., Socialdemokratų santykis su Lietuvos Respublikos demokratizacijos procesu Steigiamojo Seimo darbo metu 1920–1922, *Parlamento studijos,* 9 (2010), 79–124.
28 For more on this topic, see Mitrulevičius, G., Lietuvos socialdemokratų požiūris į rusiškąjį komunizmą 1919–1922 metais, *Gairės,* 5 (2006), 31–36; No. 6, 25–31.
29 On the approach of the LSDP to the communists, see *Socialdemokratai Lietuvos Respublikos Seimuose,* pp. 76–77.

THE SOCIALIST MOVEMENT IN BELARUS AND BELARUSIAN STATEHOOD

ANATOL SIDAREVIČ

INTRODUCTION

"Politics is the art of the possible", someone once said, but what if someone or a group of people takes it upon themselves to do the impossible? What would we call them? Political adventurers or revolutionaries? In the case of Belarus, revolutionaries did indeed take on the impossible. The Belarusian Revolution began in 1902. According to theory, any revolution has at least two stages. A political revolution is preceded by an ideological one, and if the political revolution is a success, a third stage starts, namely an economic revolution. Another theory says that every revolution after taking two steps forward then takes a step back. Belarusian revolutionaries in the period 1902–1919 took on the impossible with an ideological and a political revolution, but then they were forced to take one step back.

The revolution was initiated mainly by young people. In May 1902 Alaksandr Burbis was 16 years old, Anton Łuckievič 18, Francišak Umiastoŭski 20, Ivan Łuckievič 21, Vaclaŭ Ivanoŭski 22, Alojzija Paškievič (Ciotka) 25 and Alaksandr Ułasaŭ 27; only 34 year-old Kazimir Kastravicki (Karus Kahaniec) was a real "old revolutionary". All of them – except perhaps for Burbis – were children of hereditary nobles (šlachta), while Ivanoŭski and Paškievič were the son and the daughter of wealthy landowners. Almost all were from Roman Catholic families (Ułasaŭ was an exception). A little later other young people joined them from Orthodox families, such as Siarhiej Skandrakoŭ, and even sons of priests, such as Arkadź Smolič. Almost all were from western Belarus, Vilna, Hrodna and Minsk provinces; only one – Skandrakoŭ – was born in Čarnihaŭ province.

The first steps were taken by young people from Vilna province, led by civilian general's son Vaclaŭ Ivanoŭski, then a student at the Technological Institute in St Petersburg. In spring 1902, he and other students attempted to establish a political organisation, which they called the Belarusian Revolutionary Party. They published an appeal "To the intelligentsia", urging them to help educate Belarusians in their native tongue and to provide them with an opportunity to learn about their past. What is so revolutionary about that, a skeptic might ask? But calling the party "Belarusian" was a revolutionary act in itself, because Belarus was not officially recognised in the Russian Empire, only a North-Western *krai* (region) made up of six provinces, including Vilna, Viciebsk, Hrodna, Koŭna, Mahiloŭ and Minsk (Koŭna province was Lithuanian, and in Vilna province Lithuanians made up the majority of residents only in Troki district).

The fact that Belarusian was referred to as a language and not a dialect of the Russian language was also a revolutionary step. Officially there was no Belarusian nation but rather a Belarusian tribe which was held to be part of – together with Vialikaros (Great Russians) and Malaros (Little Russians) – the Russian nation. The fact that they wanted to teach people in their native tongue was also revolutionary, because school education in the Belarusian language was prohibited at that time. Besides, to provide education in Belarusian you have to print books, but printing in the Belarusian language was also prohibited. Only works by linguists, folklorists and ethnographers could contain Belarusian texts. Furthermore, while Ukrainians had Eastern Galicia outside Russia's borders and the Lithuanians had Transnieman Lithuania, the Belarusians had no similar cultural oasis outside the Russian Empire. And there was one more problem: division of the Belarusians into Orthodox and Roman Catholic believers. The first group used the Cyrillic alphabet, and the other group the Latin one.

Finally, we have to take into account a particular psychological aspect of this situation. The founders of the Belarusian socialist movement had to overcome the resistance of people who had been brought up Polish and Great Russian tradition. It was very much easier and more profitable to continue to accept the Polish and Russian cultures. In this situation, with scant finance and outside the law they had to start everything from scratch. Not everyone was able to stand the pressure, not everyone was willing to take risks to their welfare and health, not everyone was ready to risk prison and exile.

A first attempt to establish a Belarusian political organisation was made in spring 1902, and who knows how it might have developed if in the autumn of the same year the brothers Ivan and Anton Łuckievič had not gone to St. Petersburg from Minsk. They also had experience of work in a circle where they studied social sciences and Karl Marx's teachings. After arriving in St Petersburg the Łuckievič brothers refused from the BRP manifesto, perhaps because they were aware that in comparison with neighbouring nations Belarusians were behind in their development. The brothers could not but be influenced by the general spirit of that time and their awareness that Russia was fostering revolution. The Russian authorities were certainly aware of that.

Conflicts between peasants and landowners, workers and factory owners, the throne and the oppressed nations, the official Church and other confessions, an environment in which even the most tentative oppositional activities were impossible and it was necessary to overcome dozens of barriers even to establish a cultural and educational or charter organisation, all this ratcheted up tensions in the state.

The period of the late nineteenth and early twentieth centuries was marked by increased political activity. Representatives of the oppressed nations and advocates of the interests of the oppressed classes started to establish their first political parties. As A. Łuckievič wrote, the establishment and activities of national socialist parties in Poland, Latvia, Lithuania, Ukraine and even in Armenia gave the Belarusians many models from which to select. After arriving in St Petersburg and becoming acquainted with V. Ivanoŭski and his followers, the Łuckievič brothers proposed to establish a political party that would aim at eliminating the main cause of Belarusian oppression, autocracy. Other remnants of feudalism, in particular, large-scale land ownership, were also slated for abolition.

Culture was at a low level in Belarus. There was no Belarusian bourgeoisie, urban intelligentsia or independent scientific and literary life in the Belarusian language. In contrast to Ukraine, Belarus did not have an institution of higher education. The language of instruction for children in state schools was Russian. Clergy in Roman Catholic parishes provided education and upbringing in the Polish language. This brought home to young Belarusians the obvious fact that Belarus was the arena of Polish-Russian confrontation. The nation was threatened by denationalisation and whether it wanted it or not the political party of the Belarusian Socialists had to perform culture- and nation-forming functions in addition to its primary political function. The establishment of the party aiming at radical change in the state and political system in Russia, as well as in the agricultural sector did not in itself amount to a rejection of the BRP manifesto, but a unit within the party structure had to focus on cultural and educational goals. Rosa Luxemburg wrote that "Belarusian Hramada had to start by creating an 'educational society' to disseminate elementary education among Belarusian peasants". The society in question was the Society of Belarusian National Education and Culture, founded in autumn 1902 and headed by Ivanoŭski.

BRH/BSH: FIRST PROGRAMME – HRAMADA AND OTHER SOCIALIST PARTIES IN BELARUS AND LITHUANIA

It is difficult to describe the early history of the Belarusian Revolutionary Hramada (BRH) because the party's archive was not preserved. One can only piece together the memories of its adherents and a few materials that did not vanish with the Party records. We should also bear in mind that the party, originally called the Belarusian Revolutionary Hramada, became known as the Belarusian Socialist Hramada (BSH) in October 1904. A. Łuckievič explained the renaming of the Party in terms of the social democratic direction that was dominant among the followers of the BRH / BSH. His brother I. Łuckievič undertook to create the Hramada. Future members of the party were recruited from among young people, mainly from Vilna, Hrodna and Minsk provinces. The establishment of the party stopped after the arrest of I. Łuckievič on the eve of 1 May 1903. He remained in the St Petersburg detention centre and in "Kresty" ("Crosses") prison until September. After his release, I. Łuckievič resumed his activities and at the end of 1903 in Vilnius the First Congress of the Belarusian Revolutionary Hramada took place.

The Congress adopted the BRH/ BSH manifesto. The authors of the document did not call it a manifesto, however, but rather a programme review. The immediate goal of the BRH was, "together with the proletariat of all nations of the Russian state", to overthrow the autocracy. The second goal was stated in a note: "It is difficult at this point to say how political movements in Russia will continue, but still we will use each and every opportunity to ensure that the respective nations have as much freedom as possible, respecting their great desire for an independent democratic state in the age of capitalism".

Thus the first BRH/ BSH policy document contained provisions on the independence of Belarus and the establishment of a democratic republican system there. The BRH/ BSH stood for equal rights "for all ethnic groups, living in the same territory", for equality of "all people in the territory, both men and women, regardless of their ethnic origin and religious faith". As for the cultural provisions mentioned in the BRH/BSH policy document, they included a call for freedom of the press and "free, obligatory and comprehensive science for all at government expense" and "separation of church and state and of church and education". Nothing was said in the BRH/ BSH programme review about the languages of the peoples of Belarus, but given the provision on the equality of all ethnic groups in Belarus, it can be concluded that the Belarusian Socialists stood for equality of languages. In comparison with the statement "To the intelligentsia" the BRH/ BSII programme review can be undoubtedly regarded as a step forward, a policy document of a political party.

The Erfurt programme of the Social Democratic Party of Germany (1891) was a model for socialist and social democratic parties at that time. I. Łuckievič stated at the Conference of National Socialist Parties of Russia in 1907 that the BSH was influenced by the foundations of the Erfurt programme. The priorities laid down in the socio-economic part of the BRH/ BSH programme review indicate that the elimination of capitalism was on the agenda. This was consistent with late Marxism; in his letter to Karl Kautsky in 1882 Friedrich Engels wrote that the elimination of national oppression was a condition for any healthy and free development. In particular, he believed that the Polish socialists should prioritise national liberation in their programme.

The establishment of the Belarusian Socialist Party did not go unnoticed by neighbours. Units of the General Jewish Workers' Union of Lithuania, Poland and Russia (the "Bund"), the Lithuanian Social Democratic Party (LSDP), the Polish Socialist Party (PSP), the Social Democracy party of the Kingdom of Poland and Lithuania (SDKPiL), the Party of Socialists Revolutionaries (SRs) and the Russian Social-Democratic Workers' Party (RSDRP) were active in Belarus as well. In their manifestos, these parties did not take into account the specific circumstances in Belarus and the PSP and the LSDP mulled over plans to annex Belarusian lands to the future Polish and Lithuanian states. As for the RSDWP and the SRs, they did not event think about separating Belarus from Russia. Finally, the SDKPiL even spoke against the revival of the Polish and Lithuanian states.

The PSP was particularly interested in the Belarusian socialist movement. The emergence of the Belarusian Socialist Party led to an ambivalent response from the Polish Socialist Party. On one hand, the PSP leaders could not but be concerned about the Hramada advocating abolition of private land ownership and its transfer to those who work on it without the use of a hired workforce. Implementation of this provision from the manifesto would have damaged the economic position of Polish landlords[1] and undermined Polish workers in Belarus. In addition, the PSP leaders were not happy about the provision on an independent Belarus and the fact that the Belarusian socialists did not link the future of their country with Poland in any way. On the other hand, the Polish socialists had to engage in propaganda and information activities among the peasantry of Belarus and they needed the Belarusian Socialists as allies in the struggle against the Tsarist government. That is why the PSP had to communicate and even cooperate first with the BRH, and then with the BRH/BSH.

Also important was the fact that the majority of activists in the newly-established political organisation came from Roman Catholic families, which is why many (including the Tsarist authorities) automatically thought of them as Poles. Another factor was Lithuanian social democracy, which did not link the future of Lithuania with Poland, either. In 1902, the PSP decided to establish a branch to operate in historical Lithuania, which operated in western Belarus and ethnic Lithuania. No later than October 1904 the PSP created a new subsidiary organisation, the Socialist Party of Belaya Rus (SPBR) (*"Belaya Rus"* stands for *"White Rus"*), a competitor to the BSH. The new unit operated only in Hrodna province, however. Because October 1904 and July 1906 it published nine leaflets in Belarusian, which also contributed to the political education of the lower classes.

BSH was quite tolerant about the SPBR. Its Belarusian-language leaflets were disseminated by Belarusian socialists as well. Steps were taken to unite the BSH and the SPBR, but they were not successful. In 1906, when the revolution was ebbing away and conflicts over tactics and strategy had flared up within the PSP, both the SPBR and the PSP ceased to exist in Lithuania. The SPBR disappeared completely from the political arena, while the other party united with the Lithuanian Social Democratic Party.

COMMON RUSSIAN REVOLUTIONARY MOVEMENT: THE SECOND PROGRAMME

Even before the PSP had established the Socialist Party of Belaya Rus, the BRH was invited to Paris to take part in the Conference of Revolutionary and Opposition Parties of Russia. The Finnish Party of Active Resistance was an initiator and organiser of the Conference. The conference also had Japanese support. It was attended by representatives of the PSR, Russian liberals from the "Union of Liberation", PSP, the Polish National Democrats, the Georgian Party of Socialists-Federalists and the Latvian Social Democratic Worker Party (LSDRP). SDKPiL refused to participate in the conference, as did the RSDLP and the Revolutionary Ukrainian Party. A representative of the BRH did not attend this conference, but the party signed its resolution. Paris Conference decisions determined to a certain extent the political behaviour of the revolutionary and opposition parties in Russia during the revolution of 1905–1907.

In April 1905 in Geneva the Conference of Russian Socialist Parties took place. In addition to a BSH representative (his name was not mentioned in the conference proceedings), representatives of the Armenian Social-Democratic Party "Gnchak" and Dashnaktsutyun, the Jewish Bund, the Georgian Party of Federalists-Socialists, the LSDRP, the Latvian Social Democratic Union (LSDS) the PSP, the PSR and the Party of Active Action took part. By that time the RSDRP had split into autonomous factions, the Mensheviks and the Bolsheviks. The Mensheviks, like SDKPiL, refused to participate in the conference. The Bolsheviks were represented by Vladimir Lenin, but he did not stay at the conference for long. The formal reason for this demarche was the attendance at the conference of a representative from the LSDS, which was considered to be a "fictitious" organisation by the LSDRP. The majority did not support the LSDRP's assertions, however. The representatives of "Hunchak" and the Bund left the conference along with Lenin and the LSDRP representative. The Conference adopted two declarations and a number of other documents. The Conference called for a military uprising, a convention of the Constituent Assembly of Russia, a declaration that Russia is a democratic federal republic and land socialisation.

In calling for a Constituent Assembly in Russia, the Conference advocated that Finland and Poland not participate in the elections such a body. Instead individual constituent assemblies would be established in these countries. The Conference recognised the rights of the Caucasus (Transcaucasia) to autonomy and a Constituent Assembly of its own. As the PSP considered the historical Rzeczpospolita (the United Kingdom of Poland and Lithuania) to be not just a Polish state, and the future restored Polish state was conceived as a multi-ethnic unity, the BSH delegation issued a separate declaration in which it expressed support for establishing the historical Lithuania (Lithuania and Belarus) as separate political entities. However, the BSH delegation did not propose to the conference that this wish be included in the text of the first declaration, as this issue was to be decided jointly by the socialist parties of all nationalities residing in the territories of Lithuania and of Belarus.

A very important statement was made at the International Socialist Forum. The PSP delegation as a representative of the Polish and part of the Jewish proletariat in the territory of Lithuania and Belarus joined the BSH declaration. The PSP decision was quite simple: to prevent a joint decision by the socialist parties of Lithuania and Belarus on determining this territory as an independent political entity. The invitation to the BRH/ BSH to attend the Paris Conference of Revolutionary and Opposition Parties and the BSH's active participation in the Geneva conference show that the Belarusian Socialist Party was a recognised entity of the common Russian revolutionary movement.

The BSH was an active participant in the revolution of 1905–1907. The Party responded to the troops firing on a peace march near the Winter Palace with the proclamation "The Tsar's harvest". Calling for the overthrow of tsarism, the Party explained to the common people what a constitution was and why it was needed. In March 1905 the BSH was involved in the establishment of the Belarusian Peasants' Union, which became part of the All-Russian Peasant Union created in late July–early August. Later the Belarusian Union of Teachers' Seminaries was created with members from Maladziečna, Panevezys, Polack and Svislač teachers' seminaries. Strikes of students from these institutions were organised.

During the revolution the Belarusian Union of Teachers was also founded. At its congress in Vilna teachers demanded the restructuring of public education on democratic principles, the introduction of Belarusian as the language of instruction in schools and giving teachers the right to elect their own committees. The Belarusian Socialists formed trade unions and organised strikes. The Tsar was forced to make concessions to the revolutionary movement and in August 1905 the convocation of the State Duma was announced, and it was given legislative powers. Before that, however, certain categories of Russian crown subjects were deprived of the vote, and in any case suffrage was indirect and irregular.

The Tsar also had to make significant concessions to the revolutionary forces after the All-Russian political strike in October. This was not enough for the revolutionaries, however. In Belarus the situation became more complicated the day after the Tsar's manifesto announcement, 18 October, when a rally of citizens was fired on in Minsk. People were also killed in Viciebsk. The BSH, together with the SRs prepared an attack on Minsk governor Pavel Kurloŭ and began to gather weapons for combat units. While working on the interparty strike committee in Minsk, the BSH was involved in preparations for the joint political strike in December. After I. Łuckievič's signal at the Jacobson factory workshops and factories throughout the city ceased operations. The BSH also participated in the interparty coordination of activities in the countryside, in which representatives of the SRs and the RSDLP took part. In 1906 the Party organised agrarian strikes in Minsk, Lida, Navahrudak and other districts.

The elections to the first State Duma were held at the beginning of 1906. The BSH, like other socialist parties, hoped that the revolutionary movement would gain further ground and that the Tsarist government would introduce new concessions and therefore it decided to boycott the elections. The election boycott was subsequently recognised as a mistake, however, and the BSH took part in the elections for the second State Duma. At the end of 1906 it and the Bund, the PSR, the RSDRP and trade unions founded the left block in Minsk province. This block selected seven candidates, including S. Skandrakoŭ from the BSH. The bloc won the provincial election, but the election results were cancelled by the authorities. In some provinces, however, the authorities could not exercise their prerogative and the second State Duma was more radical than the first. On 3 June therefore it was dissolved. The same day a new regulation on elections was published. Because dissolution of the Duma and the electoral law amendment, which took place at the same time without the consent of the Duma and the State Council, were in violation of the law, the events of 3 June 1907 were considered to be a coup.

During the revolution the BSH published and disseminated leaflets in Belarusian and other languages. In 1905 it used the services of the illegal publishing offices of the PSP and the LSDP and in 1906–1907 it had its own publishing office in Minsk. This publishing office operated for almost 18 months and was not discovered by the Tsarist police. It ceased operations as the revolutionary movement came under increasing pressure and it was impossible to take risks any longer. The reactionary forces celebrated their victory with such instruments as "Stolypin neckties" (ropes) and "Stolypin" railway carriages. Many Hramada followers were imprisoned such as Alaksandr Burbis, while Karuś Kahaniec and Jakub Kołas, sent into exile from Belarus, had to join the underground movement or to migrate. There is also documentary evidence that two BSH supporters were hanged. It seems that in 1907 the BSH ceased its activities. However, a party conference took place attended by the Central Committee, and the Minsk and Vilna committees, and as A. Łuckievič wrote in his memoirs, a plan for further activities was drawn up. The party worked out a strategy of regrouping and building up its forces for the future struggle.

During the Christmas period in 1906 (NS) the second BSH Congress was held in Minsk. The Congress adopted the party's programme and elected the Central Committee of the Hramada. The BSH programme was more detailed in some respects than the "programme review" and other amendments were made. While the programme review stated that the Hramada was a socio-political organisation of the "Belarusian working people", the programme of 1906 claimed that the party would organise and unite "the working poor of the Belarusian land without regard to ethnicity". Thus, the BSH expressed its desire to represent not just Belarusian working people, but the whole proletariat (in the Hramada terminology "the working poor") of the Belarusian region. In terms of the BSH's approach to culture-, nation- and state-forming issues the differences between the 1903 programme review and the 1906 programme were quite significant.

In this programme the Hramada saw Russia's future as a democratic federal republic with free self-determination and national and cultural autonomy. The BSH rejected the provision on Belarus's independence and demanded the Belarusian region's autonomy with the Sejm in Vilna. Thus, the Party found it necessary to separate Belarus from the Lithuanian part of the Northwest krai (region). In addition, it considered Vilna to be the capital of the Belarusian region. In case of a revolutionary overthrow of the autocracy the BSH party deemed it necessary to hold the Constituent Sejm for the Belarusian region.

The switch from independence to (mere) autonomy is explained by the influence of the Austrian Marxists, who did a lot to develop the national issue, and by the decisions of the Geneva conference of socialist parties of Russia. It is also important to understand that Belarus had to pass the stages of national cultural and territorial autonomy in order to establish a strong national intelligentsia, future administrators, judges and so on to ensure an independent public sphere. While supporting the autonomy of Belarus in the Russian Democratic Federal Republic, the BSH stood for equal rights and cultural-national autonomy of all nationalities living in the same area, for equality of citizens regardless of sex, religion, nationality or race and for elimination of social class differences. The Party backed free compulsory education at the expense of the state. Nothing was said about the languages of instruction in the programme, but the statements on the equality of nationalities and national-cultural autonomy as well as more recent publications in the Party newspaper *Naša Niva* (*Our Crop Field*) give grounds to believe that the Belarusian socialists advocated instruction at schools in native languages. A. Burbis, V. Ivanoŭski, A. and I. Łuckievič and A. Ułasaŭ were elected members of the BSH central committee.

During the revolution of 1905–1907 the nationalities issue intensified in Russia. The "Russian Assembly" established before the revolution became more active and the Union of the Russian people revolted. These organisations considered Orthodoxy and autocracy to be the most important structural units of the Empire and upheld the principle of a united and indivisible Russia, under the aegis of which no issues of cultural-national autonomy, not to mention territorial autonomy, could be raised. The Russian nation (Great Russians, Little Russians and Belarusians) assumed superiority in the state, but the desire of Belarusians and Ukrainians to develop their national cultures was condemned as separatism. It was necessary to overcome the ethnic differences between Belarusians and Ukrainians and Great Russians. Previously Orthodoxy was required to be considered Belarusian. Russia's nationalities were divided into friendly and unfriendly. Among unfriendly nations Jews and Poles took first place. The BSH urged Belarusians to yield to anti-Semitic propaganda: "If someone provokes you to beat Jews, beat him, kill him like a mad dog", one BSH leaflet declared. Concerned about dangerous tendencies, at the beginning of 1907 the PSR proposed to hold a conference dedicated only to discussion of the national issue. Invitations were sent to the national socialist parties.

The conference, which took place in Finland on 16–20 April 1907, was attended by the BSH (I. Łuckievič), the Socialist Jewish Worker Party (SHRP), the Georgian Party of Socialists-Federalists, Dashnaktsutyun, the Polish Socialist Party – Revolutionary Faction[2] and the PSR. At the end of the conference an LSDS representative came and expressed support for its decisions. The parties proposed to ensure the rights of national minorities in electoral legislation in this resolution on protection of the minority rights. The Socialist Workers' Party put a question about national and territorial autonomy before the Conference. A particular issue was how to deal with extraterritorial nationalities. The SHRP offered to provide them with extraterritorial national unions under public law.

Two resolutions were adopted on this issue. In the first of them it was stated that the issue was still in the process of discussion, and therefore the socialist parties were recommended to debate it thoroughly at meetings and in their publications. The second resolution, adopted by the majority of the parties that participated in the conference (PSP and PSR abstained), supported the SHRP proposal. However, it was still necessary to discuss in detail the issue of the extraterritorial jurisdiction of the National Union and its compliance with the authority of local and territorial self-governing bodies, as well as common state institutions. Thus, most of the conference participants, including the BSH, believed that the question of the extraterritorial national unions had to be transferred from the political framework to the legal and practical arena.

The Conference also adopted a resolution on the Russian government's pogrom policy. It said,

The Conference declares that it considers it a sacred duty of the convened parties in the most decisive and active manner to fight against anti-Semitic pogroms and the policy of the Russian government and the reactionary part of Russian society, which, being a most savage expression of barbarism and violence, obscures the class awareness of the working masses and delays the class consolidation of the international fighting proletariat and the working masses.

Other documents, including congratulations to the International Socialist Bureau on the occasion of May Day, were also adopted.

HRAMADA'S CULTURAL FORMATION AND NATION BUILDING

It is hard to say what the fate of such prominent Belarusian writers as Ciotka, Janka Kupała, Jakub Kołas, Aleś Harun, Maksim Bahdanovič, Źmitrok Biadula, Maksim Harecki and dozens of other literary figures would have been if there had been no support from the Belarusian socialists. While the Łuckievič brothers were busy with party formation, Vaclaŭ Ivanoŭski began to build up Belarusian publishing to create, as Rosa Luxemburg recommended, an independent scientific and literary life in the Belarusian language. Karuś Kahaniec and his brother Ambrožy, as well as Francišak Umiastoŭski helped Ivanoŭski in this area. In 1903 the first Belarusian work of literature in the twentieth century was published, a collection of poems by Janka Lučyna, entitled "Viazanka". In order to obtain permission for this book to be published and disseminated the censorship office was told that it was written in Bulgarian.

On 12 December 1904 Tsar Nicholas II's decree "On Measures to Improve Public Order" was published, which sought to eliminate excessive restrictions on publishing. Belarusian book printing in both the Cyrillic and the Latin alphabet was now allowed. In 1906 BSH Central Committee member Ivanoŭski initiated establishment of the publisher "Zahlanie sonca i ŭ naša vakonca" *("The sun will look at our window, too")* in St Petersburg. As the head of this organisation in the period 1906–1913 he organised publication of Belarusian books, postcards and the almanac *Maladaja Belarus* ("Young Belarus"). In 1910–1913 a similar publishing house under BSH member Anton Hrynievič also operated in St Petersburg. On 1 July 1913 the Belarusian Publishing Association was founded in Vilna. Ivanoŭski was appointed its head. In addition to legal publishing, Ivanoŭski carried out illegal publishing activities. In 1906–1907 he was the head of the Party publishing house "Hramada", which issued several brochures.

Many Belarusians studied at the higher education institutions of St Petersburg, where Ivanoŭski lived and worked. As A. Łuckievič wrote, the Belarusian students were grouped round Ivanoŭski and the assistant librarian of the University Library Branislaŭ Epimach-Shypila. Ivanoŭski and Epimach-Shypila were directly involved in the foundation of the Belarusian Scientific and Literary Society of Students of St Petersburg University, whose monitor was a BSH follower Branisłaŭ Taraškievič.

The activities of the publishing group "Zahlanie sonca i ŭ naša vakonca", the publisher "Hramada" and A. Hrynievič occurred during the so-called "Naša Niva" period, when the newspaper *Naša Niva* was published in Vilna. I. Łuckievič proposed to start publishing a Party newspaper at the BSH conference in June 1906, but this idea was implemented by Francišak Umiastoŭski, who found someone willing to publish it. Thus, on 1 September in Vilna *Naša Dola* ("Our Fate") began to be published. The newspaper was issued in both Cyrillic and Latin alphabet. However, the radical left publication was not published for long. Of the six issues of the newspaper four were confiscated. Finally, on 1 December 1906 the newspaper was banned. But before "Naša Dola" was shut down the Łuckievič brothers, Vaclaŭ Ivanoŭski, Ciotka and others founded the "Naša Niva" newspaper.

The first issue of "Naša Niva" was published on 10 November 1906 in the Cyrillic and Latin alphabets. The newspaper continued until 7 August 1915. A. Łuckievič was its first actual editor and one of the main writers. After an outsider editor – Sigmund Volski – had been in charge for some time, on 8 December 1906 AlaksandrUłasaŭ became editor-publisher. I. Łuckievič tried to find funding for the publication of "Naša Niva". The members of the BSH Central Committee, the Łuckievič brothers and Ułasaŭ determined the newspaper's policy and mission. Alongside the newspaper the publishing house produced popular science, agricultural literature and fiction, as well as calendars. On the basis of the "Naša Niva" publishing house the Belarusian publishing association led by Ivanoŭski came into existence in 1913.

The "Naša Niva" publishing house started issuing a magazine for peasants "Sacha" *("Plough")* in 1912. A. Ułasaŭ became the magazine's editor, stepping aside as the "Naša Niva" newspaper editor and publisher to make way for Jan Łucevič (Janka Kupała). In 1914 Ułasaŭ also became a publisher of a magazine for teenagers and young people "Lučynka" (*"Little Torch"*). Ciotka was its literary editor.

The plans of the Belarusian Socialists included publication of a women's magazine, but the First World War prevented it. Publication of the magazines "Sacha" and "Lučynka", as well as the "Naša Niva" newspaper stopped due to the war, the recruitment of editors and publishers to the Tsarist army and forced evacuation to the east. The "Naša Niva" community became the centre around which Belarusian socialists grouped. Belarusian societies and communities from other cities kept in touch with it. BSH followers (Marxists and populists) but also people with other views were members of the editorial staff and newspaper correspondents.

The culture- and nation-forming activities of the BSH bore fruit. As historian Andrej Unučak noted, before 1915, when the Germans invaded the western areas of Belarus, the fundamentals of the Belarusian national idea had already been developed. The national idea, the notion of statehood for Belarus was now so strong that, although substantial financial and organisational resources were lacking, it could no longer be ignored by the Poles, the Germans or the Bolsheviks. It was already extremely difficult to deny the existence of the Belarusian nation, language, literature and culture. The "Belarusian issue" was no longer an internal Russian issue; it became international due to the war.

SHAPING AN INDEPENDENT
BELARUSIAN-LITHUANIAN STATE

Even before the Germans had occupied Lithuania and the western areas of Belarus, it was decided who among the BSH activists would work in the territory controlled by the Germans and who in the pro-Russian area. Central Committee member A. Ułasaŭ was enrolled in the army, members A. Burbis and V. Ivanoŭski had to leave for Russia and I. and A. Łuckievič, as well as Ciotka stayed in Vilna. In Minsk the political work was entrusted to Arkadź Smolič. After the German came into the area, the Belarusian club was established in Vilna and the Belarusian music and drama club started giving performances. The Belarusian language had equal status with Yiddish, Lithuanian and Polish. At the end of 1915 the first legal Belarusian schools opened. Training of teachers was organised, which made it possible to open 153 Belarusian schools in Vilna and Hrodna provinces by the end of 1918. From February 1916 the newspaper "Homan" ("*Noisy Talk*") was published twice a week. The Belarusian Society for Assisting the Victims of the War was a legal unit uniting Belarusians and serving as a veil for the illegal Belarusian People's Committee (BPC) headed by A. Łuckievič. The BSH branch in Vilna was operating as well. The autonomous organisation of the Belarusian Social-Democratic Worker Group was formed (BSDRH), with Belarusian workers from Vilna as its members.

The Belarusian Socialists decided to use the arrival of the Germans in Lithuania and Belarus, together with Jewish, Lithuanian and Polish democrats to implement the regional idea. On 19 December 1915 Belarusian, Jewish, Lithuanian and Polish organisations decided to establish the Confederation of the Grand Duchy of Lithuania to work together to form an independent "united" state with guaranteed rights for all nationalities in the German-occupied Belarusian and Lithuanian areas. I. Łuckievič wrote the Confederation's proclamation. In February 1916 the manifesto "Citizens" was issued, written by the Lithuanian activist Jurgis Šaulys. It declared that the structure of the Lithuanian-Belarusian state had to include at least the areas occupied by the Germans.

This noble project could not be realised, however. The majority of the Lithuanian political class dreamed of an independent Lithuania including parts of Belarus, while Polish nationalists saw both Belarus and Lithuania as part of the revived Polish state. In addition, the position of the German government was unclear. Perhaps the Lithuanian-Belarusian state project would be accepted by Berlin in early March 1917, when Anton Łuckievič, Jurgis Šaulys, Steponas Kairys and Antanas Smetona went to Berlin. At that very time the news came about the abdication of Nicholas II, and Łuckievič went to Vilna, while the Lithuanian delegates stayed in Berlin and were received by the Reichkanzler. The Lithuanians made certain promises to the Germans, and the German government was favourably disposed towards them.

Nevertheless, the Belarusians did not lose hope with regard to the establishment of a joint state with Lithuania. On 1 September 1917 at the conference held by the BPC, the BSDRH and Vilna BSH Committee the Confederation's proclamation was adopted in which the Belarusians demanded the convocation of the Constituent Sejm of Belarus and Lithuania. Now the Belarusian organisations wanted not a united (unitary) state, but a federation between autonomous Belarus and Lithuania, which would be divided in terms of the native tongue of residents. At the Belarusian conference held on 25–27 January 1918, the concept of the Belarusian-Lithuanian state was confirmed and it was proposed that "this independent state core formed in the occupied lands should be joined by the part of Belarusian territories which were still under Russian rule". The conference appointed the Belarusian Rada ("*council*") headed by A. Łuckievič in Vilna.

Meanwhile, the Bolshevik government in Russia hoped for a lightning revolution in Germany and thus delayed concluding a peace treaty with it. On 16 February 1918 the Germans launched an offensive on the Eastern Front. On the same day the Taryba (*Council*) of Lithuania declared the restoration of Lithuania's independence. On 18 February the Belarusian Rada at its meeting in Vilna adopted a resolution written by A. Łuckievič in which it demanded the joining of central and eastern Belarus to the rest of the Belarusian-Lithuanian region "in order to organise an independent public life there", for Hrodna and Biełastok could not be permitted to become part of Poland. After listing demands and the problems suffered by the people of Belarus lately, and after recalling the fact that the Belarusians and the Lithuanians lived in the Grand Duchy of Lithuania for centuries, the Belarusian Rada in Vilna declared that relations between Belarus and Russia had been broken off.

BSH IN EASTERN BELARUS: THE PARTY'S THIRD PROGRAMME

While in western Belarus the Belarusian socialists withdrew from the 1906 party programme, those in the territory controlled by Russia remained faithful to it. In comparison with western Belarus, the Belarusians in Russia could not carry out even cultural activities. By using the military situation, the Tsarist government had suppressed any initiative. The only organisation that could work legally was the Belarusian Society for Assisting the Victims of the War. Its Minsk branch was a front for the BSH led by A. Smolič.

After the abdication of Nicholas II (3 March 1917) Belarusian organisations were established in various cities of Belarus, Russia and Ukraine. The head of the Minsk organisation of the BSH A. Smolič sent them and individual activists an invitation to participate in the congress of Belarusian organisations, held on 25 March in Minsk. Before the opening of the congress, a conference of BSH organisations was conducted. The Belarusian Socialists demonstrated full loyalty to Russia. They saw the future of Belarus as "in the Federal Republic of Russia". The Conference decided "to study and work out this issue thoroughly, to establish the borders of autonomous Belarus and to open relations with neighbours (Lithuanians, Ukrainians, etc.), taking into account the decisions taken on this issue". After the conference, the congress of Belarusian organisations opened. The congress elected a 18-member Belarusian National Committee (BNC) to coordinate work. Thirteen BNC members were unquestionably leftist, Social Democrats and Socialists-Revolutionaries. Holding the majority in the BNC, but taking care of national interests, the Belarusian Socialists offered the chairmanship of the BNC to the landowner Raman Skirmunt, who was quite well-known in the political and business communities of Belarus, Poland and Russia.

The congress of Belarusian national organisations marked the beginning of a broad movement for national self-determination of Belarus in the form of autonomy. It was the start of a Belarusian political revolution and the Belarusian movement organised itself. After electing the BNC the Congress formed the first national representation (mission). The BSH's goal, stated in its programme in 1906, became the goal of the whole movement in the Belarusian territory controlled by Russia. The mistake of the Belarusian Socialists was to propose a landowner as BNC head. At a time when the country was experienced an exacerbated class struggle, this decision did not bring any benefits for the Belarusian movement. The Russian leftists seized on this faux pas to make it look as though the Belarusian movement was headed by landowners, while the right wing tried to show that it was led by the Poles, because they considered every Catholic in Belarus to be a Pole. The "Skirmunt issue" was discussed at the Party conference in Petrograd (4–6 June) and a resolution was adopted on it at the congress of the Belarusian national organisations and parties, which took place on 8–10 July in Minsk. Instead of the BNC the congress elected the Central Rada of Belarusian Organisations (CRBO). The leader of the CRBO was A. Smolič and his deputy was the editor of *Volnaja Belarus* ("Free Belarus"), Jazep Losik.

In 1917 the BSH became a member of the "Russian International", the association of national socialist parties. The Petrograd conference debated the political platform of this association. The Hramada added its provision on independence to the platform. While agreeing to the right of every nation to self-determination up to full independence the BSH still thought that secession of any part of Russia in terms of that period of time would damage the revolutionary proletariat actions. In summer 1917 the Poles and the Ukrainians fought for the creation of national units in the Russian army. This issue was also considered by the BSH conference. The conference opposed categorically the formation of national units, sharing the view of the Belarusian Socialists that they were needed only for the bourgeoisie and counter-revolutionaries. It was a mistake, which the Belarusian Socialists realised too late. The Conference elected an interim BSH central committee led by a worker and writer from Petrograd, źmicier Žyłunovič (Ciška Hartny).

In October 1917 the third congress of the BSH took place. The congress adopted a new party manifesto and elected its central committee. The new BSH programme amended the statement on a Russian Democratic Federal Republic. While the 1906 programme contained provisions on national-cultural autonomy of ethnic groups in the same territory, the 1917 programme had a paragraph on territorial and personal autonomy for all nationalities and autonomy for regions and communities that had relevant economic and social characteristics. Full political and economic equality of all nationalities living in the territory of Belarus was proclaimed.

The Belarusian Socialists were confident that social and political reforms could be successfully implemented only with a significant raising of the people's cultural level. Therefore the new BSH programme included a chapter entitled "On the national issue". The Hramada felt it necessary to carry out the following: (i) extensive development of Belarusian national culture as the only way to develop society and a general raising of the people's cultural level; (ii) legal recognition of the right of the Belarusian language to development and use in schools, courts and administrative and public institutions of Belarus. By demanding autonomy for Belarus, the BSH opposed the customs borders between Belarus and other parts of the Russian Federation. It was supposed to make the Regional Rada, not a Sejm as in the 1906 manifesto, but a legislative body of Belarus. The cooperative businessman and writer Jazep Dyła was elected chairman of the new central committee and Arkadź Smolič was elected his deputy.

OCTOBER 1917–MARCH 1918: DECLARING THE BELARUSIAN PEOPLE'S REPUBLIC

The third BSH Congress finished its work on the evening of 25 October 1917, when the Bolsheviks began their armed seizure of power. On 27 October the BSH and three other organisations issued a Letter to the Belarusian Nation. This document stated that the party saw the new government as a threat to the rights and freedoms of the Belarusian people. The Letter's authors urged sons of the Belarusian land to unite around the Great Belarusian Rada (VBR), a representative body formed at the second session of the Central Rada of Belarusian organisations in October 1917. The BSH played a leading role in the VBR. The VBR also addressed a call to the people. Adhering to the principle of federalism, it stated that within autonomous Belarus the power had to belong to the democratically elected Regional Rada. This call contained a list of activities that were to be carried out for the purpose of normalizing life in the country. Attention was paid to the fact that Belarus was at risk of being divided up between its neighbours. It was necessary for the people of Belarus to have authorised representatives at a peace congress. An army had to be mustered to ensure the integrity of Belarus and protect the vital interests of the Belarusian nation. Authority was thus needed for elections through which the people of Belarus could solve all these problems. To do this, the VBR initiated a congress of representatives of the whole Belarusian nation, to be convened on 5 December.

Members of the Belarusian Regional Committee (BAK) at the All-Russian Council of Peasant Deputies issued declarations. The BAK also called for the organisation of the Congress. By approaching the issue in terms of protecting the integrity of Belarus, it started cooperation with the new governmental institutions in Petrograd. After negotiations between the VBR and the BAK, it was decided to hold the congress in Minsk. Russia's Council of People's Commissars (SNK) agreed to the meeting, for which purpose 50,000 roubles were allocated. The SNK of the Western Region and front, which had been established, also agreed, although there was not a single Belarusian in its ranks. By giving their consent to hold the All-Belarusian congress, the Bolsheviks hoped that it would be conducted like a peasant congress in cooperation with the Minsk Soviet (Council) of Worker and Soldier Deputies, and as a result a Soviet of Worker, Soldier and Peasant Deputies of the Western Region and front would be established. Priority was given to the faction of the Left Socialists-Revolutionaries and Belarusian Bolsheviks. The hope was that the congress would split. The All-Belarusian congress was attended by 1,872 delegates. The BSH and Socialists-Revolutionaries were the leading parties and managed to work out a draft resolution on the self-determination of Belarus and interim regional authorities.

According to the resolution adopted, a democratic republican system was to be established in Belarus. The unity of Belarus and the Russian Democratic Federal Republic was proclaimed. To govern the region, the Congress decided to appoint from among its members an All-Belarusian Council (Rada) Peasant, Soldier and Worker Deputies. Thus, the Congress did not agree to cooperate with the Bolsheviks from the Western Region and front. The latter could not hold an alternative congress, as had been done in Ukraine. In this situation the SNK of the Western Region and front decided to break up the Congress, which was accomplished during the night of 17–18 December 1917.

On 18 December the All-Belarusian Congress delegates gathered at the depot of Libava-Romen railway. They decided to proclaim the Congress Rada as the interim government of the region. On 21 December the Rada of the All-Belarusian Congress recognised itself as the government and decided to supplement its composition by representatives of peasants, workers and soldiers, as well as of ethnic minorities of the region (who were represented by their socialist parties). The Rada elected its Presidium (Ivan Sierada was the chairman, Jazep Varonka was a deputy chairman, Tamaš Hryb and Kanstancin Jezavitaŭ were secretaries, all of them BSH members), as well as the Executive Committee headed by J. Varonka. The adoption of the All-Belarusian Congress resolution on regional authorities, which laid down that Belarus would be part of Russia as a federation member finally shifted the Belarusian revolution from the ideological stage to the political one.

In response to the difficult situation the Executive Committee of the Rada of the All-Belarusian Congress turned to underground action. As already mentioned, on 16 February 1918 the Germans launched their attack on the Eastern Front. On the night of 18–19 February, the Bolsheviks fled from Minsk to Smolensk. The Executive Committee of the Rada of the All-Belarusian Congress came out from the underground. On 20 February the First Regulatory Letter to the people of Belarus was adopted and published on 21 February. The Executive Committee assumed interim power in Belarus and promised to convene the Constituent Sejm. The government of Belarus was formed to manage and administer daily affairs through the People's Secretariat, headed by J. Varonka. The Letter did not mention anything about the legal status of Belarus or its relations with Russia.

After entering Minsk, the Germans cast down the Belarusian flag from the house where the People's Secretariat was located and confiscated its funds. In general, the German authorities tolerated the activities of the Belarusians. Meanwhile, the Bolsheviks were forced to return to the negotiating table with Germany and its allies, and this time to sign (3 March 1918) a peace treaty. Belarus was divided into two parts along the frontline, but was still recognised as Russian territory. The Germans agreed not to support separatist movements on Russian territory and eventually to withdraw its troops from Belarus. On 9 March the Rada Executive Committee of the All-Belarusian Congress issued the Second Regulatory Letter. Belarus in view of the preponderance of ethnic Belarusians was declared the People's Republic of Belarus (BPR). Before holding the Constituent Sejm, the Rada of the All-Belarusian Congress was declared the supreme authority of the BPR, supplemented by representatives of national minorities. The People's Secretariat was appointed the executive and administrative authority. Citizens' rights and freedoms were guaranteed: inviolability of individuals and property, freedom of speech, press, assembly and conscience, the right to form associations. All the nationalities of Belarus were granted the right to national and personal autonomy, equality of all languages was proclaimed. Belarus introduced an eight-hour working day. Forests, lakes and subsoil were declared the property of the Republic, private ownership of land was abolished.

Thus, the foundations of the state, political and economic life of the BPR as a democratic legal and welfare (social) state were laid. The second letter was welcomed by the Mensheviks, the Socialists-Revolutionaries, the PSP, the Bund and other Jewish socialist parties. All these parties sent their representatives to the Rada of the All-Belarusian Congress, which became the BNR Rada on 19 March. In the Second Letter there was still no answer to the question of the BPR's status. Was it an integral part of the Russian Federation or an independent state? The all-Russian parties and those of other nations understood that the BPR was part of the federation, which is why they welcomed its declaration. They changed their attitude completely on 25 March 1918.

DECLARING INDEPENDENCE AND THE BREAK-UP OF THE BSH

As already mentioned, on 18 February 1918 the Belarusian Rada in Vilna broke off relations with Russia. In western Belarus the intelligentsia was ready for independence, but the Belarusian socialists, who dominated in Vilna Rada, wanted an independent Belarusian-Lithuanian state. In this situation they were guided by two pragmatic ideas: the country had to have free access to the sea for its successful development and it was necessary to have a strong layer of national intelligentsia, future administrators, judges, police officers and so on to implement independence, which could be developed within the framework of national-territorial autonomy.

The situation at the beginning of 1918 forced the Belarusian socialists not to rely on evolution, but to actively make a revolution, although the conditions were not entirely favourable. Belarus was threatened with partition. The Lithuanians claimed the entire Vilna province and a significant part of Hrodna. The Latvian authorities claimed not only the Dźvinsk, Lucyn and Režyca *pavets* (counties), where Belarusians made up a minority, but also Drysa *pavet* (district). Ukraine urged the Germans to recognise its rights to the southern districts of Hrodna, Minsk and Mahiloŭ provinces. A "Belarus for Poznań" deal between Germany and Poland was also possible. Furthermore, Belarus was threatened by a potential Polis–Bolshevik deal, too.

To defend its territorial integrity, Belarus had to declare its independence. Some BSH activists in Minsk understood this well, as did some BSH members in Vilna. The Belarusian Rada in Vilna decided to send a delegation to Minsk. In his memoirs, A. Łuckievič briefly described the events preceding the adoption of the Act of 25 March. In particular, he noted that the Social Democrats (Symon Rak-Michajłoŭski, Arkadź Smolič, Jazep Losik,

Alaksandr Prušynski and others) stood for independence. But not all BSH members were ready to accept this position. The delegates of the Belarusian Rada in Vilna, basically the Łuckievič brothers, had to convince BSH members that it was necessary to vote for independence. And they succeeded. On 23 March the BSH faction in the Rada of the Belarusian People's Republic unanimously decided to vote for independence in the Rada. On 24 March at 6.00 pm the meeting of the BPR Rada began, chaired by Ivan Sierada. A report was delivered by A. Smolič. The meeting lasted until the morning of 25 March. Only then was the decision made: the Rada of the Republic declared Belarus an independent and sovereign state and issued the Regulatory Letter with this statement. The Third Regulatory Letter, drafted by A. Łuckievič, in which all the rights of citizens enshrined in the Letter of 9 March were confirmed, was adopted at the afternoon session of the Rada, which started on 25 March at 12.00 pm and was led by J. Varonka.

Belarus's proclamation of independence resulted in the withdrawal from the BPR Rada of the representatives of the All-Russian and national socialist parties, who favoured the union with Russia. They ignored the fact that the All-Belarusian Congress supported unity with a democratic Russia. Perhaps most important for the BPR government was international recognition of the Republic. Certain German officials hinted that the Republic might be recognised if the Rada and the People's Secretariat would adhere to right-wing positions. The Łuckievič brothers recommended including right-wing activists in the Rada, who (led by R. Skirmunt) were grouped in the Minsk Belarusian Popular Representative Office. On 12 April 1918 a group of members of this representative office was incorporated in the BPR Rada. It was agreed to form a new (coalition) cabinet. Before the new BPR government was formed, however, a split took place in the BSH. At the initiative of the right-wing activists on 26 April Ivan Sierada, Jazep Varonka, Raman Skirmunt, Anton Aŭsianik, Paviel Alaksiuk, Piotra Kračeŭski and Jazep Losik sent a telegram to Wilhelm II on behalf of the BPR Rada. It turned out that the whole Rada thanked the Kaiser for the liberation of Belarus from the Bolsheviks and asked him for protection as regards the Rada's desire to strengthen the country's independence and indivisibility in alliance with Germany. "Only under the protection of Germany", the telegram said, "does the Rada see the future happiness of its country". The telegram caused indignation among some BSH members and on 1 May Tamaš Hryb and Pałuta

Badunova announced their withdrawal from the Hramada faction and the formation of a separate faction of the Belarusian Socialist-Revolutionary Party (BPS-R). The new party did not break its ties with the BSH. It was still part of the socialist bloc in the Rada. And although we do not have information about any votes it held, it can be assumed that on 14 May during the election the SRs voted for a Social Democrat Jazep Losik as the chairman of the BPR Rada.

As for the new cabinet, on 9 July the Rada of the Republic approved a policy declaration by R. Skirmunt's Cabinet. It was quite a balanced programme, which is why the socialists voted for it. It should also be noted that the Rada approved the Skirmunt cabinet's programme and adopted the Pahonia ("*chevy*",) as the recognised coat of arms of the Belarusian state. J. Varonka opposed the new prime minister and his cabinet, which he was able to thwart. On 22 July 1918 the Rada appointed Ivan Sierada chairman of the People's Secretariat. Varonka instigated disorder in the Rada and the new prime minister was not able to staff his office adequately. In the course of the struggle over the prime minister's office one more faction of the BSH withdrew from it. The Belarusian Socialist Party of Federalists (BPS-F, SFs) was formed, whose most prominent members were Jazep Varonka, Kanstancin Jezavitaŭ, Vasil Zacharka, Piotra Kračeŭski and others. The SFs like the SRs were in the socialist bloc of the BPR Rada.

After withdrawal of the SRs and the SFs only the Social Democrats remained in the BSH. As a result the Belarusian Social Democratic Party came into existence, with such prominent members as Vaclaŭ Ivanoŭski, Jazep Losik, Ivan and Anton Łuckievič, Alaksandr Prušynski, Symon Rak-Michajłoŭski, Arkadź Smolič, Branisłaŭ Taraškievič and others. As A. Łuckievič wrote, the Belarusian Social Democratic Party (BSDP) did not find support among the masses, which was not surprising for an agrarian country, where there was virtually no national industrial working class and the national intelligentsia was small. Belarusian workers in St Petersburg supported the more radical Belarusian Social Democratic Workers Party. In 1919 A. Smolič drafted the BSDP programme. He published its views in pamphlet form, but no party congress took place. Although small in number, the Social Democrats played a vanguard role in the BSH in the Belarusian movement as a whole.

BELARUSIAN COMMUNISTS AND BOLSHEVIKS: BIRTH AND DEATH OF THE SSR OF BELARUS

When in spring 1917 delegates, authorised by the Congress of Belarusian National Organisations, went to Petrograd to present the proposals of the Belarusian movement, the officials of the Russian Interim Government ignored them. The party that wanted to seize power – the Bolsheviks – had a different opinion. This does not mean that the Bolsheviks were favourable towards the Belarusian movement. On the contrary, the Bolshevik activists in Belarus were its enemies. But the Bolshevik Party differed from the others in its strict discipline and the influence of its leaders.

Lenin understood that his party might play well on three issues at once: the war, land and the national issue. The reluctance of the Interim Government to give autonomy to Belarus and other regions of Russia promoted Lenin to propose in October 1917 the "immediate restoration of *full* freedom for Finland, Ukraine, Belarus, for Muslims, etc" as a goal of the Bolsheviks. In conversation with the Belarusian SR and one of the initiators of the All-Belarusian Congress Jaŭsej Kančar, however, he admitted that he held a positive attitude to Belarusian autonomy because he saw it as another channel for opposing the Interim Government. Soon after seizing power, the Bolsheviks published a declaration of the rights of peoples in Russia. This document can scarcely be called a legal act. In proclaiming the right of the peoples of Russia "to self-determination, including withdrawal and formation of an independent state", Lenin and the People's Commissar for Nationalities Stalin did not mention how such a right might actually be exercised. The promised decrees were never promulgated. In addition, the right of peoples to self-determination was recognised by the Bolsheviks only until January 1918, to be substituted by the workers' right to self-determination.

The Germans were retreating and the Bolsheviks were advancing to the west, where lay the Ukrainian and the Belarusian People's Republics, as well as the Lithuanian, Estonian and Latvian republics. The Bolsheviks were forced to invent alternatives to these entities. In creating new Soviet republics, the Bolsheviks regarded them as a buffer between Russia and the capitalist world. On 23 December 1918 the All-Russian Central Executive Committee (UTsVK) recognised the Soviet Baltic republics and Soviet Ukraine. Among this cluster of Soviet republics there was a gap, Belarus. Historian Ryhor Laźko has explained why a socialist Soviet republic was not declared in Belarus in December 1918: in contrast with Ukraine, Latvia, Lithuania and Estonia, Belarusian Bolsheviks were few in number and there were no prominent figures among them. It did not seem possible to create a government of Belarus from among the members of the North-Western Committee of the Bolshevik Party, in which there were no Belarusians at all.

In early autumn 1917 the first split occurred in the Belarusian Socialist Hramada. In Petrograd, where there were many Belarusians – workers, soldiers and sailors – a large group of members (up to 500), mostly workers, withdrew from the BSH. Then this group was joined by the Helsingfors organisation of the BSH (about 200 people, mostly sailors). Thus, the Belarusian Social Democratic Worker Party (BSDRP) came into existence. It is difficult to indicate the exact date when the BSDRP was formed but we can say for sure that Alaksandr Čarviakoŭ was its leader. The party did not break ties with the BSH. In October 1917 A. Čarviakoŭ was a delegate at the third congress of the Hramada, and in December he participated in the All-Belarusian Congress. In April 1918 the Belarusian section of the Russian Communist Party of Bolsheviks (RKP[b]) was established on the basis of the BSDRP. And even earlier on the basis of the SNK decree of 31 January the Belarusian National Commissariat (Belnackam) was established as a department of the People's Commissariat of Russia for Nationalities (Narkamnac). Čarviakoŭ was appointed the BNK Commissioner.

The Communists, Social Democrats and Socialists-Revolutionaries, non-party activists, future leaders of the BPR and the BSSR grouped round the BNK, which carried out extensive cultural and educational activities and published the first Belarusian Soviet newspaper *Dziannica ("Aurora")*. The BNK's attempts expand its work in the area of Belarus, which was not occupied by the Germans, were resisted by the Northwest Regional Committee of the RKP (b). The relations between Belkamnac and Narkamnac were not ideal, either. Suffice to say that five BNK commissioners were changed from February 1918 to March 1919. The relations between the Northwestern Regional Committee and the Belarusian RKP (b) sections were also fairly tense. The basic point of conflict was the national issue. Thus the Belarusian sections of Moscow and Petrograd appealed through the BNK to the Regional Committee with a proposal to grant the part of Belarus under Soviet control autonomy within the RSFSR or to rename the Western region the Belarusian-Lithuanian commune. In response, the Regional Committee renamed the Western Region the Western commune. The Belarusian sections could not reach an understanding with the RKP (b) leaders, either. The proposal to establish a Belarusian branch with its Central Bureau under the auspices of the Central Committee of the Bolshevik Party and expand its activities in the part of Belarus controlled by the Germans was rejected. The Belarusian branches continued their operations, however. In addition to Petrograd and Moscow, they were established at least in Voronezh, Kazan, Kozlov, Nevel, Saratov and Tambov.

After the revolution in Germany on 9 November, there was a shift in the Bolsheviks' national policy and a conference of sections was held. The Conference of the Belarusian RKP (b) sections was held on 21–23 December 1918. The Central Bureau consisting of five people was elected and included the former chairman of the BSH Central Committee źmicier Žyłunovič and former Hramada members Jazep Niacecki and Alaksandr Čarviakoŭ. The former chairman of the BSH Central Committee Jazep Dyła was a candidate for the Bureau. It is possible to say that the Belarusian national-communist direction was formed within the Bolshevik Party. And former BSH members, Marxists, played a leading role in it.

The Conference of the RKP (b) Belarusian sections, which ended on 23 December, advocated the establishment of an Interim Worker and Peasant Government of Belarus, while on 25 December Stalin invited the accountable Belnackom officers for the Belarusians to nominate candidates to the Interim Soviet Government of Belarus. The Belarusian Communists nominated 15 people. źmicier Žyłunovič was proposed for prime minister. The Belarusians wanted to occupy all positions in this government, but the Bolsheviks had other ideas; they insisted on eight Belarusian communists and eight representatives of the North-Western RKP (b) organisation to be included in the government. Then, the Bolsheviks added the names of two more activists from the North-Western organisation in ink to a list of members of the government.

On 30 December 1918 the Sixth Conference of the North-Western RKP (b) organisation opened in Smolensk, which became the First Congress of the Communist Party (of the Bolsheviks) of Belarus (the KP (b) B). The Party's Central Bureau consisting of 15 people was elected by the Congress and included only two Belarusian communists. Žyłunovič protested but it did not help. He was forced to abide by Moscow's decisions. Although the manifesto of the Interim Worker and Peasant Government, drafted by Žyłunovič, was signed only after 2 am on 2 January 1919, the day of foundation of Soviet Belarus was considered to be 1 January 1919, because that was the order from Moscow. Soviet Belarus was formed as an alternative to the BPR. Anti-BPR ideas were evident in the appeal of the First Congress of the KP(b)B to the workers of Soviet Belarus, as well as in the manifesto of the Interim Government of Belarus. Moreover, the establishment of Soviet Belarus completed the formation of a cluster of buffer Soviet states.

Two weeks after publication of the manifesto of the Interim Worker and Peasant Soviet Government of Belarus, on 16 January 1919, the Central Committee of the Bolshevik Party decided to separate the area of Smolensk, as well as Viciebsk and Mahiloŭ provinces from Belarus, and to unite the rest of Belarusian territories with the Soviet Socialist Republic of Lithuania. On 2–3 February the All-Belarusian Congress of Soviets took place. Moscow sent Lenin's right-hand man to Minsk, chairman of the Central Executive Committee Yakov Sverdlov. The Congress adopted the Constitution of the Soviet Socialist Republic of Belarus (SSRB), Sverdlov read a Resolution signed by the Central Executive Committee on recognition of the new state by Russia and then the delegates, as directed by him, voted unanimously to unite the newborn SSRB, which in the process lost three provinces, with the SSR of Lithuania. On 27 February 1919 Soviet Belarus ceased to exist. The Socialist Soviet Republic of Lithuania and Belarus (SSRLiB, LitBel) with its capital in Vilna appeared on the world map. The KP(b)B ceased to exist, too. LitBel was governed by the KP(b)LiB. There was not a single Belarusian in the leadership of this Party.

ANTON ŁUCKIEVIČ'S EFFORTS, THE GREAT POWERS AND POLAND

While a revolution took place in Germany and social democrats came to power there, in Minsk it was also decided that a social democrat had to be leader of the BPR government. On 11 November 1918 the People's Secretariat was renamed the Rada of People's Ministers. Leader of the Council of Ministers was to be A. Łuckievič, whose coalition cabinet included social democrats and socialists-federalists. A. Smolič became deputy prime minister and the Cabinet started work on 22 November. Łuckievič's Cabinet was not destined to carry out its programme, however. The German army retreated and the Bolsheviks came instead. The government thus had to evacuate Minsk. First the BPR government moved to Vilna, and on 27 December to Hrodna. A tactical alliance of the BPR and Lithuania was formed at the end of November. Lithuania received a significant part of Vilna and Hrodna provinces from Germany but it could not bring them under its control: there were not enough people who spoke the language and had the necessary administrative skills. The Taryba (*Council*) of Lithuania agreed to include representatives of the Belarusian Rada in Vilna and the Lithuanian government established a Ministry of Belarusian Affairs, headed by J. Varonka, which appointed commissioners to Belarusian districts.

In December the Polish state, restored on 11 November 1918 started to occupy Belarusian territories. The German military authorities, as directed by the Entente, did not allow the Belarusians to form military units, impeded the activities of Belarusian commissioners in districts and created a favourable environment for the Poles. To try to appease Poland, at the turn of 1919 Łuckievič wrote to the government of Poland and tried to evoke a response from the major powers. It became apparent that the fate of Belarus would be decided by others, which is why a Belarusian delegation went to Paris, where the peace conference began on 18 January 1919. Meanwhile, Poland after receiving substantial financial support from the United States and France, continued to occupy western areas of Belarus. The BPR government could not continue its operations in Hrodna, and Vilna was under the Bolsheviks' control. In mid-March 1919 Łuckievič and members of his Cabinet went to Berlin, where A. Smolič had already formed the Belarusian diplomatic mission. In Berlin Arkadź Smolič kept in touch with the prominent German Social Democrat Karl Kautsky. We can assume that it was with Kautsky's support that the BPR mission in Berlin was registered by the Ministry of Foreign Affairs of Germany on 4 May 1919.

In Paris, Łuckievič collaborated with the delegations of the states in which there were uprisings in the territory of the former Russian Empire. With the help of Zigfrīds Meierovics (Latvia) and Jaan Poska (Estonia) it was able to establish a BPR military-diplomatic mission in Riga, which was accredited by the relevant governments. The mission extended its activities to Finland as well. In Paris, Łuckievič met President-Minister of Poland Ignacy Paderewski. Paderewski invited the Belarusian Prime Minister to Warsaw. Łuckievič, guided by the principle "We have talked and will talk with all", left for Poland.

While Łuckievič was in Paris, the Polish-Soviet War broke out for Lithuania and Belarus (as Lenin defined its essence). Poland was supported by the United States and the Entente, especially France. On 24 April 1919 the Polish Army occupied Vilna and on 8 August it reached Minsk. Not knowing what to expect, the Belarusians met the Poles almost everywhere as liberators from the Bolshevik terror. On the second day after the Polish Army came to Minsk the Interim Belarusian National Committee (ChBNK), headed by Social Democrat A. Prušynski, was established. The ChBNK saw its goals as raising the level of cultural, educational and economic activities. Łuckievič, who went to Warsaw for a specific purpose ("to obtain an opportunity at any cost for our government and armed forces to be able to organise, or at least a police force"), could not know that he had fallen into a trap and that the road to Paris, where the winners were reshaping the map of Europe, was closed for him.

Łuckievič failed to ensure that the BPR Council of Ministers in Minsk get involved in the shaping of the region, but he was able to obtain permission to convene the Rada of the Republic. But before that, on 22 October 1919, Piłsudski "legalised" the Belarusian Military Commission (BVK), whose task was to form Belarusian military units. As for BVK chairman P. Alaksiuk his room to manoeuvre was limited because, as one contemporary wrote, he was doing "high policy", and thus A. Prušynski became de facto leader of the BVK. Soon Prušynski and his colleagues could see that BVK was part of the Polish political game and the Poles would not allow them to form a Belarusian army. While Łuckievič was in Paris and Warsaw, a conspiracy developed against him among the leaders of the BPR, launched by V. Zacharka and P. Kračeŭski. Łuckievič's long visit to Warsaw was interpreted by his opponents as indicating an intention to "surrender" Belarus for the benefit of Poland. While fuelling the myth of Łuckievič's political Polonophilia, on 13 December 1919 socialists-federalists and socialists-revolutionaries took over the BPR Rada and set up a "revolutionary" cabinet, headed by Vaclaŭ Łastoŭski, which operated in parallel to Łuckievič's "bourgeois" government.

The BPR Rada split. Its SF-SR part was headed by P. Kračeŭski, who acted as chairman, and Łuckievič's supporters, in difficult conditions, transferred the rights of the BPR Rada to the five-member Supreme Rada of the Republic. By means of persecution and organizing massacres the Poles forced Łastoŭski's cabinet to migrate. Łuckievič, who went to Warsaw, was detained. Unable to continue his activities, on 28 February 1920 Łuckievič asked the BPR Supreme Rada to release him from his positions, transferred his powers to A. Smolič and went to Vilna.

ANOTHER SSRB: FROM SOVIET BELARUS TO THE REPUBLIC OF BELARUS

The occupation regime established by the Polish government led inevitably to an anti-Polish backlash. The Bolsheviks skilfully used this public mood to their own advantage. With no guarantee of the BPR's recognition by Moscow, the Belarusian Socialists-Revolutionaries decided to ally with them. The Bolsheviks, who had to fight on several fronts, were ready to make significant territorial concessions to Poland. In Belarus, the Russian-Polish border could be located along the Biarezina. Warsaw wanted to see the Right-Bank Ukraine as part of the Polish state, however, and on 7 May 1920 Polish troops occupied Kyiv. But the Poles could not keep such a vast territory (from Dźvinsk [now Daugavpils] to Katerynoslav [now Dnipro]), and in June they had to leave Kyiv. The success of the Red Army in Ukraine allowed it to start a new offensive in Belarus on 4 July. The Red Army was tasked with invading Warsaw and, if all went well, to move on to Berlin. The Red Army advanced rapidly and on 11 July arrived in Minsk and on 14 July in Vilna.

The Socialist Soviet Republic of Lithuania and Belarus, established on 27 February 1919, ceased to exist de jure on 12 July 1920, having ceased to exist de facto in July 1919, when the Polish army advanced to the east. On this day the Soviet-Lithuanian Peace Treaty was signed, and Russia recognised the Lithuanian Republic. Russia transferred completely or partially Ašmiany, Vilna, Hrodna, Lida and Svianciany pavets (districts) as well as the Belarusian part of Koŭna province, with Braslaŭ and Suwalska province to the Republic of Lithuania. The power in the territories recognised by Moscow as Belarusian, which were cleared of Polish troops, passed into the hands of the Minsk Provincial Military Revolutionary Committee (VRK) headed by A. Čarviakoŭ. Representatives of the Belarusian Socialists-Revolutionaries as well as the Belarusian Communist organisation founded in January 1920 in the territory occupied by the Poles were also members of the VRK.

With the permission of Moscow the Military Revolutionary Committee got ready to declare the Soviet Socialist Republic of Belarus. Defending the integrity of the state of Belarus in its ethnographic borders and advocating the formation of a separate Belarusian army, the SRs refused to sign the Declaration of 31 July 1920, when the Soviet Socialist Republic of Belarus's independence was proclaimed. It was assumed that the power of the VRK would extend to all western Belarusian areas, which Russia had not transferred to Lithuania. France and the United States again helped Poland, however, and on 16 August the Poles and their Ukrainian allies launched a counteroffensive. On 12 October the Polish army occupied Minsk again, but on that day the armistice was signed in Riga. The Poles had to leave Minsk and retreat to the agreed line. The Soviet Socialist Republic of Belarus consisted of incomplete six districts of Minsk province (Babrujsk, Barysaŭ, Ihumien, Mazyr, Minsk and Słuck) and individual parts of Vilejka pavet of Vilna province. In December 1920 the second All-Belarusian Congress of Soviets was held in Minsk. The Congress elected the SSRB Central Executive Committee, with Alaksandr Čarviakoŭ as chairman. The SSRB government – the Soviet of People's Commissars – was formed, also headed by Čarviakoŭ, who was also People's Commissar for Foreign Affairs at the same time. A. Burbis was appointed his deputy.

The Soviet Socialist Republic of Belarus was recognised by Germany. As a recognised international entity, on 30 December 1922 Soviet Socialist Republic of Belarus signed an agreement on the formation of the Union of Soviet Socialist Republics (the USSR, the Soviet Union) with the Russian Soviet Federal Socialist Republic, the Ukrainian Soviet Socialist Republic and the Transcaucasian Soviet Federal Socialist Republic. A. Čarviakoŭ signed this agreement on behalf of the republic. Just under 69 years later, on 8 December 1991 the leaders of Belarus, Russia and Ukraine at a meeting in Biełavežskaja Pušča (Belarus) declared that the Soviet Union had ceased to exist as a subject of international law and a geopolitical reality. On 10 December, Ukraine and Belarus, and on 12 December Russia denounced the Union agreement of 1922. The Soviet Union ceased to exist de jure. On 16 December the process recognizing Belarus's independence from other states began.

In the period from the All-Belarusian Congress until 25 March 1918 the Belarusian revolution took three steps forward: Belarus seceded from Russia, it was proclaimed an independent state and then it was proclaimed a democratic state. Belarus could not become an independent and democratic state in 1918–1920, as the Western democracies, especially France, which provided Russia with a funding in the amount of about 5 billion francs, were not interested in the collapse of Russia. The Belarusian revolution, after taking these three steps forward, had to take two steps back. From 1920 Belarus was no longer part of Russia, but did not become an independent and democratic state.

In 2018, when the 100th anniversary of the BPR's independence was celebrated, on the site of the house where Ivan and Anton Łuckievič lived in Minsk, a memorial plaque was unveiled. A little later, a street was named after Arkadź Smolič. There are also streets named after Aleś Harun (Alaksandr Prušynski) and Branisłaŭ Taraškievič in Minsk. There is a street named after Jazep Losik in his native village. The names of źmicier Žyłunovič (Ciška Hartny) and Alaksandr Čarviakoŭ were rescued from oblivion long ago. The names of the Belarusian socialists who implemented a Belarusian ideological and political revolution and whose activities were so important in forming Belarusian culture, nation and state are finally returning to public consciousness.

SUMMARY

It is impossible to recount the history of the Republic of Belarus without taking into account the country's socialist movement. The Belarusian Revolution started after an attempt to create the Belarusian Revolutionary Party in 1902 and the establishment of the Belarusian Socialist Hramada (BSH) in 1903 ("hramada" means "commune" or "community"). The Party's first manifesto described its strategic goal, which became the objective of the whole Belarusian movement in the twentieth century and remains that of democratic forces in Belarus in the twenty-first century, namely the establishment of an independent democratic republic. The period from 1902 to 1917 can be characterised one of ideological revolution.

The BSH, which was the only Belarusian party at that time, remained a faction of Marxists and narodniks ("populists") until 1 May 1918. Social democrats played a major role in the Party. Aliaksandr Burbis, Vaclaŭ Ivanoŭski, Ivan and Anton Łuckievič and Aliaksandr Ułasaŭ were close to the Central Committee elected in January 1906. Social democrats Źmicier Žyłunovič, Jazep Dyła and Arkadź Smolič were in the forefront of the Party in 1917–1918. As the Belarusian nation was still not completely formed by the early twentieth century, the Party had to perform a culture- and nation-forming function as well. At the same time the Belarusian movement became part of the liberation movement of peoples in the Russian Empire, and BSH was an active participant in the Socialist movement in Russia.

The political stage of the Belarusian Revolution started after the fall of Tsarism. The Party initiated the Congress of Belarusian Organisations in March 1917 and the Congress of Belarusian Organisations and Parties in July of the same year. BSH adherents played a leading role in the Central Council of Belarusian organisations established in July, as well as in the Great Belarusian Council, which commenced activities in October.

Belarusian socialists called for the autonomy of Belarus in the Russian Democratic Federal Republic. The Party did not welcome the Bolshevik takeover. The Great Belarusian Council launched an initiative to hold an All-Belarusian Congress in Minsk. The same initiative was also proposed by the Belarusian Regional Committee at the All-Russian Council of Rural Deputies. The All-Belarusian Congress (5–18 December 1917) supported unity with democratic federal Russia and decided to form the All-Belarusian Council (Rada) of rural, soldier and worker deputies from its ranks. Bolsheviks in the "Western region" (as they called Belarus) and the war front broke up the Congress, but its delegates, who held a meeting at the Minsk depot of the Libava-Romen railway, transferred power in Belarus to the All-Belarusian Congress. The majority of seats in the Rada went to BSH members.

BSH members played the decisive role in declaring the Belarusian People's Republic (BPR) on 9 March 1918. The Rada of the All-Belarusian Congress on 19 March, became the BPR Rada after representatives of ethnic minorities joined it. On 25 March, with the help of the BSH members' votes the BPR Rada declared Belarus independent. The Republic was seen by its founders as a democratic social state based on the rule of law. The Great Powers, however, first of all France, saw no interest in Belarus and Ukraine seceding from Russia.

In autumn 1917 some BSH members left it because they supported the Bolshevik manifesto. First, they established the Belarusian Social-Democratic Worker's Party, and from 1918 they started to set up Belarusian sections of the Russian Communist Party (Bolsheviks). Ex-members of BSH initiated the declaration of the Socialist Soviet Republic of Belarus (SSRB) on 2 January 1919. The SSRB, proclaimed as an alternative to the BPR, did not last long. After its existence had been declared for the second time on 31 July 1920 it became a predecessor of the Belarusian Soviet Socialist Republic (BSSR), which was legitimised in 1927. On 25 August 1991 the BSSR became a de facto independent state. On 19 September that year the Republic of Belarus appeared on the map. On 10 December, after renunciation of the Agreement of 1922 on the Establishment of the Soviet Union, the Republic of Belarus became a de jure independent state.

---

1 When "Polish landlords" are mentioned, they refer mainly to representatives of the Roman Catholic *shlachta* (nobility) in Belarus, who were Polonised, although their ancestors were Belarusians, Russians and Litvins (Lithuanians).

2 In 1906 the PSP split into two political organisations: PSP-Lewica and PSP-Revolutionary Faction. PSP-Lewica called for the autonomy of Poland in a Democratic Federal Russia, and the PSP-Revolutionary Faction (the leader was Jusaf Pilsudski) stood for the independence of Poland.

UKRAINIAN SOCIAL DEMOCRACY AND THE UKRAINIAN NATION-STATE IN 1917-1920

YAROSLAV HRYTSAK

1899-1916: GENESIS AND BEGINNING OF UKRAINIAN SOCIAL DEMOCRACY

The history of the Ukrainian social democratic movement dates back to the turn of the twentieth century and the birth of not one, but two Ukrainian social democratic parties. This is explained not by a factional split, but by the fact that between the end of the eighteenth century and the First World War (1789–1914) ethnic Ukrainian lands were divided between two monarchies. The majority (85 per cent) belonged to the Russian Empire, the minority (15 per cent) to the Austro-Hungarian Empire. Accordingly, the two parties emerged in their respective empire. The Ukrainian Social Democratic Party (USDP) was established in 1899, in Lviv, the capital of East Galicia, Austria's biggest province, while six years later, in 1905, the Ukrainian Social-Democratic Workers' Party (USDRP) was founded in Kyiv, the biggest city of the Russian part of Ukraine.

The very fact that the local social democrats in both parts decided to include "Ukrainian" in the name of their party was an ideological statement. First, in the moment of creation of both social democratic parties neither Ukraine nor Ukrainians existed on the political map of Eastern Europe. Their official names were "Little Russians" in the Russian Empire and "Ruthenians" in the Austrian Empire. Virtually throughout the nineteenth century, there was a debate about whether Little Russians and Ruthenians were a part of the Russian or the Polish nation, two separate nations (like Serbians and Croatians) or the same nation. The Ukrainian social democrats on both sides of the Austro-Russian border declared with their choice of name that they considered Little Russians and Ruthenians to be two parts of the same nation.

The ideological dimension of the name choice goes beyond this, however. As is well known, there was no ready national theory in Marxism. The Communist Manifesto claimed that "the proletariat must first of all acquire political supremacy, must rise to be the leading class of the nation". The question for Little Russians or Ruthenians, however, was in which nation the proletariat was supposed to rise up? After all a nation presupposed the existence of a state and there was no Ukrainian state at that time. This question touched not only Ukrainians but all so-called stateless nations of Eastern Europe: Belarusians, Armenians, Georgians, Jews, Serbians, Slovaks, Tatars, Finns, Croatians, Czechs and others.

The answer given by Marxists in nation-states was quite simple. In their opinion, the purpose of the "stateless" nations was to be assimilated into the existing nation-states. As Eduard Bernstein explained later in an epilogue to a book about the beginnings of the Ukrainian socialist movement, "These were not mere national great-power whims but the expression of a fully defined view on the direction and interests of historical development."[1]

It is clear that such a solution would not please the Marxists from stateless nations. They saw it as a violation of national justice and in response created their own national parties. Their decision potentially created a conflict in the international social democratic movement, however. In the Ukrainian case, this conflict was primarily about relations between the Polish and the Russian social democrats. Even though technically Ukrainian lands were divided between the Austrian and the Russian Empire, the Polish elite retained significant political and economic influence there. It dominated in Austrian Galicia and constituted a majority in the western approaches of the Russian Empire, including Ukrainian lands, up until the First World War. There were tensions between Ukrainian Marxists and Polish Marxists concerning who had the right to operate in the cities and industrial centres of Western and Central Ukraine, where a significant part of the population was made up of Polish bourgeoisie and workers. These disputes took place in 1870–1880 between the first generations of Polish and Ukrainian Marxists from both empires. But at the time of creation of the social democratic parties, this dispute had basically been solved in both its ideological and institutional dimensions; a consensus had been reached between the Marxists of both nations to act in solidarity, but among their own national proletariats.

Meanwhile, relations with the Russian social democrats were far more problematic. As Kazimierz Kelles-Krauz, a Polish Marxist, reported from London at the beginning of the 1900s, the group of Russian social democrats gathered around *"Iskra"* ("Spark") – Lenin and the future Bolsheviks – absolutely dismissed the possible existence of a separate Ukrainian social democratic party. They could agree to have the Lithuanian Party, but to allow Ukrainians to have their own party, the members of the "Iskra" group believed, would be "political suicide". [2]

It was not only the fact that, according to the Russian social democrats, the creation of a separate social democratic party would disrupt a common front fighting the Russian imperial power. The problem was also the fact that while the Russian Marxists were the sworn enemies of the imperial power, they to some extent had taken on its centrist mind-set. In the Russian Empire, Ukrainians constituted the second largest ethnical group after Russians. The symbolic dimension also played a significant role: Ukrainians and Russians – or "Little Russians" and "Big Russians" – were very close to each other in terms of language and culture and belonged to the same Orthodox church, which could be traced back to medieval Kyiv. That is why the Russian elite saw "Little Russians" as a junior partner in ruling the empire. On the other hand, their efforts to define themselves as a separate nation of "Ukrainians" were interpreted as an existential threat to its existence. Trying to prevent this threat, the Russian imperial government prohibited the use of the Ukrainian language in public in both 1863 and 1876.

In response, Ukrainian social democrats in the Russian Empire shifted the centre of their activity to the other side of the border, to Austrian Galicia, where they could use the more liberal Habsburg regime to build their structures. There were many Marxists among them. Lviv became the main gathering place and also a centre where the documents of Ukrainian social democracy, from both the Austro-Hungarian and the Russian Empire, were published. The different political conditions in these empires had a major impact on the differences between the two Ukrainian social democratic parties. In Galicia, the USDRP grew into a well-organised parliamentary party, while in the Russian Empire the USDRP was a party only in name; in reality, it gathered together a small number of illegal or semi-legal groups. The

Galician social democrats had an ambitious goal, the political independence of Ukraine, as formulated by Yulian Bachynskyi, a Galician Marxist, in his book *Ukraina irredenta* (Lviv, 1895). The Ukrainian social democrats, on the other hand, were satisfied with a humbler formula of Ukrainian autonomy as part of the reformed Russian Empire. Mykola Porsh dedicated his book *On Ukraine's Autonomy* to supporting this thesis (Kyiv, 1909).

What the Ukrainian social democrats from both sides of the Austrian–Russian border had in common, however, were their attempts to combine social and national issues. The circumstances of daily life compelled them to do so. At the end of the nineteenth century, 90 per cent of all Ukrainians were peasants, and 90 per cent of those peasants lived in Ukrainian ethnic territories. As Moses Raphes, one of the leaders of the Jewish Socialist movement, wrote, "In Ukraine, where a landlord was a Russian or a Pole, while a banker or a merchant was usually a Jew who did not speak the 'servile language' and did not understand it, the expression 'Away with the masters!' could mean 'out with the Poles, out with the Russians or out with the Jews'." [3]

A combination of social and national demands was characteristic also of the Brotherhood of Saints Cyril and Methodius, the first Ukrainian national organisation, which appeared in Kyiv in 1845–1847. Similar to other national organisations of that time ("Young Italy", "Young Germany", "Young Ireland" and others), it promoted national slogans along with the ideas of democracy and socialism. Ukrainian poet Taras Shevchenko was the most prominent figure in the Brotherhood. His call for simultaneous national and social liberation became an ideological cornerstone of modern Ukraine. The next generation of Ukrainian figures from Kyiv known collectively as "*Hromada*" (Society) (1860–1870) was described as having the works of "Father Taras" (Shevchenko) in one pocket and Marx's *Das Kapital* in the other.[4] As proof of Marxism's popularity in the Ukrainian movement, five out of 35 translations of the Communist Manifesto into the languages of the Russian Empire were into Ukrainian.[5] Ivan Franko and Lesia Ukrainka were among the translators of Marx's works. Together with Shevchenko, they were three of the most prominent figures in Ukrainian literature in the nineteenth century.

Mykhailo Drahomanov, a leader of Kyiv society, was equal to them in terms of ideological influence. He invented a formula that became a kind of moral imperative for several generations of Ukrainian personalities until the Revolution in 1917: "According to Ukrainian circumstances, that Ukrainian is a bad one, who did not become a radical [a socialist – Y.H.], and that radical is a bad one, who did not become a Ukrainian."[6] Drahomanov's reasoning was simple: because the Ukrainian nation was a "plebeian" one (in other words, mainly consisting of peasants) and had neither an aristocracy nor a bourgeoisie, the liberation movement in Ukraine should be simultaneously national and social.

The Ukrainian social democrats accepted this formula, but only partially. Drahomanov and his followers represented the left-wing ideological tendency and movement, which can be characterised as agrarian socialism. They saw the social basis of this movement among the peasantry, whereas the Ukrainian social democrats emphasised the need to organise the industrial proletariat. They were not put off by the fact that Ukrainian workers constituted an insignificant minority both among Ukrainians and the industrial proletariat in Ukraine (see below). They believed that it was not quantity but quality that mattered; the national industrial proletariat is the most advanced class, so it should lead the fight to liberate Ukrainians from social and national oppression. In any case, the appearance of the social democrats on the Ukrainian public stage inevitably led to a conflict between youth and the older generation. In some cases, this conflict had a personal character: some Ukrainian Marxists (Dmytro Antonovych, Yulian Bachynskyi and others) were the children of Ukrainian actors. But primarily it was a conflict with the "ideological parents" of Ukrainian socialism, Drahomanov, Franko and others.

The Ukrainian Social Democratic Party in Galicia emerged from the Ruthenian-Ukrainian Radical Party (RURP), the first Ukrainian party, created in 1890 in Lviv. The first decade of this party was marked by strong conflict between the "old" and the "young" radicals. The conflict ended when in 1899 the "young" ones left the party and created their own party, the USDP. In a similar way, the Ukrainian social democrats in the Russian Empire initially (1900) were part of the Revolutionary Ukrainian Party (RUP), which was agrarian and socialist, like the Galician RURP. As early as 1902, however, the left wing proclaimed the Western European Democratic Socialism of the parties of the Second International as their guide. In 1905 representatives of this wing adopted the name "USDRP".

The Western European parties were a model for the Ukrainian social democrats, primarily the Austrian and the German Social Democrats. In particular, the programme of the USDRP was based on the Erfurt Programme (1891) of the Social Democratic Party of Germany, while the USDP was an autonomous party in the Social Democratic Workers Party of Austria. Together they took part in the congresses of the Second International in Amsterdam (1904), Stuttgart (1907), Copenhagen (1910) and Basel (1912). The Ukrainian social democrats also consciously copied the Polish left wing. For example, some of their propagandistic brochures were based on publications of the Polish Social Party (PPS). Speaking of the Russian context, the conflict between the Ukrainian social democrats and agrarian socialism was similar to the situation experienced by the first generation of Russian Marxists – Hryhoriy Plekhanov, Vira Zasulych, Pavlo Askelrod and others – who also started as agrarian socialists ("populists"). Relations between the Ukrainian and the Russian social democrats were quite tense, however. Apart from the aforementioned conflict concerning the national question, another significant fact was that they had to fight for influence in the same arena, the industrial proletariat. This proletariat was concentrated in big industrial centres in the east of Ukraine (in Donbas and Katerynslav) and was only partly Ukrainian. According to the estimates of the Ukrainian social democrats, Ukrainians constituted only one-third of the working class,[7] but even that estimate seems exaggerated. The conflict between the Ukrainian and the Russian social democrats was rather symbolic than real, however. The problem was that the majority of "workers" were indeed peasants, who worked for hire for seasonal work, whereas the class consciousness of the part that consisted of permanently based workers was very poorly developed. Speaking of the class consciousness of those workers, as surprising as it may sound, most often it manifested itself in anti-Semitism.[8] That is why it was mainly the party of the intellectuals, despite the fact that the Russian and the Ukrainian social democrats had connections with trade unions and tried to engage industrial workers in their activities.

The biggest and best organised working class was not the Russian or Ukrainian proletariat but the Jewish one. It was united into the Bund, the Jewish workers' party, which was the biggest among similar parties in the Russian Empire. It was due to the Bund's influence that the USDRP had the idea of national and personal autonomy included in their programme, which turned out to be very important later, during the Revolution in 1917.

1917: THE YEAR OF THE UKRAINIAN SOCIALIST MIRACLE

The Russian Revolution of 1917 led to a radical change in the political landscape, primarily because of the new possibilities for parties to work legally. The revolution in imperial centres, such as Petrograd and Moscow, was followed by revolutionary changes in the Western borderlands. In Kyiv, it led to the creation of the Central Council of Ukraine, a self-appointed Ukrainian Parliament. During spring and summer of 1917, it took control over Ukrainian ethnic territories. In autumn, it declared the Ukrainian People's Republic (UNR) as part of Russia.

In the Central Council, the Ukrainian social democrats played a leading part, although they were never the biggest party. The biggest was their closest allies – at the same time their closest opponents – the Ukrainian Socialists-Revolutionaries Party (UPSR), the followers of Drahomanov's agrarian socialism. At the end of 1917, the UPSR had 40,000 members, while the USDRP had only 4,500.[9] Apart from this significant advantage in numbers, however, the Ukrainian Socialists-Revolutionaries voluntarily gave up first place for the Ukrainian Social Democrats.

The reason for this was the internal weakness of UPSR party management. It consisted mainly of very young people, who did not have political experience. Mykhailo Hrushevskyi, their leader – a leading Ukrainian historian – was only 51 in 1917. Surrounded by other leaders of the USRP, however, he looked like a grey-haired grandfather among his grandchildren. It was a different for the USDRP. Most of its leaders had started their activities before the war, so they had some political experience. Two stood out: Volodymyr Vynnychenko and Symon Petliura. Together with Mykhailo Hrushevskyi, they were the three leaders of the Ukrainian revolution. Hrushevskyi was the head of the Central Council, Vynnychenko became the head of the government, while Symon Petliura became minister for military affairs.

The Ukrainian Social Democrats and Social Revolutionaries were not just the leading parties in the Ukrainian revolution. They also played the leading role among other similar governments at the margins of the Russian Empire. At the end of September 1917, the Central Council held the Congress of the Nations in Kyiv to discuss Russia's future. Belarusians, Georgians, Estonians, Jews, Don Cossacks, Lithuanians, Latvians, Poles, Moldavians, Tatars, Transcaucasian Turks and Russian Socialists-Revolutionaries (SRs) took part. Apart from Lithuanians and Poles, who set a course towards complete political independence, and Jews, who could not agree on the idea of Palestine as a future Jewish state, all other delegations agreed with the main principle suggested by the Central Council: turning Russia into a federal union of autonomous national states. That said, the Ukrainian socialist leaders saw the Russian federation as a transitional phase in the creation of a federation of European nations, which could become the federation of the whole world in the future.

The Ukrainian revolutionary government played the leading role among the governments of other non-Russian nations first because of Ukraine's size and strategic importance. Its mobilisation potential was also important. As comparative studies suggest, among all the national movements that were standing on the federative platform, the Ukrainian movement achieved the biggest success in mass mobilisation. This could be seen, for example, in the elections to the All Russian Constituent Assembly in late autumn 1917. At those elections, the Ukrainian socialist parties jointly gained about 70 per cent of the votes in the Ukrainian provinces.

This victory had international significance. Debating with Rosa Luxemburg and other communists who blamed the Bolsheviks for "corrupting" Ukrainian nationalism, Lenin pointed to the results of elections to the Constituent Assembly in autumn 1917. The four million votes that the Ukrainian socialist parties received were, in his opinion, evidence that the Ukrainian movement had to be taken into account.[10]

The Ukrainian revolutionary government also did very well in solving the national issue inside the Ukrainian People's Republic itself. Because the Central Council included representatives of the Russian, Polish and Jewish populations, it turned from being the representative body of the Ukrainian national movement into the state parliament. In addition, Ukraine introduced territorial cultural autonomy for national minorities. The achievements in providing national and cultural autonomy for the Jews were especially significant. Similar autonomy was also introduced in other non-Russian republics, but, as researchers point out, its biggest achievements were in the Ukrainian People's Republic.

Federative plans and national and cultural autonomy were achieved as part of the implementation of both USDRP and UPSR policies. Because of the similarity of their programmes, the parties could be considered twins. The USDRP, however, differed from the UPSR on one important issue: the Ukrainian Social Democrats were loyal to reformism, while the Ukrainian Socialists-Revolutionaries preferred revolutionary methods. Thus, while the Ukrainian Socialists-Revolutionaries, similar to the Russians, demanded complete abolition of private ownership of land, the USDRP agreed to this demand only in relation to the lands of the imperial family, big landlords and the church, while supporting the idea of keeping land ownership for peasants. It is believed that this difference concerning land reform played a crucial role in Ukrainian peasant support for Ukrainian rather than Russian left-wing parties at the elections to the Constituent Assembly. In contrast to Russian ethnic territories, communal ownership of land was not widespread in Ukraine, where most peasants were sole proprietors.

The year 1917 was spoken of as the year of the "Ukrainian miracle". As Volodymyr Vynnychenko wrote in his memoirs, "Indeed, at that time we were gods, who were ready to create a whole new world from nothing". [11] The miracle did not last long, however. At the turn of 1918, the numerous weaknesses of the Ukrainian revolution became obvious. The main one was its inability to protect itself. After the coup d'état in St Petersburg in October, the Bolsheviks recognised the Ukrainian People's Republic and declared war on it at the same time. By February 1918, they had captured its significant parts, including Kyiv. There were several reasons for defeat. But the doctrinarism of the Social Democrats played a role: their distrust of the idea of a regular army. In a speech at the people's assembly in Kyiv in autumn 1917, Symon Petliura explained the position of the Social Democrats as follows:

> We know what disaster this power can cause, if it falls into dangerous hands ... We do not need a standing army, but nationwide armament and police ... The danger here lies in the fact that when the bourgeoisie organises itself, the army will protect its interests against the interests of democracy and the peasantry.[12]

The idea of a people's police, which would replace the army, was part of the standard ideological package of Western European social democracy. But in the conditions of Eastern Europe, loyalty to this idea backfired on the Ukrainian social democrats. In that region, something that the theorists and practitioners of social democracy could not gave predicted appeared, namely war between two socialist governments, in this case between the Russian Bolsheviks and the Ukrainian Social Democrats and Socialists-Revolutionaries.

The main reason for the defeat of the Ukrainian revolution, however, was its reliance on the peasants, who, as Marx famously put it, one cannot lean on, "like a sack of potatos". Peasants had their own social agenda, which coincided only partially with the plans of the Ukrainian revolutionaries. Starting from spring 1917, a mass wave of expropriation of landlords' property swept through Ukrainian villages. After seizing the land and redistributing it among themselves, the peasants were willing to accept pretty much any government that would make this so-called "black partition" legal. From late 1917, they were more ready to fight among themselves than protect the Ukrainian government in Kyiv.

The political preferences of Ukrainian peasants at that time shifted from the Central Council to the Russian Bolsheviks. The Central Council with its socialist government did not hurry to adopt the land law, whereas the Bolsheviks promised to give the land back to the peasants immediately, without any preliminary conditions. That is why, during their first campaign in Ukraine, the Bolsheviks did not encounter any resistance from peasants anywhere. The resistance of the peasants started only when they experienced the Bolshevik occupation, primarily, the policy of "war communism", which was based on the abolition of market relations and taking grain away from the farms.

1918: IN OPPOSITION TO A CONSERVATIVE REGIME

While the Bolsheviks tried to take over Ukraine, they were holding negotiations in Brest with Austro-Hungarian and German commanders about Russia withdrawing from the war. The UNR government also sent a delegation to the Brest negotiations. The Ukrainian socialists wanted to get the military support of the central European states in the war against the Bolsheviks. The Austro-Hungarian and German governments were also interested in a separate peace with Ukraine, because this would have guaranteed them access to Ukrainian grain, a strategically important good in any war. But in the First World War, which turned into an all-out and exhausting conflict, grain was a question of life and death for the existing regimes. The revolution in February 1917 in Russia, as well as the later one in November 1918 in Germany started with hunger riots. As the interests of the UPR and the central European states were similar, it was quite easy for the Ukrainian delegation to sign a separate peace. A prerequisite of this agreement was a complete separation from Russia. The Ukrainian government declared full independence on 22 January, similar to the national governments of Belarus, Armenia, Georgia, Estonia, Latvia and Lithuania.

In these new circumstances, the Socialists-Revolutionaries (SRs) became the main force in the Ukrainian government. This liberated the Social Democrats from moral responsibility for the German occupation of Ukraine. The German troops drove the Bolshevik army from Ukraine without any particular difficulties. But their hope of obtaining access to Ukrainian grain turned out to be futile. The Central Council with its SR majority was helpless and ineffective in organising grain deliveries. At the end of April 1918, the German occupying government staged a military coup d'etat and paved the way to power for Pavlo Skoropadskyi, a former Russian general and descendant of the old Cossack generation. Skoropadskyi declared the creation of a Hetmanate, a conservative regime that was supposed to end "socialist experiments" in Ukraine. Although Skoropadskyi did not risk restoring traditional land ownership, he launched punitive expeditions against peasants to force them to supply grain. He reduced the rights of workers to nothing by prohibiting strikes and seriously limiting the trade unions, in particular prohibiting them from interfering in hiring and firing, as well as working conditions. As a result, the working day increased to 10–12 hours.

These repressions were nothing compared with the policy of "war communism" and the revolutionary terror conducted by the Bolsheviks in Russia. In contrast with that, Ukraine under the German occupation looked like an oasis of stability and calm. Kyiv, Odessa and other Ukrainian cities were overcrowded with refugees from St Petersburg and Moscow, mainly from the upper and middle classes. This conferred on Skoropadskyi's government not only a conservative, but also a pro-Russian character. Skoropadskyi himself believed that the German occupation was temporary. He saw his task as preserving Ukraine after the war as a part of reformed and non-Bolshevik Russia.

With its social, as well as national policy Skoropadskyi's regime provoked the radicalisation of the Ukrainian socialists. In May 1918, at their underground meeting the USDRP claimed that the Ukrainian revolution, after demanding the "state independence of Ukraine and fundamental social reforms", went beyond the national framework and declared itself part of the world proletarian revolution. Accordingly, the fate of the Ukrainian revolution would depend on the revolutionary proletarian movement in the West. In the meantime, the Ukrainian Social Democrats considered it their responsibility to overthrow Skoropadskyi's regime. To that end, they were ready to join the Ukrainian National Union with other opponents of Skoropadskyi, including Ukraine's non-socialist parties.

By joining the wider union the USDRP caused dissatisfaction among the left. They considered this step to be a betrayal of the idea of proletariat class struggle. Taking their example from the German Social Democrats, they called themselves "independent". The Independent Social Democrats called for a union with the Russian Bolsheviks. There was one condition, however: the Russian Bolsheviks had to recognise the independence of Ukraine. Leaning towards the Bolsheviks was approved by Volodymyr Vynnychenko. He even had secret negotiations with a delegation from Soviet Russia, during which they reached agreement on a common front against Skoropadskyi.

In the new circumstances, the Social Democrats renewed their leading role in the Ukrainian revolution. When in November 1918 a revolutionary body, the Directory, was created to manage the anti-Hetman coup d'état, Volodymyr Vynnychenko became its head. Symon Petliura was also a member of the Directory, which provided the USDRP with two of the five "directors".

The Directory started an uprising in the middle of November 1918, as soon as word reached Ukraine about the revolution in Germany. In just a month, the rebel troops entered Kyiv. In the revolutionary government formed by the Directory, the Ukrainian Social Democrats again had the largest number of ministerial positions. Even though the government restored the previous name of the state – the Ukrainian People's Republic – it distanced itself from the name and experience of the Central Council. First, the Central Council was allegedly responsible for inviting German troops to Ukraine and, indirectly, for everthing else that happened under Skoropadskyi. Second, Vynnychenko and the "independent" Social Democrats considered that the whole of "Europe was going through a period of socialist revolution" and the Ukrainian revolution was one of the stages of "socialist revolution in national Ukrainian form". They therefore supported the idea that the government of the UNR should be, not a "bourgeois" parliamentary republic, but a form of worker-peasant dictatorship.

At the turn of 1919, the Ukrainian Social Democrats started to lean strongly to the left. This happened under the influence of the revolutions in Germany and Hungary, whose outbreak strengthened the expectations of world revolution. In Ukraine, the popularity of the Soviet form of government grew as a reaction to the German occupation and Skoropadskyi's regime. In particular, sovietisation covered the German occupational troops returning from Ukraine to Germany. Among the Ukrainian peasantry, the popularity of the Soviet government took a specific form there: they were "for the Soviet government but without the Communists" – in other words, the Russian Bolsheviks. This created an opportunity to organise a national, Ukrainian version of the Soviet government, and the left-wing Ukrainian Social Democrats intended to seize it.

1919–1920: IN A WAR OF ALL AGAINST ALL

They did not win support either in the government or inside the party itself. Their proposal of revolutionary dictatorship was rejected. The Ukrainian People's Republic remained a democratic parliamentary republic. The main reason the UNR turned to the right was a new change in the geopolitical situation after the end of the First World War. In Eastern Europe the end of the war did not mean the end of combat altogether. The fall of the Austro-Hungarian and German Empires in November 1918 triggered new local fighting. They reached their peak in 1919 and the number of victims equalled or sometimes exceeded the First World War. In Ukraine, the Polish-Ukrainian army was active in the former Austrian part of the country, while in the East there was war between the UNR government and Bolshevik Russia.

The second war played a decisive role in the fate of the Ukrainian revolution. Despite the preliminary agreements with the Bolsheviks about the union and non-intervention, after Skoropadkyi's regime was overthrown the Red Army immediately launched a new onslaught on Ukrainian lands. During January, it occupied the majority of Ukrainian cities in the North and East of Ukraine, and at the beginning of February 1919 it entered Kyiv again. At that time, the Bolsheviks' aim was not just to bring the communist revolution to Ukraine, but also to use Ukraine as a bridge to link up with the revolutions in Germany and Hungary.

The British-French assault force landed in Odessa in spring 1919. Its aim was to take control of Ukrainian territory and stabilise the situation. At the same time, Denikin's White Army started its onslaught from the South and its route to Moscow lay through Ukraine. The White Army had the support of the Entente. The UNR also tried to get the Entente's support and started negotiations in the first months of 1919. The Ukrainian government realised that the fate of Ukrainian lands would be decided at the Paris Peace Conference and it recognised the weakness of its position. First, the shadow of the union with Germany was hanging over the UNR, and second, its radical politics created the impression that the Ukrainian government was nothing but a Ukrainian variant of Russian Bolshevism.

To make the negotiations with the Entente easier, on 9 February the Central Committee of the USDRP withdrew their representatives from the government and the Directory. Volodymyr Vynnychenko resigned as the Directory's head and withdrew his membership. His place was taken by Simon Petliura, who left the party beforehand. Petliura then became the main symbol of the Ukrainian revolution. In particular, he was connected with a wave of pogroms in Ukraine in 1919. All armies, with no exception, took part in those pogroms, including the Red Army, but the leading role belonged to the UNR army. In a situation of general chaos and "war of all against all" Petliura's influence on his army was limited and his name became a synonym for Ukrainian anti-Semitism.

The Ukrainian revolutionary government turned to the right. One factor in this development was the arrival of Ukrainian politicians from Galicia. They represented the West Ukrainian People's Republic (ZUNR), proclaimed on 1 November 1918 in the Austrian part of the country. The ZUNR developed in a completely different fashion from the UNR. It was not shaped by mass peasant movements or by pogroms, and the left-wing parties – the local Social Democrats and Radicals – did not play the main role in its government, but rather the central Ukrainian National Democratic Party. Moreover, even the Galician Social Democrats were generally more sensible than the Ukrainian Social Democrats in Kyiv. In particular, the USDP did not show signs of Bolshevisation.

On 22 January 1919, the ZUNR announced its union ("Zluka") with the UNR. This was a formality. Each of the Ukrainian states kept its own autonomy and fought their own wars: the ZUNR with the Polish army in the West, the UNR with the Bolsheviks in the East. The real union happened in mid summer 1919, when the ZUNR experienced total military defeat and its government together with its Ukrainian Galician army crossed the former Austro-Russian border and entered the territory of the UNR. For a short time, the united Ukrainian army managed to take the initiative and at the end of the summer it won Kyiv back from the Bolsheviks. On the same day, however, Denikin's army entered the capital and after brief fighting the UNR army ceded the city to its stronger rival. During the autumn, the united Ukrainian government remained in Kamianets-Podilskyi, in a so-called "death triangle". There, surrounded by enemies on all sides, without ammunition, supplies and medicine, its army suffered mass losses from hunger and disease.

Amidst plummeting morale, the Ukrainian government survived several coup attempts from the right but suffered from the permanent conflict between Western Ukrainian and Eastern Ukrainian politicians. The Ukrainian Social Democrats tried to save the situation, calling for a joint socialist government. Their hour of triumph had already passed, however. The USDRP itself survived disintegration. Some "independent" Social Democrats left the USDRP and joined the Communist Party (of the Bolsheviks) of Ukraine, created in July 1918, which was nothing other than a regional branch of the Russian Bolshevik party. Another part of the "independent" Social Democrats stayed in the USDRP, but as a separate faction. Finally, in January 1919 they created their own party, the Communist Party of Ukraine.

The Ukrainian Socialists-Revolutionaries (SRs) underwent a similar disintegration. A strong left wing also formed itself among them, which evolved towards the Bolsheviks. At that time, all of Ukraine was suffering from peasant uprisings, most of whose leaders were under the ideological influence of the Ukrainian SRs.

Being cut of from the government from both right and left, the Ukrainian Social Democrats quickly lost their positions. Their last success involved their activities in the international social democratic movement. By a decision of the Lucerne Conference (1–9 August 1919), they were accepted into the Second International, together with the USPR. This conference almost unanimously (except for the Russian SRs) recognised the independence and sovereignty of the Ukrainian Republic, protested against the Polish occupation and demanded that the Paris Peace Conference recognise Ukraine as an independent state and accept it into the League of Nations.

This external success, however, could not be exploited in internally. In the late autumn of 1919, under pressure from the Red Army's onslaught, Petliura crossed the Polish border with the remnants of his army. In Poland he made an agreement with Josef Pilsudski, the leader of a newly-created Polish state who had also renounced socialism for nationalism. In spring 1920, the union between Pilsudski and Petliura resulted in a common Polish-Ukrainian campaign to retake Kyiv. They briefly managed this, but very soon they were pushed all the way back to Warsaw by the onslaught of the Red Army. In August 1920, the Polish troops, with the participation of UNR battalions, managed to beat the Red Army at the Battle of Warsaw and stop the Bolsheviks' advance to the West. The independence of Ukraine was lost irrecoverably, however. The Ukrainian lands, according to the decision of the Peace of Riga (March 1921) were divided between Poland and the Soviet state.

Several weeks after the Battle of Warsaw, on 24 September 1920, the Central Committee of the USDRP prohibited party members from taking part in the UNR government in immigration. Those Social Democrats who refused to leave the government had to leave the party. This was the end of the USDRP's participation in the formation of the Ukrainian state.

AFTER 1921: CONSEQUENCES AND CHALLENGES

Formally, the Ukrainian national revolution had suffered total defeat. The Ukrainian Social Democrats carry some responsibility for this because for a long time they played the leading role in the Ukrainian revolutionary government. This responsibility can neither be denied nor minimised – not least when taking into account the doctrinarian position of the USDRP concerning the creation of a national army. Blaming the Ukrainian socialists for this doctrinarism became common among Ukrainians in the decades after the revolution. These accusations spread to the ideology of socialism in general and Marxism in particular. As a consequence of this, in the period between the wars and during the Second World War Ukrainian nationalism turned strongly to the right. Ironically, one of the ideologists of this turn to the right – an ideologist of integral Ukrainian nationalism, close to Italian fascism – was a former Ukrainian Marxist and Social Democrat Dmytro Dontsov.

The accusations against the Ukrainian Social Democrats are only partly true, however, because the defeat of the Ukrainian revolution was induced by factors that they could not have influenced. First and foremost there is the structure of Ukrainian society itself. It mainly consisted of the peasantry, which is an extremely unreliable basis for any kind of political movement. The Ukrainian peasants greeted every new regime in the hope that it would legalise the lands they occupied and would not interfere in their affairs. In due course they were inevitably disappointed and uprisings recommenced. The attitude of the peasants toward the UNR and the Ukrainian left parties reflected this pattern.

But the Russian Bolsheviks had even bigger problems with Ukrainian peasants. In 1918–1920 they invaded and were forced to leave Ukraine three times, and every time they left there was an outburst of mass peasant anti-Bolshevik disorder. The peasant resistance in Ukraine continued after the end of the revolution and the civil war, in the 1920s, at which time the Ukrainian peasants' biggest hopes focused not on the Ukrainian SRs but on Petliura. Eventually, the conflict between the peasants and the Bolsheviks ended with collectivisation and the disastrous Ukrainian famine of 1932–1933, which once and for all destroyed peasant resistance.

The decisive cause of the defeat of the Ukrainian revolution, however, was not the instability of its social base, but the geopolitical situation. Considering that from the beginning of the First World War in 1914 until the end of the Civil War in 1920, Ukraine was in the epicentre of prolonged military conflict the chances of building a stable nation state were next to none. It could have survived only with support from the winning states, for example, if Germany had won the First World War. On the other hand, in that case, Ukraine would hardly have been a socialist state. In any event, after the Treaty of Brest-Litovsk, Ukraine was perceived by the winning Entente as a pro-German power and thus unworthy of national self-determination. We can assume with high probability, however, that if Ukraine had been left to its own devices it would have formed a social democratic state, in which the rights of workers and national minorities would have been taken into account. This assumption is based, first of all, on the success the Ukrainian socialist parties achieved in 1917, until the Ukrainian revolution ended up in a "war of all against all".

In fact, the failure of the Ukrainian socialist project cannot be considered a complete defeat. The Ukrainian revolution was a conflict between several powers: the Ukrainian left-wing and right-wing governments, the Russian Whites and Reds, the rebellious peasantry and foreign occupiers. None of them had enough power to achieve monopolistic control over Ukrainian territories. Under such conditions it was possible to win only through compromise. Among all the revolutionary and counter-revolutionary powers, the Bolsheviks demonstrated the biggest readiness to change tack. Lenin was a genius of pragmatic decision-making. In particular, when he realised that the Soviet power was very close to death, he suggested two important compromises: the New Economic Policy (NEP) towards the peasantry and the creation of the USSR as a socialist state while accommodating the national movements on the periphery. But if we compare the pre-revolutionary programmes of the Bolsheviks and the Ukrainian socialists, as well as the experiences of the revolutionary year of 1917, we come to an unexpected conclusion, namely that the USSR was created according to a Ukrainian formula rather than a Russian one.

The modern Ukrainian nation grew from the compromise between the Russian Bolsheviks and the Ukrainian national movement. The best words to describe this formula are "enslaved, but nevertheless a nation-state". An independent Ukraine is unlikely to have emerged other than from the development of the Soviet Union, notwithstanding all the positive and negative consequences. We can debate the general balance of these consequences and hardly ever reach agreement. The only thing that is true without a doubt, however, is that we would hardly be in a position to debate the Ukrainian state at all without the Ukrainian Social Democrats and their contribution to the creation of the Ukrainian state.

The Ukrainian Social Democrats themselves had to pay a high price for their defeat, however. They disappeared as a party from the Ukrainian political stage. A small group of them were preserved in emigration between the wars, but they were a sidelined minority among the Ukrainian diaspora. When political life was radicalised and the only real option was a choice between communism and fascism, there was just no place for them. The majority did not survive the Second World War. The social democratic ideology was partially reborn at the late stage of evolution of Ukrainian nationalism (after 1944) and in the Ukrainian dissident movement of the 1970 and 1980s, but its rebirth was not accompanied by a call for Ukrainian social democracy as it was at the beginning of the twentieth century and in the revolution of 1917–1920.

There has been an attempt to revive the Ukrainian Social Democratic Party in independent Ukraine. This party does not have much in common with its namesake, however. Based on its activities, it looks more like a right-wing party than a left-wing one. Its leaders are oligarchs who support authoritarianism and are suspected of criminal activity. The real left (and also the Marxists) are the representatives of the young intelligentsia. Their activities do not go beyond intellectual discussions and occasional public campaigns, however. In any case, both the "unreal" and the "real" Ukrainian left barely rely on the experience of the Ukrainian Social Democrats, similar to the Ukrainian dissidents before them.

The only Ukrainian Social Democrats currently present in Ukrainian historical memory are Volodymyr Vynnychenko and Symon Petliura. According to sociological surveys, however, neither of them are in the national pantheon of famous historical figures. Moreover, Volodymyr Vynnychenko is often mentioned rather as a talented writer, while Symon Petliura is mentioned as a fighter for national independence – in other words, outside the context of Ukrainian social democracy.

The Ukrainian social democratic parties remain a big unknown in Ukrainian historical memory. This is especially sad because, as Ukrainian analysts and public intellectuals point out, the modern Ukrainian political stage suffers hugely from the absence of a party that is simultaneously national and left-wing. We can only hope that the Ukrainian crisis can stimulate the emergence of such a party that, in turn, might renew interest in the history of Ukrainian social democracy.

SUMMARY

The history of the Ukrainian Social-Democratic movement can be traced from the Ukrainian Social Democratic Party (1899) in the Austrian part of Ukrainian ethnic territories and the Ukrainian Social-Democratic Workers' Party (USDRP) in the Russian part. In their activities, both parties tried to combine social and national issues. This combination led to conflict with the neighboring Polish and – even more so – with Russian Marxists. Above all, this conflict manifested itself during the revolution of 1917, when, after the Bolshevik coup d'état, revolutionary Russia and revolutionary Ukraine went to war.

Even though the Ukrainian social democrats were never the largest party in the revolutionary Ukrainian government, they played a leading role. This reflected their longer political experience and higher level of sophistication compared with other leaders of the Ukrainian revolution. To a large extent, thanks to the Ukrainian Social Democrats the Ukrainian national government managed to make significant progress in mobilising the peasantry and securing rights for national minorities.

It is reasonable to assume that if revolutionary Ukraine had been left alone it would have constituted itself as a social democratic state. In the event in 1917–1920 the Ukrainian ethnic territories became the focus of several conflicts, which resulted in a kind of "war of all against all". Under such dire external and internal circumstances, the Ukrainian revolution was defeated. Its defeat cannot be considered to have been complete, however. In particular, the USSR was created as a socialist federal state by Lenin and the Bolsheviks largely in response to the challenges of national movements in the borderlands, among which the Ukrainian revolution proved to be one of the strongest.

The Ukrainian Social Democrats had to pay a heavy price for their defeat. They disappeared as a party from the Ukrainian political scene and remain a "great unknown" in Ukrainian historical memory. One can only hope that the current Ukrainian crisis can provoke the emergence of a new Ukrainian Social Democratic Party, which, in turn may restore public interest in the history of Ukrainian social democracy.

1. Е. Бернштейн, Спомини про Михайла Драгоманова і Сергія Подолиньського, in Михайло Грушевський, З починів українського соціалістичного руху. *Мих, Арагоманов і женевський соціалістичний кружок* (Женева, 1922), p. 156. (E. Bernstein, Spomyny pro Mykhayla Dragomanova I Sergiya Podolynkskogo, in Mykhaylo Hrushevskyi, *Z pochyniv Ukrayinskogo sozialistychnogo rukhu. Mykh, Aragomanov i zhenevskyi sozialistychnyi kruzhok*, Geneva, 1922, p. 156).
2. Roman Szporluk, The Ukraine and Russia, in Robert Conquest (ed.), *The Last Empire. Nationality and the Soviet Future* (Stanford, CA, 1986), p. 156.
3. М.Б.Рафес, Два года революции на Украине (Эволюция и раскол 'Бунда'). Москва: Государственное издательство, 1920, pp. 7–8 (M.B. Rafes, Dva goda revolutsii na Ukraine (Evolyuziya I raskol 'Bunda'. Moskva: Gosudarstvennoe izdatelstvo, 1920, pp. 7–8.)
4. Короткий В., Ульяновський В., упор., Син України. Володимир Боніфатійович Антонович, 3 т. Київ, 1997, vol. 2, p. 39 (Korotkiy, V. and Ulyanovskyi, V. (ed.), Syn Ukrayiny. Volodymyr Bonifatiyovych Antonovych, 3 vols, Kyiv, 1997, vol. 2, p. 39).
5. Hobsbawm, E., *How to Change the World. Reflections on Marx and Marxism*, New York & Yale: Yale University Press, 2011, p. 195.
6. Драгоманов М. П., Літературно-публіцистичні праці, 2 т., Київ, 1970, т. 1, с. 9. (Dragomanov, M.P., Literaturno-publizystychni prazi, 2 vols., Kyiv, 1970, vol. 1, p. 59).
7. Колард, Ю. Спогади юнацьких днів, 1897–1906, Українська студентська громада в Харкові. Т.1. Революційна українська партія (РУП). Торонто: Срібні сурми, 1972, с. 115-116; цит. за: Висоцький О.Ю. Українські соціал-демократи та есери: досвід перемог і поразок, Київ: Основні цінності, 2004, с. 31. (Kolard Yu., Spogady yunatskych dniv, 1897–1906, Ukrayinska studentska gromada v Kharkov, vol. 1, Revolyuziyna ukrayinska partiya (RUP), Toronto: Sribni surmy, 1972, pp. 115–16; cited after Vysotskyi, O. Yu., Ukrayinski sozial-demokraty ta esery: dosvod peremog s porazok, Kyiv, Osnovni zinnosti, 2004, p. 31.)
8. Wynn, *Workers, Strikes, and Pogroms. The Donbass-Dnepr Bend in Late Imperial Russia, 1870-1905*, New Jersey, Princeton University Press, 1992.
9. Висоцький, О.Ю., Українські соціал-демократи та есери, p. 16, 67 (Vysotskyi, O. Yu., Ukrayinski sozial-demokraty ta esery, p. 16, 67).
10. Ленин, В.И., Полное собрание сочинений. Изд. 5-е. Т.40. Москва: Издательство политической литературы, 1974, с. 18–19 (доступно за адресою: http://uaio.ru/vil/40.htm) (Lenin, V.I. Polnoe sobranie sochinenii. 5 ed. V. 40. Moskva: Izdatelstvo politicheskoi literatury, 1974, pp. 18–19 (available at: http://uaio.ru/vil/40.htm)
11. Винниченко, В., Відродження нації.Ч. 1. Київ-Відень, 1920, p. 258 (Vynnychenko, V., Vildordzennya nazii. Ch.1 Kyiv-Viden, 1920, p. 258).
12. From Висоцький, О.Ю., Українські соціал-демократи та есери, p. 66 (Vysotskyi, O. Yu., Ukrayinski sozial-demokraty ta esery, p.66).

SOCIAL DEMOCRACY AND STATE FOUNDATION: THE GEORGIAN EXAMPLE

LEVAN LORTKIPANIDZE

THE SOCIAL DEMOCRATIC MOVEMENT BEFORE INDEPENDENCE

Origins of the Social Democratic Movement in the Nineteenth Century

In 1801 the Russian Empire abolished the monarchy in eastern Georgia. This meant the end of sovereignty for the country and Georgia became part of the Russian Empire. Supporters of the Bagrationi Monarchy, members of the royal family and local nobles protested against the decision of St Petersburg. From 1801 to 1832 several military rebellions were organised in different parts of Georgia, though all of them failed. The Georgian Conspiracy of 1832 was planned by Georgian nobles, but was discovered beforehand by the Tsarist secret service. Some participants were arrested and exiled, others were given military and bureaucratic positions. All the political rebellions organised at the beginning of the nineteenth century involved monarchists, nobles and the upper classes. Lower social classes were not represented in the national liberation movement. Peasants and those from lower classes working in big cities were not thought of as a substantial political force by the nobles.

After the failure of the attempted rebellion in 1832, a period of pessimism and conformism started in Georgia. The opposition could not organise against the Tsarist system. The policy of Russification was strengthened because there were no opposition forces and newspapers in the country. Potential political actors were integrated into the state system. The Georgian language was used only to communicate in everyday life. It was barred from the civil service and public establishments, schools, theatres and churches. Publication of books in Georgian was stopped. The Russian language became dominant in the local press and all the main characteristics of Tsarism were enforced in Georgia: censorship, political repression, a violent police system and no democratic institutions. Social economic conditions for the Georgian people were hard. In the 1860s serfdom was abolished in Georgia. Before the abolition of serfdom, Georgian peasants had been a constituent element of nobles' fortunes. Peasants had no access to independent activities and opportunities for development. Only in the first half of the twentieth century were the minimum standards of an eight-hour working day and labour rights obtained by people in the Caucasus region.

In the 1860s, intellectuals returned from Russia and ended this period of pessimism in Georgia. The famous Georgian thinker Ilia Chavchavadze led a group of writers, poets and journalists whose priorities were to establish a Georgian social-political and literary press, create independent Georgian elementary and secondary schools and develop political awareness by reminding people of their history. These public figures were in favour of independence or autocephaly for the Georgian Orthodox Church from the Russian Orthodox Church. They were also in favour of establishing elective institutions of national self-government throughout Georgia. These representatives of democratic nationalism rejected the theory of class antagonism. They did not see different classes, but only one Georgian nation and called on people to maintain national integrity to counterbalance Tsarist policies. Thus, the first democratic wave in Georgia in the second half of the nineteenth century was mainly cultural. Democratic thinkers avoided discussions about economic issues and focused on language, history, literature and religion.[1] The activities of Ilia Chavchavadze and his followers did not have much in common with social democratic ideals, though they had an important influence on the creation of the left-wing movement in Georgia. The future Georgian Social Democrats received their education in schools founded by Chavchavadze's group. They familiarised themselves with illegal books in the libraries of these schools. They read about global policy and literature in newspapers founded by Georgian writers and poets. Most importantly, graduates of Russian universities established a precedent for social activism and resistance against the Russian political-military administration. They set the standard for future political leaders scattered in different regions of the Caucasus.

Social Democratic Group Formation and the Main Ideological Priorities of the Movement

The first left-wing union in Georgia was formed in 1892. They became known as the Third Group[2] or *"Mesame Dasi"* in Georgian. The constituent conference was held in a little settlement called Kvirila in western Georgia. Kvirila, is now a borough in the city of Zestafoni. Zestafoni, with its ferro-alloys factory, is one of the biggest industrial centres in Georgia. In order to deceive the police, the conference was held over Christmas and disguised as a Christmas event.

The Kvirila conference was attended by around 10 people. They were village teachers, revolutionary students of the Tiflis Theological Seminary, journalists and writers (Noe Zhordania, Isidore Ramishvili, Egnate Ninoshvili, Mikha Tskhakaia and others) who gained their fame with the help of the press created by Chavchavadze's group. Some of the conference delegates had a past in the "Khalkhosnuri" movement. This was the Georgian equivalent of the Russian "Narodniks" – "men and women of the people" – who idealised rural life and saw a return to living in village communities as a way of achieving a better, socialist society. At the first meeting the participants could not agree on the main statutes of their programme. The meeting participants assigned Noe Zhordania (who had studied in Warsaw and became a member of socialist discussion circles there) to write a manifesto for this new political movement.

The first political manifesto of the Third Group was published in 1894. Noe Zhordania called his programme "Economic Success and Nationality". The manifesto included several fundamental Marxist ideas, such as urbanisation, industrialisation and the necessity of capitalist development. The future prime minister of Georgia could not imagine the advance of socialism without a transition from feudalism to capitalism. By refusing to omit capitalism, the Georgian Social Democrats drew a line in the sand between the followers of "Khalkhosnuri" socialism and themselves.[3] Third Group members contradicted one of the main thesis statements of the 1860s national cultural-democratic movement. According to this thesis, democratic nationalists denied class antagonism. The Third Group's manifesto clearly identified a conflict in society that was caused by economic inequality, exploitation and oppression. Arguments of economic determinism had a significant place in the first programme of the Georgian Social Democrats. They tried to convince the Georgian population that economic issues and the problems of welfare distribution had to be taken into consideration when trying to explain any political or cultural event.

The main characteristic of the Georgian social democratic movement was that it appealed to various social groups. Revolutionaries from agrarian and non-industrialised regions understood that it would not be enough to rely on the working class because it was not large enough. The Third Group was in favour of a political struggle based on a coalition of rural and urban working classes. They argued that the working class had to bring together the following groups around their political agenda: landless peasants, small traders in big cities, sole proprietors, progressive intellectuals and upper class representatives of feudal society bankrupted by moneylenders. Third Group leaders believed that the working class had to be in the vanguard of revolutionary activities, although it would not be wise if they tried their chances in politics without partnership.

From 1892 to 1903, the Georgian social democratic movement was an independent political unit. Third Group members determined their political agenda without interference from any other structures in the Russian Empire. In 1903, the Third Group joined the Russian Social Democratic Labour Party (RSDLP). After joining the RSDLP, the Georgian Social Democrats were more actively involved in international left-wing discourse. The positions of the Russian and European Social Democrats were clear for the followers of the Third Group, who subsequently made the following demands: the introduction of an eight-hour working day, protection of workers' health and safety, absolute elimination of unemployment, a state-wide employment policy, equal rights for women, strengthening of local self-government and support for collective and state ownership structures. The main disagreement between the Georgian and Russian Social Democrats was about how to manage the revolutionary movement and national issues.

From the very beginning, the vast majority of the Georgian Social Democrats followed the Menshevik wing of the RSDLP. The Mensheviks disagreed with Lenin's idea of "democratic centralism". They thought it was a bad idea if only a small group of people took responsibility for managing a party that covered the whole Russian territory. They were in favour of a bottom-up organisational structure for the party. Before the First Republic was established, the whole of Georgia was covered by new organisations of the Social Democratic Party of Georgia (SDPG). By voting on different levels, these organisations had a significant influence in creating a unified position for the RSDLP Caucasus Bureau.

One of the most complicated problems for the Georgian social democratic movement was the issue of national identity, although the matter did not have much importance for Russian leftists. For citizens living under national oppression in this peripheral region of the Russian Empire, however, this issue was a great challenge. The SDPG had differing views about national identity and there were four contradictory positions in the party:[4]

(i) The radical internationalist wing of the party did not consider national identity problems as politically crucial. They believed there was only one significant issue: removing the obstacles of the proletariat. They argued that, after eliminating economic oppression, national independence and self-awareness problems would be solved naturally. The proletarian internationalist group was led by the future leader of the State Duma, Irakli Tsereteli.

(ii) In his public letters, Noe Zhordania spoke about the decision made at the Second Congress of the RSDLP. The decision was related to the development of local district self-government. At the first stage of the social democratic movement, Zhordania considered that strengthening self-governance was a way to build national self-awareness.

(iii) The first Minister of Foreign Affairs of Georgia Akaki Chkhenkeli was in favour of the national programme of the Social Democratic Party of Austria. Chkhenkeli strove to adjust the five articles of the Brno programme to the Russian Empire and its nations. These articles are:

(iv) Austria must be transformed into one democratic federal state of nations.

- Instead of historical crown lands, self-government bodies having national boundaries are created. Their legislation and governance is formed

- by national chambers. Elections of the chamber are based on universal, equal and direct suffrage.
- All the self-governing territories of one and the same nation form a unified national association, that autonomously regulates its own national affairs.
- The rights of ethnic minorities are protected by a special law that is to be adopted by the Imperial Parliament.
- We negate any national prerogative. Thus, we dismiss the request of one state language. The Imperial Parliament will determine the necessity of one intermediate language.[5]

In the 1900s a small group emerged inside the SDPG. In an open and direct manner, the group demanded political autonomy for Georgia with a view to independence. Within the SDPG there was no consensus about the national issue. In spite of this, discussions of the national programme never created a risk of the party dividing.

The Main Pillars of the Georgian Social Democratic Movement (1892–1917)

From 1892 to 1917 the SDPG developed as the main and dominant political force in the country. Progress made by the SDPG was the result of institutional activities and other events. Below, we explain the main institutions and events that had a decisive impact on the development of social democratic ideas throughout Georgia.

The Tiflis Theological Seminary

In the second half of the nineteenth century, Georgian students had several options to continue their studies after finishing secondary education. Rich citizens went to universities in Russia and Europe. For poor students, the only way to continue their education was to study at the Tiflis Theological Seminary. There was a strict regime at the Seminary. Beating students and discrimination on the grounds of nationality were common. Students were also not allowed to speak in their native language, read non-religious literature or leave the Seminary surroundings and dormitory territory without permission. Not surprisingly, the students did not obey these rules and strove to make their everyday routine more interesting and exciting. Disobedience was punished by exile, arrest or deprivation of their right to continue their studies in other institutions. This violent regime created resistance. Students formed secret groups, connected with revolutionary (at first, mainly "Khalkhosnuri", then Marxist) intellectuals and acquired prohibited publications from them. The majority of the future leaders of government and parliament in the Democratic Republic of Georgia took their first steps towards political socialisation at the Theological Seminary and had their first experiences of resistance there.[6]

The Newspaper Kvali

In 1897 the best known Georgian Marxist publicist at that time, Noe Zhordania, became the editor-in-chief of the weekly political newspaper *Kvali*. It was the first legal socialist newspaper in the Russian Empire. At the end of the nineteenth century this newspaper was the only and most effective way of communicating for social democrats. By creating their own media platform, social democrats had opportunities to present and develop new writers, journalists and columnists. *Kvali* was also actively used as a way of countering Tsarist and nationalist publications. Through it, the majority of Georgia's literate population learnt about the first social democrats. The publication also clearly presented a social democratic alternative and caused class issues to become part of public discussions. At the beginning of the twentieth century, however, the Tsarist regime decided to censor the publication and *Kvali* was closed. Through the experience they gained by publishing it, the party leaders managed to launch several new periodicals before an independent Georgia was restored. Like *Kvali*, however, most of these publications did not survive for long under imperial policies censoring freedom of speech.

The Peasant Movement in Guria and the Bakhvi Manifesto

The launch of the social movement in Guria has its origins in a series of unsuccessful strikes in Batumi. Between 1900 and 1902 workers in Batumi demonstrated against the owners of large factories, the Rothschilds and other nobles who had control over the oil industry in the city. The aim of the demonstrations was to improve workers' social conditions and win the right to participate in factory management. Unfortunately, the protesters were defeated. After numerous bloody raids, the district management exiled the workers from the city. These people, who had experienced many years of revolutionary conflict and received their education in non-formal circles, left Batumi for their hometowns in Guria and became agitators for social and political change. They travelled between villages and talked with people about the need to abolish lease fees and church taxes. Propagandists also called on the population to hold demonstrations and demand the right to use water and forest resources for free.

The Gurian people joined the social movement because they were deprived of many rights. At that time there were no advisory bodies at the village and community level. Senior leaders, administrative officials and nobles were not accountable to the local population and took decisions that were beneficial only to themselves. Local people could not fight against social oppression through legal activities. The launch of the social movement in western Georgia was due to high levels of education among the local people. There were a surprisingly high number of public schools and students in the district of Guria. Almost every large settlement had a post office that received local and imperial newspapers. The Batumi workers used their experience and established informal revolutionary educational circles.[7]

Not surprisingly, the rise of the peasant movement in Guria was partly caused by the bad harvests from 1901 to1903 and economic fluctuations after the Russo-Japanese War. Finally in 1905 after the first Russian Revolution, the social movement in Guria reached its peak. The local population showed an extraordinary ability for self-organisation. Without permission from the Viceroy of the Caucasus, they established village councils, bodies of direct democracy. The councils elected peasant courts, community governors and other officials. Each council created its own police force. The whole region elected a common revolutionary committee to fight against Tsarism. With the support of the revolutionary committee of Guria each village published its own manifesto. The first was from a little settlement called Bakhvi. According to the Bakhvi Manifesto, the rebellious population demanded the abolition of ranks, equal distribution of lands among village collectives, the establishment of a universal education system, democratic local self-government, creation of parliamentary governance based on the universal right to election and progressive taxes. After two years of fighting, the peasant movement in Guria was defeated by Tsarist military forces in a bloody battle. The existence of a democratic manifesto presenting peasants as a revolutionary class and the traumatised-heroic experience of the bloody repression became part of the Georgian social democratic narrative and determined its future political activities.

The State Duma of Russia

Before establishing the First Republic of Georgia, members of the social democratic movement used all possible methods in their political struggle in the Caucasus region. They participated in demonstrations, strikes and May Day parades; worked among the students of different institutions; supported the organisation of trade union and peasant movements; and ran a legal and an illegal press. At the same time, members of Georgian social democratic organisations actively participated in elections. After the 1905 Russian Revolution a representative body, the State Duma, was created in the Russian Empire. The State Duma advised the monarch and shared legislative powers with him. It mainly had a symbolic function and was not a threat to the Russian absolute monarchy. From 1905 to 1917 elections for the State Duma were held four times.

During these four elections, the SDPG managed to win all but one of the seats allocated to Georgia. This seat was won by the non-Marxist leftist party, the Social Federalists. The success of the leaders of the RSDLP Caucasian Bureau was the result of their strategy to create a coalition that represented all the lower classes of society. Therefore the SDPG managed not only to gain support from the working classes, but also from peasants and a small number of bourgeoisie. This is what helped to generate their electoral success. Throughout the Empire, the RSDLP was most successful in pre-industrial, agrarian Georgia. Representatives of the RSDLP's Caucasian Bureau dominated in the social democratic faction of the State Council. For decades, SDPG members – Isidore Ramishvili, Akaki Chkhenkeli, Nikoloz (Karlo) Chkheidze and Irakli Tsereteli – led the group of RSDLP parliamentary representatives.

The social democratic faction spoke for the working class, ethnic minorities and the peripheral regions of the Empire. Faction members often challenged ministers of the Empire who came to attend Duma sessions. Often, this bravery was punished by the police. From its activities in the State Council, the SDPG gained experience of campaigning during elections and recognition and influence in the Empire and abroad. By the time of the Russian Revolution in 1917, the SDPG was the strongest political force in Georgia.

THE SOCIAL DEMOCRATIC PARTY OF GEORGIA IN THE FIRST REPUBLIC

Proclamation of the Democratic Republic of Georgia

The SDPG were at the forefront of the February Revolution in 1917, participating actively in demonstrations against the Tsarist regime. The people in Tbilisi viewed the revolution with hope. Nikoloz (Karlo) Chkheidze led the Petrograd Revolutionary Council of workers, peasants, soldiers and sailors. After the February Revolution, the Petrograd Council took the role of main representative body in Russia. In some cases, it had executive along with legislative functions. After establishing the Provisional Government, Irakli Tsereteli, the leader of the social democratic faction of the State Duma, was appointed Minister of Posts, Telegraphs and Communications. Apart from Chkheidze and Tsereteli, other Georgian Mensheviks also hoped the Russian state would manage to adopt a democratic constitution that ensured equal opportunities for development for the working class and ethnic minorities. The SDPG thought the future of Georgia was in the democratic commonwealth of Russia, but the events that followed this period ran against a democratic Russia. The October Revolution drastically altered the plans of the SDPG. The party was strongly against the overthrow of the Russian provisional government by the Bolsheviks and the establishment of the Soviet regime. Caucasian social democrats had to change their plans. The South Caucasian deputies of the Russian Constituent Assembly founded a provisional parliamentary structure for the region, the Transcaucasian Sejm, in which the leaders of the SDPG formed the majority. In spring 1918, the Sejm announced the independence of the Transcaucasian Democratic Federative Republic. It was clear that the foreign policy visions of Georgia, Armenia and Azerbaijan radically differed from one another. Armenians hoped to receive the support of the Anglo-American world, while the SDPG planned to protect the country from Bolshevik aggression with the help of the German Empire. Azerbaijan planned to integrate into the Ottoman Empire that still existed at that time. Co-existence of these three nations in one state became impossible and on 26 May 1918, Georgia issued a declaration of independence.

Georgia's declaration of independence on 26 May 1918 was adopted at a Georgian National Council session. After the October Revolution, the National Council of Georgia was elected as an advisory body by the National Congress of Georgia. Two-thirds of the seats in the National Council of Georgia were controlled by the Georgian Mensheviks. Later the National Council became the Parliament of Georgia and was assigned to carry out preparatory activities for elections. The National Council also elected the first Government of National Unity of Georgia, headed by the famous Georgian revolutionary, party organiser and social democrat Noe Ramishvili. Several months later, the Government of National Unity was replaced by a social democratic cabinet. Noe Zhordania, former editor of *Kvali*, was elected Prime Minister of Georgia. Thus the announcement of the independence of Transcaucasia and Georgia was entirely dependent on SDPG members, as they controlled the absolute majority in each representative body.

The Situation in the Caucasus Region in Spring 1918

The independence of Georgia was declared against a very complicated geopolitical background. To the west of the country a civil war in Russia got under way between monarchists (the White Army) and the Bolshevik military forces (the Red Army). Independence for Georgia was unacceptable to both sides, as they considered the Caucasus an indivisible peripheral part of Russian territory. Until 1920, and before the end of the Civil War, the Red and the White armies both tried to use Georgia as a base. The SDPG refused to help either party militarily or politically. However, the Democratic Republic of Georgia was a shelter for communists escaping from monarchists, as well as for Bolsheviks fleeing from the White Army of General Denikin. The government of Georgia had to expend enormous human and financial resources to protect its western border from Civil War participants.

Turkey also had an interest in the area around Batumi in south western Georgia. In spring 1918, the Turkish army took several parts of the Black Sea coast of Georgia. Earlier, during the First World War, they had started moving towards the main cities of western Georgia, as they negotiated with German military representatives. One more threat to the Democratic Republic of Georgia was the soldiers who had demobilised from the Russo-Turkish front during the First World War. They were going back to the far provinces of Russia, were defeated, disorganised and had no other means of sustaining themselves than to rob the local population. Two revolutions and the fate of the First World War, which was still undecided, inhibited Georgia in the very first months of independence. The Georgian economy was isolated as it had been completely dependent on the Russian economy. This isolation made life very hard for the majority of people on low incomes. The SDPG started to form the Democratic Republic of Georgia against a background of numerous military threats and economic poverty. State formation began with a high level of legitimation, however, as the SDPG had full control over the government and parliament.

The Democratic Republic of Georgia and the Main Achievements of the Social Democratic Party

The Democratic Republic of Georgia and its social democratic government managed to govern the country for only three years or 1,028 days. Independence was thwarted by Bolshevik occupation and the establishment of the Soviet regime. The short life of the Republic was characterised by three political ideas.

Pluralist Democracy – An Alternative to Bolshevism

At the turn of the twentieth century, most Marxist theoreticians argued that a society had to go through several stages of development before reaching socialism. They believed that the full establishment of capitalism was a precondition of adopting a socialist system. At the beginning of the twentieth century, leftists expected socialist revolutions in regions in which large-scale industry, high levels of labour and workers' movements could be found. What happened next was the opposite of what they had expected, however. "Socialist revolution" was victorious in Russia, despite the fact it was a poor country populated mainly by peasants and lagging behind in industrial development. The instigators of the 1917 October Revolution therefore decided to experiment. The beginning of the socialist system was formed with brutal bureaucratic and military discipline, forced labour and indeed new forms of serfdom. Straight away, the Bolsheviks banned opposition parties, freedom of speech, expression and association. Leninists accused the European social democrats and Russian Mensheviks of betraying socialism. Parliamentary democracy and all attempts to change government in a peaceful way were denounced as a moral compromise and accommodation of the enemy.[8]

The SDPG decided to build an alternative regime to Bolshevism or to find another way to achieve socialism. According to the first Constitution of the Republic, Georgia had a parliamentary government. There was no president. The head of government or prime minister was elected by parliament and was the highest political representative of the country. The prime minister was elected once a year and the same person could only be elected prime minister twice, with a one-year term. The constant turnover of prime ministers was aimed at maintaining the centre of power in the Constituent Assembly, which was elected every three years. The Constituent Assembly was elected on the basis of proportional representation. After independence, universal suffrage was enacted in Georgia. Any twenty year old citizen could exercise their active and passive electoral rights. In 1918, the electoral census based on gender and wealth was abolished. In February 1919, the SDPG received more than 80 per cent of the vote in the Constituent Assembly elections. Eventually, after a series of additional elections, in mid-1920 five other parties also won seats in the Parliament. One of these parties was a political organisation representing an ethnic minority, the Armenian Revolutionary Federation or *"Dashnaktsutyun"*. It should be noted that only eight deputies out of 130 members of the Constituent Assembly belonged to the National Democratic Party, the only right-wing political force in the legislative body. Socialist forces also dominated the opposition. These forces were the Socialists-Revolutionaries Party (SRs), which favoured *"Khalkhosnuri"* ideas and agrarian socialism, and the left-wing patriotic movement, the Socialist Federalists Union.[9] The parliamentary majority, constituted by the SDPG, also included representatives from all the ethnic minorities of Georgia. Among its members in the Constituent Assembly were Abkhazians, Ossetians, Azerbaijanis, Armenians, Russians, Jews, Greeks and Germans. In addition, five revolutionary women from the SDPG were elected to the Constituent Assembly. One of them, Kristine Sharashidze, became a member of the Assembly Presidium.

Under the direction of the SDPG, a two-level system of local government was established in Georgia. There was a village level and a *"mazra"* (district) level. Simultaneously, the local government members had an opportunity to work in parliament. Thus, members of parliament could be the heads of local government bodies. Parliamentary representation gave additional political influence to local government leaders. During the three years of independence, several local government elections were held throughout Georgia. Elections were held in different regions at different times, with the political parties working within a permanent electoral regime.

The Constitution of the Democratic Republic of Georgia ensured the right to multi-level referendums and legislative initiatives driven by citizens. At popular request, referendums could be held at the village level, as well as at the unified national level. If sufficient signatures were gathered for a parliamentary mandate, a citizens' group had the right to present a draft law to the Constituent Assembly. About two hundred regional and national newspapers and journals were published in Georgia and political parties, public organisations and religious and national associations had their own press. As regards trade unions, every association had been a constituent part of the SDPG since the 1890s.

The articles of the Constitution of the Democratic Republic of Georgia on the rights of ethnic minorities were very progressive by international standards at the beginning of the twentieth century. According to the Constitution, ethnic minorities had the right to free social and cultural development. This involved the right to publish and engage in various activities in their own languages, to study in their mother tongue and to establish national unions and organisations. Ethnic minorities had equal rights to occupy positions in state, civil, military or national institutions. In a region with an ethnic minority population of 20 per cent or more, the language of this minority received official status in addition to Georgian. Under the framework of a unitarian republic and powerful local government, the SDPG also founded three autonomous units within Georgian territory: Abkhazia, Muslim Georgia (Adjara) and Saingilo (now part of Azerbaijan).

In the democratic system created by the SDPG, only one political force could not find a place. Before May 1920, until the signing the Treaty of Moscow (the agreement of recognition) between the Democratic Republic of Georgia and the Russian Soviet Socialist Republic, Bolshevik organisations were not allowed to pursue their activities on Georgian territory. Georgian law-enforcement bodies pursued Bolshevik groups, as the Bolshevik's aim was to bring down the constitutional system of the Republic. On several occasions at alternative May Day parades Bolshevik groups tried to provoke street riots and erect barricades. The government also engaged in armed conflicts with the Ossetian population living in the northern part of the

Shida Kartli region. Bolshevik ideas were extremely popular among Ossetians.

A Mixed Economy for Social Justice
The establishment of a mixed economic system was a significant achievement for the government of the Georgian Republic. The SDPG was against creating an economy that was entirely centralised and controlled by the state, though it also prevented implementation of a free market model. One of the main characteristics of the mixed economy was diversity of ownership types. The SDPG nationalised useful minerals, means of transportation, ports, railways, forests and large areas of land. The SDPG gave new cooperatives of peasants and workers the opportunity for collective ownership of small and medium-sized factories. Most important was agrarian reform. Under the reforms implemented by minister of agriculture Noe Khomeriki, first the agricultural lands of Georgia were officially documented and then peasants were allocated lands for agricultural needs in private ownership.

A key institution of the mixed economy was the High Economic Council. This was an ad hoc body created by the Constituent Assembly, aimed at developing plans for different spheres of the economy. According to the SDPG's vision, economic relations should not be regulated by markets. Factories, which were based on different structures of ownership, were to develop close relations and coordination, to be guided by the strategy developed by the state.

The Labour Code, developed by SDPG members in the Constituent Assembly, and the thirteenth chapter (on social and economic rights) of the Constitution provided a clear picture of the balance between capital and labour in economic relationships. The labour policy of the Republic included:

- an eight-hour working day;
- the establishment of labour inspection and sanitation supervision systems;
- standards for minimum wages and overtime allowances;
- involvement of factory-level trade union organisations in factory management; and
- unemployment benefit and development of an employment agency.

Operating in an environment of economic isolation, permanent military conflict and high rates of inflation made it hard for the SDPG to realise its labour policy aims. People were aware of the main aims of state policy and supported them and the press hoped that labour policy aims and improvement of the economy would be possible once greater stability had come to the region.[10]

Peace: The Main Objective for Social Democratic Foreign Policy

The years of the Democratic Republic of Georgia (1918–1921) coincided with a complicated period in terms of international policy. During these three years, the SDPG had to deal with around 10 armed conflicts, including with Armenia, Soviet Azerbaijan, Denikin's White Army, military units of the Bolshevik Red Army, Ottomans and Kemalists. The Republic never initiated a conflict; its stance was one of self-defence. Despite the permanent threat of military attack, peace was the main objective for the SDPG. Its foreign policy was based on the following principles:

- an unbiased position and permanent neutrality during international conflicts and wars;
- deployment of military forces only for self-defence and security reasons;
- supporting integration of the Caucasian states and creating good neighbourly relations in the region.

The SDPG tried its best to adhere to these three principles. The Democratic Republic of Georgia did not interfere in the Russian Civil War and never supported any party of the war. Georgian military action was initiated only for self-defence. Before Armenia and Azerbaijan became Soviet, the Georgian government initiated two unified conferences of the Caucasus. The conferences were meant to conclude by signing an agreement of military cooperation between the South Caucasian republics. According to this document the republics would have agreed not to attack each other. Unfortunately, cooperation was not achieved, as the Armenian nationalists and the Bolsheviks from Baku were actively aiming to change the status quo in the South Caucasus through violent means.

Naturally, the Democratic Republic of Georgia needed to obtain both de facto and de jure recognition. Besides, the Republic had to obtain international recognition. European republics and their leaders did not know much about the new Georgian Republic. The SDPG invited their old friends and partners to their homeland in order to assess their democratic reforms and to inform the world about the country. In 1920 a representative delegation of the Second International arrived in Georgia. The delegation was formally headed by the patriarch of the international democratic socialist movement, the famous Marxist theoretician Karl Kautsky. Due to ill health, Kautsky only arrived in Georgia after the rest of the delegation had already left. The delegation included the future first Labour Prime Minister of Great Britain Ramsay MacDonald, future Minister of Justice of Belgium Emile Vandervelde and the leader of the Irish leftists Ethel Snowden. The member parties of the Second International tried to protect Georgia's political position in European parliaments. The European social democratic press made efforts to positively promote Georgia in the West. For example, the leader of the Socialist Party of Belgium and future Minister of Justice Emile Vandervelde wrote in the French newspaper *Le Peuple*:

> If we had asked the question in the first years of the War: Where, in which European city will the first socialist government be built? Some would have named London, others Paris, Berlin, Stockholm or Brussels. But who would have thought about the capital city of Georgia, Tbilisi? In this very city the first socialist flag was raised and the formation of a real democratic system started ...

After travelling in Georgia, Ramsay MacDonald told the newspaper *Nation*:

> A real democratic state, governed by a socialist government, is being built... If the words "freedom of nations" really have meaning, if any nation deserves freedom, it's the Georgian nation. It has shown its high culture and political readiness to all mankind.

Karl Kautsky's book *Georgia – A Social-Democratic Peasant Republic*, published in 1921, is significant in this context. The book declared Georgia a real bastion of democratic socialism and told the world about the progressive state created in an unknown peripheral region of Russia.

Occupation of the Republic of Georgia

At the beginning of February, 1921, Georgia celebrated its de jure international recognition. The future of the Caucasian region was easy to foresee, however. Georgia was surrounded by hostile forces. There were Bolshevik governments in Azerbaijan and Armenia. Both the independent states of the Northern Caucasus – the Mountainous Republic of the Northern Caucasus and the Kuban People's Republic – were entirely controlled by Soviet Russia. The communists celebrated their victory in the Russian Civil War. On the southwestern border of Georgia, the Kemalist army was taking up position. Apart from that, in the second half of the 1920s, the British military forces left Batumi port. The fact that the British military contingent had controlled Batumi and the Caucasian railway was the only thing that protected the country from Russian occupation. By leaving the Caucasus region, these international forces recognised that the region was under Russian influence. The Bolsheviks rushed into the country from four directions. The Democratic Republic of Georgia managed to resist only until the end of March 1921. At the end of March several members of the government and parliament emigrated. They refused to sign capitulation documents and to give any source of legitimacy to the Bolsheviks. More than 100 members of the Constituent Assembly stayed in Georgia. Almost all of them became victims of Soviet repression during the 1920s and 1930s.

SOCIAL DEMOCRACY AND MODERN GEORGIA

From 1921, when the government of Georgia was overthrown, successive governing parties ruled. None of the governments promoted Georgia's social democratic past. The Communist Government of Georgia pronounced the social democrats enemies and fought against them. Apart from repression, a policy of suppressing the memory of the Democratic Republic of Georgia was implemented during the Soviet era. The three-year period of the First Republic was almost removed from Soviet historiography. The leaders of the First Republic – Noe Zhordania, Nikoloz Chkhenkeli and Irakli (Kaki) Tsereteli – were considered representatives of bourgeois democracy. They were denounced as opportunists and betrayers of socialism.

The first government of post-Soviet Georgia actively pursued a radical ethno-nationalist policy. They considered the leaders of the 1860s national liberation movement to be the most important historical figures. The Third Group were the main opponents and critics of Chavchavadze's group of nationalist intellectuals. Therefore under the first post-Soviet government of Georgia, social democrats and communists were considered enemies almost on an equal footing. Research and analysis of the experience of the First Republic was not an important issue for an independent Georgia. Under the Shevardnadze and Saakashvili regimes, Georgian governments were entirely focused on the ideas of a free market economy, aggressive privatisation, deregulation and a minimal state. In post-Soviet Georgia, they would not promote the mixed economy model created by the Georgian Social Democrats, which was not in keeping with their political priorities.

However, the current governing party of Georgia, "Georgian Dream", is a member of the Progressive Alliance and has observer status at the Party of European Socialists. The party's manifesto declares that it is a centre-left political organisation. Nevertheless the experiences of the First Republic find no echo in "Georgian Dream". The party leaders never talk about possible connections between the Georgian Social Democrats of the first half of the twentieth century and themselves. The current governing party of Georgia does not try to associate itself with the social democratic past.

It should be noted that the SDPG, after the death of Noe Zhordania and other members of the government, ceased to exist as a political organisation. Several social democratic parties have been created in post-Soviet Georgia, though they do not have any influence over political events.

Between 2010 and 2017, 343 people died and 678 people were injured in the workplace. The government of Georgia recently decided to reintroduce labour inspection, which had been abolished in 2006. The revived labour inspectorate is not an effective institution, however. It does not have sufficient funds or enough employees. It does not even have the right to inspect factories without warning and cannot impose significant fines on those who violate the law. Furthermore, the current statutory minimum wage is only 20 gel (8 euros). The main sectors of the economy are tourism and finance; the real economy is extremely run down. The mixed economy envisaged by the SDPG is a matter of the utmost urgency in modern Georgia.

From 1918 to 2018 every Georgian government managed to gain a constitutional majority in the legislative body for one electoral cycle. In the first Republic, the SDPG did not need even minimal support from the opposition to implement their policy agenda. Out of 130 members of the Constituent Assembly, 102 members belonged to the SDPG. The weakness of the opposition can be perceived as the most negative experience of the First Republic.

Despite its short life, poverty and constant military attacks, the Democratic Republic of Georgia was the first non-monarchist regime in the history of the Caucasian people. The First Republic instigated the tradition of Georgian parliamentarism and elective democracy. One hundred years ago, for the first time the issue of the emancipation of Georgia's oppressed lower classes made it onto the Georgian political agenda. This issue became crucial. Therefore the SDPG played a leading role in Georgian history as the first advocate of emancipation and democracy in Georgia.

SUMMARY

After the First World War several new independent republics emerged in Eastern Europe. Social democratic movements actively participated in the political constitution of many of the new states. Unexpectedly, the first social democratic government in Europe was created not in one of the western industrial nations, but in Georgia, an agricultural country formerly in the Russian Empire, adjoining the Near East.

The design of socialism and thus social democracy in Georgia was always deeply influenced by its unique conditions. While the nineteenth century was deeply imprinted by Tsarist oppression of Georgian culture and people, the first democratic movements were nationalistic and elitist as Georgia was an agricultural country with only a small industrial proletariat. It is not surprising therefore that only in 1892 was the first left-wing union formed in Zestafoni, one of the biggest industrial centres in Georgia at the time. The first manifesto of the Georgian left was published in 1894, written by Noe Zhordania, the future leading figure among the Georgian social democrats. The manifesto already exemplifies the distinct character of Georgian socialism, recognising the lack of an industrial proletariat and the need to include the peasants and other non-bourgeois classes by democratic means.

After achieving independence in 1918 the social democrats were the leading force of the fledgling Georgian republic, winning more than 80 per cent of the votes in the first democratic elections. Due to their inclusivity they created a state that was contrary to Bolshevik ideas and instead followed the lead of the German SPD and Karl Kautsky in particular. Equal rights, emancipation of minorities and women, decentralisation and a mixed economy favouring social justice were the pillars of the newly founded republic. The living conditions of workers and peasants alike were to be improved not by revolution, but through gradual progress. But the biggest challenge for the social democratic republic was the foreign threat from Bolshevik Russia, the Ottoman Empire, Armenia and Soviet Azerbaijan. In this hostile environment the social democratic government's goal was to stay neutral but still defend its territorial integrity.

Although the Social Democratic Republic of Georgia was internationally recognised and lauded as a spearhead of social democracy by many representatives of the Second International, such as Karl Kautsky, Ramsay MacDonald and Emile Vandervelde, it nevertheless succumbed to Soviet Russia in 1921 and lost its independence. Today the social democratic past is a distant memory for many Georgians. During the regimes of Shevardnadze and Saakashvili and the current government led by the "Georgian Dream" party, Georgia's focus has been on neoliberalism and a "free market economy". Despite the fact that "Georgian Dream" describes itself as a social democratic party and is registered as an observer with the European Party of Socialists, it does not portray itself as inheritor of the social democratic past.

1   Lortkipanidze, Gr. (1995), Thoughts about Georgia, TSU, pp. 100–37.
2   In the 1890s Georgian publicist Giorgi Tsereteli, father of Irakli Tsereteli – one of the prominent members of the State Duma – established the term "Third Group" ("Mesame Dasi") to denote the group of Georgian Social Democrats.
3   Matsaberidze (ed.) (2015), *Chrestomathy of Georgian Leftism*, Tbilisi, pp. 157–232.
4   Iremadze, Irakli (2016), *Ideological Transformation of the Georgian Social-democratic Party ("Third Group" "Mesame Dasi") in 1892–1905*, TSU.
5   Chkhenkeli, Ak. (2000), *Nation and We* (first published in 1915), Tbilisi: Meridiani, p. 41.
6   Jones, Stephen F. (2007), *Socialism in Georgian Colors*, Tbilisi, Ilia State University.
7   Social Movement in Georgia: Guria in 1905 and the Bakhvi Manifesto (2016), editorial article in the journal *CIVICUS*.
8   Karl Kautsky (1920), Problems and Perspectives of Socialism in Georgia, Tiflis, SDLPG.
9   Gaiparashvili, Z. (ed., 2017): First Universal Democratic Elections in Independent Georgia, Tbilisi, p. 96.
10 Alexandre Bendianishvili (2001), *First Republic of Georgia*, Ivane Javakhishvili Institute of History and Ethnology, pp. 220–57.

THE POLISH SOCIALIST PARTY: INDEPENDENCE, DEMOCRACY, SOCIAL JUSTICE

MICHAŁ SYSKA

It all started in the suburbs of Paris, in the small apartment of a Polish *émigré*, no more than one room and a kitchen. At the kitchen table, the committee elected by an 18-strong group of delegates drew up a thesis for the programme of a new political party. The thesis was the result of two weeks of deliberations. In these circumstances a declaration was issued by a workers' party whose main aim was to build an independent and democratic Polish republic. This is how the history of the most important Polish socialist workers' movement – the Polish Socialist Party (PPS) – began.

THE BEGINNINGS OF THE POLISH SOCIALIST PARTY (1892–1914)

Solidarity of the International Workers' Movement on the Issue of Poland

After the failure of the January Uprising[1] in Poland in 1864, many Polish political *émigrés* joined the international workers' movement. Socialists from a wide range of countries thus came to support Poles' independence efforts. The International Working Men's Association was established in the same year (often known as the First International), on a wave of solidarity with the January Uprising. The greatest advocate of Polish independence was Karl Marx himself, who was convinced that social liberation would not be possible without the political liberation of the working class, and that without the defeat of Tsarist Russia – "the policeman of Europe" – there would not be freedom on the continent as a whole. The philosopher from Trier wrote: "The only chance for a lasting Polish uprising and the normal development of Europe is the destruction of Russia and its Asian political habits and behaviour."

The international workers' movement acknowledged this by accepting the slogan: "For your freedom and ours", under which thousands of Poles fought in the Paris Commune. It was at this time that the word "Pole" became synonymous with revolutionary. The motives of Polish fighters can be best seen from a fragment of a letter written by one of them:

> We, as Poles, have always looked at political and social issues from a Polish perspective. Our first thought and question is always – how could Poland benefit? So when joining the Paris revolution, we saw it as a social revolution which, if successful, could completely overturn the existing state of affairs in Europe! What does Poland have to lose? Nothing. And what does it have to gain? Everything.[2]

Friedrich Engels, the closest collaborator of the author of *Capital*, wrote that "Polish independence and the Russian revolution are conditional upon each other" and in a letter to Karl Kautsky in 1882 stated emphatically that

> Polish socialists, who do not make the liberation of their country the key point of their programme remind me of German socialists who do not demand, in particular, the abolition of laws against socialists, freedom of the press, association and assembly. To be able to fight, you first need ground beneath your feet, air, light and space. Otherwise everything is just hot air.[3]

The first Polish workers' parties on Polish soil (the Social-Revolutionary Party of the Proletariat and the Union of Polish Workers) did not follow Engels' suggestion and hence the issue of independence was not in their programmes. This only happened in November 1892, in the Parisian apartment in which the eighteen socialist *émigrés* met, spending a week to create a programme for the new workers' movement. For the first time in the short history of Polish socialism, the issue of independence became a priority in a political manifesto. The meetings were chaired by Bolesław Limanowski, who wrote, over a decade later:

> Patriotism and socialism are therefore not opposites, but mutually reinforce each other. True patriotism focuses in particular on what forms the basis and actual strength of the nation, the working people, so it must be socialist; and honest socialism, which comes from a love of the nation, must be patriotic.[4]

The Polish Socialist Party (PPS), founded in 1892, was the first Polish workers' group that made the fight for its country's independence a main political priority. The PPS combined the demand for national independence with a programme of radical social and political reforms aimed at establishing socialism and parliamentary democracy. This programme led to disputes at the heart of the socialist movement. The issue of moving the fight for independence to the forefront caused arguments from the left of the party, for whom revolution was supposed to be the solution to national oppression. These differences in opinion led to splits in the party.

The First Programme of the Polish Socialist Party

The Union of Polish Socialists Abroad, which was founded at the meeting in Paris, indicated in its programme for the future party that representatives of the privileged classes and bourgeoisie had discarded the idea of fighting for independence in order to protect their own economic interests:

> Our propertied classes have clearly and explicitly started to give up the political claims they used to have. Being aware that the working masses are demanding leadership of political governments in the interests of the country, they are joining the foreign invaders so that, with their help, they can maintain their privileges over the working classes.[5]

According to the authors of the programme, only the socialist faction "can save the country from political suicide, which our propertied classes and petit bourgeoisie are forcing on us". The socialists admitted that the nobility and the bourgeoisie had previously stood at the forefront of the battle for liberation, but that those classes were unable to mobilise large parts of society with a demand for independence. The Socialist Leader Ignacy Daszyński wrote the following about the privileged class: "They tried clumsily, because they weren't able to kindle hope among people that a Polish state would be better for the Polish people than the existing foreign powers."[6] That is why, in the political programme of the new workers' party, independence and socialism were supposed to be inseparable and mutually conditional on each other. The document drafted in Paris contained specific political and economic demands. The socialists called for a sovereign democratic republic based on the following principles:

- direct, universal elections with a secret ballot; legislation for the people, in the form of both sanctions and initiatives;
- full equal rights for the nationalities that comprise the republic, based on a voluntary federation;
- self-government of municipalities and provincial councils, with elections of administrative employees;
- equality between all citizens, without discrimination by gender, race, nationality or faith;
- complete freedom of speech, publication and association;
- free judicial process, election of judges and judicial responsibility of clerks;
- free, mandatory, universal and complete education; state provision of funds for education;
- abolition of the standing army; universal conscription of the people;
- progressive tax on income and assets, and a tax on inheritance; the abolition of tax on food and essential items.

On economic issues, the new socialist party set the following goals:

- an eight-hour working day, an uninterrupted, 36-hour break every week;
- a minimum wage;
- equal pay for equal work for women and men;
- a ban on children under 14 working, restriction of working hours for minors (aged 14 to 18) to six hours per day;

- a ban on working at night in general;
- health and safety at work;
- state support in the event of accidents, unemployment, illness and old age;
- factory inspectors elected by the workers themselves;
- job centres and a workers' secretary;
- complete freedom of contract for workers;
- the gradual socialisation of land, the means of production and the media.

At the start of 1893 the Polish Socialist Party was founded, which adopted the Parisian programme. One year later, a newspaper was created for the new movement, *Robotnik* ("Worker"). Soon to be its chief editor was Józef Piłsudski, a leading figure in the growing political movement. In a famous article entitled "What is the Polish Socialist Party?" in 1895, the editor of *Robotnik* wrote:

> The expression of the experience gained by the Polish working class became the Polish Socialist Party. It was founded in February 1893 from an amalgamation of three previous workers' organisations: The Second Proletariat, the United Workers and the Union of Polish Workers, and since then has led the class fight for Polish workers. It is based on a secret, confidential organisation, comprising its own workers' forces, and its actions are focused on a uniform programme of fighting, developed by the meeting of Polish Socialists under the Russian partition (in Paris, November 1892), and supplemented by the resolutions of the annual party meetings. [...] It was created by the Polish working class, like a mother giving birth to a child.[7]

Split in the Polish Workers' Movement

At the First PPS Congress in 1893, however, there were already internal disputes about the programme, the bone of contention being the demand for an independent Poland. As a consequence of the ideological differences within the party, a group of activists left, who went on to set up the Social Democracy of the Kingdom of Poland (SDKP, later renamed the Social Democracy of the Kingdom of Poland and Lithuania, SDKPiL). During the First Congress of the SDKP it declared that "workers must grab total political power in the country. [...] This is the goal of all conscious, fighting workers in the world, and is our guiding aim."

The activists of SDKP claimed that they stood for the equal rights of nations, but they envisaged that happening through a proletarian revolution, not in the fight for an independent Polish state. Rosa Luxemburg, a key member of the party, argued that the victory of the socialist revolution would mean that "together with the complete abolition of any oppression, the subjugation of the Polish nation will be removed once and for all, and any cultural oppression will be made impossible".

Socialists in the Austrian and German Partitions.
Difficult Relations with the Austrian and German Social Democrats

The conditions in which Polish socialists operated in the Austrian and German partitions were different from those that the PPS had to deal with in the Russian partition. The Polish Social Democratic Party of Galicia and Cieszyn Silesia (PPS-D), whose origins stretched back as far as 1892, operated in conditions of openness and freedom in the Austro-Hungarian constitutional monarchy. The PPS-D had strong links with the Austrian Social Democrats, who at their Congress in 1899 replaced the demand for national self-determination with a demand to transform the centralised monarchy into a multi-national federation of nations. This could not be reconciled with the Polish socialists' view about the need to achieve independence. Due to their unwillingness to confront their Austrian comrades, the issue of rebuilding a sovereign Poland was not in the PPS-D's programme, although to the party's members and sympathisers this goal was obvious. Thanks to this tactic, Polish socialists had representatives in the parliament in Vienna.

In September 1893 in Berlin, the Polish Socialist Party of the Prussian Partition was founded (PPSzp), whose fundamental ideology became the Erfurt Programme of the Social Democratic Party of Germany (SPD). Three years earlier, the German Social Democrats decided to provide financial support for the *Gazeta Robotnicza* newspaper, which was the newspaper of their Polish comrades in the Prussian partition until 1914. The demand for independence, put forward by the Polish socialists, was often not understood in the SPD's ranks. At the start of the twentieth century, the German Social Democrats stopped cooperating with PPSzp, instead recognising the SDKP. Due to the intervention of the PPS-D's leader Ignacy Daszyński, however, conflict could be avoided and August Bebel declared "Let's shake hands on this agreement and admit that both sides have made mistakes." In 1906 an agreement was reached, based on which PPSzp became an autonomous part of the SPD. The unification of socialists in all three partitions occurred during the Sixteenth PPS Congress in Krakow, in April 1919, a few months after Poland had regained independence.

"Young" versus "Old" – Conflict within the PPS

The growth of the Polish Socialist Party in the Russian partition led to further discussions about the strategy of the group. A division between "young" and "old" started to become evident in the organisation. The latter (represented by, among others, Józef Piłsudski) believed that independence would be achieved by arming national uprisings, while the former believed that this goal would be reached in connection with the Russian revolution and in cooperation with Social Democracy in Russia. This difference in views about the party's strategy was reflected in the dispute about the role of the PPS paramilitary organisation. In 1904, the socialists set up a workers' self-defence group to protect demonstrations. This group was soon transformed into a regular fighting militia, which undertook actions against the partition powers, for example by organising assassination attempts on Tsarist officials. At its high point, the militia of the PPS had around six thousand members. In 1905, a Fighting Unit was established, led by Piłsudski. He made some organisational changes which gave the Fighting Unit a more military character and made it much more independent from the political leadership of the whole group. This caused protests within the PPS. The disparity regarding the party's strategy and the fighting force led to a split in 1906, between the PPS Revolutionary Faction (the "old"), on one hand, and the PPS Left (the "young"), on the other. The former, even though they were the minority at the Congress where the split happened, had the support of the Polish Social Democratic Party of Galicia and Cieszyn Silesia. In 1909 the PPS Revolutionary Fraction reverted back to its original name of PPS, while the PPS Left were gradually marginalised and in 1918 joined forces with the Social Democracy of the Kingdom of Poland and Lithuania, which formed the beginning of the communist party.

In its party programme in 1910, the PPS clearly declared:

> Submission to foreign powers is preventing proper social development, harming the interests of national culture, and exposing the country and its people to escalating exploitation and oppression. Only in a free, independent country can the working class develop freely and reach their potential, implement the full democratisation of the state machinery and achieve their socialist goals. That is why the PPS, by making the establishment of a democratic republic its goal, and linking this goal with independence, is fighting for an independent democratic republic.[8]

The PPS Fraction activists consistently pushed the idea of a national independent uprising. For this purpose, they aimed to create a military structure which went beyond the socialist milieu. In 1908 the Union of Active Struggle (ZWC) was founded, which included other groups from the independence movement. A year later, Piłsudski took on the formal leadership of the ZWC. In 1914, the Union had over seven thousand members and was the origin of the Polish Legions called up by the Austro-Hungarian empire.

Political Factions: the 1905 Revolution and Polish Independence

The outbreak of the Russo-Japanese war in 1904 and the revolution in Russia in 1905 evoked different reactions among the various political factions. Loyalists gave their support to the Tsar, while the SDKPiL was counting on an international revolution and was against the independence movement. Józef Piłsudski, on the other hand, was counting on Russia's involvement in the war creating an opportunity for Polish independence. He even went to Tokyo with the aim of obtaining support for the creation of a Polish Legion. His mission did not, however, achieve the expected results. Roman Dmowski, the leader of the National Democracy party (right-wing nationalists), also went to Japan and convinced his counterparts not to support the independence activities focussed around the PPS. The crisis caused by the war also triggered mass protests in which 90 per cent of workers took part, including demonstrations and strikes. The SDKPiL was active in these workers' protests and counted on their developing into an armed revolution. The PPS paramilitary organisation limited itself to sabotage, saving its strength for a future uprising. A general strike forced the Tsarist regime to make concessions and relax its policy of russification. For the conservatives and those associated with National Democracy (ND), this was a chance to increase the autonomy of the Kingdom of Poland. Loyalists from the Faction of Real Politics, and the leader of ND, Roman Dmowski, became deputies in the Russian *Duma*. At the same time, the right-wing actively worked against the left-wing parties PPS and SDKPiL. During the 1905 revolution, the ND militia attacked socialists, even killing some. The National Association of Workers was also set up, to draw workers away from the PPS and SDKPiL. The ND linked the issue of Poland to Russia. Dmowski expected that after their victory in the war, Polish land would be under Russian control and would be able to gain considerable autonomy as part of the empire. Józef Piłsudski was an advocate of the anti-Russian approach, and planned to create a Polish army alongside the Austro-Hungarian army and incite an uprising in the Russian partition. Defeating Russia and weakening the other two partition powers was supposed to provide the conditions for the founding of an independent nation.

INDEPENDENCE AND THE ROLE OF THE PPS

Regaining Independence

The PPS's stance on independence was confirmed at the secret Twelfth Congress of the party, which was held in 1916 in Piotrkow. At the same time, the socialists were attempting to increase their influence in society. In the territory of the Russian partition, occupied by German forces, the PPS was involved in the development of a union movement, which was able to act openly in this new situation. It is estimated that, by the end of 1916, around 90,000 people were involved in the union's activities on the territory occupied by Germany. The PPS supported the Supreme National Committee, established in 1914 with the objective of being a supreme authority for the Legions. It also comprised the Central National Committee, created in 1915 on Piłsudski's initiative, which represented a range of independence movements on the left (until 1917). At its Thirteenth Congress, which was held in June 1917 in Warsaw, the PPS distanced itself from Germany and Austria-Hungary, and was in favour of an independent country made up of all the Polish territory in the three partitions. In May of the same year, the socialists had already withdrawn their representative from the Provisional Council of State and refused to join other committees set up by the German and Austrian occupying authorities, the Regency Council and the Council of State. Due to the repression by the occupying forces, the party established the PPS Emergency Militia and the PPS People's Militia, who had a self-defence role. The latter was transformed into the newly-established police force in 1919 – in an independent Poland.

The Beginnings of the Nation and the People's Government of Socialists

The conditions created by the First World War provided an opportunity to build an independent Polish state. In their final years, the partition powers experienced a crisis and a process of radical change associated with the fall of the monarchy. The Polish Socialist Party decided to exploit this situation. In September 1918, at its secret Congress, the socialists recognised the need to "create a united and independent people's republic, in which the working class will join to help achieve a socialist social programme". In October, the Regency Council established by the occupying forces proclaimed Poland's independence. In response, on 7 November 1918, in Lublin, the PPS proclaimed the establishment of a Provisional Government for the Republic of Poland, which would initially be led by Ignacy Daszyński. On 11 November, the government recognised the authority of Józef Piłsudski (who by now had left the PPS) as head of state. Piłsudski entrusted Daszyński with the task of creating a government, but due to his failure to do so, on 17 November the role of prime minister was assumed by the socialist Jędrzej Moraczewski, who held this position until January 1919.

In its manifesto, the People's Government called for the convening of a legislative parliament elected on the basis of universal suffrage, based on the principles of equality, directness, secrecy and proportionality.

The socialist cabinet announced the "complete, political and civil equal rights of all citizens, regardless of origin, faith and nationality, and the freedom of thought, press, speech, assembly, demonstration, association, trade unions and strike". It also decreed an eight-hour working day and called for the establishment of democratic local councils. Furthermore, the People's Government announced that the following social reforms would before the future parliament:

- the compulsory expropriation and abolition of large and medium-sized estates and their transfer to people working under the control of the state;
- the nationalisation of mines, salt mines, oil industry and roads, as well as other factories, where that could be done immediately;
- the involvement of workers in the administration of factories not nationalised immediately;
- the right to labour protection, insurance against unemployment, illness and old age;
- the confiscation of capital obtained during the war from the illegal sale of first aid supplies and their delivery to the army;
- the introduction of universal, mandatory and free secular education.

Due to their progressive and radical-democratic programme, the governments of Daszyński and Moraczewski did not just affect the system of the country being created, but also weakened the revolutionary mood that the communists were counting on. Socialist Mieczysław Niedziałkowski wrote:

> In this tragically difficult situation, the Provisional People's Government in Lublin clearly guided, strongly and irreversibly, put the creation of the state on the pathway of democracy, to be more precise parliamentary democracy, due to the fact of its creation, its manifesto and the enthusiasm it created. On 7 November 1918, in Lublin, communism in Poland was dealt a death blow.[9]

The government of Jędrzej Moraczewski was not, however, acknowledged by the right wing, and as a result it could not be accepted by the international community. Consequently, Piłsudski came to an agreement with the leader of the right, Roman Dmowski, and appointed the government of Ignacy Paderewski in January 1919. This cabinet was acknowledged by the Allies, and consequently, the Treaty of Versailles, signed 28 June 1919, founded an independent Poland.

The Polish Socialist Party's Policy on National Minorities

In 1921 there were 27 million citizens in the newly-born Poland. It was a multi-national and multi-cultural country, in which Poles made up 69 per cent of the population. According to a census of that year the population also included Ukrainians (14 per cent), Jews (8 per cent), Belarussians (4 per cent) and Germans (4 per cent). The mosaic of faiths was just as diverse: 63.8 per cent of the population were Catholics, another 10.5 per cent were Orthodox, the same percentage of the population were Jews, 11.2 per cent were Greek-Catholic and 3.7 per cent Protestant.

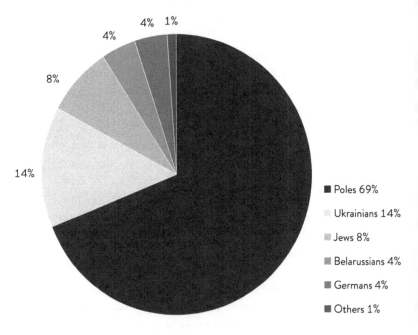

Fig. 1: Nationalities during the inter-war period

The programme of the right-wing National Democracy assumed that the Slavic minorities would undergo polonisation and eventually be assimilated, and that Germans and Jews would emigrate. This movement resorted to aggressive anti-Semitic rhetoric.

In its first programme in 1892, the Polish Socialist Party declared the "full equal rights of nations within the republic, on the basis of a voluntary federation" and political equality for all citizens, regardless of their nationality and faith. In its programme of 1910, the PPS called for the "abolition of all national suppression" and "protection of the rights of national minorities in schools, public authorities and courts". On the other hand, in the document passed at the Seventeenth Congress, the socialists declared that "the PPS shall protect the right of nations to self-determination, and in particular supports the independence of nations freed from the yoke of oppression of the old Russian Empire". At the same time, the party also demanded "the protection of the language rights of living in the affected territory" and "autonomy for national minorities living in the affected territory".

The Sixth PPS Congress in 1905 passed a resolution that focussed on the need for the Polish and Jewish proletariat to fight together. The document focussed strongly on the similarity of the PPS's independence activities to the interests of the Jewish working class: "The pursuit of a democratic and independent Poland is in the interests of Jewish workers, and not just as workers, but also as Jews. Since the republic gave Jews completely equal citizens' rights, gave them the possibility to develop freely and have an influence on public affairs." The socialists also denounced antisemitism as a "dangerous and backward" phenomenon:

> First of all, anti-Semitism is against Jews in general, while amongst Jews, like everywhere else, there are class differences, and the Jewish proletariat is subject to terrible exploitation. Secondly, anti-Semitism merely condemns Jewish exploitation, and almost exclusively as money lenders and commercially, while it supports Christian exploitation, particular exploitation in which workers suffer. And thirdly, anti-Semitism demands special laws and restrictions for Jews – and using these measures against any social group is extremely distasteful to us.

The aforementioned point of the programme was the subject of disputes with the socialist Jews from the Bund, who fluctuated between reformism, which was close to the PPS, and the revolutionary ideas of communism.

The cooperation of both groups made it easier for the Bund to accede to the Socialist International, which was confirmed by the delegates at the party Congress, which was held in June 1930.

The cooperation between the PPS and the Bund led to the establishment, in 1925, of the German Socialist Labour Party in Poland, which was active mainly in Silesia and central Poland, a fact that affected the presence of its representatives in local councils.

Class Trade Unions – The Bastion of the PPS

As early as 1916, activists of the Polish Socialist Party moved to create open trade unions during Germany's occupation of the Russian partition. At that time the Committee of Central Trade Unions was also created, which was headed by the socialist Tomasz Arciszewski (at the end of the Second World War, he became the head of the Polish government in exile in London). In 1929, in the now independent country, the trade union movement was transferred to a central agency, the Union of Trade Associations. At the beginning of its activities, the new organisation led to competition for influence between different factions on the left. The PPS soon gained a position of dominance, however. At the Congress in 1925, around 80 per cent of the delegates were supported by socialists. The members of the Bund also exerted influence in the central committee. The association called for the whole trade union movement to be merged (which was practically a success) and the organisation of strikes; it also fought for legislation guaranteeing labour and social law, and together with socialist educational organisations undertook educational and cultural initiatives.

The largest unions on the Committee of Central Trade Unions were associations for railway-workers, agricultural workers, employees in the textile and metal industries, and employees in the communal sector.

The long-term leader of the association – the Committee of Central Trade Unions – was Jan Kwapiński, who performed this role from 1922 to 1939. Kwapiński had joined the PPS in 1901. He was a member of the PPS paramilitary organisation, a Tsarist prisoner and in independent Poland a parliamentary politician. During the Second World War he was Deputy Prime Minister in the Polish government in exile, in London. After the war he worked with the PPS in exile. In 1938, the class trade unions had almost 400,000 members.

THE POLISH SOCIALIST PARTY IN THE INDEPENDENT STATE

The PPS during the Drafting of the Constitution from 1921

The party "became a factor in the state, undertaking its work by peaceful and legal means"; that is the role ascribed to the PPS in the political system of the reborn state of Poland by the distinguished socialist Mieczyslaw Niedziałkowski.

The PPS wanted to achieve socialism by means of a parliamentary battle. It rejected the revolutionary strategy. It did this by mobilising workers using strikes, mass meetings and street demonstrations to influence the political reality. The decision to go in this direction meant that, in 1919, the members of PPS were withdrawn from the Council of Workers' Delegates which had been established together with the communists, and they convened their own Council of Socialist Independence.

The Polish Socialist Party declared its own constitutional project for the new Polish state. It comprises a system of parliamentary democracy, with the parliament (*Sejm*) having authority over the government and the president. Alongside the single-chamber parliament there was supposed to be a House of Labour – a consulting body for the drafting of laws governing relations between employees and employers. The PPS project also envisioned the expansion of local councils and the guarantee of a wide range of civil freedoms. Furthermore, it also proposed "putting all the means of productions under state control or ownership", the convening of "Factory Committees as self-governing workers' body and for production control", the separation of church and state, an institution for referendums and the right to dissolve the parliament on the initiative of 300,000 citizens.

Although the constitution that was finally passed in 1921 (known as the March Constitution) diverged considerably from socialist ideals, it still introduced the democratic and republican political system that the PPS was seeking. During the work on the constitution of an independent Poland, a particularly controversial issue was the idea, put forward by the right-wing, to create a second chamber of parliament, the Senate. The socialists were able to get the support of the members of the Peasants' Party to reject this idea, although it did not block its implementation. Thanks to parliamentary and non-parliamentary efforts (mass assemblies and demonstrations), the PPS was, however, able to limit the rights of the Senate and ensure that it would be elected in universal elections. Without doubt, if it had not been for the actions of the PPS and the social organisations and trade unions associated with it, it would not have been possible to implement progressive and democratic institutional solutions. In the view of the socialists, they did not go far enough, however, and did not fulfil the party's programme. As a result, the PPS parliamentary fraction (with the exception of three people) voted against the final project. Nevertheless, in the near future the socialists would defend its provisions.

The first few years of independence were a period of PPS active collaboration in the creation of the new reality, democratic rules and institutions. In the following years, the socialists assumed the main role in defending the newly-obtained independence and the democratic values which were still to take root.

Defending Independence

In 1920 the socialists were also facing the need to defend their new country. As a reaction to the outbreak of the Polish-Soviet war, and the Red Army offensive on Warsaw, the PPS designated one of its activists – Norbert Barlicki – to the Council of State Defence, and Ignacy Daszyński to the Council of National Defence. At the same time, the party created a Central Army Division, established their local agents and introduced the enrolment of volunteers for the army and the Workers' Committee for the Defence of Warsaw.

The stability of the state and defence of its democratic character were priorities for the PPS, for which the party was willing to reach compromises with other political parties and ready to dampen radical feelings among its own electorate. An example of this approach was the reaction of the PPS leadership to the crisis caused by the death of the first President of the Republic, Gabriel Narutowicz, who was shot dead by a right-wing nationalist fanatic, and the anti-Semitic persecution of the new head of state and factions that supported him. The party leadership was able to discourage members and sympathisers of the party from a physical showdown with ND politicians, who were blamed for the hate campaign that cumulated in the President's death. In *Manifest do Ludu Pracującego* (Manifesto to the Working People) the PPS Supreme Council stated:

On 11 and 16 December two harsh blows were dealt to the young, weak nation of Poland, burdened by its recent war with an external enemy, and then weakened by the continuing civil war, incited by the reactionary group Polish Black Hundreds.[10] The working people felt as if these blows had been made directly against them [...] These people, who were being leached by a group of merciless profiteers [...] suddenly saw a huge Polish reactionary conspiracy, combining the bludgeon and the gun with a majority in parliament, killing the President of the Republic, and moving towards a dictatorship of the profiteers over the people! In front of their own eyes, the Polish nation was confronted with [the prospect of] a bloody civil war, complete economic ruin and the fall of a state, which was unable to establish the rule of law [...] Let's not look for revenge for our party, a hideous clamour for inter-party quarrels will cause us difficulties, during which many great things could be lost such as the freedom and independence of the whole nation. We don't want bloodshed, we don't want confusion, we don't want a ruined country and people, which is what the continuing and turbulent Black Hundreds conspiracy threatens.[11]

In Defence of the Constitution and Democracy

In November 1925, the PPS, motivated by a desire to save parliamentary democracy from a possible right-wing coup d'état, entered into a government for several months, in which it had to cooperate with right-wing factions. Due to a lack of consensus about economic policy, the socialists resigned in the spring of 1926. In May of the same year, the socialists supported the coup d'état of Józef Piłsudski, seeing it as a way of defending democracy, which had been threatened by right-wing forces. Soon, however, the PPS was forced to stand against their former leader in defence of the supremacy of parliament over the executive bodies. In August, amendments to the constitutions were forced through that weakened the position of the parliament and strengthened the government. The socialist Stanisław Posner in the Senate addressed the authorities:

this democracy has been in existence for just seven years, has hardly began to take shape, it's a small child which has just started to talk, and you are coming in and stamping on the young being, which needs to be raised. [...] you made holes in it. In the constitution, which clearly demarcates the rights and competencies of the three powers on which the Polish state is founded, you blurred the boundaries.[12]

In 1928, activists loyal to Piłsudski seceded from the party, founding the PPS-Former Revolutionary Fraction. The attitude of the rest of the PPS to the actions aimed at giving Piłsudski autocratic rule was explained by Mieczysław Niedziałkowski in *Robotnik*: "In the summer of 1926, the Polish Socialist Party said – Beware! In autumn it said – I reject any cooperation and am leaving! If it's later we'll fight!" In order to defend parliamentary democracy, the PPS decided to cooperate with other socialist groups (The Polish People's Party "Liberation" and the Peasant's Party), as well as groups from the centre (including the Polish People's Party "Fist"). In June 1930, the participants in a congress of a coalition of these groupings, which took the name *Centrolew* (Centre-Left), passed a resolution expressing criticism of the violation of the constitution by Ignacy Mościcki and announcing a "fight to remove the dictator Piłsudski".

The announcements by Centrolew encountered a decisive reaction from Piłsudski, who was head of the cabinet on 25 August 1930, and then dissolved the Parliament and Senate and arrested the main leaders of the opposition parties. The parliamentary elections, held in conditions that were far from democratic (with arrests of opposition politicians, the annulling of the electoral rolls of opposition parties), weakened the Centrolew coalition and consequently left to its break-up.

The PPS and the Communists

For the whole existence of the newly-reborn Polish state, the relationship between the socialists and communists was at daggers drawn. Paradoxically, however, the PPS routinely backed the legalisation of the Communist Party. This was supposed to make the political fight easier because the underground nature of the communist movement, in the opinion of the PPS' leaders, made it a clandestine legend. Furthermore, the socialists were against persecution as a method of political conflict on principle.

The PPS itself was attacked by the Polish Communist Party for "social-fascism" and "social-compromise", the betrayal of its ideals and the interests of the working class.

The growth of fascist forces in the 1930s led to the development of a strong socialist party in the PPS, which demanded across-the-board cooperation among the working class. Under its influence, there was contact between the leadership of the PPS and the Polish Communist Party in 1935, which resulted in a short-term "non-aggression pact". Just one year later, however, the socialists stated in a resolution of their supreme council that

> The Supreme Council confirms the correctness of the decision already taken to reject the opportunity to cooperate with the Communist Party. The relationship of communists to the people's front in general, and to socialists in particular, remains dishonest, sometimes even hostile. The communists continue to use their methods of diversion in the socialist movement, not shying away from undermining the authority of the organisation and the socialist or trade union leaders. In these conditions the communist slogan of a united front, which means that they cooperate with socialists everywhere, except in Russia – and in Russia there is persecution and imprisonment, and collective murders carried out on socialists and communist opposition – must be treated as a cliché, behind which there is an intention to split up the workers' and socialist movement and weaken it, in the hope that then they will submit to communist control [...] The party, in line with its principles, will carry on uniting the Polish working class in the PPS and class trade organisations, under their own banner, despite the communists.[13]

The PPS on the Electoral and Non-parliamentary Stage

In the elections to the Legislative Parliament of 1919, the PPS gained 35 seats (out of 335). Because the boundaries of the country had not yet been finalised, the size of the parliament was increased up to 1922.

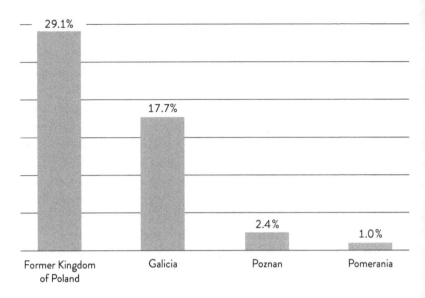

Fig. 2: Support for the PPS (in Galicia the PPS-D) in the elections to the Legislative Parliament of 1919

In 1922, the socialists received 907,000 votes, which gave them 41 seats in parliament (out of 444). In the parliament elected in 1928, the PPS became the second-biggest party, with 63 members of parliament (out of 444).

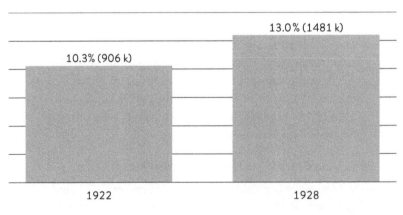

Fig. 3: Support for the PPS in parliamentary elections for the first and second term

In the parliament that commenced in 1930, there were 24 socialists from the PPS. The party did not take part in the following elections up until the outbreak of the Second World War, boycotting the undemocratic regime. Just before 1939, the Polish Socialist Party consisted of 21,000 members in 41 districts.

The PPS had considerable success in local elections in the towns and cities in the Dąbrowski basin and the central regions of Poland. Late industrialisation, together with the backward social structure did not, however, allow the party to achieve success in parliamentary elections.

Just after independence had been reclaimed, 75 per cent of people still lived in the countryside, chiefly working in agriculture. Among them the owners of small-scale farms were predominant. Only a little over one million workers were associated with large and medium-sized industry. In 1918, one in four inhabitants of Poland were unable to read and write.

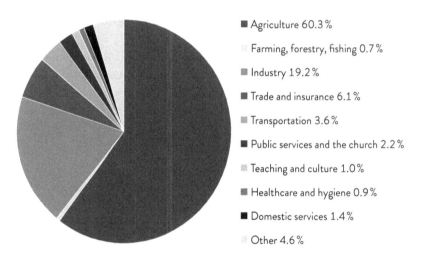

Fig. 4: Structure of the population based on the means of maintenance, based on the census of 1931

The influence of socialists in society was, however, much greater than the results of the elections or the size of the organisation might suggest. The trade unions were close to the PPS, which had around 400,000 members.

The socialists also had an effect by their activities in educational, women's, young people's, cultural and sports organisations.

The PPS engaged the younger generation of workers with the Young People's Organisation of the Society of the University for Workers, and children with the "Red Scouts". The Workers' Society of Friends of Children was also associated with the PPS, which created welfare institutions (kindergartens and schools) and organised vacations for working class children. In 1925 it convened the Polish Workers Sport Federation (which ran activities in 27 sporting disciplines). The number of members of workers' sports clubs in 1934 was 20,000. The Federation organised Polish championships and took part in Workers Olympics.

The PPS in the International Social Democratic Movement

The Polish Socialist Party saw itself as part of an international workers' movement, and in its programme, despite having a strong focus on independence, it pointed out the need for the proletariat to fight together, irrespective of nationality. In 1900, Ignacy Daszyński wrote:

> Workers are connected to unions in all countries, meaning that a Polish printer or hatter can find companions in the Czech Republic, Germany or France. ... Socialism calls on the whole nation, while at the same time linking it in a fraternal manner with other nations. Socialists understand that just as capital is international, labour must also link all the nations.[14]

In the programme from 1910, socialists declared that the "PPS has taken the position of international solidarity with the working class". The party indicated that the "situation of workers in one country has become dependent on the situation of workers in other countries". "Fraternal support in the fight against exploitation and oppression, theoretical and practical cooperation of the conscious proletariat without national differences – all of this comes under the great slogan: Workers of the world, unite!", declares the aforementioned party document.

In an article from 1921, socialist Mieczysław Niedziałkowski pointed out that the members of the party were focussing mainly on the issue of independence and the boundaries of the new country:

Until independence was regained, Polish socialists were so preoccupied with the political revolution in their homeland that they paid relatively little attention to universal problems and did not endeavour to obtain an influential position on a larger scale in the pre-war International. This preoccupation with more arcane issues did not play well.[15]

At its Congress in 1920, the party underlined the essence of the supranational sense of the fight for socialism: "The PPS appreciates the international nature of the social upheaval, in which the leading role will be played by countries who are leaders economically and socially." According to Polish socialists, this fight had to be coordinated: "The PPS is adding its strength to the actions of a conscious proletariat of all countries, thereby working to rebuild the international links between workers and the respective organisational forms."

The embodiment of these programme points was the affiliation of the PPS to the Second International of 1889. After the end of its activities in 1916, Polish socialists were involved in the activities of the Socialist Workers International convened in 1923. The PPS was therefore part of the social democratic and reformist tendency.

In issues of international harmony, the PPS consistently opted for the right of nations to self-determination. In the 1920 programme it declared that the "PPS is aiming to secure lasting peace between nations by creating a League of Nations, based on mutual understanding and equal rights of all nations, removing the hegemony of the great powers". At the same time, the party demanded the "removal of clandestine international pacts and the application of complete transparency in international relations".

The response to the growth in fascist tendencies in the 1930s was the radicalisation of the PPS programme, which found expression in the so-called Radom programme passed in 1937. The introduction of this document includes a vision of a socialist international society: "In connection with the working masses around the world, and as a member of the Socialist Workers' International, the Polish Socialist Party aims to create a Polish Socialist Republic, consisting of all Polish territories, connected with the other Socialist Republics by long-lasting peace and close fraternal economic, political and cultural cooperation."

HERITAGE

In September 1939, facing attack by Nazi Germany, the Polish Socialist Party created its own defence force, and its members were present in army and underground structures for the whole duration of the war, providing further evidence of their patriotism. During the occupation, socialists were also represented in the *émigré* government of the Polish Underground, and the national political bodies of the Polish Underground State. After 1945, some of the activists decided to cooperate with the communists, forming the so-called Reborn PPS, which in 1948 was forced to merge with the Communist Party on the latter's terms. The PPS existed in exile. Its previous activists, who stayed in Poland, were active in opposition democratic activities, including the Workers' Defence Committee established in the 1970s, whose newspaper was called *Robotnik*, referring to the PPS tradition. In 1987, socialist activists associated with Solidarity undertook an attempt to reactivate the party in clandestine conditions, which was repressed by the Communist authorities at its Congress. After the democratic changes the national and émigré parts of the PPS were united, but the movement has been unable to play a key role in democratic Poland.

When the Communist Party underwent a realignment toward social democracy in 1990, after the fall of the authoritarian system, the newly-created successor party invoked the PPS tradition in its ideological declaration. This kind of axiological-historical reference appeared in other programme documents of the party, together with the organisational changes in post-communist social democracy, which obtained a position of hegemony in the democratic party system. Linking itself to the heritage of the Polish Socialist Party was undoubtedly supposed to help make it more credible as a party that respects the rules of parliamentary democracy and political pluralism, as well as one that stands up to defend the country. In 2018 those associated with the SLD convened a Social Committee of Socialists, which wants to remind people of the role played by socialist groups in building the state, on the one hundredth anniversary of its independence. Politicians from the SLD are also involved in an initiative to build a monument to Ignacy Daszyński in Warsaw.

The PPS also remains a legend and reference point for other socialist groupings in Poland, however. The party *Razem* (Together) also refers back to this tradition; *Razem* was founded in 2015, looking for modern inspiration in Spain's Podemos and Greece's Syriza. Particularly for the younger generation of progressive activists who dominate the ranks of *Razem*, the achievements of the Polish Socialist Party are an important weapon in the fight against the disturbing right-wing "politics of memory", which in recent years has been able to count on strong support from state institutions. The legacy of the PPS could help socialists halt the right-wing appropriation of concepts such as patriotism, country, independence or nationalism, thereby enabling it to mobilise votes from social groups that once formed the basis for social democracy.

CONCLUSION

The Polish Socialist Party was the first workers' movement to put the demand for an independent and democratic republic at the top of its political programme. It stuck unwaveringly to its position of consistently fighting for a sovereign nation, unlike the right-wing parties, who were closer to a loyalist approach to the partition powers or set weaker goals, such as autonomy within a foreign empire. The PPS's demand for national liberation linked a programme of radical social and political rebuilding to socialism and parliamentary democracy. This was the agenda of two provisional governments led by the socialists in November 1918, which introduced the principles of a democratic political system and a social system based on the protection of workers' rights. The constitution accepted by the parliament elected in democratic elections in 1921 guaranteed a wide range of political and social rights thanks to the socialists who, although they did not make up the majority in parliament, were able, due to the activities of their members of parliament and pressure from the trade unions close to the PPS, to put their foot down when it came to the institutional principles of the reborn republic.

In the following years, the socialists had to defend both independence and democracy. In 1920 they actively took part in the defence of Warsaw against the Red Army. A year later they had to stand up to the nationalist right-wing, which tried to discredit the democratic election of the first President of the independent Poland by means of an anti-Semitic campaign. After the coup in May 1926, the PPS came out against the institutional changes that were heading towards authoritarianism, devised by their former leader. At the same time, along with the rise of fascism in Europe, the challenge became the radicalisation of the Polish right-wing. For socialists that meant regular confrontations with fascist militia on the streets and at colleges.

The social structure of the new republic meant that socialists were unable to count on the support from voters that the peasant and right-wing parties received. The socialists' possibilities for expansion were restricted by the country's later industrialisation, compared with the West, and the large majority of the population who lived in the countryside. The non-parliamentary activities of the PPS stood out, however. Thanks to a whole network of social organisations (for children, young people, women, cooperatives, culture and sports) the party had an effect on a larger part of society than their election results would indicate.

The PPS was a diverse party, with an eclectic ideology; its ideological principles were more often subordinate to political goals than vice versa. It was in particular the ongoing political activities that created the party's ideological image and identity. The constant points of guidance were: independence, democracy and social justice. The party often sidelined its principles concerning socialism in order to achieve and defend its primary goals. Undoubtedly, Poland would not have been reborn in 1918 as a democratic state with a wide range of political rights (including the right of women to vote) and social rights, if not for the involvement of the Polish Socialist Party in the fight for independence and the design of the new state system. And although the socialist goal could not be achieved, democracy only survived one decade and independence was lost after 20 years, the PPS never capitulated in the struggle for its goals. That is why the heritage of this party is now an axiological inspiration for all the democratic socialist groups in Poland.

SUMMARY

After the failure of the January Uprising in 1864, many Polish political emigrants joined the international workers' movement. Socialists from various countries therefore supported the Poles' independence efforts. The International Working Men's Association was established in the same year (often called the First International), on a wave of solidarity with the January Uprising. The greatest advocate of Polish independence was Karl

Marx himself. The closest collaborator of the author of Capital, Friedrich Engels, wrote that "Polish independence and the Russian revolution are conditional upon each other" and in a letter to Karl Kautsky in 1882 stated emphatically:

The Polish socialists, who do not make the liberation of their country the key point of their programme, remind me of the German socialists who do not demand, in particular, the abolition of laws against socialists, the freedom of the press, association and assembly. To be able to fight, you first need ground beneath your feet, air, light and space. Otherwise everything is just hot air.

The Polish Socialist Party (PSP), founded in 1892, was the first Polish workers' group that made the fight for its country's independence a political priority. The PSP combined the national-independence demand with a programme of radical social and political reforms aimed at establishing socialism and parliamentary democracy. This programme led to disputes at the heart of the socialist movement. The issue of moving the fight for independence to the forefront caused arguments from the Left of the party, for whom revolution was supposed to be the solution to national oppression. The difference of opinion led to splits in the party.

Among all the political movements, PSP was most consistent in its position on independence. Conservatives favoured a loyal approach to the foreign occupiers, while the National Democrats (right-wing nationalists) were in favour of Polish autonomy within the Russian Empire. These differences became evident during the 1905 revolution, when militia associated with the right-wing nationalists attacked socialists from the PSP and the revolutionary left-wing movement.

In 1904 the PSP created its own militia organisation, which was supposed to form the nucleus of an army of uprising, according to its supporters in the party management. On the day before the First World War broke out, Józef Piłsudski, then leader of the PSP, began to create military organisations with a wider political platform than a socialist one, to fight alongside the Austro-Hungarian empire.

In the first days of Poland's independence in 1918, the socialists took the political initiative by creating the Provisional People's Government of the Republic of Poland, with Ignacy Daszyński at its head and a progressive manifesto demanding political and social rights. The cabinet of the socialist Jędrzej Moraczewski – nominated by new head of state Józef Piłsudski – which followed afterwards, introduced democratic electoral law (including the right of women to vote), equal rights for ethnic and national minorities, an eight-hour working day, social insurance and institutions to protect jobs.

In the following years, due to the country's agricultural basis and thus the huge number of rural voters, PSP was unable to count on mass support, so it defended the country's independence and parliamentary democracy as an opposition force. In 1920, the socialists were in involved in the defence of the country against the Red Army. They protected democratic institutions from the right-wing nationalists and the political groupings focused around the former socialist Józef Piłsudski, who created an authoritarian political system in the 1920s. The wide influence of PSP on society continued through the trade unions and social organisations (for young people, education, women, housing, culture and sport).

1. The Polish national uprising against Russia, which lasted from 22 January 1863 to the middle of 1864, ended in defeat, with tens of thousands killed in battle, nearly a thousand missing, around 38,000 sentenced to penal servitude or exiled to Siberia, and around 10,000 emigrating.
2. Myśliński J., Swobody, fabryk i ziemi!, Warszawa 1988.
3. Myśliński J., Swobody, fabryk i ziemi!, Warszawa 1988.
4. O co walczy PPS? Zbiór dokumentów ideowych i politycznych PPS, Warszawa 2012.
5. O co walczy PPS? Zbiór dokumentów ideowych i politycznych PPS, Warszawa 2012.
6. Potocki P. (red.), Niezbędnik Ignacego Daszyńskiego, Warszawa 2016.
7. O co walczy PPS? Zbiór dokumentów ideowych i politycznych PPS, Warszawa 2012.
8. O co walczy PPS? Zbiór dokumentów ideowych i politycznych PPS, Warszawa 2012.
9. Niedziałkowski M., Demokracja parlamentarna w Polsce, Warszawa 1930.
10. Black Hundreds – A Russian political movement from the start of the twentieth century, based on a nationalistic and conservative ideology, including xenophobia and antisemitism.
11. Michałowski S., Polska Partia Socjalistyczna w systemie politycznym II Rzeczypospolitej, Annales Universitatis Maria Curie-Skłodowska, Vol. XLV I/XLVII, 17.
12. Michałowski S., Polska Partia Socjalistyczna w systemie politycznym II Rzeczypospolitej, Annales Universitatis Maria Curie-Skłodowska, Vol. XLV I/XLVII,17.
13. Michałowski S, Polska Partia Socjalistyczna w systemie politycznym II Rzecypospolitej, Annales Universitatis Maria Curie-Skłodowska, Vol. XLV I/XLVII, 17.
14. Potocki P. (red.), Niezbędnik Ignacego Daszyńskiego, Warszawa 2016.
15. Niedziałkowski M., Zadania polskiej polityki socjalistycznej (1921), www.lewicowo.pl (dostęp 20.07.18).

Bibliography

Jerzy Holzer, PPS, szkic dziejów, Warszawa 1977.

Marzec W., Rewolucja 1905 roku i plebejskie doświadczenie polityczne, Łódź – Kraków 2016.

Stanisław Michałowski, Polska Partia Socjalistyczna w systemie politycznym II Rzeczypospolitej, Annales Universitatis Mariae Curie-Skłodowska, Vol. XLV I/ XLVII, 17.

Jerzy Myśliński, Swobody, fabryk i ziemi!, Warszawa 1988.

Mieczysław Niedziałkowski, Demokracja parlamentarna w Polsce, Warszawa 1930.

Mieczysław Niedziałkowski, Zadania polskiej polityki socjalistycznej (1921), www.lewicowo.pl (dostęp 20.07.18).

O co walczy PPS? Zbiór dokumentów ideowych i politycznych PPS, Warszawa 2012.

PPS- Wspomnienia z lat 1918–1939, Warszawa 1987.

Przemysław Potocki (red.), Niezbędnik Ignacego Daszyńskiego, Warszawa 2016.

Roman Stefanowski, PPS 1892–1992, Warszawa 1992.

Włodzimierz Suleja, Polska Partia Socjalistyczna 1892–1948. Zarys dziejów, Warszawa 1988.

Michał Śliwa, Polska myśl socjalistyczna (1918-1949), Wrocław 1988.

Jan Tomicki, Polska Partia Socjalistyczna 1892-1948, Warszawa 1983.

Michał Trębacz, Bund – Międzynarodówka – PPS. Historia współzależności, Biuletyn Instytutu Pamięci Narodowej, nr 7 (128), lipiec 2011.

Feliks Tych, Rok 1905, Warszawa 1990.

Anna Żarnowska, Geneza rozłamu w Polskiej Partii Socjalistycznej 1904–1906, Warszawa 1964.

Żarnowski J., Polska Partia Socjalistyczna w latach 1904–1906, Warszawa 1965.

THE "AUSTRIAN" REVOLUTION OF 1918 AND THE ROLE OF THE SOCIAL DEMOCRATIC PARTY OF GERMAN-AUSTRIA 1918–1920

OLIVER RATHKOLB

STARTING OUT LOOKING BACKWARDS – PARLIAMENTARY DEMOCRACY IN AUSTRIA 1918/19

Even such a manifest break as the end of the monarchy in the Habsburg Empire of Austria-Hungary, in tandem with the end of the First World War, did not signal a totally new beginning. Centuries-old cultural and social traditions and authoritarian constraints imposed by Cisleithania's political and religious structures were anchored too strongly in the various social strata and had imbued everyday life at every level. In what follows we shall reconstruct some aspects of the changes that shaped social democracy up to 1918.

DEVELOPMENT OF SOCIAL DEMOCRACY SINCE 1888/1889

As early as 1908 Christian Socialist journalist Karl Schwechler from Graz stated that

> the conditions of existence for social democracy were particularly favourable in the second half of the previous century. The triumphal march of industrialism, which thanks to the prevailing views of economic liberalism knew no bounds and whose sole morality was profit had brought a new class into being, the industrial proletariat, which, constantly troubled by feelings of insecurity had no other wish than to eliminate these social circumstances.[1]

The 1848 February revolution that had finally been crushed by military force in October of that year was a middle class/student movement with some involvement of the workers. Key political hubs for the emergence of an institutionalised social democratic workers' movement were the many clubs authorised as a concession by the Habsburg government in a law on association after the military defeat at the hands of Prussia at Königgrätz/Sadowa in 1866. The Austrian constitution of 21 December 1867, too, which dealt with the general rights of citizens in the kingdoms and countries represented in the Imperial Council strengthened this development, although the electoral law was confined to a few dominant classes and de facto excluded the workers.

In the Habsburg Empire turboglobalisation got under way, albeit after some delay, around 1870 – at the same time educational organisations boomed, including the one in Mariahilf in Vienna or the "Equality" club in Vienna Neustadt. With the Coalition Act of 1870 trade unions began gradually to emerge after the first big demonstrations. The first attempt at social democratic organisation in 1874 in Neudörfl in Burgenland failed and was also suppressed by the authorities.

In Hainfeld in 1888/89 Victor Adler, a doctor who administered to the poor and whose father had been a successful Jewish businessman, was the first to bring about the amalgamation of two disparate factions of the labour movement between moderate and radical groups that wanted to organise a proletarian class-based party. Key to the organisation of workers was the press, which Victor Adler co-financed and shaped – first with "Equality" and then, after it was banned, with the *Arbeiter-Zeitung* as main organ. General male suffrage was achieved for the first time in 1905 by mass demonstrations, while the goal of female suffrage was sidelined for purposes of expediency.

At the Imperial Council elections in 1907 the Social Democrats obtained 87 seats out of 516, including 10 seats in Vienna with 38 per cent of the votes. In 1901 only two Social Democrats had managed to get elected to the Imperial Council in Vienna. The Christian Social Party and Conservatives were a little stronger in 1907 with 96 representatives. There were just under 20 factions altogether, although they were weaker than the growing mass parties. At the municipal level, by contrast, the old "curia" suffrage still prevailed, linked to tax payment, and safeguarded Christian Social dominance in the Imperial and Residential City of Vienna until 1919.

In 1909, the Social Democratic Party was completely reorganised, by means of direct contributions and direct membership, as well as hierarchical sub-organisations (district organisations, regional organisations, local organisations, as well as a party conference at which 20 people were elected to form the national party leadership, as the party executive). This single-minded centralisation was strengthened in 1907 by the acquisition of a party headquarters, when an apartment house was purchased and turned into a party building, which housed both the editorial offices of the *Arbeiter-Zeitung* (Workers' Newspaper) founded in 1889 and the printshop of the publishing house Vorwärts, Swoboda & Co. This new building, designed by two pupils of Otto Wagner, Hubert and Franz Gessner, and located at 97 Wienzeile (on the right or southern bank of the Vienna river) also symbolised the self-confidence of the Social Democrats, with its two gilded flagpoles and large statues of a male and a female worker. It was also home to the party secretariat and the women's central committee, as well as the trade union committee.

Although the election results in 1911 were somewhat disappointing for the Social Democrats, in Vienna itself they emerged as the strongest party, with 43 per cent of the votes, overtaking the Christian Social Party in the Imperial Council. The German National Party and the German Liberal Party were still the strongest group in parliament, however. At the same time, it did not prove possible to implement social policy reforms, such as the creation of social insurance or reform of the law on associations. Demonstrations against a wave of price increases ended in bloody clashes with the police. In tandem with this the government increasingly resorted to emergency decrees and suspended the Imperial Council. Harsh press censorship was also imposed.

Before the world war the Social Democrats had already founded six daily newspapers, in Vienna (*Arbeiter-Zeitung*), Graz (*Arbeiterwille*), Salzburg (*Salzburger Wacht*), Innsbruck (*Volkszeitung*), Reichenberg in Böhmen (*Vorwärts*) and Linz (*Wahrheit*). In addition there were several weekly and five illustrated papers, as well as the theoretical journal *Der Kampf* (The Struggle), a local periodical, two youth papers, two social policy papers, two cooperative newspapers, three sports papers and a magazine for political satire (*Neue Glühlichter*). The combined circulation of these papers was 548,000. Another 53 trade union papers had a combined print run of 366,050. The women's organisation had 20,058 members in 316 locations and its official mouthpiece, *Arbeiterinnenzeitung* (Women workers' newspaper), had a print run of 26,500. The youth organisation had 12,061 members in 355 associations.

Despite massive political persecution, by the end of June 1913 the "German Social Democratic Party" had 142,027 registered members in 1,365 places in Cisleithania, 42,000 of them in Vienna.[2] A total of 194 specialist associations with a membership of 648,497 wielded considerable mobilising force through strike action. Another important socio-political element were the 882 consumer cooperatives with their 250,000 members, 284 of which, with 100,000 members, joined the Central Association of Austrian Consumer Cooperatives.

Nevertheless during the First World War the majority of Social Democrats remained loyal to the war aims of the imperial household and the government, although parliament was not permitted to convene and was recalled only in 1917. The party leadership made the case for a struggle for the "national survival of German culture" and against the exploitation of the workers in Tsarist Russia. The minority group with a clear anti-war stance were represented publically by Friedrich Adler, Max Adler, Robert Danneberg, Therese Schlesinger and Gabriele Proft. In protest Victor Adler's son physicist Friedrich Adler assassinated the authoritarian Minister-President Karl Graf Stürgkh. Only in 1917 did the "truce" (*Burgfrieden*) collapse and mass strikes break out in response to the serious supply problems caused by the war, culminating in June 1918 across the monarchy.

After the erosion of the Habsburg Monarchy in 1918 and the declaration of the German-Austrian Republic on 12 November 1918 the following Social Democratic organisations were still in existence:[3]

Cooperative movement
- Central Association of Austrian Consumer Cooperatives (1904)
- Wholesale Purchase Company of Austrian Consumer Cooperatives (1904)
- Credit Association of Austrian Workers' Associations (1912)

Welfare and benevolent societies
- Workers' Cremation Society "Die Flamme" (The flame) (1904; 167,315 members)

Sports organisations
- Naturfreunde (Friends of Nature) (1895; 75,018)
- Arbeiter Turn- und Sportbund (Workers' Gymnastics and Sport Federation) (1893, 28,909 members)
- Arbeiter Radfahrer Verein ARVÖ/ARBÖ (Workers' Cyclist Club) (1899)
- Arbeiter Turnerbund (Workers' Gymnastics Federation) (1907)
- Arbeiter Stemm- und Turnverein (Workers' Weightlifting and Gymnastics Club) (1906)
- Arbeiter Schwimmverein (Workers' Swimming Club) (1909)
- Verband der Arbeiter-und Soldatenvereine VAS (Federation of Workers' and Soldiers' Clubs) (18.5.1919)

Occupational group organisations
- Sozialistische Mittelschüler (Socialist Secondary School Students) (–; 2,525)
- Sozialistische Studenten (Socialist Students) (1895; 1,576)
- Sozialistische Mittelschullehrer (Socialist Secondary School Teachers) (–; 480)
- Gewerbetreibende & Kaufleute (Merchants and Tradesmen) (1898/99; ca. 19,600)
- Bund sozialistischer Akademiker (Federation of Socialist Academics) (10.4.1919)
- Verein jugendlicher Arbeiter (Young Workers' Club) (1894)

Educational and cultural organisations
- Arbeiter Stenographen (Worker Stenographers) (1895; 1,232))
- Arbeiter Abstinenten (Worker Teetotallers) (1905; ca. 4,500)
- Arbeiter Sänger (Worker Singers) (1902; 11.624)
- Verein der Konfessionslosen (Non-religious Persons' Association) (20.11.1887)
- Arbeiterinnen Bildungsverein (Women Workers' Education Association) (1890)
- Volksbildungsverein "Volksheim" (Adult Education Club) (1886)
- Arbeiter Symphonie Konzerte (Worker Symphony Concerts) (1905)
- Freie Volksbühne (Free People's Theatre) (1908)
- Freie Schule (Free School) (1905)

- Kinderfreunde ("Friends of Children") (1908)
- Volksbuchhandlung (People's book shop) (1893)

After 1918 the members of the trade union committee formed the "free trade unions" together with the Social Democrats and cooperated with the chambers of blue- and white-collar workers, as well as the trainee sections (1913, 428,363 members, but by the end of 1921 already 1,079,777 members). The number of party members rose rapidly in 1919 to 332,000 (including around 70,000 women).[4]

PARLIAMENTARY REVOLUTION 1918

Austria was suffering great hardship when, after intensive negotiations, the last Kaiser, Karl, issued a written declaration on 11 November 1918 to the effect that he was renouncing "any participation in affairs of state". There had been talk of a possible continuation of the monarchy right up to the last moment. The deciding factor in the emperor Karl's withdrawal from government affairs, which was only supposed to take effect if "German-Austria" opted to become a republic, was not the extremely serious economic and political situation, but the fact that not only had the war been lost but the victorious allies (France, but above all the United States and Great Britain) showed no interest in backing the monarchy or the Habsburgs. Despite a multitude of proposals on resolving the nationality conflict at the end of the nineteenth century the ruling elites in Austria-Hungary were not willing to implement a proper federalisation of the Dual Monarchy or take into account the fact that the "Germans", but also the "Hungarians" were in a numerical minority in their respective domains, or possessed only relative majorities. The Social Democrats, too, were unable to come up with particularly viable proposals. For example, Karl Renner had suggested that the Imperial Council should be elected in accordance with ethnic criteria, not according to the territorial principle. Otto Bauer, in turn, took the view that the nationalities question would resolve itself via the class question and the classless society. Realpolitik meant that the Social Democrats were unable to prevent a split between Czechs and Germans. Until 1918, in the wake of the Brunner programme, the pragmatic long-term goal was to restructure the monarchy into a democratic federation of nationalities. Ultimately, this would not have challenged the Habsburg state. In the end, however, German-Austrian workers were given precedence and the solution of the nationalities question had to make way for a revolutionary upheaval. Only Otto Bauer, after his return from a Russian prisoner of war camp, voted for the dissolution of the Habsburg state, in contrast to Victor Adler, who tabled union ("*Anschluß*") with Germany only as second-best option.

Closely linked to national subjugation by the German minority was the lack of democratic decision-making in the Monarchy. There had been universal suffrage for the chamber of deputies in the Imperial Council only since 1907. Furthermore, this "right" applied only to men and bore no relation to the national balance of power.

Besides the lack of experience with democracy and the nationalities conflict a further, largely negative element of a psychological nature entered into the First Republic: the after-effects and trauma of the war. Austria-Hungary had mobilised around 8.5 million men for war service, which was 75 per cent of the male population between the ages of 18 and 50. As many as 1.6 million of them gave their lives for the great-power politics of Austria-Hungary and the German Empire, while another 3.9 million were wounded, went missing or were made captive (as of 6 November 1918). In his memoirs, former Austro-Hungarian finance minister Alexander Spitzmüller wrote that "the greatest crime" during the war was the destruction of the legal order, made manifest, among other things, in the countless court martials. Otto Bauer, in turn, described the changes in the "structure and frame of mind of the proletariat" brought about by their experiences in the trenches: "during their years in the trenches they still had faith in the powers-that-be. Then came the revolution, then came the day of homecoming. But at home hunger, cold and unemployment awaited them."

But it was with problems of this kind that the young Republic had to cope, having been legitimised on 12 November 1918 by those deputies who had been elected members of the Cisleithanian Imperial Council in 1911 in the (overwhelmingly) German-speaking elections. These representatives – 111 for the German National Party, 70 Christian Socials and 39 Social Democrats – had convened on 21 October 1918, in parallel with similar assemblies in Prague, Agram (Zagreb) and Laibach (Ljubljana), in the Lower Austrian Landhaus in the Herrengasse in Vienna as a "provisional national assembly for German-Austria". On 30 October the provisional national assembly had adopted the "provisional constitution" framed by Karl Renner, which proclaimed union with Germany ("Resolution on the fundamental institutions of state authority").

Up to 11 November, formally speaking, two governments were functioning because even after 27 October the last Imperial government under prime minister Lammasch had still not resigned. Lammasch, a renowned expert in criminal, constitutional and international law at the University of Vienna, was a convinced pacifist and throughout the First World War and even before it had protested vehemently against the war. At that time he was a lone voice but he had clearly recognised the terrible consequences of the world war. On 1 November the Lammasch government had handed over its official duties to the Renner government, but there was still only a "people's state" (*Volksstaat*) and there had been no clarification of whether it was a constitutional monarchy or a parliamentary republic. Only on 11 November did the emperor Karl sign a declaration to the effect that he had renounced "any participation in affairs of state". The provisional state government elected a 22 person state council with three presidents: first president Franz Dinghofer (German National Party), second president the Christian Social prelate Johann Hauser and as third president Social Democrat Karl Seitz. These three functioned as a kind of federal presidency.

The Crown Lands themselves had previously been dependent on directives from the imperial government and now reconstituted themselves through provisional provincial assemblies, demanding and exercising much more independence of the central power. In this sense 1918 represented a federal revolution. The assembly of 30 October 1918 was accompanied by mass demonstrations by soldiers and officers. Soldiers wore red cockades on their caps, while the officers wore black, red and gold ones, symbolising, respectively, the socialist revolution and union with Germany.

While a provisional state government, whose highest organ was to be the German-Austrian State Council, was established only on 30 October, agreement had already been reached on the name of the new state entity: "German-Austria". With regard to the form of the state the Christian Social Party was still debating the monarchy, although this was no longer really an option, given Karl's 11 November renunciation of any part in government affairs. The Social Democrats around Victor Adler and the supporters of a Greater Germany clearly advocated the establishment of a parliamentary republic.

They were keen on union with a Germany led by a Social Democrat/centre-right coalition. German National Party supporters also favoured unconditional merger with the German empire or the German Republic (declared on 9 November 1918). A demonstration by the German student body at the University of Vienna on 30 October 1918 illustrates the kind of political views prevailing during that period on what kind of state people wanted. Social Democratic member of the Imperial Council and State Chancellor Karl Renner declared that "the German-Austrian people that hitherto has been ruled now wants to rule itself". His speech was greeted with jubilation by those assembled there. It is thus easy to see why a German National Party representative Franz Dinghofer, as president of the provisional national assembly, proclaimed the republic at 3 pm on 12 November 1918. The new national flag of red, white and red, conveyed continuity because these had been the colours of the Duchy of Austria since the thirteenth century. Around 150,000 people had been milling around in front of the parliament since midday, not to mention armed bands of various political stripes. During Dinghofer's speech Red Guardists hastily cut the white section out of the flag and hoisted up the red remnants, which they had tied together. Later on, communist soldiers (Red Guardists) rushed the parliament to hand over their resolution to establish a socialist republic. In the ensuing gunfire between five and ten people were seriously wounded, 32 slightly injured, including many women and young people. The violence was to continue.

The events surrounding the proclamation of the republic reflect the revolutionary mood that accompanied democracy during that period and would continue to dog the First Republic, although in more moderate form. While the Social Democrats under Victor Adler and, after his death shortly before the proclamation of the republic, under Otto Bauer had endeavoured to divert any revolutionary tendencies into democratic channels the Christian Social Party and the German National Party interpreted the revolutionary workers' and soldiers' councils as instruments of the "Red Terror" and a possible "putsch from the left". This misperception of social democratic policy ultimately led to the disintegration of the coalition in 1920. It has to be remembered in this context that Otto Bauer and, as regards the workers' and soldiers' councils above all Friedrich Adler had been able to thwart revolutionary developments, sometimes, it's true, by adopting a somewhat belligerent manner.

The founder of the Austrian Social Democrats, Victor Adler, formulated Bauer's political position most clearly in a letter of 9 July 1918. Bauer's presence ensured that "there will be no rightward excesses, while his intelligence, which is much more clearheaded at the council table than, at times, in the heat of the struggle, ensures that he will perpetrate none to the left". The outcome of the first elections to the National Council on 16 February 1919 revealed how political camps were increasingly taking shape in the young republic: 72 Social Democrats, 69 Christian Socials, 26 German Nationals of various stripes, a Czech, a centre-right Democrat and a Zionist. State Chancellor Renner formed his second government, a coalition of Social Democrats and Christian Socials. In March 1919 women entered the legislative assembly for the first time: seven Social Democrats (Anna Boschek, Emmy Freundlich, Adelheid Popp, Gabriele Proft, Therese Schesinger, Amalie Seidel, Maria Tusch) and one Christian Social (Hildegard Burjan), which represented a major political breakthrough.

The fire of "Austrian" parliamentary revolution was soon extinguished, however, and the extreme economic and social crises and the prohibition of union with Germany by the Paris Peace Accords imposed a heavy burden on the First Republic and split the, after all, very successful first national unity government and later the grand coalition.

Despite the formal work on a joint constitution and the multi-layered legislative functions of the constituent national assembly mistrust grew steadily. On the centre-right/conservative side the development of socialist council republics in Hungary (21 March 1919) and Munich (5 April 1919) was viewed with consternation, while the Social Democrats strove to deter the workers' movement from revolution by means of pragmatic reforms. Above all the fear of a "Bolshevik" revolution like the one in Russia in 1917 encouraged cooperation. Besides the concern of the centre-right and conservative parties that too far-reaching changes in the distribution of wealth were on the cards there was another factor that heightened the political tensions. Most of the civil service, which remained largely intact from the period of the Monarchy, viewed the envisaged democratic reforms with considerable scepticism and distrust. Consequently, many reforms were "watered down", obstructed or simply not implemented.

In the first few months of 1919 centre-right fears of a revolution and left-wing fears of a counterrevolution were stoked not least by the skyrocketing unemployment, which in Vienna shot up from 24,503 in December 1918 to 113,905 in February 1919, and communist machinations, which were aided and abetted by Hungary's communist council republic.

There is too little public, but also political awareness of the fact that the First Republic emerged through a largely peaceful "Austrian revolution", based on the parliamentarism of the Monarchy and the 1848 Revolution, represented by the German-speaking Imperial Council representatives elected in 1911. The national unity government up until the first National Council elections in February 1919, in which women were allowed to vote for the first time, functioned very well as a "state builder", despite the incredible difficulties and problems it faced.

The efforts to keep above all Sudetenland, but also South Tyrol and Lower Styria within the territory of the new state, not to mention the "union" with Germany foundered on the opposition of the Entente powers. Only in the case of Carinthia was it possible through force of arms and, above all, the referendum of 1920 to stave off the territorial claims of the Kingdom of Serbs, Croats and Slovenes, with the votes of the Slovenian-speaking Carinthians ultimately proving decisive. In 1921 Hungarian parts of what is Burgenland today adhered to Austria after a referendum.

SOCIAL POLICY AND EARLY FORMS OF CONSOCIATIONAL DEMOCRACY IN AUSTRIA, 1918–1920

The coalition was able to withstand the multifarious pressures, however, and even managed to implement a series of important social policy reforms. In his 2016 study *The Habsburg Empire: A New History* Pieter Judson rightly noted the cultural and administrative strengths of Cisleithania and of the Habsburg Monarchy in general. This formed the basis of the brief window for reform after the nomination of Ferdinand Hanusch, a Social Democratic trade unionist from the textile sector, as Ignaz Seipel's successor as state secretary for social affairs under the First Republic. From the outset he was able to rely on an innovative and experienced "imperial" bureaucracy, which included, among others, the jurist and economist Karl Přibram, who had been working in the Habsburg ministerial bureaucracy since 1909 and from 1911 to 1917 as deputy secretary at the Central Committee for Statistics. In 1918 he became head of the department of the State Bureau for Social Affairs responsible for social legislation and was closely involved in, among other things, drafting laws on the introduction of the eight-hour day, state unemployment insurance, the law on works councils and the chamber of labour.

The ministerial "think tank" around Hanusch also included Heinrich Kautzky, former board member of the Imperial and Royal (Austro-Hungarian) Office of Labour Statistics, as well as a member of the standing advisory labour council in the Monarchy. Max Lederer, in turn, had a profound knowledge of social legislation and during 1907–1916 accumulated intensive social policymaking experience as jurist and secretary of the newly established Central Office for Child Protection and Youth Welfare. Section head Julius Kaan was an established expert on social insurance, while another section head Otto (von) Gasteiger had originally worked from 1907 at the trade ministry, latterly as advisor on blue- and white-collar worker protection, then working at and from 1918 heading the section for victims and surviving dependents of war at the Ministry of Social Affairs. Section head Dr Franz Meinzinger (Edler von Meinzingen) had already been responsible for housing assistance at the Austro-Hungarian Ministry for Public Works and prior to that had been responsible for the census of 1900 as court secretary of the Central Statistical Committee. Ferdinand Hanusch, a former journeyman weaver born into a poor family in Silesia, was able to complement this extensive social law and social policy expertise with many years of political experience. He had been active in the labour and trade union movement since 1891. As secretary of the textile workers' union and chair of the Trade Union Commission, the executive body of the Social Democratic trade union movement, as well as a member of the Imperial Council since 1907 he had for decades been calling and arguing for the introduction of the eight-hour day, the abolition of so-called "work books" and many other social policy legislative reforms.

The fact that it proved possible at this particular time, first of all from 30 October 1918 in the national unity government under chancellor Karl Renner, with the Christian Social Party, the Social Democratic Party and the Greater German People's Party, and then from 15 March 1919 to 7 July 1920 in two coalitions with Social Democrats and Christian Socials, to press ahead with this social legislation reform was naturally also due to international developments and fears of a council (soviet) regime or even a communist revolution, like the one that had taken place in Russia in 1917. Section head Max Lederer formulated this openly: "in the interest of maintaining order and tranquillity and avoiding eruptions of despair we had to do everything possible at least in the area of social policy. This was the order of the day and Hanusch seized it with both hands. " Ferdinand Hanusch himself stated in 1919 that "if we were to have any chance of avoiding extremism we above all had to engage the trust of the working class that this state was different from the one that preceded it ... The sacrifice that industry had to make barely registers in comparison with the billions in losses that one day of revolution visits upon a big city". At the same time Hanusch was well aware, that social reforms would not usher in a socialist state.

Inside the Christian Social Party, furthermore, the workers' faction prevailed during this period and between 1917/1918 and 1920 an intensive first phase of social partnership commenced among workers' representatives in negotiations with trade union representatives and Imperial Council members or, later on, National Council members. After the establishment of the General Commission for the War and Transition Economy a house committee was set up, whose members included, among others, representatives of industry, the trade unions and sickness insurance. As early as 1898 then trade minister Joseph Maria Bärnreiter had set up a "standing advisory working committee", also on a parity basis. It was the working committee of this steering committee that subsequently, at the instigation of the Social Democratic MP Jakob Reumann, made arrangements for the establishment of a parity-based industrial committee. This committee discussed numerous draft bills, ranging in 1919, for example, from the law on workers' holidays to the law on works councils.

An important communication channel between Hanusch and private industry ran through the freemasons' lodge "Lessing zu den drei Ringen", to which the director of the Federation of Industrialists Josef Trebitsch belonged as Worshipful Master and Ferdinand Hanusch as Senior Warden (*zugeteilter Meister*). Social Democratic MP Franz Schuhmeier was also a member of this lodge and later on also professor of anatomy and subsequently Vienna city councillor Julius Tandler.

The social policy reforms in 1918–1920 included the following major laws:

- 4 November 1918, industrial district commissions for organising employment agencies/setting up conciliation panels

- 6 November 1918, disability care, state aid for the unemployed
- 19 November 1918, expansion of the labour inspectorate, law on the eight-hour working day in factories, law on working at home
- 20 November 1918, state unemployment benefits for salaried workers
- 25 January 1919, abolition of work books (*Arbeitsbücher*) and penalties for breaches of contract/establishment of a state benefits fund for housing
- 4 February 1919, law on appropriation for residential purposes
- 25 April 1919, disability compensation law
- 14 May 1919, ban on night work for women and young people
- 15 May 1919, law on the establishment of works councils
- 30 July 1919, law on workers' holidays
- 17 December 1919, law on the standard eight-hour working day
- 18 December 1919, law on conciliation panels and collective agreements
- 28 February 1920, establishment of chambers for blue-collar and white-collar workers
- 24 March 1920, law on unemployment insurance

A total of 83 social laws were adopted and by 1920 Chancellor Karl Renner had established Austria in the front rank of Europe's welfare states.

The first measures were intended to tackle the major problems facing those returning home from the war and the growing army of unemployed (160,000 people as early as February 1919). In the teeth of criticisms from business unemployment benefits, which made up only a small part of the necessary state food subsidies, were raised twice. As the Christian Social politician and Hanusch's successor Josef Resch put it, "these social policy measures came at a time when it would not have been possible to maintain domestic peace and order without state intervention".

Three laws in particular should be highlighted. First of all, the laws on the eight-hour working day and on works councils. The latter, as leading Social Democrat Otto Bauer saw it, was also supposed to form part of a training initiative to provide works councils with some insight into production and sales mechanisms, thereby enabling them to prepare staff for socialised companies. Käthe Leichter, who was later to become a renowned Social Democrat social expert and worked at the State Committee for Socialisation, summed up Otto Bauer's aims concisely:

1. Trade union efforts to legalise their representatives in firms. 2. To put an end to absolutism in the firm and business owners' "master of the house" mentality, giving workers a say in all matters that concern them. 3. Establish participatory bodies in the socialisation process.

This law took up a number of elements of the council (soviet) movement, while attempting to channel it politically. Ultimately, however, the socialisation project foundered on the opposition of the Christian Social Party and works councils remained largely confined to advisory activities and workers' protection. In Austria today, however, works councils play an important role in company supervisory boards.

The third ground-breaking law concerned the establishment of the Austrian chambers of labour, adopted virtually on the same day as the chamber of commerce law of 26 February 1920. At this time the Social Democrats under Otto Bauer had already decided to terminate the coalition, which no longer considered it feasible to press ahead with measures such as a wealth tax or grain management. There was also pressure from the party base. But a number of measures were still to be quickly agreed on and implemented. They included the decree on the employment contracts of female household employees and the employment conditions of individual categories of worker (catering sector, law offices), as well as the Unemployment Insurance Law of 24 March 1920.

After the collapse of the first grand coalition, Christian Social Party–dominated governments continued to propagate clearing away the "revolutionary debris" (Ignaz Seipel, 29 February 1924), but ultimately it was not carried out wholeheartedly, despite numerous cuts and deterioration. Fears of revolutionary developments remained, although they subsided significantly from 1920 onwards. The municipal elections of 4 May 1919 exacerbated the differences between Social Democrats and Christian Socials and conservative groupings. On the basis of universal suffrage the SDAP won an absolute majority, with 54.2 per cent of the vote and 100 out of 165 seats. The Christian Social party came second, with 27.1 per cent and 50 seats. The nationalities conflict continued with the swearing-in ceremony conducted in German because representatives of the Socialist and Democratic Czechoslovaks Party (PSDČ), which won 8.4 per cent of the vote and eight seats, securing third place, partly spoke Czech and protested against the wording of the oath, which also contained a promise not to endanger Vienna's German character.

A new power factor emerged in the form of "Red Vienna", which until the separation of Lower Austria from the capital city in November 1920 gave the Lower Austrian regional assembly a Social Democratic colour. In Vienna, on the basis of the extensive municipal infrastructure that can be traced back to Christian Social mayor Karl Lueger, a comprehensive municipal house-building programme grew, together with a social policy welfare model. Subsequently a luxury tax was introduced to fund it, although the sharpest point of conflict was the challenge to the total control over divorce exercised by the Catholic Church. This made divorce de facto impossible with the exception of a loophole in §83 Austrian Civil Code (ABGB), which enabled the administrative authorities to set aside this obstacle to remarrying "for pressing reasons". Both the Social Democratic governor of Lower Austria (1919/1920), Albert Sever, and Social Democratic mayor of Vienna Karl Seitz made copious use of this option. This *Kulturkampf* with the Christian Social Party would ultimately lead to political control over the Constitutional Court.

A second deep-seated area of conflict was the schools issue, on which conservative religious views dominated Christian Social policy. From 15 March 1919 to 24 October 1920 Social Democrat Otto Glöckel headed the school administration as under secretary of state for education in the Renner-Fink coalition government. Within the framework of his reform efforts, among other things, compulsory attendance of religious tuition was abolished. Glöckel had been a teacher himself and in 1897 had been dismissed as a trainee teacher by Karl Lueger for "political radicalism" in Vienna. In 1917 he had published his main school policy aims: independence of schools from excessive red tape, separation of church and school and introduction of comprehensive schools. At the same time, all talents were to be supported, teaching and study materials were to be provided free of charge and modern pedagogical methods were to be implemented.

From 28 March 1922 to 1934 Glöckel as executive president of the City School Council implemented his school reform programme in Vienna, within the constraints of what was legally possible, aiming to replace learning by rote with modern teaching methods, in close cooperation with the latest developments. As undersecretary, however, he was unable to bring in comprehensive schools, with streaming, for all children between the ages of 6 and 14, even though it was the centrepiece of his reform plans, aimed at educating "proficient, upstanding, morally stable 'doers' who were eager to work".[5]

In conclusion, between 1918 and 1920 the Social Democrats in Austria, on the basis of wide-ranging policy preparations before 1914, both ushered in comprehensive parliamentary democracy under Karl Renner and, also with Ferdinand Hanusch, created the social policy framework of a welfare state, even though the requisite financial resources were unavailable at the time. From 1920, after the failure of the coalition, Social Democratic political influence was limited to Vienna, where it proved possible to implement at least some of these reforms on housing and education. While leading Social Democrats such as Otto Bauer continued to preach the principal goal of Austromarxism, the classless society, they behaved pragmatically in everyday political practice with a view to stabilising liberal parliamentary democracy and were able to head off short-sighted attempts by workers' and soldiers' councils to stir up socialist revolution.

It therefore makes perfect sense that in 1928, as Health Care Councillor of the City of Vienna, Julius Tandler instigated the placement of commemorative busts of Victor Adler, the first Social Democratic mayor of Vienna Jakob Reumann and social reformer Ferdinand Hanusch outside parliament on the Ring, all of whom had played key roles in setting the post-war agenda up to 1920.

SUMMARY

The Social Democratic Workers' Party of Austria (Sozialdemokratische Arbeiterpartei Österreichs, SDAP) became a decisive political force within a few decades after the unification party congress at Hainfeld in 1888/1889 and, in the wake of the 1907 elections, was the second largest party in the Imperial Council (Reichsrat) of the Cisleithanian (northern and western) part of Austria. Under the leadership of Victor Adler there was a change of course towards a peaceful transition from the wartime Habsburg dictatorship to a democratic republic and the transformation of the state bureaucracy at central-state and federal level towards the end of the war in 1918. Although after the 1911 elections the Social Democratic MPs were the weaker grouping in the provisional National Assembly, over against the Christian Social Party and the German National Party, Karl Renner was nevertheless elected state chancellor on 30 October 2018. The central departments in the areas of foreign relations and social affairs were taken by Social Democrats Victor Adler and Ferdinand Hanusch. Otto Glöckel and Julius Deutsch were dominant undersecretaries in the areas of home affairs and the armed forces. Karl Seitz served as both president of the National Assembly and state president.

Cooperation with the centre-right parties worked surprisingly well because of the extreme external pressure exerted by fears of a communist revolution and because the problems involved in transforming parts of the former Cisleithania were virtually unmanageable. Given the economic dependence on the Entente powers and the centrifugal trends in individual conservative-dominated *Länder* such as Salzburg, Tyrol and Vorarlberg to leave the federated state again a socialist revolution seemed an illusion.

Despite its revolutionary wing the majority of the SDAP remained loyal to a coalition with the Christian Social Party even after the successful elections of February 1919, in which it garnered around 40 per cent of the vote. At the same time, Julius Deutsch was able, with the help of Friedrich Adler, to channel the anarchist-revolutionary tendencies in the army and to implement some of the most progressive social policy legislation in Europe. An eight-hour working day and a law on a chamber of labour and works councils are only a few examples of their achievements. Nationalisation projects such as in coal mining, the iron industry and the large forested estates were planned but were unable to command a majority.

It did not prove possible to integrate the German-speaking territories of the newly established Czechoslovakia into the new federated state on the basis of President Wilson's 14 Points or to bring about union (*"Anschluß"*) with Germany. The territorial claims of the Kingdom of Yugoslavia to parts of Carinthia, however, were averted by military means and by a referendum. In the end the German-speaking South Tyrol was affiliated to Italy in the peace accords.

Already under the Habsburg Monarchy the SDAP's orientation was pan-German, entirely in the spirit of the 1848 revolution, whose political symbolism had been adopted by the liberals, and despite its Marxist rhetoric the party was politically pragmatic and sought to stabilise democracy. Despite the resignation of Otto Bauer, who had taken over from Victor Adler – who had died on 11 November 1918 – as secretary of state for foreign affairs, and the collapse of the coalition in June 1920, a collective constitutional compromise was achieved in parliament on 1 October 1920. This still provides the basis for the current constitution of the Austrian Republic, with amendments.

Although, despite the severity of the circumstances, the SDAP was able to influence social issues, introduce social policy innovations, prevent a communist revolution and help shape a democratic parliamentary constitution, it ultimately ran aground on the national question; in other words, the attempt to create a pan-German state including all German-speaking territories together with the German Reich. The peace treaty of Saint Germain-en-Laye in 1920 set in stone the small independent state of Austria and prohibited the name "German-Austria" and the "union" with Germany.

1 Karl Schwechler, Die österreichische Sozialdemokratie. Eine Darstellung ihrer geschichtlichen Entwicklung, ihres Programmes und ihrer Tätigkeit (Austrian Social Democracy. An Account of its Historical Development, its Programmes and its Activities), Graz 1980, 1f.

2 Ludwig Brügel, Geschichte der österreichischen Sozialdemokratie. Fünfer Band: Parlamentsfeindlichkeit u. Obstruktion/Weltkrieg/Zerfall der Monarchie (1907–1918) [History of Austrian Social Democracy, Vol. 5, Hostility of parliament and obstruction/world war/fall of the monarchy], Wien 1925, 140.

3 Selection of organisations up to 1919: Wolfgang C. Müller/Wolfgang Maderthaner: Die Organisation der österreichischen Sozialdemokratie 1889–1995, Wien 1996.

4 Julius Deutsch, Geschichte der österreichischen Arbeiterbewegung: Eine Skizze [History of the Austrian Workers' Movement: An Outline], Vienna 1947, 106.

5 Otto Glöckel, Die österreichische Schulreform (Austrian Education Reform), Vienna 1923, 4.

HUNGARIAN SOCIAL DEMOCRATS IN A PERIOD OF REVOLUTIONS AND COUNTER-REVOLUTIONS (1918–1921)

PÉTER CSUNDERLINK

FROM WORKERS' ASSOCIATIONS TO A POPULAR PARTY ONE MILLION STRONG – HUNGARIAN SOCIAL DEMOCRACY FROM THE EARLY DAYS UNTIL 1918

The Hungarian labour movement followed the German template, the ideas of the leaders of the Hungarian workers' movement were chiefly influenced by the firebrand advocate of self-help Ferdinand Lassalle (1825–1864), the revisionist Social Democrat (who once spoke in Budapest) Eduard Bernstein (1850–1932) and the centrist Karl Kautsky (1854–1938) (Lenin was not known in Hungary until 1917 and the philosopher György Lukács [1885–1971] became the leading ideologist of the communist party in 1919 only after the failure of the dictatorship of the proletariat, having read Lenin's *State and Revolution*). Although organisations along similar lines had already existed (the General Workers' Association founded in 1868 and the Non-Voters' Party founded in 1878), the Social Democratic Party of Hungary (MSZDP) was established in 1890 and Friedrich Engels (1820–1895) and Wilhelm Liebknecht (1826–1900) sent a letter of congratulations at the news of the first planned congress. Engels, who was at the time celebrating his seventieth birthday in London and could only attend the congress "in spirit", wrote:

> The existence of the Social Democratic Party of Hungary is yet another confirmation that modern large industry cannot settle in a country without causing the older pre-capitalist societies to revolt, and lead to the creation of not only a capital-

ist class, but a proletariat, too, and thus a class war for both, as well as a functioning workers' party aiming to change the bourgeois capitalist world order.

The MSZDP entered politics following the example of the Second International founded in 1889, whose primary goal was not to seize power, but to establish a populist party and enter parliament. The Hungarian party's programme was formulated in their 1903 manifesto, using the Erfurt programme of the Social Democratic Party of Germany (SDP) as a template. According to it the MSZDP

> does not wish to create a new ruling class or privilege, but means to eliminate all class privilege, and intends to grant equal rights to all people based on equal needs, regardless of nationality, ethnicity, religion and sex. It will dismantle the cause of inequality, that is, the private ownership of the means of production, and by removing the laws, mores and customs based on such inequality, give new substance to human life by placing the means of production under public ownership.

Because the intention was to achieve this ultimate goal via parliamentary rather than revolutionary means, one key demand was the secret ballot in every municipality for every citizen over twenty years of age, regardless of sex, and also that elections be held on public holidays, so that workers could not be hindered in the exercise of their democratic right by their work and their employer.

The leadership of the Social Democratic Party therefore differentiated between a maximalist manifesto – promoting revolutionary change – and a minimalist manifesto (bringing about the conditions of revolutionary change through democratic means). The leaders of the party may have been hopeful because in the 31 December 1899 issue of *Budapest Napló* ("Budapest Journal"), which represented the views of the social democrats' opponents – the liberals ruling Hungarian political life towards the end of the nineteenth century – the paper somewhat regretfully paid farewell to the nineteenth century, the "century of democracy", predicting that it would make way for the age of socialism: "Democracy is under siege from socialism; the sanctity of individual rights and the legitimacy of individual power are under attack by the concept of collectivism."

At the same time, in an article welcoming in the new century published in *Népszava* ("People's Voice"), the labour movement was described as the "Christianity of the age":

> In an age in which society was rotten to the core and the culture of the old was striding towards dissolution, one offshoot of the loathed and oppressed working people, the son of a carpenter spoke out as a reformer, promoting charity and equality. He wanted to be the redeemer of the poor and the oppressed. And the rich and powerful treated him as a subversive, rebelling against state and social order. [...] our time has revealed one manifestation which provides assurance to rational people, striving to work in the spirit of fairness, that humanity can move towards a brighter future. This is the labour movement. As it was in Nazareth when those languishing in poverty and oppression were full of thoughts of a self-proclaimed revolution, now, too, the masses of the proletariat have seized the notion of democratic socialism and made it their own, and they constitute the force that guarantees progress.

The "red monster" according to the Right, and the "red giant" according to the Left was tensing its muscles. The MSZDP became a popular party relatively quickly, even though apart from in Budapest and a few rural industrial centres (for example, Timisoara, now in Romania) there were not many industrial workers. Further development of the trade union movement aided the transition to a popular party: trade union members counted as party members, but anyone was considered a "socialist" if they read the daily party paper *Népszava*, first published on 1 April 1905. The editor was the party chairman, the moderate centrist, wary of extremists, Ernő Garami (1876–1935). The social democratic daily's column entitled "Forward!" (*Előre!*) proudly promoted the party:

Let's unfurl our red flag and fly it high over the workers of Hungary. Let us thank them. Let us thank them as the warriors of a belief whose flag now soars above us. [...] The daily paper of the Social Democratic Party of Hungary is in motion. It carries with it the triumphant beliefs of the coming times – beliefs which only a few years ago were laughed at, mocked and looked down on by the powers-that -be. Beliefs whose conquering strength is so devastating there is fear behind the mockery of the powerful. Beliefs whose warriors are persecuted in every way possible by the fearful authorities, and this paper bears witness to one of the most beautiful triumphs of these beliefs. Yes: we bring news of victory in our first issue! This paper is not the fruit of commercial profiteering, nor is it a tool squandered for money and bought to serve hidden agendas. This paper is a medal of victory won in the fire of fierce fighting and desperate, bloody struggle, and pinned by us to the ramparts of our enemy's battlements.

Besides the daily paper in Hungarian, the Hungarian labour movement published newspapers in other languages, too, for example the German-language *Volksstimme*, and in 1906 the party launched a theoretical journal "Socialism" (*Szocializmus*) for publishing longer writings and studies, which was edited by Ernő Garami and Zsigmond Kunfi (1879–1929), but ideas were also spread in the "Worker's Library" (*Mukások könyvtára*) series (for example, in 1909 Ernő Garami presented the lives of Marx and Engels).

Garami and Kunfi were both excellent speakers, and spoke multiple times for the "Galilei Circle" (1908–1919) which sought to enrich free-thinking young minds. The politicians of the labour movement, the social scientists of social democracy and the leftist radical youth were active in educating workers. For example, in workers' homes in the outskirts of the city world-famous mathematicians – such as Pál Dienes (1882–1952) – taught the first four rules of arithmetic to illiterate proletarians on the "edge of the city", often spending a great deal of time with them "at night on the outskirts", to quote the great modern poet Attila József's proletarian poems. After the publication of his 1897 collection *Proletár versek* ("Proletarian poems"), however, the most famous workers' poet of the early twentieth century Sándor Csizmadia became the resident poet of the MSZDP and was celebrated as a "worker's Petőfi", after the national poet and liberal revolutionary Sándor Petőfi (1823–1849), for poems such as the following, roughly translated:

People without a homeland

Brothers and sisters, left behind,
motherland and fatherland, no goodbye.
Gone to find a new home abroad.
A new poverty, the old poverty gone.

No tears are shed, or sighs are heaved,
their hearts unpierced by pain.
Forced to steal away, to flee that earth
where their own fathers bled.

Their only benefactor is the dark,
cloaking them beneath its robe.
Because their good and honest masters
won't let our starving patriots leave.

Leave in peace, there's nought to mourn,
abandon poverty and servitude.
Somewhere across the ocean soon
a better life might bloom for you.

And lest you're simply swapping pains,
moving from one penury to another,
don't be sorry, you'll still have gained,
far away from Hungarian freedom.

Our flag

Our flag is red
let's fly it high:
and offer shelter
to the oppressed and exploited,
equality's our motto;
we bear no masks,
we only ask for bread,
for rights, for justice.

Our banner is red,
and hangs rigid as a cliff,
born home from work by the people's
broken, thin and horny hands;
come rain, come shine,
we'll stand our ground,
and should we lose,
our names be lost,
but never our cause.

Our banner is red,
we have fallen beneath it;
soldiers of freedom,
in heart and soul.
Master and commander are the people
and sacred is their will.
Oh, tyrants in affluence,
Oh, corpulent loafers, do not think us fools.

In response to the use of the "blood-red flag", to internationalism and to Hungarian industrial workers' multi-ethnic composition – both the German *Wahlfond* and the Slovakian *Volobny Základ* featured under the Hungarian *Választási Alap* ("Election Fund") on the cover of the MSZDP's collection booklet – the "Hungarian lords" branded the Social Democrats "traitors, disloyal rogues" who felt free to impose their own ("socialist") stamp on their "country".

In retaliation against the continuous accusations, Ernő Garami wrote in his 1903 pamphlet entitled "Patriotism and Internationalism":

> the socialists, who allegedly renounce their country, are in fact perfectly capable of answering the question of what our country means to us: our rights and our bread. When my rights are taken from me, and the bread is stolen from my hands I'm robbed of my country. Those who rob me of it, they are the true traitors, they are the true disloyal rogues, and if I fight against them for my own rights and my own bread, then I'm fighting for my country! In a nation in which rights are a privilege, there the people have no country!

And once more with emphasis:

> Today's people have no country. They are rogues in the saddest sense of the word. And those who call themselves patriots have robbed these people of their country – in the country's name. And today, fighting for the country, and for those oppressed as the enemies of the country, are the international social democrats!

At the beginning of the twentieth century an entire labour counter-culture came into existence with its own press, its own literature, its own matinees, its own public holidays – most significantly, 1 May – and its own historical heroes (György Dózsa, Ignác Martinovics, Sándor Petőfi), as well as its own stirring demonstrations and its own provocative pamphlets and booklets. The MSZDP held to the basic thrust of the party's 1890 statement of principles, that it "would employ all means in the public sphere, the press, assemblies etc., in the interest of spreading socialist beliefs and it would strive against all obstacles that inhibited free speech, against press laws, and against any regulation that limited the rights of association and assembly". The MSZDP protested against the strict press law of 1914, whose censorship embittered the lives of the newspaper's journalists during the First

World War. The legendary, "Franz Joseph I is dead" front-page obituary of the 22 November 1916 issue of *Népszava*, contrary to public belief, was not left blank out of respect for the deceased ruler, rather censorship had removed the social democrats' obituary.

The first constitutional political party in Hungarian history was therefore founded by the social democrats. Until then Hungarian parties had been merely clubs without any statutes or constitution. It was this new constitutional nature which made possible the efficient organisation and execution of mass strikes and labour demonstrations. As Lajos Kassák (1887–1967) wrote in his memoirs *A Man's Life* (*Egy ember élete*): "There was a time when we organised a demonstration every day of the week." A favourite destination of the demonstrators, or revellers, rather, who marched along Andrássy Avenue (bearing Gyula Andrássy's name since 1885) and turned into (Queen) Elisabeth Boulevard, was the tavern, the *Trieszti Nő* ("Triestina"), where, over a few pints of beer, they could discuss the day's events, or simply pass the time with working women, who since 1905 had had their own paper *Woman Worker* (*Nőmunkás*). The editor was Mariska Gárdos (1885–1973), the first chair of the Women's Workers' Association of Hungary, founded in 1903.

In 1905, the festivities of the 1 May public holiday drew to a close in the same tavern, as reported in *Népszava* concerning the march that had attracted the members of fifty-six trade unions:

> Quite a sensation was caused by the group of goldsmith and jeweller comrades, whose flag bearing broad fluttering red ribbons was carried by four 12–14 year-old girls in red dresses. The 300 railway comrades, who were participating in the demonstrators' procession for the first time, were also received with interest. The procession led along Kerepesi Street, Erzsébet Boulevard, Andrássy Avenue and Stefánia Street into the city park, singing workers' songs along the way. There was only a demonstration in front of the independent party office, which was booed and chants were heard for electoral reform. In the park the procession broke into three. The iron and metalworkers went to the *Zöldvadász* tavern, where Comrade János Vanzcák gave an official speech. The

woodworkers, tailors and printers went to the Reklám garden where Comrade Dezső Bokányi spoke. The construction workers and smaller trades went to the Trieszti Nő, where Comrade Jakab Kardos was the speaker.

But regardless of the fact that the social democrats of Hungary had organised themselves into a party, for decades the representatives of the Hungarian state saw the labour movement as a threat to security, rather than as a political entity. Ernő Garami wrote in his memoirs *Hungary in Revolt* (*Forrongó Magyarország*): "similar to unacknowledged [religious] groups the Social Democratic Party [...] belonged to the ranks of unacknowledged political parties and the party had contact with the government only through the police or the public prosecutor". The police were watching the social democrats – or as they mockingly named them the *cucilistas* ("the dummy-suckers") – and every year between 1902 and 1913, the commissioner of the Budapest police informed the prime minister or the minister of the interior about the activities of the Socialistic labour movement of Hungary. The year 1905, however, brought a change, when during a crisis of Hungarian politics, the significance of the MSZDP's ability to mobilise large crowds grew. The police superintendent Dezső Boda, who censured the *Népszava* editorship frequently, wrote in his annual report:

> This year the Social Democratic Party of Hungary had a significant role in the Hungarian political crisis. All of the parliamentary political parties regard the party as a political force and for their own benefit have striven to guarantee its continued activity.

Due to the 1905 Russian Revolution, the MSZDP became more active than ever before, a crisis in Hungarian politics presented an opportunity for politicians, seeking allies, to "lift the labour party to their level". Minister of the Interior József Kristoffy (1857–1928) – appointed to the illegal 1905 "guardsman government" or "professional government" by Franz Joseph I, who had not accepted the results of the elections, naming the real winners the "national enemy" – wanted to establish funding for Fejérvár county in such a way as to hold out the prospect of electoral reform. The Kristóffy–Garami pact – which promised extension of the suffrage and the removal of limitations affecting MSZDP – led to the first truly large mass demonstration in the MSZDP's history, "Red Friday" on 15 September 1905. The next day *Népszava* wrote optimistically about the demonstration held in front of the Parliament:

> A great day has come: a parade of the troops, Red Friday. It went as we planned, and passed in as grand a manner as possible, and was as productive as could have been imagined. Above the crowds, the roof, the tower, the cupola, and the thousands of adornments of the parliament building loomed menacingly, and that menace gave rise to an awful tension in the air, which was returned by the piercing eyes of one hundred thousand people roaring below. The anger in the eyes, the occasional flourish of the Marseillaise, otherwise silence and calm; the calm of swallowed rage, the confidence of determined force.

Relations with the MSZDP could no longer be seen as merely a question of criminal law, alliance with the party had become a political dilemma for the bourgeois or centre-right parties.

Even though, in the 1890s, the social democrats were successful in introducing workers' insurance and improving working conditions, they were unsuccessful in their fight to obtain universal suffrage and the secret ballot. August Bebel and Jean Jaurés (1859-1914) both spoke of the MSZDP's struggles with electoral reform (naturally both letters were published in *Népszava*) but to no avail. After the "national enemy" – who attacked the socialists relentlessly – came to an agreement with the ruler, the "guardsman government" that had promised electoral reform was forced to resign, with severe consequences.

At the beginning of the twentieth century a mere 5–6 per cent of the Hungarian population could vote as a result of the strict rating of voters according to property and educational qualifications. In 1913 and again in 1918 changes were made in the strict electoral law, but no elections were held under the new rules due to the First World War. As a result, the Social Democratic Party of Hungary, who wished to carry through their demands by means of popular representation, were unable to acquire a single seat in parliament until 1918, despite the fact that the MSZDP had become Hungary's strongest and most organised party, and its membership had soared since 1917. The number of union members (and at the same time party members) was only 55,000 in 1916, but had grown to 215,000 by 1917 and to 721,000 party members by 31 December 1918.

One important reason the popularity of the party experienced a significant boost was that MSZDP party members did a lot to improve living conditions during the "pauperization" of the First World War. While the bourgeois newspapers often only got as far as propagating "beech-nut soup" as a flavoursome and nourishing dish, the Social Democrats were actually doing their best to weigh up the gravity of the situation. Through surveys, the national union of woman workers of Hungary inquired about the situation of women working in factories, and the results were shocking. One example was a seventeen-year-old girl supporting ten (!) people from her wages, who had coffee (most likely coffee-substitute) for breakfast, and soup and vegetable pottage for lunch and dinner. Another was a fifteen-year-old who commuted an hour and a half to work, was supporting six, had bread for breakfast, beans and sometimes potatoes for lunch and dinner. They also cited an older married woman who lived on meatless soup.

It was thanks to the success of the MSZDP that by the end of the war even without parliamentary representation the party leaders were regularly invited to the prime minister's study. In the summer of 1917, István Tisza's replacement, the new prime minister, Móric Esterházy, personally visited the editorial office of *Népszava* on Conti (now Tolnai Lajos) Street, to discuss matters with the Social Democrats, who were also able to have meetings with the monarch, Karl I.

THE SOCIAL DEMOCRATS IN
THE 1918 DEMOCRATIC REVOLUTION

Defeat in the First World War swept away not only the Austro-Hungarian Monarchy, but also the old Hungarian political elite: the general populace supported the Hungarian National Council, a consolidation of the oppositional powers that called for an end to the war, and the Social Democrats played a role in the coalition government, Károlyi's government, which came to power on 30–31 October 1918 with the Aster Revolution. When the leader of the bourgeois radicals and the Károlyi government's foreign minister without portfolio, Oszkár Jászi (1875–1957) held a "review of the troops" before the democratic powers, looking back on the 1918–1919 period of revolutions, the Social Democratic Party received their first mention due to their "preeminent organization". Following the Aster revolution *Népszava*'s print runs were one million copies and the Social Democrats' "merits in the organization of the working people and in the undermining of the old Hungary were undeniably great". But Jászi criticised the party's opportunism and excessive restraint: "The greater majority of this party leadership would never have brought about a revolution, had not the sudden actions of many soldiers, students and workers brought the situation to a head."

In the beginning the revolution was widely supported. In *The Book of the Victorious Revolution* (*A diadalmas forradalom könyve*), published in late autumn 1918, not only were left-wing writers and poets – or those thrown in with the left-wing, such as Mihály Babits (1883–1941), castigated for his banned pacifist poems of peace – published, but right-wing, conservative writers, too. In this volume, the memories of the revolution's participants were reported; for example, it is from this volume that we know how close the members of the National Council had come to being arrested: the exploited telephone girls, unable to vote – whose work was physically burdensome due to the repetitive lifting of heavy cables – had decided they would stop forwarding the orders of the city's commanding officer, Géza Lukachich (1865–1943). As opposed to the "backstabbing" theory of the extreme right who believed Germany and the Austro-Hungarian Monarchy lost the world war because the "traitorous" freemasons and social democrats triggered the revolution, the revolution broke out because the central powers had lost the war.

The Aster Revolution – named because Budapest was full of autumnal flowers due to the approaching All Saints' Day – was not planned. On the night of 30 October 1918, among the National Council members trapped in the Astoria Hotel, Zsigmond Kunfi could not be certain he would not end the next day hanging from the gallows. As Oszkár Jászi summarised the unpredictable and unaccountable revolutionary atmosphere in his memoirs *Hungarian Calvary – Hungarian Uprising* (*Magyar kálvária – magyar föltámadás*):

Reason, debate, the thorough consideration of circumstances, logical planning and the strict execution thereof, the rational distribution of roles and the rest of the familiar intellectual concomitants of political actions in normal times, as if by magic, disappear, and in their place, mysterious magnetic fields form in society, which draw the masses towards themselves with tremendous power, and the vast majority of so-called "personalities" are swept into their power.

According to Jászi, it was necessary that István Tisza – named the official responsible for the war – die in October 1918; similarly Béla Kun (1886–1938) could not have escaped that fate had he stayed in Budapest in August 1919. The prime minister, Mihály Károlyi (1875–1966) had a wreath delivered for the catafalque of István Tisza bearing the words "to my greatest political opponent" (which was thrown out by Tisza' widow), while in his memoirs *Faith without Illusions* (*Hit, illúziók nélkül*) he wrote of the dandy aristocrat turned socialist: "The cowardly murder of Tisza was the first and only bloody stain to taint the honour of our October revolution."

Mihály Révész (1884–1977), a *Népszava* journalist – and later in the period of the Hungarian Soviet Republic, the keeper of the minutes of the Revolutionary Governing Council – summarised the events from the Social Democrats' perspective in his pamphlet "The Victorious Hungarian Revolution" (*A győzelmes magyar forradalom*), published not long afterwards. But the children were not forgotten either, and today we can read with amusement Lili Ringer's "children's book of tales" *Pepper in the Revolution* (*Pukkancs a Forradalomban*) in which she tries to introduce the revolutionary parties to children:

> The socialists [...] are urgently demanding their rights. Theirs is the red flag and they're mostly workers. Oh, Pip, if you saw how beautiful it is when they march at rallies in rows, four by eight... I'm sure you'd want to be a worker, too. It's so pretty. I'll probably be a worker, too. I'm going to talk to Daddy about it this afternoon.

> I don't know the social democrats, I only saw them today, when we proclaimed the republic. I don't know whether they were workers or state officials, but everyone was wearing a red tag on their hat, and on it was written:
>
> Long live the national Social Democratic Party! They sang the national anthem with us when Count Mihály Károlyi spoke. Oh, Pip, they love Károlyi. But it's no wonder, he spoke so well! He said we want to live in peace!... That land ought to be given to the people, that we should support the government in this difficult task.
>
> I swore I would! ... Will you?

The Social Democratic Party strove to consolidate the efforts of the revolution. *Népszava* wrote: "Wherever possible, the work must begin!", and in his speech, which created a great stir and was met with some astonishment, Zsigmond Kunfi, talking as the leader of the labour movement, announced the temporary suspension of the class struggle, after the popular government was sworn in before the National Council:

> We ask for your help for just seven weeks so we can create peace and a government of the people. All counter-revolutionaries will be regarded as accomplices of the old system. It's difficult for me as a stalwart social democrat to say this, but still I must, but during these seven weeks we do not wish to live in class hatred and class struggle. And we ask everyone to put all class interests aside, to put all denominational considerations to the back of one's mind and to help us with the job in hand

Ernő Garami thought that after a successful revolution a longer democratic period had to follow until eventually the Hungarian working class – which the leader of MSZDP in autumn 1918 did not consider mature enough for the exclusive leadership of the country – could take power into their own hands. As he wrote in *Hungary in Revolt*, "it would be impossible for a Hungary previously under feudal governance to immediately skip all intermediate developmental steps, and to arrive at such a social and state system in which the class interests and wishes of the relatively small industrial working class are of critical importance".

In the catastrophic economic situation and the atmosphere of panic caused by foreign occupation – in December 1918 the Czechoslovakians occupied Upper Hungary, the Romanian army Transylvania and in the south the Allies had pressed as far as the cities of Pécs and Baja – there was, however, not the time or the possibility to build the country slowly. With the fall of the Austro-Hungarian Monarchy Hungary, too, was under threat of falling to pieces as a result of the separatist activities of national minorities. The MSZDP supported the drawing of ethnic lines on the grounds of national self-determination. At the February 1919 international social democratic conference in Bern, the MSZDP delegation sided with national self-determination and demanded a referendum in Hungary's nationally diverse territories.

Party representatives promoted pacifist policies and trusted in the good intentions of the Allies. Throughout the proclaimed Hungarian Soviet Republic, only once did they resolve to take up arms in March 1919, when the social democrats temporarily united with the communists. It was later a rather uncomfortable memory for the counter-revolutionary Horthy regime that against the occupying Czechoslovakian and Romanian forces, it was not the National Army that fought, but the Red Army. The only campaign of the last century comparable to the May–June 1919 northern campaign – to reclaim Sátoraljaújhely, Nové Zámky, Košice and Prešov led by chief of staff Aurél Stromfeld, a left-wing sympathiser who joined the Social Democratic Party in January 1919 – was Artúr Görgey's 1849 Spring campaign. Following the successful military campaign – the peak of which was the proclamation of the Slovak Soviet Republic – Stromfeld had stepped down, when Béla Kun naively accepted Clemenceau's peace offer and retreated from the reclaimed territories. The Romanians did not do the same, however, although according to the Clemenceau pact they should have done so. Without Stromfeld's expert leadership and demoralised as a result of the voluntary retreat, the Red Army's July 1919 offensive east of the River Tisza against the Romanians was soon utterly defeated.

ATTEMPTS TO IMPLEMENT THE SOCIAL DEMOCRATIC PROGRAMME AND TO BUILD THE "NEW HUNGARY"

The MSZDP demanded resolutely that a Hungary independent of the now-collapsed Austro-Hungarian Monarchy be a republic, with a single-chamber parliament, free of any upper house of aristocrats and church dignitaries. On 1 November 1918 Zsigmond Kunfi announced the government manifesto that heralded the republican form of state, and the next day the headline in *Népszava* was "We demand a republic!" On 16 November 1919 Hungary was proclaimed a "people's republic" (on 12 November in Vienna and 14 November in Prague the Austrian and Czechoslovakian republics were proclaimed, after Karl I withdrew from participation in the management of state affairs in his Eckartsau Proclamation).

At the celebration held on Parliament Square (now Kossuth Square), after prime minister Mihály Károlyi and János Hock chairman of the National Council had spoken, Ernő Garami gave a speech as a representative of the Social Democrats, though he stressed that it was "no longer time to speak", but "to work, and to work hard, for some of us, for all of us, for hundreds of thousands, for millions, right away, right now. To work, and to work hard. To work for the free, independent, democratic people's republic of Hungary!"

The old parliament was dissolved, and until the first assembly of the new democratic parliament the expanded National Council took over as lawmaker. This "Greater National Council" published the first "popular verdict" on the formation of the Hungarian People's Republic in the central hall, and also compelled Mihály Károlyi to lead the "popular government" to urgently deliver new laws on electoral rights, the freedom of the press, trial by people's jury, freedom of association and assembly and land reform. But the task of the National Council was assumed more and more by the Budapest Workers' Council, formed 2 November 1918, and led by the familiar trade-union officials of the MSZDP, whose significance grew swiftly over several months until the proclamation of the Soviet Republic. The Budapest Workers' Council resolved the year-end government crisis – a result of the difficulties of coalition government and of debates about confronting far-left communists and militant right-wing counter-revolutionary groups – on 8 January, with an assembly that began at three and ended the next day at seven in the morning, where instead of Ernő Garami's motion urging that they leave the centre-right government, the workers' representatives who were present accepted Zsigmond Kunfi's proposal of compromise. Accordingly, the Social Democrats did not shoulder the task of governance in its entirety – a move that was eventually supported by Sándor Garbai (1879–1947), withdrawing his own proposition – but remained in the coalition government and continued to appoint ministers to it.

The MSZDP demanded universal, equal and secret suffrage for every citizen over 20 years of age, regardless of sex. This was achieved only within limitations: only women over 24 who could read and write were given the right to vote, while all men over 21 years of age could vote. After the country was made a Soviet Republic in spring 1919 in collaboration with the communists, every man and woman over 18 years of age was given the right to vote, but "reactionaries" were excluded, not only clerics and wealthy peasants, but also "exploiters", that is, anyone who had employees, and thus, according to the interpretation of the lawmakers, had work-free access to income. But despite the severe restrictions, a record-breaking number of voters made it to the polls in the elections on 7 April 1919, and more than two million voted. The majority of women still stayed at home, however, because although they had been granted the right to vote, some did not dare and others had been forbidden, which men justified on the grounds that women were incapable of taking it seriously.

Besides electoral rights the most burning issue in Hungary was land. In the MSZDP's manifesto, published on 8 October 1918, they demanded "radical agrarian reform"; "the government must strive to achieve radical and fundamental *agrarian reform*, which *will put the land in the hands of those who work it.*" As soon as they had entered government the Social Democrats had pressed for the expropriation of medium-sized and large estates and their transformation into farmers' cooperatives, but during the Károlyi government they were not able to convince others. According to the 1919 XVIII People's Act regarding "the allotment of land to land-workers" – which was publicised in the promotional pamphlet entitled *The Shorter Catechism of Land Law* written by Zsigmond Móricz – "not one big landowner may keep more than five hundred *hold* (1.42 acres) of estate". Or as Móricz wrote:

> These five hundred *hold* can be selected by the landowners themselves from their estates, as they please. Therefore, the landowner must be permitted and aided to select in such a

way as to best make use of the farm and farming equipment. However, it is not free for the landowner to choose in such a way that might hinder the development of, for example, a community.

Thus, where the given community was in need of it due to a lack of land, anything above a large estate's first two hundred *hold* could be divided up. The church's large landholdings were definitely slated for such treatment. Zsigmond Móricz wrote with excitement: "Here, in our hands now is the first law since the rulers of the House of Árpád which gives something to the people! This land law is the first which doesn't forbid, or hinder, or steal anything from the people, but *gives something to them!*" Gyula Krúdy wrote about the "second Magyar conquest" in his report on the redistribution of the parish estate of Mihály Károlyi who, as president of the republic, began the land reform with his own property. There was not enough time for the nationwide enforcement of the law, however.

The redistribution of land was dismissed in the Soviet Republic: the Social Democrats leading the People's Committee on Agriculture had formed state farming cooperatives from large estates, which reduced support for the "dictatorship of the proletariat" among poor peasants who had expected to receive allotments. Placing the means of production under public ownership was a long-standing MSZDP demand, because not only did the party find a society based on private property unfair, but they believed that the economic model founded on it was inevitably anarchistic as a result of conflicting economic interests. As Dr Jenő Erdély wrote, while outlining the manifestos of the various political parties in preparation for the 1919 elections, which were never held:

> in the wake of the inevitable crises caused by the disorder in the capitalist system *homelessness, mass poverty, and universal insecurity* have become permanent phenomena in society. Class conflict will only heighten and all efforts towards the nationalisation of the capitalist means of production will intensify, as the only means towards abolishing exploitation and poverty, and *a new social order* will become necessary.

Hence according to the Social Democratic manifesto:

> There is no private ownership of the means of production. Let it be put under public ownership and let the capitalist system of production be made into a *socialist system of production*. Public ownership ought to be gradually expanded with the nationalisation of the forests, the water works, the mines and transport. The right to fish and hunt must also be made public.

Nor were the factories nationalised under the coalition government, but only during the Soviet Republic (when every factory consisting of more than ten workers was nationalised), and management of the factories was given over to the workers' councils. During the Soviet Republic, the eight-hour working day was introduced (a longstanding demand of the Second International), wages were raised and the pay gap between the lowest and the highest paid was radically reduced, although as a result there were negative consequences for the country, which was suffering from production problems, and the social democrat (but later communist) economist Jenő Varga (1879–1964), former editor of *Népszava's* economics column and People's Commissar for Finance, was forced to back down at the National Assembly of the Councils in June 1919, and the performance-based piece wage was reinstated at the expense of idealistic plans.

FROM "RED MONSTER" TO GOVERNMENT PARTY – THE SOCIAL DEMOCRATS IN GOVERNMENT AND IN THE ELECTIONS

The great tragedy of the Károlyi government – and the Social Democrats within it – was that although the governing left-wing radical intellectuals had been planning the construction of the "New Hungary" for almost a decade and a half in the "first Hungarian workshop for sociology", the journal *Twentieth Century* (*Huszadik Század*), as well as polishing the manifesto, their chance to build it came at a disastrous time following defeat in a world war, in the middle of the complete collapse and part-occupation of the country and, if that was not enough, the Spanish flu pandemic. Before the Károlyi government the Social Democrats had only had one appointment:

Ernő Garami was made Minster of Commerce – the editorship of *Népszava* was taken over by Jakab Weltner (1873–1936) – Zsigmond Kunfi was made Minister of Labour and Welfare and Vilmos Böhm (1880–1949) became Minister of Defence. Böhm was a mechanic by trade and according to a comical, but presumably false anecdote, he was met by state officials with a very warm welcome as they thought that Böhm had come to repair the typewriters. Joking aside, however, it was one of Böhm's strengths, besides being an excellent organiser, that the tiny engineer, who practised his politician's mannerisms in front of the mirror, still gave thought to such matters as axle-grease when he was put at the head of the Red Army during the Soviet Republic.

From the beginning a huge and fundamental dilemma was posed by the question of what role the Social Democrats should play in the government of a democratic revolution. However much it might represent a step forward compared with the political and economic regime prior to the revolution, could they build a bourgeois capitalist system, if in the long term they were striving to surpass it? Ernő Garami answered "no" and it was only at Mihály Károlyi's request that he brought the Social Democrats into the coalition government. He would have found it more appropriate if the MSZDP had supported Károlyi's politics from outside the government. The "appetite" of several social democratic politicians had grown, however, and they wanted MSZDP participation in the government to match their authority. As bourgeois support for the Károlyi government fell, the importance of the Social Democrats grew: in the "petit bourgeois" Berinkey government formed in January 1919, five ministries were led by Social Democrats; Ernő Garami and Vilmos Böhm remained Minister of Commerce and Minister of Defence, Zsigmond Kunfi and Gyula Peidl were made Minister of Education and Minister of Labour, and Oreszt Szabó was appointed Minister of Ruthenian National Affairs.

Despite the passing of the new electoral law by the Károlyi government, the elections were postponed, as significant territories within Hungary were still under the occupation of Czech, Romanian and French forces. The elections were finally held in April 1919, in the Soviet Republic, after the Social Democrats joined forces with the communists, but in these elections it was possible to vote only for candidates of the united party, the MSZDP. Under the Soviet Republic government, at first the communists only held one commissarial position in the Revolutionary Governing Council – Béla Kun was made Commissar of Foreign Affairs – while the rest of the commissars were Social Democrats and Sándor Garbai was elected president. The de facto leader was the communist Béla Kun, however. Later the proportion of communists in the government rose to half when the deputy commissars became commissars.

Because the proportion of members of the Revolutionary Governing Council who were of Jewish origin was well above 60 per cent – which meant that the Jewish community was almost ten times "overrepresented" according to national statistics – the dictatorship of the proletariat was widely labelled a "Jewish dictatorship" during the counter-revolutionary period. It is important to clarify, however, that as members of an atheist and internationalist political movement the commissars could hardly be said to have a Jewish identity. At the National Assembly of Soviets, Béla Kun stated that "my father was a Jew, yet I didn't remain a Jew, I became a socialist, I became a communist", implying that the secular faith of Bolshevism had replaced his Jewish faith. The large proportion of the Jews among participants in the labour movement needless to say could not be explained by the "Judeo-Bolshevist" theory, but simply because, despite legal emancipation – the Jewish religion had become a recognised denomination in 1895 – Jews still regularly encountered discrimination. For them, joining an internationalist movement presented them with the opportunity to leave behind the disadvantages caused by their "Jewishness", which hindered their full social integration.

When the dictatorship of the proletariat failed, the communists and left-wing Social Democrats emigrated from Hungary. The moderate Social Democrats who remained formed the Peidl government, which was overthrown on 6 August 1919, after only one week, by a right-wing putsch. And so began the "White Terror" – the persecution of left-wing actors in the 1918–1919 revolutions – in response to which the MSZDP boycotted the 1920 elections. In the 1922 elections the Social Democrats ran again, after their leader, Károly Peyer, had reached an agreement with the right-wing prime minister, István Bethlen, in 1921. The MSZDP were the legitimate opposition of the Horthy regime.

"SISTER PARTY" OR "RIVAL PARTY" – THE RELATIONSHIP OF THE SOCIAL DEMOCRATS TO THE COMMUNISTS

The relationship between the Social Democratic Party of Hungary and the Communist Party was first one of opposition, then one of allies and after the 1918–1919 revolutions again one of opposition. The Communist Party of Hungary was organised by Bolsheviks sent from Soviet Russia to Hungary. Following the formation of the party on 24 November 1918, led by Béla Kun, the party were fierce critics of the government, and of the Social Democrats in particular.

The Communists attacked the Social Democrats for forming a coalition government with the bourgeois parties, suspending the class struggle in November 1918, and striving to strengthen the bourgeois democratic system, while the Communists promoted the necessity for a dictatorship of the proletariat. In articles critical of the government in the communist *Vörös Újság* ("Red Paper"), launched in December 1918, the Communists accused the Social Democrats of betraying the workers, while in *Népszava* the Social Democrats accused the Communists of endangering the achievements of the revolution through incitement and hatemongering. Due to these attacks the Social Democratic ministers decided to get even with the seemingly demagogic Communists, and so in February 1919 the Communist Party leadership were arrested. In prison Béla Kun was beaten half to death by police officers, and so was made a martyr: the popularity of the Communist Party soared among workers and war veterans when a reporter of the most widely read tabloid, *Az Est* ("The Evening") carried out an interview with the "half-dead" Béla Kun. Sentences from this interview became legendary, and the leader of the Communist Party was made a martyr by the labour movement overnight:

> "What were you beaten with?"
> "A rifle butt", Béla Kun answers quietly.
> "Would you recognise the police officers who beat you?"
> "That doesn't matter", he says calmly, "they were misguided men."

In March 1919, when the crisis reached a climax and the Berinkey government resigned, the Social Democrats were not confident enough to form a government themselves and they reached an agreement with the imprisoned communists. Contrary to public opinion this happened without the knowledge of Mihály Károlyi, who as president of the republic wanted to appoint a purely social democratic government with Zsigmond Kunfi as prime minister. The left-wing Social Democrats who favoured uniting with the Communists led a coup against Károlyi, however, with the help of Secretary Pál Kéri (1882-1961), by writing a statement of resignation as the president of the republic in his name and forging his signature. By the time Mihály Károlyi realised it, they had already formed a dictatorship of the proletariat, and the Social Democratic Party and the Communist Party had united under the name of the Hungarian Socialist Party (MSZP). (The party changed its name in June 1919 to the Socialist-Communist Worker's Party of Hungary.)

A leading figure in the history of Hungarian social democracy Ernő Garami did not ask for a position in the united party as he did not want to be a member of a party whose name did not feature the word "democracy". He decided to leave the country – just as later Oszkár Jászi and Mihály Károlyi would leave during the Soviet Republic. Béla Kun wanted Garami to travel to Switzerland by appointment of the Revolutionary Governing Council to write reports on international affairs, but Garami did not accept. Jakab Weltner, editor of *Népszava* believed that the Social Democrats had no other choice but to "restore the workers' unity". As he later wrote in his 1929 memoir *Revolution, Bolshevism, Emigration* (*Forradalom, bolsevizmus, emigráció*), after the presentation of the Vix Note, on 21 March 1919, the MSZDP could choose between two methods of "suicide": uniting with the communists or backing down, as advised by Ernő Garami. In the end the MSZDP chose the "most respectable means of annihilation" by "attempting to save the situation".

At the beginning, however, there appeared to be no talk at all of "suicide": the Soviet Republic had widespread public support in its first weeks because it was expected that the dictatorship of the proletariat would defend Hungary's borders. The "honeymoon period" lasted until the Romanian attack on 16 April 1919, when the leadership of the Soviet Republic panicked, and tried to ward off the organisation of counter-revolutionary movements by unjustifiably taking hostages and the "red terror" began. The Social Democrats consistently played a backseat role. Overall, during the Soviet Republic, as long as any hope remained of maintaining the dictatorship of the proletariat, the Social Democrats cooperated with the Communists successfully. After the fall of the dictatorship of the proletariat in August 1919, the Social Democrats and Communists blamed one another for its failure, and they became hostile once again for the following three decades.

RED HORIZONS – THE MSZDP'S RELATIONS WITH SOCIAL DEMOCRATIC PARTIES ABROAD

Because Hungary contained multiple national minorities, within minority-led sectors of the MSZDP, Czech, Slovakian and Romanian social democrats were politically active and printed social democratic papers in their own languages (for example, *Volkstimme*). The MSZDP demanded the emancipation of national minorities. They were frequent participants in international social democratic conferences, representing Hungarian social democratic politicians, and during the First World War they took part in social democratic conferences held in neutral countries. In the interest of foreign affairs they strove to strengthen relations with the workers' parties of the allied nations. The MSZDP's strongest relationship was with the Social Democratic Party of Austria (SPÖ), which had survived the fall of the Austro-Hungarian Monarchy. Consequently, after the fall of the dictatorship of the proletariat Austria provided refuge to persecuted communist and left-wing social democrats fleeing Hungary.

WHAT CAN BE LEARNED FROM THE SOCIAL DEMOCRATS DURING THE PERIOD OF REVOLUTIONS AND COUNTER-REVOLUTIONS?

Although they may be harshly judged by posterity, in an extraordinarily difficult period following defeat in the First World War and a time of crisis among the revolutions of 1918–1919, Hungary's Social Democrats set an example for today. Their efforts to improve the education of the poor and those at the bottom of society so they could make responsible decisions, their efforts to democratise public administration, their support of progressive taxation and finally, their belief in the beneficial effects of international communication, must be acknowledged and are still worth pursuing.

SUMMARY

The Hungarian labour movement sought to emulate its German counterpart and its leaders were influenced by the ideas of Lassalle, Kautsky and Bernstein (the name of Lenin was unknown in Hungary until 1917). The Social Democratic Party of Hungary (Magyarországi Szociáldemokrata Párt, MSZDP) – which was founded in 1890 – commenced its political activities in accordance with the directives of the Second International.

The aim of the Hungarian Social Democrats was not a revolutionary takeover, but becoming a mass party and entering the Hungarian parliament. The MSZDP easily became a mass party, but their most important demand, the universal, equal and secret ballot, was rejected. For this reason, the MSZDP, which wanted to achieve its demands in a democratic way, did not manage to get even one MP into the Hungarian Parliament until 1918, even though it had become the strongest and most organized party of Hungary by then, with a rapidly growing membership. Membership of the party soared after 1917, reaching almost 1 million by autumn 1918.

After defeat in the First World War and the "Aster Revolution" on 30–31 October 1918, the opposition came to power and the Social Democrats were included in the government under the leadership of the so-called "red count", Mihály Károlyi. Ernő Garami, leader of the MSZDP, became Minister of Commerce and later on other Social Democrat politicians entered the government. The MSZDP firmly demanded that the independent Hungary become a republic, and on 16 November 1918 Hungary was proclaimed a "people's republic" with a unicameral parliament (without a House of Lords).

The MSZDP wanted a universal, equal and secret ballot for every citizen over the age of 20, regardless of gender. But this demand was realised to only a limited extent: only men over 21 got the right to vote and literate women over 24. After transforming the "people's republic" into a Soviet Republic with the collaboration of the Communists in the spring of 1919, everyone over 18 got the right to vote, but the so-called "reactionaries" (including clerics and "kulaks") were excluded.

The issue of land was the other hot topic in Hungary at that time. The Social Democrats demanded the nationalisation and collectivisation of medium-sized and large estates, but they were unable to prevail in the civic democratic Károlyi regime. The old demand of the MSZDP, the nationalisation of factories, was not accomplished either during the period of coalition government, only later, during the Hungarian Soviet Republic, when every factory employing more than 10 workers was nationalised.

The Social Democratic Party of Hungary had hostile relations with the Party of Hungarian Communists ("Kommunisták Magyarországi Pártja", KMP), resumed after an interlude of rapprochement in the wake of the revolutions of 1918–1919. When a hostile occupation by the entente powers threatened Hungary in March 1919, the Social Democrat and Communist parties were unified under the name of the Socialist Party of Hungary ("Magyarországi Szocialista Párt", MSZP), in order to create a "worker unit" to defend Hungary in alliance with Soviet Russia. The "dictatorship of the proletariat" was proclaimed. Although the Social Democrats and Communists could work together successfully in the Revolutionary Government Council, the Hungarian Soviet Republic was short-lived due to the catastrophic internal and external situation, which could not be managed either peacefully or with violence. When the dictatorship of the proletariat failed, the Communists and the left-wing Social Democrats emigrated from Hungary.

The moderate Social Democrats, who remained in Hungary, formed the Peidl government, but this was overthrown by a right-wing coup after only a week on 6 August 1919. A "White terror" started – persecution of leftists who played a role in the revolutions of 1918–1919 – and for this reason, the MSZDP boycotted the election of 1920. The Social Democrats participated only in the election of 1922, after the new Social Democratic leader, Károly Peyer, made a pact with the rightist prime minister István Bethlen. The MSZDP became the legal leftist opposition of the Horthy regime for two decades.

SOCIAL DEMOCRACY AND THE CZECHOSLOVAK REPUBLIC, 1918–1938

MARTIN POLÁŠEK

ORIGIN AND EARLY DEVELOPMENT OF SOCIAL DEMOCRACY

All over Europe, social democratic parties grew up first and foremost as interest parties. They defended the concrete material interests of working people, above all factory workers, although in time also those of other groups. In general, they sought to help people without privilege, whether that means privilege of family or of property. The strength of these parties for the most part developed from the strength of the workers. Things were no different in the Czech lands, which formed the industrial backbone of the Habsburg monarchy. It was for this reason, too, that the social democrats emphasised the social and political emancipation of the non- or underprivileged. This is evident in demands for improvements in working conditions, a new role for the state in economic policy and political democracy.

At the same time, however, the social democrat movements were, from the start, movements of cultural or social development in the broadest sense of the word. The social democrats understood that people's lives are not confined to work or politics and that they cannot be emancipated in one area and left without rights in another just because they are used to it. Many social democratic demands were pioneering in the context of the time. The ending of the death penalty, the right of women to have an abortion, the possibility of being cremated and equal rights for children born in and out of wedlock or the right for "each to be ensured an education in keeping with their abilities".

A social democratic party was founded in the Czech lands in 1878, part of the first major wave of such parties. It was thus founded only a little later than the social democratic parties in Germany and at about the same time as those in the Netherlands, Belgium and Denmark. It was also founded earlier than, for example, the social democratic parties in Sweden and Britain (Labour).

This does not mean much in itself because many social democratic parties faced, immediately following their foundation, such severe repression that they almost fell apart. This was also the case of the social democratic movements in Austro-Hungary. Thus although we consider 1878 to be the symbolic beginning of our historical story, in the 1880s the party had to be de facto refounded.

These early attempts to suppress the social democrats entirely were unsuccessful, however, and in time the pressure eased, although social democrats continued to face all kinds of limitations and bullying from the state. Nevertheless, the social democrats themselves changed their approach. From the 1880s they started to focus on the democratisation of Austro-Hungary and participation in elections as the main tool for implementing their demands. They thus strove for full and fair suffrage. At the start of the twentieth century it was social democrat demonstrations, together with the impact of the Russian revolution of 1905, that in the end led to the introduction of general suffrage. At the same time, however, the social democrats kept a certain amount of distance. In practice this could be seen in the way they participated in all types of elections and tried to solve everyday problems, but it was also able (and willing) to formulate a vision that went beyond the needs of the electoral struggle and the boundaries of an electoral term. In this it was helped above all by Marxism.

THE BIRTH OF CZECHOSLOVAKIA

During the First World War, the Czechoslavonic social democrats gradually abandoned their original idea of the democratic transformation of the Habsburg monarchy. Instead, the idea of national independence took over, in the form of a common state of Czechs and Slovaks. Towards the end of 1918 the party expressed this in a change of name; instead of Czechoslavonic, it was now the Czechoslovak Social Democratic Workers' Party. Social democrats abroad had taken on the idea of an independent state even before this. In autumn 1917 it also gained ground among social democrats in the Czech lands. However, since 1915 there had been ties between the social democrats and the resistance movement abroad.

On 14 October 1918 the social democrats, together with the National Social Party, led the workers in the Czech lands in a general strike. This halted the export of food from the hungry Czech lands to the centre of the monarchy and set in motion the administrative collapse of Austro-Hungary. The organisers of the strike talked in their declaration about "new state sovereignty" and a "free Czechoslovak republic". This was the first time that it had been publicly declared that the new state would be a republic. On the same day the provisional Czechoslovak government in Paris gained recognition and four days later Masaryk made the Washington Declaration. The path to 28 October lay open.

One of the five "men of 28 October" was the social democrat František Soukup. He was justice minister in the first Czechoslovak government and later became deputy chairman (1920–1929) and deputy-speaker (1929–1938) of the Senate. The first legislative body (the Revolutionary National Assembly, 1918–1920), which among other things gave the Czechoslovak Republic a constitution, was headed by the social democrat František Tomášek. In 1920–1925 he was also speaker of the Chamber of Deputies of the National Assembly. The social democrat Vlastimil Tusar was prime minister in two successive governments during the toughest post-war period, from spring 1919 to autumn 1920. His main achievement was that he managed to ensure the relatively smooth creation of Czechoslovakia from the former monarchy in the historical borders of the Czech lands, while at the same time creating stable relationships with both Austria and Germany.

The social democrat Alfréd Meissner was elected chairman of the constitutional law committee of the first legislative assembly. He was the author of the provisional constitution of 1918 and one of the most active creators of the 1920 constitution. Most of the fundamental elements of the constitutional order formed part of the ČSDSD's long-term programme and many of them were also taken on by other political formations, some earlier, some not until the end of the First World War. To take a few examples: the republic as the state form, with the people being the only source of state power and no state power ensuing as it were "from God's grace"; general, equal, direct and secret suffrage for both men and women; a proportional electoral system; a government that answers to parliament; and legislative assemblies – in the end both the Chamber of Deputies and the Senate – that are elected, not appointed. (When the constitution was being drafted there was no lack of people suggesting that the Senate be appointed by the president or that its members be voted for indirectly.)

The democratic, republican and parliamentary nature of the Czechoslovak Republic was seen by the social democrats as part of their final aims, one of the manifestations of national and social emancipation. It was not supposed to end only with the national right to self-determination and liberal democracy, however; to no less a degree, democracy was meant to penetrate other areas. In this, however, the social democrats were not as successful.

Since the start of the twentieth century, the ČSDSD had pushed for "direct legislative activity by the people, in terms of both the right to make legislative proposals and the right to reject them". This implied holding plebiscites and the idea was duly included in the Czechoslovak constitution. In special situations, in which legislative assemblies were unable to decide a certain problem, it was to be decided by referendum. An accompanying law that would have actually enabled referendums to be held, however, was never approved; indeed, no bill for such a law was even put forward.

Legislation on the army was also not forthcoming. The social democrats had long opposed the idea of a standing army, which after experience of the Austro-Hungarian army they associated above all with the belligerent whims of the political and economic elites. They did support a militia, however, in the sense of brief periods of military service for the entire male population, with the army to be mobilised only if the country was threatened. They saw soldiers as citizens who used weapons only temporarily. It was for this reason that they were in favour of soldiers having voting rights, but the idea did not take hold under the First Republic. The ČSDSD recognised the significance of the troops in the creation of the state, but did not wish to expand their number. The defence law of 1920 set up a standing army but at the same time declared itself to be a temporary solution before a militia system could be prepared. This temporary provision lasted for the whole of the rest of the First Republic. In the 1930s the social democrats themselves abandoned the idea of militias. The opinion took hold that if the army was a based on the home defence principle, if it contained some democratic elements and if it was under the full control of elected politicians it would not serve the aims of national or state aggression. As such, the social democrats were able to support it.

The social democrats wanted church and state to be separated. There were various currents of opinion; the Slovak social democrats even recommended that the issue be dealt with later, once Czechoslovakia had been established. The idea that the state should be separated from the church did not in the end make it into the constitution, however, although there was also nothing in the constitution to prevent it. In some ways it at least paved the way for the separation of church and state, for example in its declaration that no one should be forced to take part in any religious act (which means, for example, that no one would have to take part in school prayer or in the army if they did not want to). The result was a compromise. The education system was gradually separated from the church, albeit not completely. On the other hand, when the ČSDSD was in opposition in the second half of the 1920s, the right-wing government put forward a law ensuring that clerics were paid out of the state budget, and in the 1930s the intended civil code did not cover marriage and family law, out of regard for the clerical parties.

The social democrats believed that democracy also ought to penetrate economic relations. The constitution did not contain this principle at all, however. Partial success in this regard came in 1920–1922 with the laws on factory councils and employee profit shares, but the effect was not substantial and did not go beyond a few small sectors of the economy. During the First Republic there were no major nationalisation projects that would have brought certain sectors of the economy into public ownership, and there was also no control of financial capital (such as suggestions for a state banking sector or the nationalisation of the central bank as a key instrument of economic policy).

There were only two spheres in which the idea was realised. In neither was it something new, but during the First Republic it became substantially more widespread. The first was the idea of public enterprises: enterprises created and operated by the community or state. The reasons for such enterprises varied: in order to ensure equal access to all, because private initiatives would never venture into these spheres, or because they had a purpose other than financial profit. During the First Republic they were mostly municipal companies such as electricity, water and gas concerns.

The second form in which economic democracy was realised was in self-help activities, above all cooperative enterprises. In this the social democrats led by example. The social democratic Central Association of Cooperatives, which at the beginning of the twentieth century had about 80 member cooperatives, had over 700 by the end of the 1930s, with almost 500,000 members and 14,000 employees. These were consumer cooperatives, whose members could purchase everyday goods at wholesale prices or have them supplied at cost. There were also production cooperatives, which produced goods for the wider market. If you had a share in them, you had a share in the profits – but also in the losses. There were many sectors in which cooperatives functioned, including bakeries, agricultural concerns and the manufacture of orthopaedic aids, to name but a few. The association gradually built up and expanded the network to include the General Cooperative Bank and the Czechoslovakian People's Insurance Company.

SOCIAL DEMOCRATIC POLITICS IN THE CZECHOSLOVAK REPUBLIC

With the creation of Czechoslovakia, the social democrats showed in practice what they had earlier claimed in theory. If there is democracy, then it is possible to demand one's rights by peaceful means, through elections. The social democrats' greatest electoral successes came in the early period of the Czechoslovak Republic. In the 1920 parliamentary elections the ČSDSD gained over 25 per cent of the vote nationwide. From today's point of view this may not seem like much, but during the whole of the First Republic no other party ever came within 10 per cent of this result. In the Czechoslovakia of the time there were, in fact, two parallel party systems, Czechoslovak and German. There were Czechoslovak and German social democratic parties, Czechoslovak and German agrarian parties and so on. If we recalculate the ČSDSD's 1920 election win in terms of Czechoslovak votes, it was over 37 per cent. By way of comparison, the German social democrats in the Czechoslovak Republic gained approximately 11 per cent of the vote, which meant over 43 per cent of the "German" vote.

The social democratic movement was badly damaged by internal splits and the creation of the Communist Party of Czechoslovakia (KSČ). In the 1925 elections the ČSDSD fell nationwide to less than 9 per cent, beaten not only by right-wing opponents from the Agrarian and People's Parties, but also by the KSČ. The most dramatic fall was in Slovakia. It was only in the second half of the 1920s that the ČSDSD started to grow again, stabilising at around 13 per cent; in other words in second place. In 1935 it was the third strongest party in the First Republic.

The party membership developed accordingly. Shortly before the First World War the ČSDSD had around 150,000 fully paid-up members, while the estimate of the total membership was around 240,000. The period of the creation of Czechoslovakia saw a sharp increase in interest in membership. Precise statistics were not kept during the tense years of 1918–1920, but there were an estimated 500,000 members. After the party split and the KSČ was formed, the social democrats were left with some 190,000 members. During the remainder of the First Republic the number grew again, until by the end of the 1930s it had reached 230,000 members.

The social democratic movement's internal turmoil in 1919–1921 was not specific to Czechoslovakia. The same thing was going in other social democratic parties during the same period. In all of them it ended in the same way, with the creation of communist parties alongside the social democrats. In some countries the new communist parties remained on the fringe (in Austria and Sweden, for example); while in others, such as Germany and France, they were as strong as or stronger than the social democratic parties. The Czechoslovak social democratic party was badly damaged by the split (see p. 296).

In September 1920 the government led by Vlastimil Tusar had to step down. The internal disagreements in the party escalated during the autumn, and the left of the party – the future communists – started to take over the party's buildings and to take the fight to the streets. The police intervened, people were injured and some even killed. In some parts of the country there were even local revolutions in December 1920. They ended as quickly as they started, but they had a long and drawn-out sequel, not so much for the state as for the social democratic party. The split had many twists and turns, and many of those who at first left for the KSČ ended up returning to the social democrats in the following years. Still, although the ČSDSD later became a powerful party once again, only gradually did it regain the strength that it had had in the early 1920s.

The ČSDSD was not the first social democratic government to share in

Social democrats in the ČSR	Communists in the ČSR
The path to the achievement of socialism has to be chosen in accordance with the conditions in each country, in this case the economically-advanced Czechoslovakia	A universal approach based on the experience of the October revolution and Soviet Russia; expectations of world revolution
Gradual socialisation using various forms; reform approach	Massive and immediate socialisation in the form of nationalisation; social tensions need to be escalated
Parliamentary democracy, with certain elements of direct democracy	Parliament is meant to serve only as a tribune, with power to be taken over by workers' and military councils... and then see what happens next
In a situation of a 'balance of class forces' there has to be a coalition government with non-socialist parties	No government with non-socialist parties, indeed no cooperation with them in general
International cooperation between socialist parties on the basis of the renewed Second International; shared experiences and coordination of approaches, but each party to be fully independent	National parties to be only branches of the International (Third International) directed from the centre... which as it happens was in Moscow; the leadership issues binding guidelines and parties must expel anyone who disagrees with the approach
In organisational terms a mass political party, in which the lower level delegates power to higher levels	Heavily centralised party organisation; as well legal organisations there have to be illegal organisations

Tbl. 1: Social democrats and communists in the ČSR

government power. In Belgium, Denmark and Sweden the social democrats had entered coalition governments during the First World War. The Czechoslovak social democrats were not only a governing party, however, but also the creators of a whole new political order and a key pillar of the new political system. A similar role was played by the social democrats in Germany and Austria.

For most of the First Republic the ČSDSD was a governing party (1918–1925, 1929–1938). Repeatedly and for a long time it held what we would now call the ministry of social affairs, the ministry of education, the ministry of transport (at that time mainly railways) and the ministry of justice. If we add the ministries that in the 1930s fell to the German social democrats as coalition partners, then the social democrats also ran the health ministry. For a shorter time the ČSDSD ministers also ran further ministries, such as the ministry of public works (in charge, for example, of urban planning, but also mining) and the ministry of supply.

The social democrats were also the main driving force behind projects such as the new system of health, invalidity and old age insurance, land reform, the eight-hour working day, the 32-hour minimum weekend, unemployment insurance (the Ghent system), safety at work, a number of educational reforms (including the coeducation of boys ad girls, parents' associations and courses for the unemployed) and the creation of a modern civil code. In the 1930s this was intertwined with an attempt to deal with the Great Depression and its mass unemployment.

It is true that opposition from other parties meant that these projects went through in forms less ambitious than the social democrats had originally intended. The proposal for unemployment insurance, for example, passed with a lower level of compulsory payments than was the case in the former Austro-Hungary; accident insurance did not cover employees in services and agriculture; old-age pensions were granted only if pensioners did not do any work at all; and so on. In a similar vein, land reform did not go as far as the Social Democrats had planned and private farmers were given preference over cooperatives. Not even the proposed civil code corresponded to the original aim because it did not cover collective agreements, not to mention family law.

It should also be mentioned that some of the social democrats' proposals did not succeed at all, for example the proposal for a minimum wage or for a law on the recultivation of mining areas. In addition, many of the proposals for dealing with the economic crisis – such as state labour exchanges (the predecessors of today's Labour Offices), the relaxation of monetary policy and the creation of state organisations to support export and state investment projects – came late and in a weaker form than had been proposed, and so their effect started to be seen later, or more diluted, than had been expected.

The social democrats also managed to successfully govern municipalities, in particular in larger cities. Some cities during the First Republic had no mayors other than social democrat ones (such as Plzeň, Moravská Ostrava, Kladno and Znojmo). Other larger cities were administered by the social democrats only for a time (such as Olomouc, Brno and, if we count the German social democrats, Ústí nad Labem). In other cases they shared in the administration for many years, but did not manage to het a social democrat elected mayor (for example, Prague, Hradec Králové). In their work at the local level they showed in practice how effective the public ownership of companies could be, what a well-thought-out regulatory plan could achieve and what social housing meant.

We should also not forget that during the First Republic some functions that are today performed by the state or, on the contrary, by private companies, were carried out by special public organisations. So, for example, health and social insurance were administered by health and social insurance organisations set up on the principle of self-administration. The state monitored them, but the administration was carried out by the insurance organisations themselves, and those insured were represented in them. Unemployment support was also transferred to the insurance principle during the 1920s. Unions paid out benefits to their members partly from funds provided by the state. The social democrats were extremely active in all these organisations, which was perfectly logical: ČSDSD members were often also union members, and many social democrat deputies were also chairmen of the various trade union organisations. For many years the unions supplemented the functions of the state, providing their members with insurance through their own efforts, and their employees were professionally equipped to organise insurance operations. Finally, the First Republic differed from today's republic in that political parties had mass membership and did not limit themselves to purely political activities. This was particularly visible in the case of the social democrats. The ČSDSD owned a number of buildings that it made available to the public as community spaces (conference halls and restaurants, to a lesser extent cinemas, gyms and libraries).

The party's publishing house issued not only newspapers and theoretical literature, but also entertaining reading, including the classic works of Victor Hugo and Charles Dickens, as well as Burroughs' Tarzan novels or the detective fiction of Van Dine. More demanding readers could go for George Orwell's debut *Down and Out in Paris and London* or Gabriel Garcia Lorca's poetry. The ČSDSD also organised a whole range of interest and hobby associations. Within the party framework it was possible to enjoy cut-price railway travel, go skiing, join an amateur theatre group or choir, stay at a hiking chalet, attend sexology lectures or listen to the radio together (radio was a relatively new medium and sets were not readily available to the less well-off).

During the Austro-Hungary era this model had been a way of shielding oneself from the power of the state and at the same time against the exclusion of social democratic party members and supporters from social life. It is almost possible to talk about a parallel society or way of life. After the creation of the Czechoslovak Republic, the originally defensive function of this network of associations took something of a back seat, and they started to play a greater role as islands of exemplary behaviour which would be gradually enlarged. Both before and after the creation of the Czechoslovak Republic, however, these associations had one common feature: whatever people did not manage to get through public institutions, the ČSDSD tried to ensure for them through its own resources. In doing so, it was thinking both of their needs and of the spreading of its ideas.

SOCIAL DEMOCRATS ON THE INTERNATIONAL SCENE

The social democrats had been active on the international scene long before the creation of Czechoslovakia. Since the nineteenth century the ČSDSD had been part of the Second International, which united social democratic parties across Europe, later across the world. Two echoes of this can still be found in the Czech calendar in the form of 1 May as Labour Day and 8 March as International Women's Day. After the First World War the social democrats became involved in the renewal of the International.

The ČSDSD regularly hosted socialists from other countries at its congresses. In addition to representatives of the large parties from Germany, the United Kingdom, Austria, the Netherlands, Belgium, the Scandinavian lands and Spain, they included guests from smaller parties, often parties that were not allowed to operate legally in their own countries. Speeches at the ČSDSD congress were one of the few ways in which they could let the world know what was going on in their countries. And so the congresses featured speeches by Hungarian social democrats, Romanian social democrats and Polish socialists, all of whom were persecuted by authoritarian right-wing regimes. There were also the Ukrainian radical socialists, the Russian socialists-revolutionaries (SRs) and the Russian social democrats, the Latvian social democrats and the Georgian social democrats, who had been subjugated by Soviet Russia.

There was also close cooperation with social democrats of other nationalities within Czechoslovakia. First and foremost this included the Czech and German social democrats, although it was a relatively long time before the two parties found common ground, a point we shall return to in more detail later. In addition, there was cooperation with the Polish social democrats, who were active in the Těšín area, and with the Zionist movement Poale Sion, which was close to the social democrats; Poale Sion deputies were guests in the social democrat deputies' club.

The ČSDSD's foreign political programme corresponded to the Czechoslovak Republic's foreign policy. The social democrats preferred the peaceful ordering of international relations and international disarmament. They focused on the idea of collective security and the functioning of the United Nations, and they rejected military intervention in Soviet Russia, as well as the attempts by the Habsburgs to return to the throne in some countries of central Europe. It was above all due to the social democrats that Czechoslovakia as a state took an active part in the creation and functioning of what is now the International Labour Organization (ILO). The ILO was created in 1919, as part of the newly-founded League of Nations. Its purpose was to monitor and recommend approaches to social policy. The subject of work actually formed a part of the peace treaties, and the relevant parts of the Versailles and Saint German treaties have lost nothing of their urgency.

It was thanks to the social democrats that the international congress of social policy took place in Prague in 1924, set up by the International Association for Social Progress (IASP, IVSF). It was an umbrella association for a wide spectrum of state and non-state organisations and individuals engaged in developing a social policy agenda, ministries of social affairs, municipal councillors, social insurance organisations, employee and employer associations and individual progressive employers, academic organisations and individual academics.

The social democrats set their sights still higher, however. They called for the democratisation of the League of Nations, so that the organisation could become a real joining of nations, not just of the governments of member states. They recommended gradual decolonisation, even in the case of colonies that had belonged to the winning powers of the First World War (although at the same time it was possible to detect, in relation to the colonised nations, a slightly dismissive, paternalistic tone). As part of their attempts to achieve international disarmament they called for the nationalisation of weapons industries and their international control. Some social democratic currents aimed in the long term at Europe-wide integration on a democratic and socialist basis, the creation of a United States of Europe.

The social dimension of international cooperation was something that in any case the social democrats intended to continue to highlight. They wanted participation in negotiations on international trade treaties just by business people, but by trade union organisations and consumer associations. They demanded that workers be included in the ČSR's representation at the League of Nations and at international conferences. The social democrats also recommended that Czech diplomatic offices should have social attachés, who would be tasked above all with ensuring the labour rights of Czechoslovak workers abroad. Of all these things, however, only a very few came to pass, indeed almost nothing.

SOCIAL DEMOCRACY AND ISSUES OF NATIONALITY

In 1918 the fates of the Czech and Slovak social democrat movements came together for a while, as the Slovak part of the originally Hungarian social democratic party joined the ČSDSD. They were later joined by the Hungarian-German social democrats in Slovakia, who had also originally belonged to the Hungarian social democrats. The ČSDSD's membership in Slovakia was not large, however. Being a social democrat in the Czech lands meant something different from being one in Slovakia: whereas in the Czech lands and Moravia the social democrats were largely a movement of industrial workers, in Slovakia their backbone consisted of state employees. In the Czech lands the ČSDSD's profile was highest in social policy, while in Slovakia there was a greater emphasis on education and cultural policy.

The social democrats were the bearers not only of socialist thought, but also of the idea of "Czechoslovakism", the notion that Czechs and Slovaks form two related branches of a single nation, the nation-state of the ČSR. This was based on a simple conjecture: Slovakia was a largely agricultural country, in which the church had a major influence and there were also major social expectations; if they were not a firm part of Czechoslovakia, they would either create a reactionary regime on the basis of simple slogans, or a communist dictatorship. And then Slovakia would sooner or later be swallowed up by Hungary, something which still had its supporters in Slovakia. The Czechoslovak unit was best equipped to maintain the idea of a single Czechoslovak nation, the social democrats believed. The ČSDSD thus repeatedly held ministries designed for the special administration of Slovakia, and for the gradual unification of the laws and rules in the Czech lands and Slovakia.

The ČSDSD was thus always seen in Slovakia as a governing party, a party of the ruling order, even when it was in opposition. Its nationality programme was not so radical as to be able to compete with the reactionary (*Hlinka*) Slovak People's Party and its slogan of "autonomy". Furthermore, its social programme was not so radical as to be able to compete with the communists and their slogan of "social revolution" under the conditions then prevailing in Slovakia. The electoral results of the Czechoslovak social democrats were thus weaker in Slovakia than in the Czech lands.

An even greater long-term role was played by the question of the relationship between Czechs and Germans, however; or more precisely, between the Czechoslavonic branch of the social democratic movement – the Czechs originally emphasised joint Slavonic roots and from the nineteenth century their party was called "Czechoslavonic" – and its German-Austrian branch.

Until the late nineteenth and early twentieth centuries, there was a federation of Austrian social democratic parties that included the Austrian Germans, Czechs, Poles, Croatians, Slovenians and Italians. The federal Austrian social democratic movement was thus sometimes called the "little International". From the very beginning, however, this federal party was dominated by two "national" parties, the German-Austrian and the Czechoslavonic. The Czechoslavonic was the second strongest after the German-Austrian, especially after it started to build an independent organisational structure in the 1890s. During the early years of the 1920s the Czechoslavonic trade unions gradually separated from the Austria-wide unions, and the Czechoslavonic party then immediately split from the Austria-wide party.

The bone of contention was the national question. For the German-Austrian social democrats, national questions played a less fundamental role; for them, the main problem was social. The workers were faced by capitalists and their interests were fundamentally at odds. Language and culture were something they largely had in common, however. The issue of nationalities was seen as being derived from the social problem. It was assumed that as soon as social problems were solved, national ones would be solved more or less automatically.

Socialists from nations or nationalities that were not governing ones, or which were in a minority, saw things differently, however. Czech or Polish workers faced not only capitalists, but for the most part capitalists with different languages and cultures, as well as a state power with a different language. Under the heading of state power we may include not only the government, army, police and courts, but also a wide range of activities that may not be directly repressive, but if they take place in a language other than the native language it may cause significant problems, such as taking a parcel to the post office, going on the railway, registering a plot of land in the land register, the payment of damages in the event of an accident at work, not to mention schools and various cultural institutions.

The Czechoslavonic social democrats thus felt doubly oppressed: first for their social status, then for their nationality. Sometimes, as a result, they gave priority to language and cultural identity ahead of social issues. Or they demanded that social position and nationality should be considered at the same time. They emphasised the safeguarding of national minorities from the power of the majority, and generally promoted the decentralisation of the state. And regardless of anything else, they demanded that their language and cultural identity be respected by the pan-Austrian social democrats. In organisational matters regarding the social democrat party they gave priority to a federative or confederative model. They wished to see autonomy for the various national components of the Austrian-wide social democratic movement and restraint when it came to central coordination.

The Austro-German social democrats saw the matter differently, however, and in both the unions and party policy they pushed for a centralised model. German seemed to them to be the most suitable language for the socialist movement because everybody in Austria understood German, which was far from the case for Czech or Polish. And because social questions seemed to them to be the only important ones, it seemed logical to them that the whole party should be represented by a single leadership, in practice largely German.

Despite every attempt, the Czechoslavonic and Austro-German social democrats failed to reach agreement on the matter. The Czechoslovak social democrats were also often attacked from both sides. Their German-Austrian comrades accused them of succumbing to the influence of national chauvinism, splitting a movement that was united. A small part of the Czechoslavonic social democrats, who supported the policy of the German-Austrian party, even split off and created their own political party, which was meant to compete with its mother party (the "centralists").

The other Czech parties, on the other hand, accused the social democrats of betraying the nation. Here, too, a rival socialist party sprang up, the Czech National Social Party. In everyday affairs it had a number of goals that were similar to those of the social democrats, but while the social democrats defended the idea of social emancipation across the nations, the "national socialists" limited their efforts to the Czech nation. The "national socialists" claimed that the nation was one large family and that it was necessary to achieve harmony within it. To this the social democrats replied that such a family stuck together only until the chips were down and then it was always the poor who had to the make sacrifices. They said the national question was often only another way of hiding from those at the bottom the fact that someone was deliberately keeping them there.

After the creation of the Czechoslovak Republic, the roles changed in some ways. In the old Austria, the Germans had been in the majority and the Czechs in the minority, albeit a large one. Within the Czech lands, however, the Czechs had been in the majority and the Germans in the minority. Because Czechoslovakia had been created largely within the historical borders of the Czech lands, the Czechs were once again in the majority there, and the Germans in the minority – although again a large one. With the construction of the Czechoslovak nation, including both the Czechs and the Slovaks, the Germans became much more of a minority.

The now truly "Czechoslovak" social democrats supported the creation of the Czechoslovak Republic within its historical borders. The reason was not that they hankered after tradition and the age-old rights of the Czech kingdom. The Czechoslovak social democrats recognised the right of nations to self-determination, but added that this right was guaranteed to the great majority of Germans precisely because Germany and Austria existed. On the contrary, Czechs and Slovaks would be denied the right to self-determination if the Germans were to split away from the Czech lands and join

Germany or Austria. The new Czechoslovak state would then be practically incapable of life. For this reason a small number of Germans had to stay within other states, including in Czechoslovakia, but as a minority their position had to be firmly anchored. The path to this lay in enshrining minority rights directly in the constitution, and further by the language law of 1920, which had the status of a constitutional law.

Now, however, it was the German social democrats in the Czechoslovak Republic who called for issues of nationality to be dealt with as a matter of priority, who leaned towards the splitting off of predominantly German areas, and later at least to extensive administrative decentralisation of the ČSR. And this time it was the Germans, including the social democrats, who pointed out that national advantage was to be found in a number of everyday situations that were not covered by minority rights and the language law.

The result was that although the Czechoslovak and German social democrats in the ČSR had the chance to imprint on the country a more democratic and social character, they were unable to reach agreement on national questions and proceeded separately, sometimes even in conflict. It is, however, true, that over the course of the 1920s their positions grew closer. In 1928 there was even a joint congress of social democrats of all nationalities in Czechoslovakia. Czechoslovak and German social democrats had worked together in Czechoslovak governments in 1929–1938. They exerted no little effort on resolving the economic crisis. Together, and with a major effort, they helped refugees from Nazi Germany after 1933, and from Austrofascist Austria after 1934. Together they also tried to find a new way of organising the state that would allow Czech Germans to feel that Czechoslovakia was their state, while preserving its democratic character and its existing borders. Some Czechoslovak and German social democrats thus also started to draw the future of the Czechoslovak nation along civic, not ethnic lines; as a nation of whom Czechs, Slovaks and Germans would form an equal part. The chance for major change that opened up at the start of the 1920s never repeated itself, however, and attempts in the late 1930s were not destined to last for long.

WHAT STILL REMAINS ALIVE?

The Czech/Czechoslovak social democrats wished for a political democracy and an independent Czechoslovak state. They helped to build both and provided both with powerful support, not only in their emphasis on the need for a democratic approach if social democratic ideas were to put down firm roots in the conditions of central Europe. Democracy was not just a means to an end for them. Gradually they started to lean towards the conviction that democracy was one of the movement's ultimate aims. Or, to put it differently, that the same principles that were usually called "democracy" in the political arena were known as "socialism" in the economic one.

The policy of the social democrats was to satisfy the material interests of the social classes on which the ČSDSD leant – in terms of membership and electoral results, as well as symbolically – and in which at the same time they saw the backbone of the future society. This policy thus included sickness, invalidity and old age insurance, an eight-hour working week, days of rest from work, unemployment insurance, health and safety at work, the introduction of a minimum wage, state labour exchanges and so on. During the period in question, this policy thus served the interests above all of the workers in the population but not even at this time did this mean workers in the narrow sense of manual workers or even employees. It referred to a broad group of people who might be referred to as "people of work". The social structure of society and the character of work have changed since then (although in a number of directions far from what the social democrats would have liked). Some solutions of the time are still viable, others not.

More fundamental is the meaning of social democracy. Policies were designed to satisfy more than material interests and the immediate improvement of material conditions. They were meant to be a means of emancipating and liberating the individual. If you are forced to rely on long and exhausting work for a low wage, work that you are not in a position to lose or you will be plunged into poverty, then you will hardly have the energy and interest to follow public affairs, think about books or to put yourself into someone else's situation (such as a foreigner or someone with a rival opinion) in order to understand them. The social policy of social democracy was meant to free people in order to allow them to devote themselves to something other than work. Or rather, so that instead of working to survive, they could devote themselves to working for satisfaction, for some sort of social end or for themselves.

The social democrats focused on the organisation of production, not just on the redistribution of what was produced. This also applied to private companies through government regulation and the introduction of employee participation in decision-making, as well as with the aid of cooperative principles. Even at that time, however, they were less successful in this than in social policy. A factor in this was the ČSDSD's inability to assert themselves, something that applied to socialist parties in general. Similarly, the social democrats also found themselves lacking capable people and well-thought-out, concrete plans.

The ČSDSD was also a party with a cultural agenda in the broad sense of the word (for example, the position of women in the family and the labour market, coeducation in schools, public libraries and so on). In this it struggled with a lack of interest on the part of its members, indeed its voters; and it really was more of a lack of interest rather than any sort of self-aware cultural conservatism of the sort that its bearers might even have been proud of. For the culturally-liberal parts of society, on the other hand, the ČSDSD was too strongly fixed in their minds as the party making economic demands on behalf of the workers.

As can be seen, the situation in today's social democracy is not too different in terms of the problems it faces. The clearest difference is in terms of will. Once again, there is no need to hark back to the specific themes of that period or to their solutions. What is important is not to lose sight of its basic direction. In other words, social democracy did not want to stop at the gates of factories, schools or houses; it wanted the democratic principles of equality, justice and freedom to permeate social relations in general.

Finally, the social democrats well understood that social democratic politics may be based in sovereign states, but it should not close itself off within their boundaries. As one of the then leaders of the ČSDSD said, a few years ago social democrats of all parties had been attacked as guilty of treachery to the nation and high treason to the state, and now suddenly the things they supported were being laid down in international treaties. Indeed, in connection with the peace treaties of 1919–1920 we should once again clearly point out that they not only created new states, but included social concords that are still valid today. They created not only the League of Nations, but the International Labour Organization.

On this particular point, the social democratic position towards the nation as a category is also important. National identity was and is extremely important, but this identity is not something given once and for all, it is something people create. The Czech/Czechoslovak social democrats showed this well in relation to the subject of Czech–German relations, the search for a common "state nation" of Czechoslovakia and a social agenda as the basis of cooperation. It was a long and painful process and during the First Republic it was not crowned with success. But the social democrats at least started out along that path.

CONCLUSION

Czechoslovakia was created a hundred years ago, and much has changed since then. The Czech Republic's official state public holiday is still 28 October, however, both in fact and symbolically. The Czech Republic feels in many ways that it is the continuation of the Czechoslovak Republic. The story of the First Republic (1918–1938) may, in this context, be read as the story of the first major attempt to bring the social democratic idea into practice. At the same time, it may be seen as the story of unfulfilled visions, both for Czech policy and for social democracy as a world movement.

SUMMARY

Czech social democracy, as an ideological current, broad social movement and political party (ČSDSD) was formed in the last third of the nineteenth century. It developed along similar lines to social democratic movements in the other industrialised countries of central and western Europe. During the First World War, the Social Democrats abandoned their original aim of the democratic transformation of Austro-Hungary in favour of the creation of an independent democratic state, the Czechoslovak Republic (ČSR). They made a significant contribution not only to the creation and stabilisation of the ČSR, but during the whole period of its existence they provided it with firm support, even in the face of the decision by one wing of the party to split off and form the Communist Party, which then competed fiercely with the Social Democrats.

Social democratic ideas on political democracy played a significant role in shaping the constitutional order of the new state, and for most of the period from 1918 to 1938 the Social Democrats were participants in coalition governments. The party was the driving force behind projects such as the new system of sickness, invalidity and old age insurance and pensions, land reform, the eight-hour working day, days off, unemployment insurance, health and safety at work, a number of education reforms and the introduction of a modern civil code. In the 1930s this developed into an attempt to cope with the Great Depression and its mass unemployment. The Social Democrats also exerted influence through their strong representation at regional and municipal level and their broad base resulting from cooperative enterprises and the unions.

The ambitions of the social democratic movement were greater than this, however. They wanted democracy to penetrate economic relationships, or more precisely, the sphere of production, as well as social relationships in general. In this, however, the ČSDSD was not as successful as it had hoped; its policy was realised only in certain areas or for short periods of time. The Social Democrats also believed that while social democratic policy should issue from sovereign states, it should not be confined to their borders. Still, although the movement undertook more international activities than any other political force in the ČSR, here, too, it was more a question of beginnings and unrealised visions.

The complicated relations between minorities in the ČSR, which were the legacy of previous historical developments, at first hindered cooperation between social democratic currents, especially the Czech/Czechoslovak and the German ones. Attempts to find common solutions gradually grew stronger, however, and by the end of the 1920s the German Social Democrats in the ČSR had become a governing party. At the same time there were increasing attempts to find a new order that would allow Czech Germans to see Czechoslovakia as "their own" state, while preserving its democratic character and its existing borders. The opportunity to impose more of a social democratic imprint on the ČSR that existed in the early 1920s was not to be repeated in later years.

The Czechoslovak Republic of 1938 to 1938 represents the first major attempt in the Czech lands to implement social democratic ideas in practice. It is an attempt that is still inspirational today, both where it succeeded and where it remained unfulfilled.

THE ROLE OF SLOVAK SOCIAL DEMOCRACY IN THE FORMATION OF THE FIRST CZECHOSLOVAK REPUBLIC (ČSR)

ZUZANA POLÁČKOVÁ

THE RISE OF THE SLOVAK SOCIAL DEMOCRATIC MOVEMENT AND THE NATIONALITY ISSUE

The social democratic movement in Slovakia took shape gradually during the second half of the nineteenth century in a particular social and economic context. The territory of the present-day Slovakia – known as "Upper Hungary" at the time – was part of the Kingdom of Hungary. Upper Hungary was a rural country dominated by agricultural production and only a fledgling industry. Most of its Slovak inhabitants worked as seasonal labourers in agriculture or as vegetable merchants, day labourers, masons, travelling tinkers or craftsmen, servants or bonded labourers. Many people left to find work in the Monarchy's capitals Vienna and Budapest. A large number of Slovaks emigrated to the United States and Latin America, mainly Argentina and Brazil. Between 1880 and 1919, nearly 600,000 out of the total Slovak population of less than 2 million emigrated.

Although the 1867 Austro-Hungarian Compromise meant liberalisation, partial democratisation of social life and strengthening of the rule of law, it also brought increased Hungarian oppression. The new social reality was also reflected in the workers' movement in Hungary. In addition to economic and social hardships, Slovak society was confronted with Magyarisation efforts on the part of the Hungarian elite, which complicated the development of national self-consciousness and building a modern Slovak nation. The pace of modernisation of Slovak society was therefore slower, with social and national issues intertwined.

The language and ethnicity issue thus became the main impediment to the formation of a unified socialist political entity in Hungary, and also hindered effective integration of the Slovak workers' movement into the all-Hungarian one. Because of Slovakia's lagging industrialisation, the Slovak workers' movement was correspondingly weaker and unable to assert itself more vigorously in the all-Hungarian socialist movement. The gradual industrialisation of Upper Hungary in the second half of the nineteenth century, however, brought an increase in the number of workers, who soon started to organise themselves politically. The first association of workers on Slovak soil worth noting was *Napred/Vorwärts/Elõre* founded in the trilingual city of Pressburg/Bratislava/Pozsony. The worker population in this relatively industrialised city was ethnically mixed, made up of Germans, Hungarians and Slovaks. Bratislava's rapid economic growth also attracted workers from Vienna and Budapest. The *Napred* association and its members thus came in contact with the international workers' movement and its ideas. After the Austro-Hungarian Compromise in 1867, Budapest became the centre of the workers' movement in Hungary and the Social Democratic Party in the Kingdom of Hungary was formed there in 1890. The birth of a strong socialist party in Hungary, which also included members of the Bratislava *Napred* association, contributed to strengthening the Slovak workers' movement, the consolidation of its organisational structure and trade union organisation. In Budapest, Slovak socialists established contacts also with the representatives of Czech workers, jointly publishing the journals *Nová doba* and *Zora*. In response to the growing organisational base of the workers' movement in Hungary and to industrial and agricultural strikes, the government resorted to persecution and Slovak workers' representatives had to leave Budapest. Thus, in the early years of the twentieth century, an important change took place in the organisation of the workers' movement in Hungary as Bratislava's significance rose as the centre of the Slovak workers' movement.

Importance of Bratislava for the Development of the Slovak Social Democratic Movement

In the early years of the twentieth century, the centre of gravity of the organised Slovak workers' movement started to shift from Budapest to Bratislava. The multicultural Bratislava of that period was a small metropolis that maintained lively cultural, political and economic contacts with neighbouring Vienna. It lay at the crossroads of three ethnolinguistic regions: German, Hungarian and Slovak. The predominant element in the social and economic fabric of the city was its traditionally German-speaking population; around 1900, however, the influence of its Hungarian-speaking inhabitants and of Slovaks from the surrounding areas, working in the city, was growing. Bratislava was able to preserve its cosmopolitan character even during the strong Magyarisation campaign. Hungarians dominated Bratislava politically, Germans and Jews economically, while Slovaks constituted the bulk of the working class. The social democratic movement in Bratislava became the second most important in Hungary, after Budapest.[1] Hungarian government elites were increasingly concerned about the rising influence of Vienna's more advanced social democratic movement and the increasing impact of the idea of Czechoslavonic mutuality on the workers' movement in Bratislava.[2] According to Hungarian statistics of 1910 (notoriously biased and exaggerating the number of inhabitants of Hungarian ethnicity in the Kingdom of Hungary), Germans and Jews represented 42 per cent, Hungarians 40 per cent and Slovaks 15 per cent of the 80,000 people who lived in Bratislava. It was in this tumultuous period that young worker Emanuel Lehocký became active in the Social Democratic Party and played an important role in setting up of the first Slovak social democratic organisations in Bratislava and its vicinity in the period 1902–1903.

After *Nová doba* and *Zora* ceased publication he set out, together with Štefan Martinček, Ján Pocisk and Ferdinand Benda, to launch a socialist-oriented Slovak-language periodical. They openly stated at the ninth congress of Hungarian Social Democrats in 1902 that the party's success was jeopardised by the lack of organisation of non-Hungarian workers. According to the leaders of the Social Democratic Party in the Kingdom of Hungary, however, there was no need for individual national factions to have a press organ in their own language.

The Rise of Autonomous Slovak Social Democracy and the Launch of *Robotnícke Noviny*

The breakthrough occurred at the eleventh congress of Hungarian Social Democrats in 1904, at which the Slovak delegation formed a central committee of the Slovak workers' organisation, with Lehocký as chairman. The most important task the committee had to tackle early on was to secure funding to issue a periodical. They asked social democratic organisations in Vienna, Bratislava and Budapest for help, but without success. In the end, the central committee received financial support from the regional secretariat of the Czechoslavonic Social Democratic Party for Lower Austria, and was thus able to start publishing *Slovenské robotnícke noviny* (Slovak Workers' News), which hit the streets of Bratislava on 1 October 1904 in two thousand copies. Its key topics were universal suffrage in Hungary and nationality issues. Rather than being narrowly focused on the working class, it gave considerable space also to cultural and language issues. The paper's success encouraged the central committee to take another decisive step, organisational independence. Slovak socialists were inspired by the example of Czechoslavonic social democrats, an important vanguard of the Czech struggle for equal status as a nation. On 11–12 June 1905, Slovak social democrats held their constitutive congress in Bratislava with the participation of 44 delegates. In his keynote address Lehocký challenged the party leadership's policy of centralism and assimilation. To support his arguments, he referred to the Austrian Social Democratic Party, which respected national factions. Slovak social democrats were able to preserve their independent status for less than a year, however. Due to organisational shortcomings and financial problems caused largely by the Budapest leadership of the party, they had to rejoin the social democratic party of Hungary in March 1906.

Vienna – Mediator of Democracy and of Czechoslovak Cooperation

In the run up to the First World War, Lehocký and other Slovak socialists concentrated mainly on organisational matters. In *Robotnícke noviny* they explained the importance of fighting for universal suffrage, encouraged contacts with Czech socialists, helped mobilise and organise workers also outside major industrial centres and passed on information about strikes and their brutal suppression. The hegemony of the Budapest leadership in Bratislava was weakened under the influence of the Czechoslavonic Social Democratic Party (the ČSS) and the Austrian Social Democratic Party in Vienna. Slovak social democrats took as their model the German social democratic movement in Bratislava, which proved able to resist Magyarisation. There were also Slovak social democrats among the members of the Czechoslavonic Social Democratic Party (ČSS) in Vienna. The party was in close contact with and provided political and financial support to social democrats in nearby Bratislava. Solid foundations were laid for strengthening Czechoslovak mutuality in the cultural and political spheres.

The idea of Czechoslovak mutuality was shifting to the political level, taking the form of cooperation between the various political parties of the Austrian and Hungarian parts of the monarchy. Important visitors to Bratislava included such representatives of the Vienna workers' movement as Andreas Scheu and Eduard Niemczyk, a close friend of Karl Liebknecht. The geographical proximity between Vienna and Bratislava favoured cooperation. The ČSS provided ideological and financial support to the Slovak social democrats' drive for independence in 1905. Antonín Němec, the ideological leader of the party, which he also represented in the Austrian Imperial Council and in the Second International, arrived in Bratislava on 10 June 1905, on the eve of the constitutive congress of Slovak social democrats. His speech "The Substance and Development of Social Democracy and its Importance for Slovak Workers" made it clear that cooperation with the Slovaks was aimed not only at strengthening Czechoslavonic mutuality, but also at fostering the idea of a united Czechoslovak nation. Czechoslavonic social democratic representatives viewed this idea also in its political context, as a way of strengthening their base in Austria and helping them to fend off the allegations made especially by the Russian members of the Second International that they lacked a spirit of internationalism. With the financial assistance of Vienna-based Czech social democrats, Lehocký was able to launch *Slovenské robotnícke noviny* in Bratislava in 1904. In Vienna, Slovak workers Vojtech Lojdl, Jozef Jamriška and Jozef Pajger founded the associations "Slovenská vzdelávacia beseda" and "Dispozičná a tlačová základňa triedne uvedomelého dělníctva slovanského" in 1901 and 1903, respectively. Slovak social democrats held their first congress on 11–12 June 1905 in Bratislava at the Petöfi Court on Dunajská Street. Among its participants were Antonín Němec from Vienna and Karel Světlík who represented the Social Democratic Party for Lower Austria. The 1905 Russian revolution had a marked impact also on the workers' movement in Slovakia and in the whole of Hungary. It was reflected not only in a widespread strike movement that took on the character of a political struggle (especially because of the call for universal suffrage), but also in workers' strengthened class consciousness, socialist ideas and the expansion of workers' organisation in trade unions. The year 1912 saw also the creation of a Slovak section of the ČSS in Vienna.

Slovak Social Democracy before the War and Its Struggle for Democracy and National Autonomy at the Fourth Congress

Its unsuccessful struggle for voting rights in Hungary (pursuant to Article 5/1848 and its amendments, only around 6 per cent of the population had the right to vote) and the growing Hungarian oppression after 1907 led the social democratic party to fall into passivity. Not long before the outbreak of the First World War, Slovak social democrats in Bratislava stepped up their campaign for universal suffrage among the working population. In May 1912, they initiated the formation of a canvassing committee that played an important part in the organisation of retaliatory demonstrations and workers' rallies in Bratislava, Žilina, Košice and Trenčín, called in response to the bloody suppression of the 23 May 1912 general strike in Budapest. To be able to fight against growing expenditure on armaments and conduct a universal suffrage campaign, social democrats needed to cooperate more closely with other Slovak political parties. They held their fourth congress on 12–13 April 1914 in Bratislava. Lehocký focused his keynote speech on the issue of nationality and the need to address it both within the workers' movement and at the national level. He stated that the ultimate goal was to achieve democracy and autonomy. He recommended a federal arrangement not only for Hungarian social democracy but for the entire monarchy. In closing, he denounced the state's Magyarisation policy and criticised Hungarian social democrats for condoning it. The congress demanded equal status for all national sections in the party and all nations in the monarchy. Because, just as the war began, the government of Hungary paralysed political life in the country, Slovak social democratic leaders focused their efforts on saving and continuing to issue *Robotnícke noviny*.

The First World War and Its Impact on Slovak Social Democracy

The outbreak of the First World War in 1914 polarised and demoralised the European socialist movement. The ideas of socialist internationalism confronted defence of the state and national interests. Although the Second International called on all workers to organise anti-war demonstrations when the war began in 1914, the leaders of German, Austrian and Hungarian social democratic parties voted in parliament to give full support to their governments in seeking war loans. *Robotnícke noviny* protested the war shortly after the Sarajevo assassination of 28 June 1914 and wrote prophetically: "the catastrophic warmongering policy endangers the very existence of the Austro-Hungarian Empire whose dire state makes it necessary for social democrats to protect it from the stupidity and dullness, insolence and impotence of the ruling elites".[3] Thus, even though social democrats in small nations of the Austrian and Hungarian parts of the monarchy did not immediately and unconditionally support Hungarian and Austrian social democrats, they did not have the courage to oppose government policies in the tense situation later in 1914. On 22 October 1914, *Robotnícke noviny* published the following appeal on the part of Slovakia's social democrats to the membership base: "at this time of war, the aspirations of the working class must yield before the strong determination of the state to defeat and destroy the state of the enemy. ... naturally, the working class must also aim at the victory of the state they live in, the state that gives them the opportunity to develop and to work". An anti-war mood was evident in Slovakia as soon as the war started, as evidenced by numerous court proceedings and prisons filled with ordinary citizens and engaged politicians and journalists who publicly spoke out against the war and its consequences. At that time, the Slovak social democratic party withdrew into passivity, while outwardly declaring loyalty to the Hungarian government.[4] The war also prevented the functioning of trade unions because most of their members had enlisted in the army.

Activation of Slovak Social Democrats under the Impact of the Russian Revolutions in 1917

In the course of 1917, Slovak social democrats started to enter public and political life more actively and deepened their cooperation with the Czech social democrats. The revolution of February 1917 toppled the Russian Tsar and led to the formation of a provisional government. These events, and the form of the February Revolution itself, also affected the situation in Austria-Hungary, manifested in numerous strikes and hunger demonstrations. The starving war-decimated population was becoming radicalised and 14 strikes were held in Slovakia in 1917 alone.[5] The Social Democratic

Party in the Kingdom of Hungary called a general strike in January 1918 to support the Brest-Litovsk peace, and 40 strikes were held in all major Slovak towns. These strikes significantly weakened the war-stricken economy of the Monarchy. The army was rocked by revolts and desertions incited by returnees from Russian captivity.[6] Slovak social democrats needed some time to really understand the revolutionary developments in Russia. This is evident from articles in *Robotnícke noviny*, alternated between positive and negative assessments of events. At first, the social democratic movement was impressed by revolutionary slogans demanding national self-determination and peace without annexations. Social democratic positions on the Russian revolution were influenced by the Czech social democrats and by articles by Karl Kautsky, whose criticisms of the October Revolution were taken seriously by the Slovak social democratic leadership. Information about the US President Wilson's initiative and his Fourteen Points stressing the right of nations to self-determination and the importance of a post-war peace settlement, also found its way to the social democratic movement. Its representatives viewed both initiatives in a more or less positive light, considering them a sign of the early cessation of the conflict. They realised that a separate Brest-Litovsk Peace Treaty between Russia and Germany would quash their hopes for the demise of Austria-Hungary, and would prevent the nations of the monarchy from asserting their right of self-determination.[7] Internal tensions started to increase gradually also within the Social Democratic Party in the Kingdom of Hungary. Its leaders were not willing to soften their position concerning the exclusively Hungarian leadership of the party. Social democrats representing non-Magyar nations in Hungary were outraged by the exclusion of their political and trade unions leaders from decision-making inside the party and in the trade unions.[8] This came clearly to light in the preparations for the Stockholm congress of the Second International in the summer of 1917. In the absence of the representatives of non-Magyar nations at the congress, Hungarian social democratic representatives contested the right of national self-determination and called for the preservation of a united Hungary. Their call was challenged by the delegation of the Czechoslavonic Social Democratic Party of Workers which demanded that the Kingdom of Hungary be transformed into a federation of equal nation-states. Moreover, it called for the unification of the Czech and Slovak nations.[9] From then on, the idea of a united

Czechoslovak nation underpinned cooperation between Slovak and Czech social democrats.

SLOVAK SOCIAL DEMOCRACY AND ITS ROLE IN THE FORMATION OF THE CZECHOSLOVAK STATE IN 1918

Strengthened Cooperation between Czech and Slovak Social Democrats

In the post-Stockholm period, Hungarian social democratic leaders partly modified their approach to the Slovak section and offered Lehocký a place in the delegation to the upcoming congress of the Second International, with a proviso that he would defend the integrity of Hungary and the preservation of the Austro-Hungarian Empire. Lehocký decided to consult on his participation in the next Second International congress with František Tomášek of the ČSS for Lower Austria, a leading representative of Czech and Slovak minorities in Vienna and deputy of the Imperial Council.[10] At their meeting in Hainburg, they agreed that Slovak social democrats would not be part of the Hungarian delegation and that they would refuse to support the preservation of the Austro-Hungarian Empire. They also agreed to work towards building a state union of Czechs and Slovaks. Because of the growing controversy with their Hungarian counterparts in the Hungarian Social Democratic Party, Slovak social democrats strengthened their cooperation with Czech social democrats and in this way with the Czechoslovak national liberation movement. The new leadership of Czech social democrats entered into closer cooperation with the Czechoslovak resistance abroad. In parallel, Slovak social democrats renewed their cooperation with the Slovak national liberation camp. The first to respond to their offer for cooperation was Vavro Šrobár who had been cooperating intensively with the Czech resistance at home and abroad from the beginning of the First World War. *Robotnícke noviny* started to publish his articles, in which he condemned the passivity of the Slovak National Party and its policy towards the Hungarian government. Lehocký in his articles also denounced Slovak parochialism, writing: "for God's sake, let's learn something from our history and from what's going on in Europe. May democratic equality, social justice and self-determination rights become our motto!"[11]

Cooperation between Social Democrats and the Slovak Political Camp and Its Role in the Creation of a Common State of Czechs and Slovaks

The Hungarian Social Democratic Party's efforts at safeguarding its integrity and obstructing the unification endeavours of Czech and Slovak social democrats reached its peak in the first half of 1918. The Slovak National Party (SNS) – the key representative of the Slovak nation – remained passive until the spring of 1918. Its position on Tsarist Russia was decisively shattered only by the revolutions of February and October. Slovak social democrats challenged the SNS as early as 1914 when, somewhat unscrupulously, they harshly condemned its policy vis-à-vis Austria and Russia. Later on, however, Lehocký joined the initiative of Matúš Dula and Slovak social democrats participated in the creation of the Slovak National Council (SNR) as a nationwide representative body in 1914 in Budapest. All through the war, the SNR remained practically inactive. The same goes for Slovak political currents that had emerged before the war (such as the *Hlas* or the *Prúd*) and did not manage to re-assemble and take action during the war. The ensuing political vacuum on the Slovak political scene opened up room for cooperation between progressive Slovak political forces and social democrats and for creating a platform for the self-determination struggle fought together with domestic and foreign Czech resistance in pursuit of creating a common state of Czechs and Slovaks. The Slovak social democratic party thus became a major player on the domestic political scene during and especially towards the end of the war. This is evident from a number of articles written by conservative politicians.[12] Cooperation between political entities had its limitations, however. In their contacts with political Catholicism and the Slovak People's Party (the SĽS) as its political representative, social democrats had to abide by the limits given by the SĽS' religious stance, which was in conflict with their socialist and liberal secularism. The SĽS considered the workers' movement to be its ideological enemy and socialism an "immoral, Jewish scheme". Among the movements and currents constituting the Slovak political spectrum before and after the First World War, Slovak social democrats were clearly the closest to those representing the liberal current. Their ensuing cooperation led to a call for recognition of the Slovak nation's right to self-determination in a common state with the Czechs.

The first public manifestation of their endeavours was the May Day celebration in Liptovský Mikuláš. The event, organised by Slovak social democrats, drew massive participation from factory workers and other inhabitants of the town and the surrounding areas. Among the speakers was Vavro Šrobár, an active proponent of the idea of a common state of Czechs and Slovaks, and collaborator of leading Slovak and Czech politicians in Vienna and Prague. He drew up a resolution on self-determination of the Hungarian arm of the Czechoslovak community, namely the Slovak nation, the full text of which was published in *Robotnícke noviny*. The Czech press then disseminated the content of the resolution throughout the world, presenting it as proof of the Slovaks' desire to leave Hungary and form a common state with the Czechs. The Mikuláš resolution sent waves through the entire Slovak political camp, prompting the SNS to convene a confidential meeting in Martin on 24 May 1918. At the meeting, the SNS instructed its chairman Matúš Dula to establish contact with the social democrats. The discussion led to the adoption of a resolution whereby the SNS stated its firm support for the right of the Slovak nation to self-determination and for the creation of a common state with the Czech lands, Moravia and Silesia. The Mikuláš resolution greatly increased the prestige of the social democratic party, which became a state-building element. A prominent Slovak politician of European renown, Milan Hodža, wrote about the Mikuláš resolution: "Slovak socialists demonstrated their political maturity ... as well as their commitment to the struggle for the rights of people of Slovak nationality."

During the remaining months of the war, Slovak social democrats closely cooperated with the SNS in setting up the Slovak National Council (the SNR) – the representative body of the Slovak nation and a common platform for Slovak political entities – aware of their important role in the process of building a new state. Social democrats had three members in the SNR (Adolf Horváth, Ján Maršálko and Emanuel Lehocký); Lehocký was appointed a member of its Executive Committee.

Creation of the ČSR and the Declaration of the Slovak Nation

Although Slovak political representatives had their own ideas about Slovakia's independent status and the degree of its autonomy in the new state that came into being on 28 August 1918 in Prague, they accepted the idea of Czechoslovak national unity and conformed to the centralistic model of the new state. On 30 October 1918, the Slovak National Council (SNR) adopted the Martin Declaration proclaiming allegiance to the united Czechoslovak nation, for which it demanded unlimited self-determination right on the basis of total autonomy.[13] Ivan Dérer, by that time already a sympathiser with social democracy (he joined the party only in August 1919), who came to the meeting from Vienna, conveyed the position of the Czech delegation, which called for the creation of a common state.[14] As a member of the SNR, Dérer brought the Martin Declaration to Prague. Lehocký, who took the floor after Dérer, stressed the need to work together in building a Slovak national political bloc and the importance of the workers' movement in that bloc.

Creation of the United Czechoslovak Social Democratic Party of Workers and Institutionalisation of Social Legislation

After they withdrew from the all-Hungarian party at the beginning of December 1918, Slovak social democrats convened a congress on 25 December 1918 in Liptovský Mikuláš. Prominent speakers at the congress included Lehocký, Korman, Benda, Pocisk and Horváth. All of them expressed support for the Martin Declaration and subscribed to the idea of Czechoslovak national and state unity. The congress sent a 25-member Slovak delegation to the unifying Twelfth Congress of the ČSSDSR in Prague. After unification, the Slovak Social Democratic Party was governed by the Bratislava-based Country Executive Committee of the Czechoslovak Social Democratic Party in Slovakia, directly reporting to the Prague headquarters. The attempt to use the congress to unite all socialist parties and movements of the new state failed because of the opposition of minority socialist parties. The congress issued a call to urgently introduce social reforms and democratic procedures in administration and legislation, as well as the disbanding of the army and the establishment of armed militias, the expeditious adoption of the constitution and electoral law and expropriation of large estates, mines and industrial enterprises. It also called for the secularisation of education and separation of church and state. Shortly after the war, the Social Welfare Ministry led by social democrat Lev Winter (his ministry followed up on the activity of a Vienna institution created in 1917) issued several laws on social policy. The Ministry's remit included care for widows, orphans, war victims, disabled persons, rental flats, the unemployed and job mediation services. A set of laws passed in 1920 regulated works councils and coal field councils in mining and metallurgy, and miners' share in net profits. A law on arbitration courts was adopted to deal with the situation in heavy industry. The Czechoslovak Republic enacted an eight-hour workday in 1918, the second state to adopt such a measure, after Austria. Also adopted in 1918 were the unemployment support system, the tenant protection act and the child protection act. The situation of agricultural labourers in Slovakia and their relationships with their employers also had to be tackled. This was partly achieved through a decree on the protection of their employment rights introduced by social democrat Ivan Dérer as minister plenipotentiary for the administration of Slovakia. Social, accident and sickness insurance were modernised as well. A left-wing platform was formed at the congress by "Red Legionnaires", members of the Communist Party of Czechoslovakia newly created in Russia; a left-wing Marxist faction was formed in December 1919. Their programmes before the first parliamentary elections in Czechoslovakia in 1919 and 1920 diverged from those of social democrats because of their differing positions on the October 1917 Russian Revolution. Although social democrats never completely renounced the idea of revolution, they did not approve of the revolutionary methods for installing the dictatorship of the proletariat, which they considered to be unsuitable in the conditions of Czechoslovakia.

Social Democracy and the Minorities Issue after the Creation of the ČSR

The international situation had an impact on the development of the Czechoslovak Republic from the moment of its creation. The new state was recognised de facto before it was established de iure. But the country's success on the international level was not matched by the political reality at home. The situation in both parts of the republic was tense. The four German provinces created in 1918 in the "historical Czech lands" sought to separate from the ČSR and be annexed to Austria. More than 50 people died fighting the Czechoslovak brachial power. In Slovakia, the situation was even more complicated. Hungarian troops occupied almost two-thirds of Slovak territory; state borders were definitively settled only as late as June 1920 at the Trianon conference. For this reason, Slovakia could not hold municipal elections, as Bohemia and Moravia had done in June 1919. According to the 1921 statistical data, Hungarian nationality was claimed by 634,827 persons, German nationality by 139,900 and Czechoslovak nationality by 2,013,372.¹⁵ Under minority clauses of peace treaties concluded in Saint-Germain and Trianon, Czechoslovakia guaranteed minorities not only civil rights but also special rights in the area of education and language. Effective enforcement of these rights depended on the existence of a functioning democracy, a productive economy and social legislation. Ivan Dérer focused his political work mainly on the social aspects of the newly adopted common Czechoslovak legislation. The main problem that arose after the creation of the new state and the determination of its borders was state citizenship, which marked the lives of tens of thousands of people, especially members of ethnic minorities. The number of stateless persons in the ČSR in that period was close to 80,000. This means that, in real life, those persons were not entitled to social and health insurance and even to pensions for which they had saved and paid contributions their whole lives. Social democrats consistently pushed for a modern understanding of the civic principle and ethnicity. The recognition of civil rights and codification of the Constitutional Act on the statehood of the inhabitants of individual parts of Czechoslovakia – the state composed of two entities that belonged either to Austria or to Hungary before the war – was an important factor in the process of unification of public administration and law-making. Dérer's name and his role in the passage of the act was often cited by leading European politicians and cultural personalities at congresses of minority representatives all over Europe.¹⁶

The Social and Democratic Movement in Slovakia during 1918–1920 in relation to the Hungarian and German Minorities

Minority political parties were not represented in the Revolutionary National Assembly (RNZ) and became integrated into the parliament as late as after the April elections of 1920.¹⁷ After the Czechoslovak Republic was established, the Hungarian Social Democratic Party was divided according to nationality. The Slovak arm of the former Hungarian social democrats merged with its Czech counterpart in December 1918 and accepted its programme of building a united democratic Czechoslovak state with a social focus. In this way the unity of the republic and the nation, as well as the unity of social democracy in the Czechoslovak nation and state was to be proven. Room opened up for Hungarian and German social democratic organisations in the Czechoslovak state to join social democrats in Czechoslovakia; however, most of them did not do so. The Hungarian social democratic organisations were not united. Two organisations were functioning in Slovakia: one a pro-Hungarian and a pro-Kingdom of Hungary organisation in Košice, and the pro-Czechoslovak social democratic organisation in Bratislava. They responded differently to the establishment of the new state and could not reach a common platform. Social democracy in Bratislava was of a cosmopolitan nature and linked to headquarters in Budapest and Vienna and to European social democratic institutions. At the end of 1918, a Hungarian-German social democratic party was formed in Bratislava, led by Paul Wittich, Gyula Nagy and Antal Svraka. The party became a relevant entity in the 1920 elections. It won more than 108,000 votes and four mandates. It founded an independent faction in the parliament, headed by Paul Wittich. Its candidates for the Senate had been included in the list of the Czechoslovak Social Democratic Party. After 1921, the left wing of the party joined the Czechoslovak Communist Party (KSČ), which was also joined by a large number of Hungarian social democrats. The outstanding members joined the ČSSDSR (the Czechoslovak Social Democratic Party of Workers) and the German Social Democratic Party, and their integration into the political scene of the First Czechoslovak Republic took place slowly and with difficulty. Their efforts to maintain independence did not bear fruit. Crisis and polarisation of social democracy in the Czechoslovak Republic, completed by the creation of the KSČ, also greatly harmed minority parties. Their members either joined the KSČ or went over to new minority parties that had social issues in their programmes; however, their dominant aim was to revive the Kingdom of Hungary.[18]

SOCIAL DEMOCRACY AND BUILDING THE NEW STATE

Two state legal acts determined the new stage of Slovakia's modern history after 1918 as part of an independent Czechoslovak state: the Declaration of the Czechoslovak National Committee on 28 October 1918 in Prague and the Declaration of the Slovak Nation on 30 October 1918 in Martin. At that time, Slovak territory was still occupied by the Hungarian army and the state's public administration was still accountable to the Hungarian government. By making it hard for Slovakia to become part of the new state, the Hungarian government and its activities at the same time strengthened, in practice, the application of a state political theory of Czech and Slovak national unity. When dealing with military intervention, an important role was played by proposals from the Hungarian government supporting Slovakia's autonomy. The situation in Slovakia could not be solved even by the SNR (the Slovak National Council) or the Temporary Cabinet or the National Committee and out of all this arose (with no elections) the Revolutionary National Assembly (RNA) in Prague. In the RNA, the Slovak political parties had no independent position; they were associated in the Slovak faction of MPs (SCMP). It was in this forum that the Slovak social democrats pursued a swift organisation of elections based on universal, equal and secret ballot and the creation of a legitimate parliament with representation of Slovak MPs. United Czech and Slovak social democrats were quickly becoming part of the political structure of the new state. They contributed to the drafting of the Constitution, the Election Act and acts related to public administration, unification and the rights of minorities. The representatives of social democratic parties responded to mass radicalisation with revolutionary language, but in practice they were pursuing reform policies.

Creation of Ruling Power Institutions and Slovak Social Democracy

Until February 1920, the Temporary Constitution applied in ČSR, which was endorsed by the Czechoslovak National Committee (ČNV) on 13 November 1918. Based on the Temporary Constitution, government institutions were established. Legislative power was embodied in the Revolutionary National Assembly (RNZ), which was transformed from the National Committee by political parties, bringing in members of parliament based on the elections of 1911. In the Czech and Moravian territories, the government of the Coalition of All Nations (Vláda Všenárodnej Koalície) was formed. There were three social democrats in the government, none from Slovakia. Slovakia was represented in the cabinet by Milan Rastislav Štefánik (with no party affiliation) as the Minister of War; he was in charge of Czechoslovak legionnaires. Another Slovak minister was Vavro Šrobár (member of the Hlas movement and a farmer) who first served as minister of health care, later as minister plenipotentiary with full authority for Slovakia's administration. The RNZ had 270 MPs; Slovakia was represented by the faction of Slovak MPs (KSP) who had been nominees of Vavro Šrobár from SNR and its branches, as well as from the Slovak National Party. In this faction, social democracy was represented by 10 prominent people from Slovakia: Ferdinand Benda, Ivan Dérer, Adolf Horváth, Jozef Cholek, Andrej Kubál, Emanuel Lehocký, Ivan Markovič, Ján Maršalko, Jozef Oktávec and Ján Pocisk. There were three women in the RNZ from the Czech and Moravian territories, and from Silesia. Only one woman from Slovakia represented social democracy in the Revolutionary National Assembly, a young worker from a tobacco-processing plant, Irena Káňová. She was the youngest MP. There were no German and no Hungarian MPs in the RNZ. In Slovakia, the executive power was assumed by the Temporary Government appointed by the Czechoslovak National Committee. Its term was brief (from 4 November to 14 November 1918); after the adoption of the Temporary Constitution it was replaced by the Ministry with full authority for Slovakia (MPS) which was one of the ministries of the Czechoslovak government and directly subordinate to it. The parallel existence of the faction of Slovak MPs (KSP) and the Slovak National Council (SNR) created a two-track environment, which was ended by the abolition of the SNR and all national councils representing minorities in January 1919. The MPS had broad competencies as it was necessary to consolidate the situation in Slovakia. State borders were not determined; a big part of Slovakia was still occupied by Hungarian troops and the economic and social conditions were disastrous.

Election Preparations, Endorsement of the Constitution and Social Democracy

Even though universal suffrage was a basic demand of social democrats in the Hungarian Kingdom – in Slovakia this had been the case since 1890 when the social democrats began to emerge – it materialised for the first time only after the establishment of the ČSR in its first parliamentary elections in 1920. Until the 1920 elections, Czechoslovakia did not have a duly elected parliament, in contrast to the surrounding newly-formed states. Those in power argued that the post-war situation was complicated, relations with the German and Hungarian minorities were hostile and the border of the ČSR had not been determined, particularly its Slovak part. In February 1920, the state-forming powers that were associated in the Revolutionary National Assembly (RNZ) adopted the Constitution of the ČSR. The Constitution was adopted without the votes of the German and Hungarian minorities because these were not represented in the RNZ. Motions to the parliament were submitted by the Cabinet as a whole, led by a social democrat, Vlastimil Tusar (it was established after social democrats had won in communal elections in June 1919 in the Czech Republic and Moravia; no elections were held on the occupied territory of Slovakia). In the interest of pursuing the Constitution and maintaining its application in the long run, the socialists gave up their radical claims for socialisation and property expropriation without compensation. The wording on the legal restriction of property should have meant a gradual and evolutionary transition from capitalist to socialist ownership. Similarly, the socialists did not succeed in pushing through the original wording of the Act on Regional Administration to provide for the widest possible participation in public administration. The concept of administrative autonomy for Slovakia, which was pursued by the Slovak social democrats Markovič and Derér, did not materialise. The authors of the draft Constitution took as baseline the constitutions of the agreement states and the United States. Minority rights were regulated by minority clauses of the Saint-Germain Agreement that were incorporated into the Constitution.

Course and Election Results

Municipal elections in 1919 and parliamentary elections in 1920 brought victory for the Social Democratic Party on a national scale. The election campaign was characterised by strong socialist rhetoric and populist slogans. Social democratic sections of various ethnic groups agreed to engage in pragmatic cooperation during the election campaign. The election programme of the Slovak social democratic parties contained a statement that social democracy would strive to gain a majority in the parliament in order to secure a social legislature. The programme tried to address the broadest spectrum of the population and therefore combined nationalisation of industry and radical land reform. It underlined material needs and their fulfilment as the population in Slovakia was "politically illiterate" and many citizens cast their vote for the first time in their lives. Social democrats pursued the economic and legal equality of women and men to create appropriate conditions for the development of work, including day-care facilities.[19] In the 1920 elections to the Chamber of Deputies of the National Assembly, 27 women were on the list of candidates for the Social Democratic Party, which accounted for exactly 10 per cent of all 270 candidates. On behalf of Slovakia, three women were on the candidate lists of the Social Democratic Party, for Liptovský Mikuláš, Martin-Vrútky and Nové Zámky. Only one of them made it into the Chamber of Deputies, however, journalist and author Anna Sychravová. In the April parliamentary elections, the Slovak social democratic party won 510,341 votes cast for the Chamber of Deputies (38.1 per cent), and 21 out of 74 MPs (for comparison, in the Czech and Moravian lands, the Social Democratic Party won 26 per cent of the votes). It also gained six mandates for the German and Hungarian social democrats. The results were confirmed by the elections to the Senate, which took place one week later; out of 57 social democratic senators 13 were elected in Slovakia. Because the list of candidates of the social democratic party for the National Assembly and to the Senate in Slovakia was a compromise between the left and the right, there were several distinct personalities of Hungarian, German, Slovak and also Czech ethnicity. The party nominated to the parliament also left-wing party officials: Karol Svetlík, Hermannn Taussig, Ľudovit Surányi, Jozef Schiffel and Štefan Daruľa. In the Senate, Slovakia was represented by Anton Svraka, Václav Chlumecký and Teodor Matuščák. After the elections, a coalition of social democrats and agrarians was again formed. The contrast between the Social Democratic Party as the ruling party and its radical election agitation was criticised not only by the left within the party but also by other parties in Slovakia. The 1920 election campaign was the last time the moderate and pro-communist wing and the radical wing of the Czechoslovak German and Hungarian social democratic movements managed to present themselves jointly and maintain the impression of unity in the workers' movement. After this, joint action of the moderate and the radical wings of social democracy came to an end.

Outstanding Social Democratic Women Politicians in Slovakia in 1900–1925

The participation and organisation of women in the structures of the social democratic movement in Slovakia evolved gradually. This was an expression of the party's maturation and social development. The beginnings of the social democratic movement, when it had a relatively small membership, were also characterised by a low participation of women. No women held leadership positions or more prominent posts. But even the German Social Democratic Party in Bratislava, which was the most highly developed pre-war social democracy structure in Slovakia, had only one prominent social democrat of German ethnicity in its ranks, Elsa Grailich (1880–1968). She was a nurse and later became a journalist and writer. In 1918 she was at the helm of the women's section of the German Social Democratic Party in Bratislava. She was an active member of the Workers' Council and was arrested in March together with Vavro Šrobár and Paul Wittich for supporting Bolshevism. In the 1920s, she published a book about Bratislava's interiors and during the Second World War rescued Jewish children. After 1948, her entire property was confiscated and, as an ethnic German inhabitant of Bratislava, she was threatened with deportation from Czechoslovakia. She lived an interesting but far from easy life.

In the Revolutionary National Assembly (RNZ), the social democrats of Bohemia, Moravia and Silesia were represented by three women. As mentioned in the previous section, the Social Democratic Party in Slovakia had only one woman representative in the Revolutionary National Assembly (14 November 1918 to 25 April 1920), a young tobacco factory worker Irena Káňová (5 April 1893 to 8 April 1965). She was the youngest deputy and lived all her life in Banská Štiavnica, with the exception of a short period when she participated in top-level political work and in the building of a common state of Czechs and Slovaks. She joined the Slovak Social Democratic Party in 1917. In the RNZ, she replaced Alica Masaryková, the daughter of President T.G. Masaryk. Alica Masaryková, who represented Slovakia in the RNZ, was so impressed by young Irena that she gave up her seat for her. Káňová did not get re-elected to the National Assembly in the 1920 elections, however. In 1921, she joined the KSČ and was extremely active in the strike movement. She took part in the anti-fascist uprising and continued to be an active member of the Communist party and a fighter for equality and emancipation of women until the end of her life in 1965.

As mentioned in Section 3.3 only one of the three female social democratic candidates for Slovakia was elected to the Chamber of Deputies, journalist and writer Anna Sychravová (7 July 1873 to 22 February 1925). This prominent social democrat of Czech origin worked actively in the workers' movement in Slovakia. She was a regular contributor to the daily paper *Právo ľudu* and was immersed in the struggle to preserve the unity of social democrats in 1920–1921. Even before the First World War, she was politically active in the field of planned parenthood and education for blind and deaf-and-dumb children. She strove to improve the situation in Slovakia by, for instance, banning the sale of alcohol to juveniles.

Among the social democratic candidates in the 1920 Senate elections there were only two women, representing electoral districts of Prague and Hradec Králové. Not a single woman was nominated as a candidate on the Slovak social democrats' candidate list for Senate elections, however.

Party Polarisation and the Birth of the Communist Party (KSČ)

The social democratic party started to become internally polarised in 1918. A radical leftist group was formed within the party as early as the unifying congress of the Slovak and Czech democratic parties in December 1918. In this process, a significant role was played by differing attitudes towards the revolution in Russia and the Third International. Other factors in this process were the Hungarian Soviet Republic, the Slovak Soviet Republic and the mass arrival of Hungarian communists to the Czechoslovak Republic as a result of a dictatorship and the counter-revolutionary regime in Hungary.

The strike in Rumanová village at the end of March 1919 also influenced the situation: after the intervention of the Czech police, in cooperation with the Ministry Plenipotentiary for Administration (MPS) of Slovakia, two people were killed. Even though the leadership of the Slovak Social Democratic Party condemned the MPS and stated that the extraordinary MPS regime was the "source of all evil", the party changed its position after the change in the MPS leadership when an Agrarian Party member, Šrobár, was replaced by a social democrat Dérer and the MPS returned to the previous authoritarian way of administering Slovakia. The situation was alarming, Slovakia's southern borders were threatened and supplies were complicated. Even Dérer was confronted by the issue of wheat supply in the southern Slovak districts in the summer of 1919. Although he began his term of office with the best of intentions on how to administer Slovak territory democratically, he was soon criticised across the board. The main critics were primarily the left-wing pro-communist trade union leaders in the town of Ružomberok. The gap between the Country Executive Committee in Bratislava and members of local organisations who criticised the coalition politics of the party and its non-compliance with the party programme was growing wider.

During the summer of 1920, the Social Democratic government and the party in the Czechoslovak Republic found itself on the defensive domestically. The International Workers' Movement began to radicalise. In Moscow, the delegates to the Second Congress of the Communist International were engaged in talks on the necessity of pursuing 21 conditions laid down for the left-wing movements in social democracies. Bohumír Šmeral, a significant representative of social democracy before the war, withdrew from public life during 1918–1920 due to allegations of Austro-Marxism. He re-entered political life in autumn 1920 after his return from Russia and after being elected to the parliament as a social democrat. His main objective was to establish an independent communist party that would then absorb rank and file members of the social democratic parties. As a split in the Social Democratic Party was expected, the Social Democrats withdrew from the ruling coalition and began to fight for party unity. The crisis in the party continued, however, and congresses on the left and right wings in autumn 1920 brought a final disintegration, sealed by the establishment of the Communist Party of Czechoslovakia (ČSSDSR) in May 1921. In Slovakia, the left organised a congress in Martin in September 1920 with trade union participation, with 152 delegates representing 178,000 workers from Slovakia and Carpathian Ruthenia. Members of the Hungarian and German organisations also took part; they were not members of ČSSDSR. At the meeting, supporters of the Communist International delivered speeches and elected Karol Svetlík as chairman. Dérer also came to Martin and supported the idea of dividing participants into sections according to ethnicity so that the majority in the Slovakia supporting social democracy would not be taken over by the radical Hungarians and Germans.

The Second Congress of the Country Executive Committee of the Slovak Social Democracy was held in Bratislava on 7–8 November 1920 with 112 delegates, 89 of whom represented 76 political organisations with 83,994 members. German and Hungarian left-wing organisations responded to the congress in Bratislava with a strike that was actively supported by MP Svetlík and Senator Svraka from the left. In Slovakia, the Communist Party was established at the Congress of the Marxist left from Slovakia and Carpathian Rithuania, which took place on 16–17 January 1921 in Ľubochňa and Ružomberok. In May 1921, at the Prague Congress, the Slovak Communist Party joined the Marxist left in the Czech Republic and the

Communist Party of Czechoslovakia was formed. After the Czechoslovak Communist Party was established, social democracy in Slovakia found itself in crisis. In the eastern and southern parts of Slovakia, social democratic organisations basically fell apart. The party maintained its position only in Bratislava and in the central region of Slovakia. Its falling membership also reduced income to the party treasury and partly paralysed it. In 1924 various proposals on how to solve the ongoing party crisis were discussed at the fourteenth congress of the Social Democratic Party in Ostrava. Principles of gradual transition to collective ownership were adopted; hired labour was to be eliminated and Leninism was rejected, in particular, the concept of a workers' revolution and dictatorship of the proletariat. The parliamentary elections of 1925 in Slovakia resulted in a significant drop in votes for social democrats. In Slovakia, the party won only 60,635 votes (4.25 per cent), a distinct weakening compared with the result in 1920. The social democrats lost their votes to the Communists and the People's Party. According to records from December 1925, 197 organisations were active in Slovakia, with members totalling 12,349.[20]

International Cooperation of the Slovak Social Democrats and European Ideas

The most beneficial cooperation within the social democratic movement in Central Europe after the disintegration of the monarchy was undoubtedly that between the Czechoslovak Social Democratic Party and its Austrian counterpart. This applies not only to the years 1918–1920 but also to the watershed geopolitical periods (1945–1948, 1968, 1989). Cooperation between the Czechoslovak social democratic movement, based in Austria, was renewed in 1918, new ties were formed and old contacts with the Czech social democrats in Vienna were strengthened, as well as with the Social Democratic Party, which was renamed the Czecho-Slovak Social Democratic Party.

The Austrian government, which was led by social democrats, did not support the armed resistance of the German population in Czechoslovakia. It adopted a pragmatic approach, laying a firm basis for future cooperation. Thanks to the cooperation of social democratic governments of both countries the so-called "Brno Agreement" was signed, the first bilateral inter-governmental agreement providing for reciprocal guarantees of civil rights and rights of minorities. The agreement focused on the rights of the German minority in the Czechoslovak Republic and of the Czech and Slovak minorities in Austria. It also contained complementary provisions to minority clauses of the Peace Treaty of Saint-Germain signed in 1919. The ideas of prominent Austrian social democrats, Otto Bauer and Karl Renner, had a significant influence on the social democratic movement in Slovakia, primarily in Bratislava, already before the war. After the war, cooperation was renewed and reached its peak in the 1930s during the process of granting asylum to emigrant-social democrats in 1934 after the outbreak of the civil war in Austria and abolition of social democracy in the country. As a result of the elections in Austria in 1919 the Czech social democrat František Dvořák, who maintained strong ties with the Bratislava workers' movement, was elected to parliament. He organised several lectures in Bratislava on the topic of elections and how to vote. Dvořák also cooperated with the pan-European movement led by Richard Coudenhove-Kalergi, the author of one of the first projects on European federalisation. In the multi-ethnic Czechoslovak Republic the idea of pan-Europeanism fell on fertile ground and was supported also by social democrats. It was Bratislava, with its proximity to Vienna that was pre-determined for the organisation of the series of lectures held by Coudenhove-Kalergi in the 1920s in cooperation with representatives of the local social democratic movement.

The Legacy of Social Democracy Today

The history of the twentieth century clearly shows that democratic political systems in Europe fell prey or were susceptible to various forms of authoritarian, even totalitarian regime. Democracy, political openness and maximum participation of citizens in public and political action, as well as social processes, are the most important values of the twenty-first century.

In this regard, the most valuable message and collective intellectual legacy of the social democratic movement is the awareness of the social democratic tradition. But how are we to understand the content and meaning of this dualistic concept? In practice, it means that during the current global crisis of democracy it is important to draw on the tradition of social equality and efficient handling of the public space with the aim of accommodating the interests of all social strata. In short, social democracy's legacy from a hundred years ago has left us two fundamental messages: to maintain and strengthen social justice and social consensus; and to reinforce political democracy and political culture. The ever growing and deepening differences between the rich elites and the poor strata of society bear witness to how relevant these messages are today. In the period from 1918 to 2018, Slovakia has experienced alternations of authoritarian or even totalitarian regimes that hid their nature under the mask of implementing socialist ideas. Therefore, it is now necessary to consider the historical role of the Social Democratic Party after the formation of the Czechoslovak Republic in 1918; in other words, coming to understand how social democracy contributed to the foundation, creation and establishment of democracy in the broadest sense of the word, as we know it today. As a political movement, social democracy was set apart from the communist regime by the fact that it promoted actual participation of the working class and the trade union movement in political and social processes. In contrast to the communists, and the model of social arrangements they tried to enforce through a dictatorship of the proletariat, which in reality meant the dictatorship of a new elite – the new political caste of one party – social democrats have always advocated efforts to establish democratic socialism on the basis of a functioning civil democracy. Social democracy has striven to improve and broaden the existing democratic base in society. Without a doubt, in 1918 social democracy played an important role in the establishment of a democratic state. In the inter-war period, it contributed momentously to the reinforcement of a pluralist and democratic political culture, which was then continued in Slovakia after the authoritarian regime of the war-time Slovak State was defeated in 1945. It lasted for only three years, however, until the Communist Party seized power in 1948. In the 1960s, the ideas of the social democratic tradition gradually matured again until they were reborn in 1968, while the Communist Party was being slowly reformed into a social democratic one. These ideas were not successfully put into practice, however. In 1989, following the "Velvet Revolution", Alexander Dubček revived the ideas, considering them to be a necessary requirement of the transformation process. After 1989, the legacy of social democratic ideas found its roots in Slovakia only gradually and very slowly. Although several leftist movements were formed in this period, their content and form were typical of the political context of that time, post-socialist and still seeking final shape. After all, these political subjects vanished fairly quickly from the political scene. Since 2005, the Smer-Social

Democracy party has claimed to be the main heir of social democratic traditions, a role it is partially fulfilling in practice. It has major populist features, however, that have been criticised by the Socialist International, as well as by the socialist faction in the European parliament.

CONCLUSION

Since the formation of a social democratic organisation in 1905, the dual concept and focus of social democracy in Slovakia have remained more or less the same. Cooperation between the Slovak social democrats with other ethnic sections within the unified Social Democratic Party in the Kingdom of Hungary set the conditions for subsequent international cooperation. The Slovak social democrats benefited from cooperating with the Hungarians in Budapest, Germans in Bratislava and Czechs in Vienna. Big cities, a multicultural atmosphere and relative freedom provided sufficient room for Slovak social democrats and their supporters, and allowed them to pursue political and national emancipation, activation and implementation of their goals in society. The autonomous operation of Slovak social democracy created the conditions for political experience also for ordinary party members and supporters. Collaboration with the Czech social democracy in the Austrian part of the Monarchy significantly contributed to strengthening and pursuing the idea of Czech and Slovak mutuality. Consequently, a joint state of Czechs and Slovaks was formed in 1918. The basic structures of the social democratic movement in Slovakia were relatively poorly developed; the political party itself as well as the trade unions had very few members. The political core of the party also had a small number of members (in 1908, the Slovak Committee in the Social Democratic Party in the Kingdom of Hungary had 6,346 members; in December 1918 the Slovak social democrats reported 15,000 members prior to the unifying congress; in 1920, after the left wing had split it reported 84,000 members; and after the drop in numbers in the elections of 1925 only a little more than 12,000 members). The influence of the social democratic movement in Catholic Slovakia was weakened also due to its anti-religious focus and secular efforts in education. And so it is worth noting that the Slovak Social Democratic Party became the strongest political party in Slovakia after the parliamentary elections of 1920. The first elections to the Chamber of Deputies in the Czechoslovak

Republic took place on 18 April 1920 covering almost the whole territory of the republic. Temporarily, some border areas were excluded from the elections; the Peace Conference, held as part of the negotiations on the determination of new borders, was also seeking a solution to the status of these territories. The elections to the Chamber of Deputies took place in 23 electoral districts (seven in Slovakia) with 22 political parties taking part in the race. The Czechoslovak Social Democratic Party, winning 25.7 per cent of all valid votes and 74 mandates) became the strongest political party in the Czechoslovak Republic. Social democrats then won the elections in Slovakia, too. They gained 39.8 per cent of the votes and jointly with the Hungarian and German Social Democratic Party won more than 46 per cent. In the elections of 1925, however, the social democrats lost more than half of their votes, which indicates that their base was unstable and uncertain.

In 1920, after the formation of the independent Czechoslovak state, a mood marked by euphoria and positive, quite often even naive expectations was palpable. Socialist ideas were in keeping with the post-war radicalisation of the population, a bad economic situation and lack of food, as well as overall pauperisation. The victory of social democracy in Slovakia was not only a direct reflection of the party's organising efforts, popularity and political power, but also of the national revolution and the immature behaviour of the electorate characterised by a mass psychology of "naive expectations". The fact that the majority of voters in Slovakia participated in elections for the first time (the right to vote in the Kingdom of Hungary was limited and in the territory of Slovakia – Upper Hungary – only 6–7 per cent of the population could vote before 1918) helped political parties simplify their election campaign along populist and aggressive lines and social democrats were no exception. After the elections in 1925, the Czechoslovak Communist Party followed up on its populist campaign, benefiting from the fact that social democrats did not fulfil the promises they made during the previous campaign and running a much more moderate campaign than in 1920. The elections in 1925 and the ever-present populism brought great political success to the Slovak People's Party (SĽS), which profited from the fact that issues of nationality and ethnicity were not addressed in Slovakia. The centralist social democrats did not deal with the issue and many voters turned to the SĽS led by Catholic priest Andrej Hlinka. The SĽS used religious rhetoric and propaganda and advocated national demands.

Social democracy has contributed to Slovakia's development because it has always advocated thorough and comprehensive social, political and economic emancipation of the working class. It has fought for social justice, universal suffrage and political democracy. Nevertheless, we have to be critical of its centralist policy, opportunistic attitude to Slovak national demands and unrealistic enforcement of the Czechoslovakist political doctrine until the end of the first Czechoslovak Republic in 1938. During the existence of the pre-Munich Czechoslovakia, social democrats in Slovakia defended the idea of Czech and Slovak national unity, a centralist political doctrine. This seemingly pragmatic attitude, which the social democrats maintained until 1938, prevented the movement from actively interfering in political developments while the country disintegrated. The Social Democratic Party was banned in Slovakia on 16 November 1938.

The essential fact is, however, that social democracy made an important contribution to the formation of the first common state of the Czechs and the Slovaks. In 1918–1920, the first two social democratic governments laid the foundations of a modern and democratic political system, functioning parliamentary democracy and democratic political culture.

SUMMARY

Prior to 1914, Slovak social democracy was formed in cooperation with Hungarians in Budapest, Germans in Bratislava and Czechs in Vienna. Its contacts with Czech social democracy in the Austrian part of the monarchy contributed substantially to the growth and implementation of the idea of Czecho-Slovak mutuality and, ultimately, the idea of a common Czecho-Slovak state.

After the Czechoslovak Republic (or Czechoslovakia) was established in October 1918, the Czech social democratic party merged with its Slovak counterpart in December 1918 to form the Czechoslovak Social Democratic Workers Party. Unified Czecho-Slovak social democracy became firmly embedded in the political structure of the new state. It participated in the drafting of the Constitution, electoral law and laws related to public administration, unification and the rights of ethnic minorities. Even though the leaders of social democracy used revolutionary rhetoric in response to the post-war radicalisation of broad swathes of the population, they pursued reform policies in political and social practice.

The first elections to the Chamber of Deputies in Czechoslovakia were held on 18 April 1920. The social democratic party emerged as the strongest political party in Czechoslovakia. In Slovakia, social democrats achieved electoral victory as well. They obtained 39.4 per cent of the valid votes and, combined with the votes for the Hungarian-German Social Democratic Party, more than 46 per cent. Social democracy played a major role in the creation of the first common state of Czechs and Slovaks. Between 1918 and 1920, the first two social democratic governments laid the foundations of a modern and democratic political system, functioning parliamentary democracy and democratic political culture.

1 Gosiorovský, Miloš, Dejiny slovenského robotníckeho hnutia 1848–1918 (The History of the Slovak Workers' Movement), Bratislava, 1958, p.153.
2 Babejová, Eleonóra, Obraz Bratislavy v diskusii uhorského parlamentu o elektrickej dráhe do Viedne (Bratislava's Image in the Debate of the Kingdom of Hungary's Parliament on Electric Railway to Vienna), Historický časopis 51, No.1/2003. 3 For more details see Provazník, Dušan, V prvom desaťročí v ČSR (In the First Decade of the ČSR), in Lehotská, Darina and Pleva, Ján, Dejiny Bratislavy , Bratislava, 1966, p. 350.
3 Robotnícke noviny, 9 July 1914.
4 For more details see Hronský, Marián, Robotnícke hnutie na Slovensku po roku 1918 (Workers' Movement in Slovakia after 1918), in Kapitoly z dejín sociálnej demokracie na Slovensku, Bratislava, 1996, pp. 42–43.
5 Ibid., p. 43.
6 For more details see Hronský, Marián, Robotnícke hnutie na Slovensku po roku 1918 (Workers' Movement in Slovakia after 1918), in Kapitoly z dejín sociálnej demokracie na Slovensku, Bratislava, 1996, p. 50.
7 Robotnícke noviny, 3 January 1918.
8 For more details see Van Duin, Pieter, Central European Crossroads, Berghahn Books, 2009, pp. 143–52.
9 The same position was presented by the Český zväz (the Czech Union) on 30 May 1917 at the Vienna Imperial Council.
10 After the creation of the first ČSR František Tomášek was appointed member of the National Committee and later on Chairman of the Revolutionary National Assembly, the first parliament of the newly formed Czechoslovak Republic.
11 Robotnícke noviny, 22 November 1917.
12 For instance, in his article entitled 'The New Year', published in a January 1918 issue of Národné noviny, Ján Škultéty wrote about the need to join forces with the social democrats in the struggle for Slovak independence.
13 The Slovak National Council (SNR) created in 1918 was the supreme representative body of the Slovak nation. It was created on 12 September 1918 in Budapest in response to the demise of Austria-Hungary. The SNR was officially constituted on 30 October 1918 in the town of Turčiansky Svätý Martin on the occasion of the proclamation of the historical Declaration of the Slovak Nation (the Martin Declaration) whereby the Slovak people joined

the newly formed Czechoslovakia. Vavro Šrobár as the Interim Government Chairman who represented the interests of the Czechoslovak Government in Slovakia dissolved the SNR by decree on 23 January 1919. https://sk.wikipedia.org/wiki/1919

14 See Hronský, Marián and Pekník, Miroslav, Martinská Deklarácia. Cesta slovenskej politiky k vzniku Česko-Slovenska (The Martin Declaration. The Path of the Slovak Politics to the Creation of Czechoslovakia), pp. 268-70.

15 Tóth, Andrej, Novotný, Lukáš and Stehlík, Michal, Národnostní menšiny v Československu 1918–1938. Od státu národního ke státu národnostnímu? (Ethnic Minorities in Czechoslovakia 1918-1938. From a Nation State to an Ethnic State?), Prague, Charles University, Prague, Faculty of Philosophy, 2012.

16 17 Poláčková, Zuzana, Za oponou slovensko-rakúskych vzťahov v 20. storočí (Behind the Curtain of Slovak-Austrian Relations in the 20th century), Bratislava, SAV Publishing House, 2013, pp. 68-69.

17 For more details see Krajčovičová, Natália, Slovensko na ceste k demokracii (Slovakia on Its Path to Democracy), Bratislava, 2009, pp. 59-73.

18 Zelenák, Peter, Maďarská sociálna demokracia na Slovensku (Hungarian Social Democracy in Slovakia), in Kapitoly z dejín sociálnej demokracie na Slovensku, Bratislava, 1996, pp. 146-91.

19 For more details see Osyková, Linda, Sociálni demokrati kontra komunisti v 20. rokoch 20. Storočia (Social Democrats vs. Communists in the 1920s), in Forum Historiae, http://www.forumhistoriae.sk/documents/10180/11520/osykova.pdf

20 For more details see Krajčovičová, Natália, Slovensko na ceste k demokracii (Slovakia on Its Path to Democracy), Bratislava, 2009, pp. 9-49.

A HISTORY OF UNREALISED POSSIBILITIES: SOCIAL DEMOCRACY AND THE CREATION OF THE KINGDOM OF SERBS, CROATS AND SLOVENES (1918–1921)

ANA RAJKOVIĆ / TVRTKO JAKOVINA

WHY DON'T HISTORIANS SEE SOCIAL DEMOCRACY?

After the Second World War, interest in the labour movement and labour parties in the historiographies of all the states that once made up Tito's Yugoslavia almost always concerned communists and the Communist Party. The domination of such topics by Croatian and other historiographers was due to the interest and incentives of politics, transmitted to the institutes for the history of the workers' movement, which existed in every federal unit of the former Socialist Federal Republic of Yugoslavia (SFRJ), built an official and ruling ideology that was founded upon self-management socialism and Marxism. Thus arose an extensive, often hermetic and unusually detailed reconstruction of strikes, the press and illegal activities perpetrated by the Communist Party of Yugoslavia (KPJ). The historiographical attitude towards social democracy bore the imprint of ideological struggles. The fact that social democracy had found itself on the losing side of the ideological conflict would have pushed it to the margins even without state intervention. It was argued that the Socialist Party of Yugoslavia "did not represent the working class anyway, but only a thin layer of well-paid officials in institutions for the protection of workers or labour exchanges",[1] and that their policy was "antiproletarian and inhumane".[2] Likewise, it was alleged that the Slovenian social democrats were obsessed with "reformism" and "opportunism" and thus blamed for the betrayal of the revolution.[3] This was an exaggeration to say the least because, by participating in government at various levels between the two world wars, the social democrats nevertheless managed to improve conditions for workers, primarily by insisting on labour regulation.

Among the most important works by historians who have written about this issue are Toma Milenković's *Socijalistička partija Jugoslavije (1921–1929)* [The Socialist Party of Yugoslavia (1921–1929)], Vujica Kovačeva's *Ideološke i političke borbe u radničkom pokretu Hrvatske i Slavonije 1917–1919* [Ideological and political struggles in the labour movement of Croatia and Slavonia, 1917–1919] and Vlado Strugar's *Socijaldemokratija o stvaranju Jugoslavije* [Social democracy during the creation of Yugoslavia], published in 1965. The most important female Croatian historian, Mirjana Gross, wrote her doctoral dissertation on the role of social democracy in the political life of Croatia from 1890 to 1905.

After the end of the Cold War, with the collapse of Yugoslavia and the establishment of a formally full democracy, when taboo topics should have ceased to exist and historical studies of national histories increased fivefold (from two to ten) in the Republic of Croatia alone, not only was social democracy not reinterpreted or researched, but it was forgotten. Croatian historiography on left-wing parties and leftist movements for the most part has remained silent, just as it has been silent on the Second World War, except in describing the Ustasha movement. Extensive syntheses of the "long nineteenth century" barely even mention the history of the Social Democratic Party of Croatia and Slavonia.[4] This practice is similar to that of 1943, when Pavičić's *Hrvatska vojna i ratna poviest i Prvi svjetski rat* [Croatian military and war history and the First World War] completely omitted the Italian front, so that Croatia's then military allies would not be offended.[5]

The situation is similar in the other countries of the former Yugoslav federation, which is no surprise because in some places even the word *"radnik"* (meaning "worker") became taboo (and hence was replaced by *"djelatnik"*). In most countries, unemployment is increasing so workers and ideas that refer to that segment of the population are being marginalised. Historiography in the successor states of the former Yugoslavia, rather than explaining what happened – which is its whole purpose – much more often follows the assumed interests of the ruling elites. In such a situation, the values of social democracy, which are often said to have been realised in most of the Western world, are in some countries of the "Old Continent" seriously endangered or so weak that they need to be nurtured or even fought for.

THE NEW STATES OF 1918 AND THE RENEWAL OF WORKERS' PARTIES

The Kingdom of Serbs, Croats and Slovenes came into being on 1 December 1918, when politicians from countries that until recently had been constituent parts of Austria-Hungary travelled to Belgrade and presented the Address of Unification to the regent, Aleksandar Karađorđević. Thus the Kingdom of Serbs, Croats and Slovenes was created before the talks in Paris began, although it was often said that Yugoslavia was only a "creation of Versailles". In fact, the idea of creating independent states, including the unification of the South Slavs, was a decades-old idea entertained by numerous politicians from different parts of the new state, although primarily Croats within Austro-Hungary. The Yugoslav Committee, which consisted of politicians who had fled from Austro-Hungarian territory at the beginning of the Great War, advocated the dissolution of the Monarchy, much like the national committees of other peoples, such as the Slovaks and the Czechs. At the end of the war, what was supposed to become the new state was threatened primarily by the Italian forces that invaded the territory promised to Italy by the London Treaty of 1915 in order to get Italy to enter the war on the side of the Entente. On the other hand, Serbia, which had been under occupation in 1915, and whose government and army withdrew across Kosovo to Albania, and then (on Italian ships) to Solun, returned and began to conquer Austro-Hungarian territory. Montenegro, another independent state, as well as an ally of the Entente, which fought bravely until 1916, lost its sovereignty. The Montenegrin king, Nikola Petrović, was the grandfather of Regent Aleksandar Karađorđević, the future king of the Kingdom of Serbs, Croats and Slovenes, but he could no longer return to the country from France, and Montenegro, although a victor, was erased from the political map of Europe. Thus, regions that had been independent for decades, those which had been part of the Ottoman Empire until a few years before (Kosovo, Macedonia, the Sandžak), and countries that had been part of the Austrian and Hungarian political space with varying degrees of independence for several centuries (the Slovenian and Croatian lands) finally became part of the same state in 1918. It was a merger of different traditions and different state philosophies.

The new state was a unification of regions inhabited by members of different faiths (Roman Catholic, Orthodox Christian and Muslim) and different nations (Serbs, Slovenes and Croats, as well as a large number of Albanians, Turks, Germans and Hungarians). The country became part of a system that was supposed to prevent Bolshevik ideas from penetrating the rest of Europe and to function as a barrier against the possible recovery of an aggressive Germany, but also against the possible return of the Habsburgs. All men were granted the right to vote, which resulted in rapid changes on the political scene. Unlike other states, the complex, multinational Kingdom of Serbs, Croats and Slovenes was not clearly dominated by any one nation, although the population of Serbs was twice that of Croats, the second largest nation. Still, Serbs made up much less than half the population of the new state, which presented insurmountable difficulties for a nation that was unprepared and had no experience in ruling over a multinational community. The new state encompassed "areas that differed greatly economically (with different stages of capitalist development), socially (especially urban vs rural structures) and culturally (primarily in terms of literacy and education) ... as well as in terms of political institutions (the level of bureaucratisation and the rule of law)".[6] Although the Croatian lands were among the poorest in Austria-Hungary and had very high illiteracy rates, they were much more wealthy and developed than the territories with which they were united in 1918. In Serbia, Bosnia–Herzegovina and Croatia–Slavonia, social democratic parties had existed before the First World War. The experience of most European social democratic parties also applied to conditions within the Kingdom of Serbs, Croats, and Slovenes.

After the First World War, social democratic parties found themselves in deep ideological controversies. Old questions were opened and it became clear that the differences between moderate/right and radical/left currents had not been resolved, but were more keenly felt than ever. In part, this was because of the success of the October Revolution in Russia (1917), which had showed that the methods of the left, such as strikes and revolutions, could lead the working class to power. The rightist current of the social democrats continued to advocate evolutionary socialism, the gradual replacement of capitalism by socialism, primarily through parliamentary methods of struggle. This was the theory of the German Social Democrat Eduard Bernstein (1850–1932) from the end of the nineteenth century, with which the revision of orthodox Marxism began, and thus the division of the social democratic parties of that time into left and right wings.

The end of the war pushed this conflict to its final showdown. The leader was the German workers' movement, within which, according to the Yugoslav workers' press, fratricidal war broke out in 1918. The social democratic government of the defeated Germany, led by Philipp Scheidemann (1865–1939), or rather his confrontation with the leftist Spartacus League of Rosa Luxemburg and Karl Liebknecht (1871–1919), caused additional discord within social democratic parties in which the leftist current, inclined towards revolutionary conquest of power and averse to cooperation with bourgeois or centre-right parties, became more radical but also more powerful politically. Many European countries were in a difficult political situation at the same time. Canadian historian Margaret MacMillan, depicting Paris in the post-war period, writes: "Strikes and protests were an everyday occurrence. That winter and spring, through the streets marched protest processions of men and women dressed in the traditional blue clothing of French workers, which were opposed by processions of members of the middle class."[7]

The new Yugoslav state also faced a number of difficulties, from the appearance of so-called "green cadres" (deserters from the Austro-Hungarian army engaged in banditry) and the problems of implementing agrarian reform amid strong communist activity, to tough negotiations about the organisation of elections for the future Constitutional Assembly. Workers were particularly critical of the situation in the new state. Osijek's *Radničke novine* [Workers' news], for example, wrote that everyone was feeling their way in the dark and that "whoever thought that peace was fully assured by the armistice and that the slaughter had stopped was fooling themselves".[8] The historian Bogdan Krizman, in his review of the "Telephonic and Telegraphic Announcements" coming in from various parts of Croatia to the central office of the National Council, shows that in Osijek at the end of October 1918 there were "riots and terrible days. The masses got hold of arms and began to plunder. Agitated peasants from the surrounding villages attacked the city as well as landowners' estates in the vicinity. Three dead and many wounded."[9]

Nevertheless, the leaders of the pre-war workers' movement, primarily the social democrats Vitomir Korać (1877–1941), Slavko Henč (1879–1955) and Anton Kristan (1881–1930) began working towards the unification of the Yugoslav proletariat. The renewal of the workers' movement was led by the Social Democratic Party of Croatia and Slavonia (founded in 1894) and the Social Democratic Party of Serbia (1903). These countries were home to the most developed part of the movement. Elsewhere, such as in Macedonia, Montenegro or Bosnia and Herzegovina, the labour movement had developed mainly under the influence of the Croatian or Serbian movements. Slovenia, the most developed part of the new state, in part followed the Croatian social democrats, although in Styria there was never a distinct differentiation between social democrats and communists. The most obvious manifestation of the renewed activity of workers' parties and politicians was the revival of labour newspapers. These included *Radničke novine*, *Socijalista* and *Sloboda* in Croatia; *Radničke novine* in Serbia, *Glas slobode* [Voice of freedom] in Sarajevo and, from May 1920, *Rdeči prapor* [Red banner] in Slovenia.

The Yugoslav social democratic parties continued their pre-war policies, which were in line with the principles of the Second International (1889–1916). Thus, some social democrats still rejected revolution as a modus operandi despite its victory in Russia. In this way the differences between the leaders of the workers' parties from the late nineteenth and early twentieth century began to deepen. The dispute was visible already at the time of the revival of the movement even in relation to the General Workers' Union (ORS), which the leftist current thought should be a temporary solution as an umbrella organisation, whereas the non-radicalised members that felt the ORS would be a good permanent organisational solution. Thus, according to Toma Milenković, parallel to the process of reconstruction was the process of ideological and political differentiation, which culminated in the establishment of the Socialist Workers' Party of Yugoslavia (communists), later the Communist Party of Yugoslavia (KPJ), as well as the unification of the social democrats in the Socialist Party of Yugoslavia (SPJ). This new party dropped the adjective phrase "social democratic" from its name and introduced the term "socialist", which would remain the name of the social democratic current throughout the following period.[10] In the first period, the most prominent individuals in Yugoslav social democracy were Vitomir Korać, Živko Topalović (1886–1972), Dragiša Lapčević (1867–1939), Anton Kristan (1881–1930) and the brothers Jovan and Sreten Jakšić.

Despite the separation of the left wing from the Social Democratic Party, ideological struggles within it continued. A portion of the left-wing current, known as the centrists, approached the Social Democrats in 1920 and began to advocate cooperating with the Communists. Such policies soon began to weigh on Yugoslav social democracy. Vitomir Korać, a great opponent of such an approach, believed that unification with the Communists would lead to the total disappearance of the Social Democrats. On the other hand, Dragiša Lapčević, who had a great reputation and authority in the party, began to move away from the leadership, as he was committed to the unification of the entire working class. This would ultimately result in his departure from the party.

Although the Communist Party of Yugoslavia (KPJ) was banned in 1920, the conflict between the two currents continued to be the main feature of the activities of the Socialist Party of Yugoslavia in the first few years after the war. For this reason, not only in historiography but in real life as well the history of social democracy has been inseparable from the history of the (illegal) KPJ. In parallel with the ideological struggles, social democrats worked on building party structures and recruiting workers into their ranks, primarily through youth and women's associations. Most of the workers' societies, such as chambers of labour and similar institutions, were run by social democrats. Despite their obvious effort in the elections, they achieved exceptionally poor results and were never able to amass a significant membership.

SOCIAL DEMOCRATIC IDEAS AND THE SOUTH SLAVS UNTIL 1918

The first workers' organisations in the area inhabited by the South Slavs appeared in the mid-nineteenth century. Thus, in the territory of the Kingdom of Croatia, Slavonia and Dalmatia,[11] various societies were established, such as the Society for the Care of Sick Sales Assistants. In Serbia, such societies were founded somewhat later. It was not until 1896 that the Society of Moccasin Workers for Mental Growth and Fraternal Aid was set up; the following year a similar society was founded in Kragujevac. In this period, the most common such organisations were patients' societies, which were established in most parts of the future Kingdom of Serbs, Croats and Slovenes, but the only chamber of labour before 1914 was founded in the Kingdom of Serbia. In 1878, at the Berlin Congress, Serbia became fully independent and thus acquired the prerequisite for independent socio-political development. The workers' movement was late to appear in the Principality of Montenegro, where the first workers' organisations, such as the Workers' Federation, were founded in 1903, but no political party was established. In Macedonia, the first workers' organisations did not begin to appear until the beginning of the twentieth century, under the strong influence of Serbian labour; with the support of the Main Workers' Federation (GRS) of Serbia, a trade union of footwear workers was established in Skopje in 1909.

In Croatia, the first workers' organisations were founded at the instigation of employers, but they nevertheless provided a foundation for further labour organisation on a class basis. The main reason for this was the social position of the workers themselves, which was written about by, among others, the champion of workers' rights on the territory of Croatia, Miloš Krpan (1862–1931). In a description of the state of workers in the town of Brod na Savi, he pointed to the example of the "Zvjernica" [house of beasts] near the railway station, in which the exploitation and abuse of workers was particularly inhumane. "In the summertime, the stacking and unloading starts at 2:30 in the morning and finishes at 8:30 in the evening, and there is a break at noon when one can chew on a piece of bread. (...) The poor man who is late (...) is mercilessly excluded from work. Thus, 17 hours of hard labour for miserable pay."[12] Although an 1852 law banned the establishment of political societies throughout the Austro-Hungarian Monarchy, after the introduction of constitutional government workers started to found social-democratic clubs in the second half of the nineteenth century.[13] This was largely linked to the activities of Austrian and Hungarian socialists, whose illegal publications (such as *Volksstimme*) reached even the periphery of the Monarchy.

The first steps towards organised activity on the part of workers occurred in cities, primarily in Ljubljana, Belgrade, Zagreb and Osijek. In Osijek, the first workers' society in Croatia was founded in 1867, the Osijek–Workers' Education Society. The next important event was the organisation of typographers in Zagreb. Traditionally more educated than other workers, typographers played an important role in political labour activism, especially in terms of launching newspapers. They launched *Radnički prijatelj* [Workers' friend], a newspaper especially widespread among workers in the then Kingdom of Croatia and Slavonia, as well as in Serbia.

During this period, South Slavic socialists were making contacts, mainly thanks to the activities of Vasa Pelagić (1833–1899). This is documented in numerous arrest warrants issued by the authorities of the then Kingdom of Croatia and Slavonia, in which Pelagić is labelled a socialist agitator and an anarchist. These warrants were quite detailed; for example, one from 1880 states that Pelagić especially liked milk and boiled eggs. Governing structures were very much aware of the existence of socialist thought, especially its potential for disruption. Therefore the central authorities sent numerous communications inviting local authorities to keep track of Pelagić's movements and to arrest him on sight. Pelagić influenced the development of the labour movement throughout the entire area of the future kingdom. Among others, Krpan emphasised in his letters that Pelagić had had a significant role in his own ideological formation.

Stojan Kešić points out that, apart from foreign workers, the influence of information coming from Zagreb and Belgrade was crucial for the penetration of socialist thought in Bosnia and Herzegovina. This penetration, as in other regions, occurred primarily through the smuggling in of labour newspapers, which was then strictly punished by the authorities. Kešić also states that "the authorities in Croatia and Bosnia and Herzegovina collaborated closely in monitoring the expansion of socialist ideas and the smuggling of socialist reading material. They communicated with each other about whether inhabitants of Bosnia and Herzegovina had participated in socialist activities in Croatia and vice versa."[14]

With a certain delay after the German lands, following the events in the international labour movement during the second half of the nineteenth century, the first social democratic parties were organised. The workers' movement in the South Slavic regions took on the appellation "social democratic" because that is what German workers named their party in 1869, and the German workers' movement had been a spiritus movens for the entire European workers' movement. As historians would write during the Cold War, "The German political movement began to call itself social democratic in the 1860s based on the tradition of 1848. This movement demanded the sovereignty of the people on the basis of general electoral rights and the transformation of society in the interest of the working masses."[15] On 8 September 1894, the Social Democratic Party of Croatia and Slavonia (SDSHiS) was founded in secrecy under the leadership of Ivan Anceló (1870–1922).

Somewhat later, in 1903, just a few months after the May Coup and the fall of the Serbian Obrenović dynasty, the Serbian Social Democratic Party (SSDP) was founded, whose first president was Dragiša Lapčević. Along with the party, the Workers' Union was established. In Bosnia in 1909, the Social Democratic Party of Bosnia and Herzegovina was founded under the leadership of Sreten Jakšić. The organisation of workers in Bosnia and Herzegovina was greatly influenced by the arrival of Jerotije Plavšić and Mićo Sokolović (1883–1906), the founder of the modern workers' movement of Bosnia and Herzegovina.[16]

At first, the social democrats' primary task was trade union activity. Very soon, in 1905, critics of this policy appeared, primarily Dimitrije Tucović, who considered that party and union activities should be represented equally. This was also the opinion of Triša Kaclerović (1879–1964), who also emphasised that the party organisation had grown weak because of the union's rise in power.[17]

One pioneer of sorts in the penetration of socialist ideas in the South Slavic region was Serbian Socialist Svetozar Marković (1846–1875), who also initiated the first socialist newspaper in the Balkans, *Radenik* [Worker]. Marković, among other things, dismissed clericalism, considering that intellect must play a major role in the socialist movement. Because of this, he was the target of criticism from Serbian literary historian Jovan Skerlić (1877–1914), who wrote that Marković overestimated the role of the intellect, putting his thought into the wider context of the socio-political situation in Serbia during the second half of the nineteenth century. According to Mira Bogdanović, Skerlić concluded that, because of economic and cultural backwardness, when social oppositions did not yet exist, Marković's socialism could have been nothing but an "intellectual and ethical appeal to reason and feelings".[18] "Marković's basic thesis was that Marx's views about capitalism were valid for Western European societies, but for the South Slavic areas, where neither the mode of production nor the ownership forms were comparable to those in Western Europe, were less useful than the Russian theory of agrarian socialism."[19] Svetozar Marković was an exceptionally prolific theorist who published many books and articles, including the notorious *Ništavilo parlamentarizma* [The pointlessness of parliamentarism] (1872), *Otkuda dolazi naša siromaština* [Where our poverty comes from] (1873) and Slobodana Štampa i Žandarmerija [The free press and the gendarmerie] (1973).

After Marković, a group of young Orthodox Marxists led by Dimitrije Tucović (1881–1914) and Dragiša Lapčević, who had also participated in the establishment of the SSDP, appeared in Serbia. At this stage of the development of social democratic ideas, there was a departure from Marković's ideas, which were proclaimed utopian, and whose followers were called "old socialists". In this ideological confrontation, Tucović was extremely active, pointing out that "the activities of the Serbian social democrats are not ideologically compatible with the activities of Svetozar Marković and his followers", who according to Tucović had no understanding of new forms of struggle that had not previously been possible.[20]

In the Kingdom of Croatia and Slavonia, unlike the Kingdom of Serbia, the workers' movement did not have intellectual leaders. It was mostly represented by workers, craftsmen and junior clerks. After Ancel, the Social Democratic Party of Croatia and Slavonia was taken over by the clerk Vitomir Korać (1877–1941), the joiner Slavko Henč (1879–1955) and the typographer Vilim Bukšeg (1874–1924). Despite their unstructured theoretical background, they occasionally printed brochures. Hence, in 1907, Henč published a manual entitled *What Is Universal, Equal, Direct, Secret, and Proportionate Electoral Law?*, and 1912, Korać published *Goals and Paths of Social Democracy*, in which, among other things, there are demands for freedom of speech and association, social equality of the sexes and enlightenment.[21] They succeeded in legalising trade unions (1907) and establishing the General Workers' Alliance (1908). One particular success was in 1907, when they won their first parliamentary seat: Vitomir Korać became the first worker representative in a legislative body in this region.

In Bosnia and Herzegovina, the workers' movement relied largely on the poor peasantry and foreign skilled workers – people of different nationalities who came to the region when it became part of Austria-Hungary – and who were especially active in larger cities such as Sarajevo and Banja Luka. These cities were also the most vibrant part of the Bosnian workers' movement, primarily in terms of organisation, but also in terms of strikes. The movement in Bosnia and Herzegovina experienced some major leadership coups, especially after the ban of Labour Day celebrations on 1 May 1906, which failed to prevent the vast majority of workers from taking to the streets and starting a strike. The authorities responded by making arrests, and the workers' leaders who were then at the helm of the movement, because of Sokolović's death, primarily Stevo Cvijanović Obilić and Vilim Prates, did not handle the situation well. After the end of the strike, there was a showdown that resulted in their ejection, upon which the typographer Nikola Vukojević assumed the leadership.

The homogenisation of the workers' movement and the founding of social democratic parties also opened up intra-party controversies. Most of the parties accepted the official line of the Second International, in which German Social Democrats dominated. This was most visible in their relation to strikes, which was the main stumbling block in the international workers' movement. The question of striking was becoming a key issue throughout Europe. This topic was discussed at the Congresses of Brussels (1891) and Zurich (1893), where strike action was mentioned mainly as a weapon of political struggle. In the discussions, different ideas about moderation conflicted with each other, especially between German socialists and the somewhat more radical views of the French, Dutch and Norwegian delegations. Here, the labour movement found itself at a crossroads. In the Netherlands, there was a division between moderate socialists who had left the SDB (*Sociaal-Democratische Bond* or Social-Democratic League) and in 1894 founded the SDAP (Social Democratic Labour Party). The SDB objected to the adoption of a parliamentary struggle which, in the opinion of the party, enabled bourgeois influence to penetrate the workers' movement.[22] The more moderate current maintained that strike action could be used only in exceptional cases as a means of putting pressure on employers, because the authorities could use frequent striking as an excuse for further repression against the movement itself. Other, somewhat more radical currents considered that striking should be the basic means by which workers seek to realise their demands.

Similar processes occurred in the SDSHiS, which culminated in conflict. Krpan advocated using the strike as the main means of labour struggle. When a general strike broke out in Brod na Savi (1906/1907), however, the social democratic leadership completely distanced itself from it. They feared that during the strike there would be conflicts with the authorities, so they argued for calm. After that, Krpan wrote in *Hrvatski branik* [Croatian Sentinel] that the actions of the leaders in Zagreb were not driven by humanity and solidarity but rather by "revenge" because the strike was launched without their permission.[23]

On the other hand, Serbian social democrats made an ideological departure from Svetozar Marković's ideas. Before the Great War, the Serbian workers' movement had "never been well organized and steady ... where the membership pay dues, attend meetings, ... where the leaders agree on the basic orientation, etc."[24] The most pronounced disagreements among Serbian social democrats arose over relations with the countryside, in other words, the inclusion of peasants in the workers' movement, an issue they had faced since the very first days of the party's organisation.[25] The main figure in these discussions was Dragiša Lapčević, who initially opposed the inclusion of the countryside in the workers' movement, considering that the movement must be oriented exclusively towards the *pure proletariat*. In one document entitled "Proposition on the Resolution of the District List" he stated, indirectly, that no agitation should be conducted in rural districts as they were not proletarian and "do not feel socialist".[26] Over time, opposition against such action grew. Thus, Momčilo Janković from Niš stood up against Lapčević, declaring that the peasants in Serbia are nothing other than a "pure proletariat". Though tensions grew over time as part of the membership became increasingly active in the effort to spread party agitation to rural areas, these struggles ended, primarily because Lapčević changed his attitude towards the rural population, and eventually the party, at its eighth congress in 1910 in Belgrade redefined its relationship to the peasantry. Živko Topalović and Dimitrije Tucović played a big role in this.

In addition to internal party turmoil, a great blow was dealt to social democratic parties in the area of the future Kingdom of Serbs, Croats, and Slovenes (Yugoslavia) by a ban on socialist activities on the outbreak of the First World War. "The workers' movement in the Yugoslav lands stopped ... their operations at the beginning of the war or when it broke out, either because they were banned by the authorities (Slovenia, Croatia–Slavonia, the Slavic part of the movement in Banat, Bačka, and Baranja), or because the situation made it impossible (Bosnia–Herzegovina and Serbia)".[27] Political life actually faded out as the world entered the Great War, especially until it became clear that the conflict would last a long time and that its consequences would be dramatic. Dimitrije Tucović and Triša Kaclerović were Serb Social Democrats who took up a decisive position against the war in 1914 in Parliament, describing it as an imperial conflict that could not do any good for the workers.[28] This fact was often emphasised later because it was relatively unique. Dimitrije Tucović was buried in the centre of Belgrade's Slavija Square, where his remains stayed until 2017.

Despite the difficulties faced by social democrats when organising workers until 1914, they succeeded in building party organisations. They were also successful in building bridges both conceptually and organisationally, influencing the development of social democracy in the Yugoslavian region during the following period. As each of the countries of the future Kingdom of Serbs, Croats and Slovenes had numerous specific characteristics, so the workers' movement differed, depending on the political and economic circumstances of each environment. The union movement was more developed in more developed lands in Slovenia, Croatia and Serbia, but there were also big differences between them.[29]

THE REVIVAL OF THE WORKERS' MOVEMENT AND THE BEGINNING OF THE RIFT WITHIN THE SOCIAL DEMOCRATIC PARTIES

The stimulus for renewal of the movement, as Vitomir Korać writes, came from Bosnia. Already in February 1916, social democrats in Bosnia proposed the launching of a weekly newspaper in Zagreb that would report on events in the Socialist International. The minister of foreign affairs of Austria-Hungary, Count Ottokar Czernin (1872–1932, in service from 1916 to 1918), was at that time trying to include social democrats in the rescue of the Austro-Hungarian Monarchy. The minister demanded that Korać visit the Socialist Conference in Stockholm (5–12 September 1917),[30] where Austro-Hungarian socialists were supposed to argue for the Monarchy's survival. According to Korać's testimony, he rejected the offer. The conference triggered deep divisions in the party itself. They discussed whether or not socialists from the Yugoslav region should even attend the conference. In the end, a compromise was reached: the Action Committee, which had been established in the meantime, decided that two delegates, right-wing Mijo Radoševic and left-wing Stjepan Turković should participate. Eventually, for financial and organisational reasons, only Mijo Radošević left for Stockholm. Serious conflicts soon followed. At the beginning of July 1917, *Sloboda* [Liberty] began to be published in Zagreb; according to Korać, the newspaper immediately took a clear stand against Bolshevism and explicitly advocated cooperation with bourgeois parties in order to achieve Yugoslav national unity. During 1918, many labour newspapers were already launched, including another *Sloboda* in Novi Sad, *Radničke novine* [Workers' news] in Split, *Aprovizacija* in Osijek, *Radničke novine* in Belgrade and *Glas Slobode* [Voice of Liberty] in Sarajevo.

In addition to the press, the social democratic parties began to work on revitalising party organisations. Already in 1918, the Temporary Action Committee was founded, which set three goals: the revival of workers' professional organisations, the revival of party activities and the launch of a socialist newspaper. The members of this committee included Vitomir Korać, Stjepan Batt, Mijo Radošević and Stjepan Turković. Korać states that, although attitudes had not yet fully crystallized, they were already confronted by two currents: a sympathetic and an antipathetic view of Russian Bolshevism. Shortly thereafter, in Zagreb, the annual general assembly of the General Workers' Alliance (ORS) was held in August 1918; its aim was to determine the state of the movement itself and to lay down guidelines for further development. The historian Bosiljka Janjatović points out that the social democratic leadership of the ORS immediately after the creation of the State of Slovenes, Croats and Serbs was the main organiser and initiator of many of the workers' actions and the general strike in February 1919, which led to an eight-hour work day for all workers in Croatia.[31]

Although the differences between the separate currents were still not obvious because of the collapse of one state and the creation of a new one, the end of the war and the generally difficult situation, the ban on printing *Sloboda* brought to light a serious rift within the social democratic party. After the ban, the party launched a new paper entitled *Pravda* [Justice], which was also quickly banned, now on the charge of spreading Bolshevik ideas. Everything became even more visible when it came to deciding whether the socialists should enter the National Council. This was a new body, the supreme authority in the State of Slovenes, Croats and Serbs, a community that included the South Slavs living on the territory of the former Austria-Hungary after local politicians broke relations with Vienna. The new, unrecognised state was proclaimed 29 October 1918, and its capital was Zagreb.

The Workers' Council, which was founded in 1917, passed a resolution allowing the entry of social democrats into state bodies at its session on 20 December 1918. This caused a stir among the Yugoslav proletariat. Thus, the Social Democrats in Bosnia and Herzegovina, through their press, primarily *Glas slobode*, spoke out against the participation of Croatian social democrats in the National Council. On the other hand, strong support for Korać and his politics was provided by the Slovene Social Democratic Party, which on 8 September 1918 issued a statement that it was joining the National Council organisation and accepted cooperation with bourgeois parties. Accordingly, the founding conference of the National Council was attended by Vitomir Korać and Vilim Bukša, as well as the representatives of the Slovenian Social Democrats, Anton Kristan and Josip Petejan (1883–1960). This elicited a fairly sharp response from the Social Democrats of Bosnia and Herzegovina, who distanced themselves from this policy and the SDS of Slovenia by means of a special declaration.[32]

After the unification of the Yugoslav lands – that is, the establishment of the Kingdom of Serbs, Croats and Slovenes on 1 December 1918 – Korać entered the royal government on behalf of the social democrats as Minister of Social Policy. This triggered a wave of left-wing protests that regarded such a policy as *"fruitless ministerialism"*, while in later Yugoslav historiography everything that happened at that time was interpreted as contributing to the final dissolution of the party and trade unions. The leftist current still believed that the workers' movement must apply more radical forms of struggle for the ultimate creation of a communist society, arguing that there was revolutionary potential on the territory of the Kingdom of Serbs, Croats and Slovenes. This was proven first of all by widespread peasant disorder in Slavonia. Thus, the pre-war conflicts became clearer than ever. Later on, even historiography developed a narrative in which the judgements of the leftist current – the future communists – on the potential for revolution, the liquidation of feudalism, national oppression and the realisation of complete democracy had not been correct. This implied that there had been a profound split and that the election of Korać and other social democrats had been a poor choice.[33]

Korać emphasises that, in 1919, "the workers' movement, in the new relationships, began ... to thrive with unprecedented strength. The number of trade unionised workers rose to 50,000. Political organisation took place in about 100 localities."[34] The movement was spreading, but the party was on the verge of schism. This was particularly apparent on 16 January 1919 during a conference of fairly militant workers' occupational associations (typographers, railroad workers, store employees, leatherworkers, builders and bookbinders) in Croatia, who refused to join the General Workers' Alliance (ORS) and instead founded the Cartel of Professional Organisations. These unions would later become the core of the communist trade unions in Croatia. A further split in the party manifested itself at the end of January 1919. At the Provincial Conference of Croatian Social Democrats held in Zagreb, which "turned into a decisive battle over the decision of whether to approach Bolshevik tactics or continue with opportunistic tactics", two bodies were present: the General Board of the party in which the rightist current had the upper hand, and the Action Committee, dominated by members of the leftist current.[35]

Cooperation among Yugoslav social democrats continued. Dragiša Lapčević and Filip Filipović were at the Conference in Zagreb as representatives of Serbia's social democrats, while Sreten Jakšić and Bogdan Krekić came in the name of Bosnian social democrats. It should be noted that all of these guests supported the leftist current. After the introductory speeches, the main issue was discussed, tactics. Two resolutions were presented in this regard. The reformists repeated their position that the participation of members of the social democratic parties in the government was justified, because this strengthened the proletariat. In this resolution, every form of terrorism and chauvinism was condemned. On the other hand, the leftists in their six-point resolution highlighted the aspiration of unifying all Yugoslav social democratic parties, on the principle of an irreconcilable class struggle, without collaboration with the bourgeoisie. Among other things, they emphasised their disapproval of social democratic party members participating in the Yugoslav government, and at the end of the resolution they voiced their demand that the party join the Third International.

On this occasion, Vitomir Korać highlighted the basic principles of the policy of *ministerialism*. In his opinion, for a socialist revolution to occur, economic factors must be mature; he pointed out that uprisings represent only water in the mills of foreign imperialists and domestic reactionaries. He stressed that his faction did not rule out the method of armed uprising, but advocated this "only when we think that by this method we can achieve the victory of democracy, the victory of a majority with no rights over a tyrannical minority".[36] He concluded: "My politics derive from my deepest beliefs, so you can even stone me, but I will not change my mind."[37]

After a vote, the rightist resolution won out. It rejected Bolshevism in its second point, stressing that an antidemocratic principle was incompatible with party principles. It was repeated once again that the party condemned all forms of terrorism. This, of course, was directed against the left-wing current and its policy of accepting Bolshevik methods of gaining power. The conclusions of the Conference inspired a particularly sharp reaction from Zagreb's *Pravda*, which criticised the "lamblike politics" of the social democrats, identifying them with civil liberalism. They considered that all tactics were allowed in the creation of socialism. Here, it is evident that the leftist current of the party had positioned itself against the policy of ministerialism; that is, it considered that the participation of social democrats in government was the root cause of the split among its membership. After the resolution, the leftist current with Dragiša Lapčević and Filip Filipović established the Leftist Action Board as a counterweight to the Main Board.

The social democrats in Croatia were extremely divided. The rightist current considered that the leftists' tactics had developed under the influence of opponents from Russia and were trying to separate the right from the masses, to compromise them, and so the entire workers' movement lost out under their "factional dictatorship".[38] Although probably a few more Croatian and Slovene social democrats were among the rightists, and Serbs and Bosnia-Herzegovinians were more on the side of the leftists, it is difficult to make generalisations. Older historiography claimed that the SDSHiS was strongly marked by opportunistic politics under the influence of the Second International and Austro-Marxism. Within all the parties, there were strong ideological controversies and both streams were represented. For example, within the Social Democratic Party of Croatia and Slavonia there was a strong leftist current from which the Communist Party would be formed. At that time, numerous newspapers of the leftist current, later the Communist Party, were published within the territory of Croatia, but this may not have been representative. These included: *Radničke straže* [Workers' sentinels] (Vukovar), *Radnička riječ* [The worker's word] (Osijek), *Narodna volja* [The will of the people] (Požega) and *Oslobođenje* [Liberation] (Split), as well as the Zagreb papers *Novi list* [New paper] and *Plamen* [The flame].

The Slovenian social democrats stuck with the right wing of the party. They cooperated closely with similar groups in Croatia and Vojvodina and were ready for unification. The Slovenian workers' movement was under the strong influence of Austria's socialists, who had already fully accepted the tenets of evolutionary socialism. Anton Kristan, together with Vitomir Korać and Vilim Bukša, joined the first government of the Kingdom of Serbs, Croats, and Slovenes of Ljubo Davidović (16 August–18 October 1919). The social democrats had three ministers in this government: Kristan was minister of forests and mines, Korać was minister for social policy and Bukšeg was minister for the nourishment and restructuring of the country. Thus continued the policy of ministerialism, and ideological conflicts themselves became a constant feature of the Yugoslav workers' movement.

THE BELGRADE AND NOVI SAD CONGRESSES – THE DIE IS CAST

The Osijek *Radničke novine*, in its issue of 24 February 1919, published at the initiative of the Serbian and Bosnian social democratic parties a declaration inviting all *comrade parties* to attend a congress in Slavonski Brod, which was supposed to be held "at Easter" in order to unify all the Yugoslav social democratic parties. On that occasion, rightist newspapers, such as *Socijalist*, criticised Belgrade's leftist newspapers for creating an open split in the party, calling them "terrorists". Because the authorities banned holding the congress on the territory of Croatia and Slavonia, it was held in Belgrade from 20 to 23 April 1919. Vitomir Korać had left the government (on 24 February 1919), but regardless of the fact that the main reason for objections – the social democrats' "ministerialism" – no longer existed, part of the membership still wanted to break away and establish a new party. On this occasion, the social democratic press, which included the Osijek *Socijalist*, wrote that the leftist current had caused unrest among the workers, something that the major landowners and other reactionaries were waiting for. In this period a new reason for disagreement between the two currents appeared: agrarian reform. Under circumstances of great rural unrest and the demands for land reform, the authorities realised that solving this issue would be one of the key political problems after the war.

The government of Stojan Protić passed the issue of agrarian reform on to the Ministry of Social Policy, headed by Korać. The labour press put further pressure, pointing out that large estates had to be divided because otherwise many of them would remain uncultivated, which could lead to even greater food shortages. In February 1919, the Preliminary Provisions for the Preparation of Agrarian Reform were published. The committee for the solution of the agrarian issue proposed the main principles of agrarian reform, which included the expropriation of large estates, with compensation for the previous owners. The leftist social democrats sharply criticised the payment of compensation, asserting that this was too generous to the wealthy class and demanded collective ownership of the land. The leftists felt that social relationships were set for upheaval and that the revolutionary potential of the rural masses should be used, while the rightists emphasised that in the Kingdom itself there were no large estates except in Slavonia and that therefore there was no revolutionary potential. As a counter-argument in the debates on the need to create a more radical peasant proletariat, the thesis was raised that the Yugoslav peasant, in the event that he is able to solve his problems in the Russian manner, tends to stand against the workers, hoping for higher prices for "grain, livestock and milk" while the latter of course desire lower prices. Due to widespread opposition to such reform, Korać resigned.

The internal rift between social democrats was partly conditioned by international circumstances. In most countries, the leftist current had been isolated from party structures and, on the pattern of the Russian Bolsheviks, founded communist parties. Among other things, in 1919 the Communist Party of Germany was established and after that the Communist Party of Bulgaria, while in 1920 communist parties were established in France and Switzerland. The revolutionary events in Hungary and the Hungarian Soviet Republic of Béla Kún, as well as the return of many Yugoslav soldiers from prison in Soviet Russia often infected with the ideas of the Bolshevik revolution, were radicalising the workers. In April 1919, 450 delegates from all over the Kingdom of Serbs, Croats and Slovenes attended the Congress in Belgrade. At that time, the Socialist Workers' Party of Yugoslavia (Communists), or SRPJ(k), and a trade union body called the Central Workers' Trade Union Council of Yugoslavia (CRSVJ) were founded. The new party was made up of former members of social democratic parties, or parts of them, who opted for the revolutionary path to socialism and the acceptance of the revolutionary experience in Russia, and groups who condemned cooperation with the bourgeoisie in any form.

The following parties entered into the SRPJ(k): the Serbian Social Democratic Party, the Social Democratic Party of Bosnia and Herzegovina, the Social Democratic Party of Dalmatia, the left wing of the Social Democratic Party of Croatia and Slavonia, gathered around the Action Committee of the Left, socialist organisations in Vojvodina, the Yugoslav Revolutionary Communist Alliance Pelagić and socialist organisations in Macedonia and Montenegro.[39] The social democrats in Bosnia-Herzegovina were fiery advocates of the Belgrade Congress and considered that the whole breakup had been caused by Korać's ministerialism.

On the other hand, the social democratic parties continued to oppose revolution and sought national concentration and cooperation between the classes. Social Democrats reacted to the Belgrade Congress in the press, pointing out that there was "much ado about nothing", as all the talk about the congress was mere radicalism and collective revolutionary psychosis. At the same time, Korać emphasised that no one should count on the current rebellious state of the working class as a given. Soon the rightist current of the party held its congress of unification in Novi Sad on 21 and 22 June 1919. That congress marked the foundation of the Yugoslav Social Democratic Party (JSDS), which Korać described as a counteraction against the Bolsheviks. The Social Democratic Party of Croatia and Slavonia, the Yugoslav Social Democratic Party (Slovenes) and the Vojvodina Social Democratic Party all joined the JSDS in Novi Sad.[40] During the Congress, it was concluded that the social democrats would continue to participate in the work of state bodies and thus defend the interests of the working class. Particularly emphasised was the need for active political engagement to ratify a new constitution. Thus, along with many other parties, the social democrats submitted their constitutional proposal, which was based on "socialisation of the big estates" and decentralisation. On the other hand, this draft of the future constitution did not reject the system of private property; it left open the possibility of the socialisation of some means of production, but only through a gradual, evolutionary process,[41] as was the case with the programmes of all the social democratic parties.

A year later, in Zagreb, from 2 to 4 April 1920, the social democrats from Banat, Bačka, Bosnia and Herzegovina, and the remaining rightist currents from Croatia and Slavonia were united. The new party was called the Social Democratic Party of Yugoslavia (SDSJ). Thus, at the end of 1920, there were two social democratic parties in the Kingdom of Serbs, Croats and Slovenes:

the JDSJ and the SDSJ. "The first organisations were concentrated only in Slovenia, primarily in Carinthia and Styria, while the membership of the other was scattered throughout Croatia, Slavonia, Bosnia and Herzegovina, and Vojvodina."[42] The JDSJ was also active internationally. The party's delegates, among others, participated in the founding conference of the "Second-and-a-Half International" in Vienna. On that occasion, they accepted its programme documents and assumed the obligation "to work on the unification of the Yugoslav working class on its platform".[43]

The Belgrade and Novi Sad Congresses did not mark the end of turmoil. New clashes occurred at the second congress of communists in Vukovar in 1920, where the SRPJ(k) was renamed the Communist Party of Yugoslavia (KPJ), while the social democrats, because of major disagreements, would unite several more times. Congresses largely defined the major ideological postulates of the main currents in the workers' movement. They did not halt the process of ideological differentiation, however, either in the Social Democratic Party or in the Communist Party.

THE JOINING OF THE *CENTRUMAŠI* AND THE PATH TOWARDS CREATING THE SPJ

Although the majority of social democrats joined the JSDS, they still failed (not unlike the communists, in fact) to build a stable party structure. This was largely related to what was going on in the SRPJ(k). At the second party congress held in Vukovar (20–26 June 1920), at which the party was officially renamed the Communist Party of Yugoslavia, part of the membership separated themselves. This group would later be called the *centrumaši* ("centrists") and were closer in their opinions to the social democrats. This faction published a *Manifest opozicije* [Manifesto of the opposition], which clearly opposes fundamental communist principles.[44] Shortly after the elections to the Constitutional Assembly on 28 November 1920, the *centrumaši* were excluded from the KPJ under the leadership of Živko Topalović. At the end of March 1921, they founded the Socialist Workers' Party of Yugoslavia (SRPJ).

The aspiration to bring the KPJ and the social democrats together was most dominant among the Slovenian social democrats, especially those from Maribor. There had never been a complete break with the Communists in that region, so it was possible to quickly and easily bring together "social democratic and left-socialist organisations".[45] At the beginning of October 1921, a meeting was held at which it was concluded that the two currents were not separated by any principle or tactical differences. This was because Maribor's social democrats were under the influence of the Austrian social democrats, who thought that unification should be carried out in accordance with the Vienna policy, namely the Second-and-a-Half Socialist International, which was convened between the Second and Third Internationals (Comintern). That policy was not in line with the views of the party leadership, however, who at a round-table conference at the end of 1921 completely ignored the conclusions of the Maribor meeting.

Efforts to cooperate were obviously being made, but there were a number of obstacles along the way. The *centrumaši*, for example, mostly reproached the social democrats for insisting on ministerialism. Topalović considered pure ministerialism, without relying on the broad proletarian masses, to be most damaging to the working class because it helped the bourgeoisie to strengthen its position. Such criticism was directed mainly at Korać, the most prominent proponent of ministerialism. Korora, however, rejected the criticism, calling the *centrumaši* "verbal revolutionaries" and reproaching them with allowing the communists to gain the ascendancy in the workers' movement.

Negotiations between the two social democratic parties nevertheless occurred on 1/2 August 1921, shortly after the assassination of Interior Minister Milorad Drašković (1873–1921) by the communist Alija Alijagić. During these negotiations, the Socialist Community of Yugoslavia (SZJ) was founded, whose basic document was the *Protocol of the Agreement of Socialist Parties*. This text defines the relationship with ministerialism, internationalism and communism, but it completely rejects a socialist revolution. The Bosnian *centrumaši* were against this document. They thought that such unification was artificial and that it was not a step towards the unification of the working class. The newly formed SZJ was expecting a large influx of membership. After the assassination of the interior minister, the royal government passed the *Obznan* [Proclamation], a law that banned the KPJ. Such a development never occurred, however. Therefore, the leadership of the Socialist Party on one hand had to work on making the party stronger and on the other to tighten the party's positions. Most importantly, however, they had to define the party's relationship with the *centrumaši*.

Because of all this, the SZJ was understood as a temporary solution to the founding of an umbrella party, which all social democratic currents could accept. As the KPJ was banned, the SZJ's infrastructure became stronger. After the dissolution of the communist administrations of workers' clubs, they were handed over to the social democrats, giving them a material and organisational boost. Apart from workers' clubs, social democrats now also ran workers' printshops. Nevertheless, there was confusion and incoherence in the ranks of the SZJ. Thus, at the time decisions were being taken in Belgrade about the unification of all *centrumaši* and social democratic currents, the Zagreb District Council only managed to recommend the creation of a Socialist Community that had in fact already been founded four months beforehand.

Due to the conflicting views on ministerialism, Korać did not hesitate to unite. That is why the unification committee, which met in Belgrade on 23 October 1921, set up a commission to work on the unification programme. The commission consisted of Lapčević, Topalović, Korać, Divac, Korun and Golouh. At the session of the unification committee on 14 December, the drafts of the unification were adopted, thus removing the last obstacle to the unification of all the Yugoslav social democratic parties.

The act of unification was not achieved at the congress, but at a conference of representatives of the central committees of three parties (JSDS, SDSJ and SRPJ), held on 18 December 1921 in Belgrade. On that occasion, three documents were adopted: the *Manifesto and the Decisions of Unification*, the *Programme* and the *Party Charter*. As its main objective, the new party designated the awakening of class consciousness and the organisation of the proletariat. On this occasion, once again, the communist tactic of proletarian dictatorship was condemned and the unbridgeable difference between social democrats and communists was emphasised.

Greater friction arose when it came to the question of the party's name. Korać's supporters demanded that "social democracy" be highlighted in the name of the party, while the *centrumaši* opposed this, pointing out that this name was tainted. In the end, a compromise was reached and the party was named the Socialist Party of Yugoslavia (SPJ). The leaders of the party were Dragiša Lapčević, president of the executive, and Vitomir Korać as political secretary. It was decided that, in order to make work easier, the party would be organised regionally, with seven members to be elected at regional assemblies, and that the party newspaper, *Socijalističke radničke novine* [Socialist workers' news] would be renamed *Radničke novine* [Workers' news].

The social structure of the party, according to Toma Milenković, consisted mainly of officials from labour institutions,[46] such as labour exchanges, chambers of labour and the like. In Croatia, mainly industrial workers joined the party. In Slovenia, the party initially had many supporters among the peasantry. Their number eventually fell, but the party organisations remained in those areas because they were close to larger industrial facilities. In Vojvodina, most of the party membership consisted of peasants, making this area stand out in comparison to the overall social image of the party. In Serbia and Bosnia and Herzegovina the situation was more or less similar, because the membership came from the ranks of craftsmen, with a slightly smaller number from the ranks of intellectuals and industrial workers. According to available data for Belgrade, at the end of May 1921, the party had 153 members, of whom 101 were hired workers, 31 craftsmen and 10 clerks, as well as members of the intelligentsia.[47]

The creation of the SPJ marked the completion of one phase in the development of social democracy in the Kingdom of the Serbs, Croats and Slovenes. In this way, this political current took on clear party contours within which it needed to take advantage of the free political space with which it was provided. Severe infighting, as well as constant battles with legal communist organisations during the 1920s, above all with *independent workers*, prevented the SPJ from developing or creating a social democratic politics of the kind that existed primarily in Germany. Therefore, the SPJ was never able to develop recognisable political patterns, and for this very reason, it failed to attract broader masses among the working class.

THE SOCIAL ACTIVITIES OF THE SPJ

Social organisations of social democrats, such as the Union of Socialist Youth of Yugoslavia (SSOJ) or the Secretariat of Women Socialists, played a major role in the education of future members of the party. Initially, the parties did not pay much attention to these organisations, so it was not until late in 1921 that an action was organised in Zagreb to establish a youth organisation. It should be noted that the Action Committee of SSOJ did not have a well-defined structure. This is apparent from the decision of the SPJ, according to which that committee should be active solely on a cultural and educational level. The first representative of the Action Committee was Mirko Kus-Nikolayev (1896–1961), who worked there until 1925, when he withdrew from the party. He later became a well-known ethnologist and one of the founders of sociology in Croatia. The Social Democratic Youth was primarily concerned with studying the writings of Karl Kautsky (1854–1938), in which they found ideological inspiration. According to the Committee's charter, which was adopted sometime later, the membership was to be divided into two age groups: 5 to 12 years and 14 to 28 years. It should be emphasised that the SPJ leadership sought to link this organisation to party structures. This would cause a number of problems in the future, especially when Antun Schmidt, a former member of the Union of Communist Youth of Yugoslavia (SKOJ) became the head of the SSOJ.

The social democrats were somewhat more adept at organising women. In this, the *centrumaši* had a major role. Even before its official unification in the SPJ, this group expressed a need for the political organisation of women. In this field as well, the social democrats fought with the communists. At their first conference (1920), the communists also held the Conference of Women Socialists, which adopted the then SPJ(k) programme and began printing newspapers aimed at attracting women to the party.

The social democrats acted similarly. The culmination of their endeavours was the period immediately prior to the establishment of the SPJ. On 30 January 1921, the first Conference of Women Socialists was held, at which Milica Đurić-Topalović (1893–1972) gave the main speech. In November 1921, a temporary secretariat was established. Besides Đurić-Topalović, Sofija Levi and Mara Timotić were also members. Although this organisation had the necessary structure and party support, few women joined the Secretariat. In Croatia and Vojvodina, almost no one joined this organisation, while in Slovenia, especially in Maribor, women were organised into "special organisations and in early May 1921, they had about 300 members. ... The work of women socialists was overseen by a committee of 16 members elected by special rules."[48] Over time, however, their numbers diminished, primarily because of ideological conflicts.

There are only two passages in the SPJ Charter that refer specifically to women. One states that women are equal to men legally, politically and socially, and the other that women are banned from night working. At the first congress of the SPJ, a new charter was adopted. This one mentions the possibility of "creating organisations of women socialists for the achievement of certain educational and propaganda goals".[49]

THE SOCIAL DEMOCRATIC LEGACY

The social democratic idea in the Yugoslav space faded completely at the beginning of the Second World War, and it was not institutionally restored until the early 1990s. Regardless of the fact that the Yugoslav communist system was probably the softest in Europe during the Cold War, it was not a social democracy: it was not a system that rejected revolution. At the beginning of the 1990s, former members of the League of Communists, as the Communist Party was called after 1952, began to establish parties in their respective republics, which in various forms incorporated the name "social democracy". Among others, the Social Democratic Party of Croatia (SDP) and the Social Democratic Party of Bosnia and Herzegovina (SDPBiH) were founded, while in Serbia a party named the Social Democratic Party of Serbia was founded in 2014. At least two other parties in Serbia recall their social democratic legacy (the Socialist Party of Serbia, the Socialist Party).

Similarly, in Croatia and Bosnia and Herzegovina, social democratic parties invoke the years 1894 and 1909, respectively. Nevertheless, the existence of a social democratic legacy is rather questionable. This is supported by the fact that today no one marks any of the anniversaries or personalities that are truly related to social democracy. The first death of a worker during political unrest in Croatia, 16-year-old Srećko Kulundžić (1889–1905), who was killed during the first general strike in Osijek in 1905, has been completely forgotten, for example. In general, the social democratic parties relate to the past awkwardly, if at all. On the other hand, the removal of the monument to and grave of Dimitrije Tucović as part of the reconstruction of Slavija Square in late 2016 caused great interest among the public in Serbia. The public interpreted it as a renunciation of the socialist past and of Tucović's ideas, which no longer fit the postmodern image of the city, nor the current extreme-right, nationalist ideology. It should be noted that a certain slowness to embrace the social democratic idea probably comes from the fact that some party members compromised themselves by joining the fascist movement (Živko Topalović), while others left the party for good government positions, such as the Slovene Etbin Kristan, who left the SPJ to become a government commissioner in New York. All this has contributed to the general ignorance about the social democratic legacy, though appearances imply otherwise, at least in terms of party names.

Historiography has written sporadically and not always particularly positively about Yugoslavia's social democracy. This does not mean, however, that the idea did not exist, that there were no politicians or politics or that there was no socio-political influence. This field is still potentially interesting for research, primarily because of numerous theoretical writings, but also with a view to obtaining a better understanding of the complex political life of the Kingdom of the Serbs, Croats and Slovenes, which has not been exhausted in the assigned, binary paradigms of nationalist/bourgeoisie and communists. Finally, today it would be important to establish the communist and social democratic legacies, especially in the area of the former Yugoslavia, where this is more dynamic and more venerated than in most of Eastern Europe. Because many of the emancipatory ideas of social democracy have to date been realised only in this area, the whole story is current, alive and worthy of attention.

SUMMARY

There were several social democratic parties in the territory of the Kingdom of Serbs, Croats and Slovenes, a complex state that came into existence on 1 December 1918 with the unification of the Kingdom of Serbia, Montenegro and the lands inhabited by South Slavs within Austria-Hungary. The oldest was the Social Democratic Party of Croatia and Slavonia (founded in 1894). In Serbia, the Social Democratic Party of Serbia had existed since 1903, while in Slovenian territory and in parts of Istria inhabited by Croats, the Yugoslav Social Democratic Party had been active since 1896.

The last to be founded was the Social Democratic Party of Bosnia and Herzegovina (1909). Workers' parties were relatively small and weak in countries that were minimally industrialised, predominantly agrarian and poor. The role of social democrats was thus relatively invisible when Austria-Hungary began to disintegrate and a new country emerged. Soon, as in the rest of Europe, impressed by the October Revolution and then by the activities of Béla Kun in Hungary, the Left experienced a split between the Communist Party of Yugoslavia (KPJ) and social democrats. The KPJ, which had attracted a large number of members, was banned in 1921 following its success in the first general elections, after which it had become the third strongest party in the parliament. Politicians who were more inclined to parliamentarianism and opposed to revolution entered the government and were attacked as "sterile ministers". One faction of the social democratic parties united in 1919 to form the Yugoslav Social Democratic Party (JSDS), while in 1920 another group founded the Social Democratic Party of Yugoslavia (SDSJ), which had somewhat fewer supporters.

The two social democratic parties began negotiations in the summer of 1921 and finally merged at the end of that year as the Socialist Party of Yugoslavia (SPJ). This was a united social democratic party led by Dragiša Lapčević and Vitomir Korać (as political secretary), whose platform was decidedly against revolution and against communism. Although it profited materially when the authorities distributed all the property of the outlawed communist parties and their trade unions to the social democrats, the effects were small.

Though illegal, the KPJ continued to operate through trade unions and organisations that were de facto under its control, causing a rift among social democrats, who had difficulty reaching the working class. The SPJ never became a significant factor in the political life of the Kingdom of Serbs, Croats, and Slovenes (later renamed the Kingdom of Yugoslavia), although it fought for the interests of workers and participated in the theoretical debates of that time.

---

1   Bosiljka Janjatović, *Sindikalni pokret u Jugoslaviji do 1941* [The union movement in Yugoslavia until 1941], Varaždin: Sindikalna škola Hrvatske and NIU, 30.
2   Toma Milenković, *Socijalistička partija Jugoslavije* [The Socialist Party of Yugoslavia], Belgrade: Institut za savremenu istoriju and NIP Export-press, 1974, 580.
3   Josip Cazi, *S puta reformizma na put klasne borbe. Ujedinjeni radnički sindikalni savez 1929–1934* [From the path of reformism to the path of the class struggle: The united workers' union alliance], Radničke novine, Zagreb, 1977, 17.
4   See, for example, the anthology *1918. u hrvatskoj povijesti* [1918 in Croatian History], MH 2012, p. 543, or *Temelji moderne Hrvatske. Hrvatske zemlje u "dugom" 19. stoljeću* [The foundations of modern Croatia: The Croatian lands in the "long" nineteenth century], MH 2016, p. 741.
5   Slavko Pavičić, *Hrvatska vojna i ratna poviest i Prvi svjetski rat* [Croatian military and war history and the First World War],

Zagreb: Hrvatska knjiga, 1943. Most of this book covers the First World War, but the Italian front is intentionally skipped over. The Independent State of Croatia (NDH) was an ally of Hitler's Germany and Mussolini's Italy.

6   Srđan Milošević, Od stagnacije do revolucije [From stagnation to revolution], in *Jugoslavija u istorijskoj perspektivi* [Yugoslavia in historical perspective], Belgrade: Helsinški odbor za ljudska prava u Srbiji, 2017, 327–365.

7   Margaret MacMillan, *Mirotvorci*: Šest mjeseci koji su promijenili svijet [Peacemakers: Six months that changed the world], Zagreb: Naklada Ljevak, 2008, 55–56.

8   Politički pregled [Political overview] *Radničke novine. Socijalističko glasilo* [Workers' news: The socialist organ], (Osijek), no. 14, 29 November 1918, 1.

9   Bogdan Krizman, Građa o nemirima u Hrvatskoj na kraju g. 1918 [Sources on the unrest in Croatia at the end of 1918], *Historijski zbornik*, 8/1957, nos. 1–4, 111–129.

10 This was probably in great part due to inherited negative opinions of social democracy: because they had voted in favour of war loans in July 1914, these parties were often denounced as traitors of the working class who had contributed to the outbreak of the First World War.

11 The Triune Kingdom of Croatia, Slavonia and Dalmatia was a territory ruled by the Ban in Zagreb, who functioned as head of government, and included only Slavonia and Croatia (the northwestern part of today's Croatia). It had a high degree of autonomy and after 1868 was part of the Hungarian half of Austro-Hungary. Dalmatia, whose capital was Zadar, was in the Austrian part of the state. The Military Frontier territory was not formally united with the Triune Kingdom until 1881. Until 1908, Bosnia and Herzegovina was formally part of the Ottoman Empire but had been occupied (or liberated?) by Austria-Hungary since 1878. After the Young Turk Revolution, Vienna ended this situation by officially annexing the territory, causing a deep crisis in Europe, but not a great conflict, because Russia, after its defeat in the war with Japan, was not prepared to help Serbia, which was dissatisfied with the taking of lands it considered Serbian.

12 Dejan Dedić (ed.), *Miloš Krpan. Izabrani spisi* [Miloš Krpan: Selected writings], Zagreb: DAF, 2010, 19.

13 The first secret social democratic club that the authorities discovered was in Zagreb. It was run by Wolfgang Hiža and Franjo Srnec. Both were convicted. After they had served their prison sentences, Srnec was banished to Slovenska Bistrica, and Hiža to Bohemia.

14 Stojan Kešić, Hrvatski i srbijanski radnički pokret i stvaranje prvih sindikalnih organizacija u Bosni i Hercegovini [The workers' movement in Croatia and Serbia and the creation of the first labour unions in Bosnia and Herzegovina], in *Materijali naučnog skupa Prvo radničko društvo u jugoslavenskim zemljama – Osijek 1867* [Materials from the scientific conference on the First Workers' Association in the Yugoslav countries – Osijek 1867], (main editor Zdravko Krnić), Slavonski Brod, 1969, 291–315.

15 Marijan Britovšek, Radnički pokret u periodu između Prve i Druge internacionale [The workers' movement in the period between the First and Second Internationals], *Priručnik za istoriju međunarodnog radničkog pokreta* [Manual for the history of the international workers' movement], (ed. Ljubinka Krešić), Belgrade: Rad, 1964, 281–331.

16 Stojan Kešić, Hrvatski i srbijanski radnički pokret i stvaranje prvih sindikalnih organizacija u Bosni i Hercegovini [The workers' movement in Croatia and Serbia and the creation of the first labour unions in Bosnia and Herzegovina], in *Materijali naučnog skupa Prvo radničko društvo u jugoslavenskim zemljama – Osijek 1867* [Materials from the scientific conference on

17 the First Workers' Association in the Yugoslav countries – Osijek 1867], (main editor Zdravko Krnić), Slavonski Brod, 1969, 291–315.
17 Mira Bogdanović, *Srpski radnički pokret 1903–1914: naličje legende* [The Serbian workers' movement 1903–1914: The other side of the legend], Zagreb: Globus, 1989, 33.
18 Isto, 165.
19 Đorđe Tomić; Krunoslav Stojaković, *Iz povijesti jugoslavenske ljevice od početka 19. stoljeća do izbijanja Drugog svjetskog rata. Skica poglavlja koje nedostaje* [From the history of the Yugoslav Left from the beginning of the nineteenth century to the beginning of the Second World War: A sketch of the missing chapters], Belgrade: Rosa Luxemburg-Stiftung, 2013, available at: http://dordetomic.de/wp-content/uploads/2013/12/Perspektive-07_Online.pdf, accessed 20 July 2018.
20 Idem.
21 Vitomir Korać, *Ciljevi i putevi socijalne demokracije* [Goals and paths of social democracy], Zagreb: Naša snaga, 1912.
22 Henny Buiting, The Netherlands, The Formation of Labour Movments 1870–1914, *Contributions to the History of Labour and Society*, 2 (main ed. Jurgen Rojahn), Leiden, 1990, 57–85.
23 Ivan Kovačević, *Radnički pokret u Slavonskom Brodu* [The workers' movement in Slavonski Brod], Slavonski Brod, 1976, 163.
24 Mira Bogdanović, *Srpski radnički pokret 1903–1914: naličje legende* [The Serbian workers' movement 1903–1914: The other side of the legend], Zagreb: Globus, 1989, 259.
25 Desanka Pešić, Dragiša Lapčević i "seljačko pitanje" (1903–1914) [Dragiša Lapčević and the "peasant question"], in: *Prilozi za istoriju socijalizma* [Contributions for a history of socialism], vol. 3, Belgrade: Institut za izučavanje radničkog pokreta, 1966, 65–102.
26 Idem.
27 Toma Milenković, *Socijalistička partija Jugoslavije* [The Socialist Party of Yugoslavia], Belgrade: Institut za savremenu istoriju and NIP Export-press, 1974, 21.
28 For more on Serbian socialists in the nineteenth century, see: Latinka Perović, *Srpski socijalisti 19. veka* [Serbian socialists of the nineteenth century], Belgrade: Rad, 1985.
29 Bosiljka Janjatović, *Sindikalni pokret u Jugoslaviji do 1941* [The union movement in Yugoslavia until 1941], Varaždin: Sindikalna škola Hrvatske and NIU, 20.
30 Konferencija u Stockholmu trebala je okupiti sve socijalističke stranke u Europi, a predstavljala je svojevrstan odgovor lijevoj struji i njezinoj Zimmerwaldskoj konferenciji (5–8 rujna 1915.).
31 Bosiljka Janjatović, *Sindikalni pokret u Jugoslaviji do 1941.* [The union movement in Yugoslavia until 1941], Varaždin: Sindikalna škola Hrvatske and NIU, 15.
32 Josip Cazi, *S puta reformizma na put klasne borbe. Ujedinjeni radnički sindikalni savez 1929–1934* [From the path of reformism to the path of class struggle: The United Workers' Union Alliance], Zagreb: Radničke novine, 1977, 16.
33 Ibid., 17.
34 Vitomir Korać, *Povijest radničkog pokreta u Hrvatskoj i Slavoniji. Od prvih početaka do ukidanja ovih pokrajina 1922. godine* [History of the workers' movement in Croatia and Slavonia: From the early beginnings to the repeal of these provinces in 1922], Vol. I., Zagreb: Radnička komora Hrvatske i Slavonije, 1929, 256.
35 Idem.
36 Stranačka konferenca u Zagrebu [Party conference in Zagreb], *Radničke novine. Socijalističko glasilo* [Workers' News: The socialist organ], (Osijek), no. 7., 13 February 1919, II.
37 Idem.
38 Vitomir Korać, *Povijest radničkog pokreta u Hrvatskoj i Slavoniji. Od prvih početaka do ukidanja ovih pokrajina 1922. godine* [History of the workers' movement in Croatia and Slavonia: From the early beginnings to the repeal of these provinces in 1922], vol.

39 I., Zagreb: Radnička komora Hrvatske i Slavonije, 1929, 263.
39 Stanislava Koprivica-Oštrić, Programi radničkih političkih stranaka osnovanih u Jugoslaviji 1919. – 1929. (uporedna analiza) [Programmes of workers' political parties founded in Yugoslavia 1919–1929 (comparative analysis)] *Zbornik*, no. 7–8/1970, 219–54.
40 Vitomir Korać, *Povijest radničkog pokreta u Hrvatskoj i Slavoniji. Od prvih početaka do ukidanja ovih pokrajina 1922. godine* [History of the workers' movement in Croatia and Slavonia: From the early beginnings to the repeal of these provinces in 1922], vol. I., Zagreb: Radnička komora Hrvatske i Slavonije, 1929, 272.
41 Ferdo Čulinović, *Jugoslavija između dva rata* [Yugoslavia between the two wars], vol. I, Zagreb: Jugoslavenska akademija znanosti i umjetnosti, 1961, 326.
42 Toma Milenković, *Socijalistička partija Jugoslavije* [The Socialist Party of Yugoslavia], Belgrade: Institut za savremenu istoriju and NIP Export-press, 1974, 25.
43 Ibid., 28.
44 Manifest opozicije KPJ [Manifesto of the opposition KPJ], available at: http://www.znaci.net/00001/138_19.pdf; accessed 18 August 2018.
45 Toma Milenković, *Socijalistička partija Jugoslavije* [The Socialist Party of Yugoslavia], Belgrade: Institut za savremenu istoriju and NIP Export-press, 1974, 67.
46 Toma Milenković, *Socijalistička partija Jugoslavije* [The Socialist Party of Yugoslavia], Belgrade: Institut za savremenu istoriju and NIP Export-press, 1974, 562.
47 Ibid., 559.
48 Toma Milenković, *Socijalistička partija Jugoslavije* [The Socialist Party of Yugoslavia], Belgrade: Institut za savremenu istoriju and NIP Export-press, 1974, 506–507.
49 Idem.

SOCIAL DEMOCRACY AND THE REPUBLIC OF ICELAND

BJÖRGVIN G. SIGURÐSSON

INTRODUCTION

Social democrats in Iceland founded both the Social Democratic Party (SDP) and the Icelandic Confederation of Labour in 1916. The former was established as the latter's political wing, a role in which it continued until the labour movement severed its ties with the SDP in the early 1940s. Following the SDP's founding, significant strides were made in spreading and increasing the influence of social democracy and trade unionism.

Frequent splits and conflicts within the SDP would later hamper its political power, but it still exerted a major influence in shaping Icelandic society, including the enactment of legislation on fishing vessels' working hours, social security and workers' dwellings in the party's earliest years and during the first years after Iceland regained sovereignty. The SDP formed various coalitions with other parties, implementing a range of social democratic policies. The party split five times, first of all in 1938 when one of its most prominent members joined forces with the Communists. From that time onwards, a powerful party to the left of the SDP always existed, fragmenting the left wing of Icelandic politics until the parties reunited as the Social Democratic Alliance at the end of the twentieth century. The labour-based parties' combined share of the vote, excluding the Progressive Party, ranged between 35 and 40 per cent, compared with the SDP's average share of 15 per cent until the formation of the Alliance.

The biggest milestone on Iceland's journey towards sovereignty and independence was achieved in 1918 when the Act of Union with Denmark was passed. Up to that point, Iceland was part of the Kingdom of Denmark. Through the Act of Union, Denmark officially relinquished its claim to Iceland and declared it a free and sovereign state in a personal union with the Danish King. Although this formally ended foreign control over Iceland, the last step remained, the founding of a republic completely independent from Denmark and with an Icelandic president as head of state. During the First World War, a new, class-based party system emerged in Iceland. All the parties avoided making electoral promises on the relationship with Denmark, and Iceland's first coalition government, formed in 1917, can be said to have settled the issue without party-political conflict. The resolution of the sovereignty issue was thus not a party-political issue for the new class-based parties.

The SDP and Icelandic social democrats in general made a substantial mark on the conclusion of the Act of Union and the sovereignty agreement with Denmark, however. The contributions made by representatives of the fledgling social democratic movement were even critical to reaching an agreement with the Danish negotiation team. The greatest of these contributions was made by the SDP member Ólafur Friðriksson, who travelled to Denmark to win support from members of the Social Democracy party. Different views on the founding of the Republic of Iceland during the Second World War were to prove problematic for the SDP, whose approach to how and when to found the republic was opposed by the majority of Icelanders and all the other parties. The debate was not about whether to found a republic, but how and when, with Denmark under German occupation. At the centre of the debate was the choice between a rapid separation between the two countries or a divorce along legal lines based on the 1918 Union agreement, with the SDP favouring the latter option. The Social Democrats in Iceland have a proud and colourful history reaching back to the SDP's founding over a century ago. They have had a profound influence on many aspects of Iceland's social model, shaping it in the form of classical social democracy in the face of fragmentation into two to three parties for over six decades.

A NASCENT LABOUR MOVEMENT AND PARTY

Iceland's Social Democratic Party (*Alþýðuflokkurinn*) was founded on 12 March 1916, together with the Icelandic Confederation of Labour. The

Confederation's role was both to develop trade unionism and spread social democracy, with the SDP initially serving as its political arm. The two remained under one rule until 1940, structured as both a trade union centre and a political party until that year.[1] This organisation's structure was modelled on British and Nordic trade union centres. Trade unions had existed in Iceland since the late nineteenth century, but had not gained much of a foothold. This changed dramatically with the advent of the Confederation and the SDP. Over the next two decades, the party and movement went from strength to strength to become a major shaping force for Icelandic society at large, as we shall see below.

Five Reykjavík trade unions prepared the Confederation's establishment. At its founding meeting, unions from the nearby town of Hafnarfjörður also joined the Confederation, with unions from other regions of Iceland gradually following suit. Icelandic workers' first attempts to found trade unions were the seamen's unions (*Bárufélögin*), which were the Confederation's precursor. The union *Báran* ("The Wave") was established in 1894 in reaction to the formation of a federation of fishing vessel operators in Faxaflói Bay. In 1907–1910, a Confederation of Icelandic Workers operated. This was the first comprehensive association of Icelandic labourers and in many respects the forerunner of the Confederation of Labour's political activities and thus a prelude to the founding of Iceland's first socialist or social democratic party, the SDP.

During the First World War, members of the Dagsbrún General and Transport Workers' Union sought cooperation with other unions to prepare the founding of a confederation of trade unions. A ten-strong preparatory committee worked on the confederation's founding in the winter of 1915–1916. The committee launched a candidacy for the Reykjavík Town Council in the January 1916 elections, with union representatives winning three out of the five seats up for election. The founding meeting of the Confederation of Labour and the SDP was held at the meeting house for the seamen's union Báran, and was attended by a total of 20 representatives of seven unions. Ottó N. Þorláksson was elected General Secretary of the Confederation, Ólafur Friðriksson was elected Deputy General Secretary and Jón Baldvinsson was elected Secretary. They served in their respective roles until the first regular congress of the Confederation later that same year, when Baldvinsson took over the reins as General Secretary and Jónas Jónsson took over as Secretary.

Just over two decades later, the SDP split for the first time when Héðinn Valdimarsson, one of its most influential figures, formed a splinter group that merged into a new party with the Communists. The split was to prove consequential and was the first of five such schisms. Such fragmentation would hamper the social democrats' influence and strength considerably in Iceland compared with the other Nordic countries, whose parties remained united and became a dominant force on the political scene.

The split and related conflict within the trade unions also led to a rupture between the party and the movement, culminating in the separation of the SDP from the Confederation of Labour. The SDP thus became an independent party 24 years after the party-cum-movement was established. "Following conflict within the trade union movement, the Confederation of Labour's constitution was amended in 1940 to separate the party from the Confederation. Thereupon, all the party's member organisations left the Confederation, which became solely a trade union centre, all of whose members had equal rights within it regardless of party affiliation. At the Confederation's next congress, held in 1942, all workers in Iceland were then united into the Confederation", reported daily newspaper *Morgunblaðið* on 12 March 1996 to mark the 80th anniversary of the party and movement.

THE "FEAR ALLIANCE"

In 1920, Jón Baldvinsson, one of the two leaders of the SDP and General Secretary of the Confederation of Labour, was elected to Iceland's parliament, the Althingi. For five years, he served as the only Member of Parliament for the SDP. He was the first to introduce many reform bills championed by the SDP in ensuing decades, which would mark a series of watersheds in the struggle for workers' rights. Among his achievements as the SDP's sole MP in his first term in office was legislation on mandatory rest periods for seamen, one of the party's key policies in its first years. The Progressive Party was formed in the same year as the SDP. One of the initiators of the foundation of both parties was Jónas Jónsson from Hrifla, later MP and minister, who was to become one of the most controversial and influential Icelandic politicians of the twentieth century. The idea was for the general rural populace to support the Progressive Party, and that of the urban coastal areas to support the SDP; together these two parties should be able to form a powerful bloc dominating the Icelandic political scene.

In two elections in the 1920s, the two parties ran in an informal electoral alliance, called the "Fear Alliance", whereby they committed generally not to run against each other in individual constituencies. The parties were later to diverge in markedly different directions, not least owing to their different views on rural depopulation and migration to coastal towns. The Progressive Party moved to the political centre and later to the right of the political spectrum, becoming increasingly opposed to Iceland's membership of the European single market, which the SDP supported and fought for. The July 1927 parliamentary elections marked a milestone in the SDP's history when it gained four new MPs in addition to Jón Baldvinsson, the party's nationally elected leader. In Reykjavík, the party won nearly 35 per cent of the vote and two of the constituency's four seats in parliament. This strong showing was largely due to the SDP's influence within the trade unions, which had become widespread at this time. For instance, prominent SDP members wielded substantial control within the Dagsbrún General and Transport Workers' Union, the Reykjavík Seamen's Union and the Framsókn Working Women's Union.

The SDP's biggest victories in this historic election were won in the town of Ísafjörður in the West Fjords, where the party gained 59 per cent of the vote, and in Iceland's "northern capital", Akureyri, where it won 54 per cent. The SDP would also hold a clear majority in Hafnarfjörður and Norðfjörður, which together with Ísafjörður were called the "red towns" because of the party's strong base there. Following the 1927 election, the SDP shielded the Progressive Party's position as the governing party by not opposing it in parliament in return for the advancement of key SDP policies. These included amending the poverty relief legislation, extending the voting franchise, amending the law on mandatory rest periods for trawlermen to ensure eight hours of rest per 24-hour period, establishing state-owned enterprises in various sectors and legislation on workers' dwellings.

A SOVEREIGN ICELAND

Iceland's parliament, the Althingi, was first convened in 930 AD, just over a century after the country's settlement began. In its first few centuries, Iceland was a republic ruled and governed by chieftains. In 1262, however, it became part of Norway after a bloody civil war in Iceland, which ended in the country submitting to the authority of the Norwegian King, thereby losing its sovereignty. This was followed by nearly seven centuries under foreign rule. The biggest milestone in Iceland's return to sovereignty and independence was passed in 1918 in the form of a new Act of Union with Denmark, up to which point Iceland had been part of the Kingdom of Denmark. The process of repatriating sovereignty had begun in earnest in the early nineteenth century, when Jón Sigurðsson and the *Fjölnir* group of Icelandic intellectuals launched an active struggle to regain the country's independence and reinstate the Althingi. The Althingi was restored in 1843, followed by home rule in 1904, with the country gaining an Icelandic minister resident in Reykjavík.

The struggle for independence gained increasing momentum from its beginnings in the nineteenth century until the early twentieth century, when home rule and, subsequently, recognition of Iceland's sovereignty were achieved on the back of growing economic prosperity and the new self-confidence that this produced. By agreeing to the 1918 Act of Union, Denmark officially relinquished its claim to Iceland, declaring it a free and sovereign state in a personal union with the Danish King. This formally ended foreign control over Iceland, but the last step remained: the founding of a republic completely independent of Denmark and with an Icelandic president as head of state. Sovereignty came at the end of the First World War. The war affected relations between Iceland and Denmark in a number of unforeseen ways, including foreign affairs, as the United Kingdom usually chose to interact with the Icelandic government directly, thereby bypassing the Danish government. Having declared neutrality in the war, Denmark was in an awkward position vis-à-vis the warring parties.

This chain of events brought Iceland increased control over its foreign affairs, which could scarcely be withdrawn at the end of the war. In effect, the regaining of formal sovereignty was thus partly a confirmation of a fait accompli. The founding of a republic, the obvious form of government for newly independent states, was bound to follow. The 1918 sovereignty agreement with Denmark was the culminating moment in Iceland's struggle for independence. After a defined period, the country would be entitled to declare full independence. Iceland had been growing away from and loosening its ties to the Danish state in the course of the independence campaign and as a result of economic progress and various other factors, in addition to the circumstances brought by the war. The industrial revolution had finally reached Iceland at the turn of the twentieth century and brought Icelanders the knowledge and technology needed to engage in modern economic activities at sea and on land, thereby transforming the country's economic and social make-up.

Although sovereignty meant a substantial constitutional change for Iceland, in fact its independence had been increasing in practical terms since 1904 with growing domestic parliamentary control and ministerial power. The events leading up the 1918 Act of Union and its conclusion occurred in piecemeal steps towards independence, each of which was negotiated with Denmark. Home rule had brought Iceland real control over its own affairs, with only limited Danish interference in its governance thereafter. Nevertheless, the big leap to formal sovereignty remained to be taken as the stepping stone to an independent republic.[2]

During the First World War, a new, class-based party system emerged in Iceland. A shared trait of all political parties at that time was avoidance of making electoral promises concerning the relationship with Denmark, an issue that can be said to have been settled without party-political conflict by Iceland's first coalition government, formed in 1917. Over the preceding decades, the relationship with Denmark had been the subject of fierce debate in Iceland, dividing people into factions. Now, however, new parties were being formed around class-based politics: the interests and rights of workers, on one hand, and those of the ruling class, on the other.

NEGOTIATING THE UNION WITH DENMARK

The SDP and other social democrats in Iceland made a substantial mark on the sovereignty negotiations with Denmark and the conclusion of the Act of Union at the end of the First World War. The contributions made by representatives of the fledgling social democratic movement were critical to reaching an agreement with the Danish negotiation team. The greatest of these contributions was made by the SDP member Ólafur Friðriksson, who travelled to Denmark to win support from members of the Social Democracy party there. Prime Minister Jón Magnússon is said to have beseeched the SDP leader Jón Baldvinsson that an SDP representative travel to Copenhagen in a bid to convince members of the Danish sister party to conclude an agreement on the Union issue between the two countries. The Danish Social Democrats were deemed to be resistant to the Icelandic entreaties, but Friðriksson had been working with the SDP's Danish counterparts for a number of years, so was chosen for the trip.[3]

Two days after arriving in Denmark, he met Thorvald Stauning, leader of the Social Democrats. Stauning initially refused outright to support the Icelandic effort. Several days of negotiations with other influential members of the Danish party ensued, which finally led to their approval of Friðriksson's request and the formation of a negotiating committee. It is obvious from the SDP's written sources, reports and minutes of meetings that its relations with the Danish Social Democrats were extensive from the outset. The SDP sought support from and modelled itself on its Danish counterpart, and clearly the SDP's efforts were instrumental in reaching the 1918 sovereignty agreement.[4] Many Nordic social democrats took the view that the Nordic countries should be united into a single state rather than split up. This view sprang from the internationalism that was prevalent in social democratic thinking, and also had its adherents among many active members of the newly formed Icelandic party.

SOCIAL DEMOCRATS AND ICELAND'S SOCIAL MODEL

In the decades following the repatriation of sovereignty, social democrats, through the SDP and the trade union movement, played a decisive role in developing a modern society in Iceland, their influence being discernible in most aspects of Iceland's social model. In an interview marking the SDP's 75-year anniversary in the social-democratic newspaper *Alþýðublaðið*, one of most influential leaders in the party's history, Dr Gylfi Þ. Gíslason, said: "Without the Social Democratic Party, Icelandic society would not be what it is today. Iceland is a modern, industrialised country whose living standards are among the highest in the world, a society shaped by welfare policies. This is what the Social Democratic Party has been working for."[5]

Ever since the SDP's inception, the party, and later the Social Democratic Alliance, has had a profound and lasting influence on society that far exceeds its size and share of the vote. Its frequent splits and the fragmentation of the Left have enabled the conservatives and rightists of the Independence Party to take centre stage in the political arena, but always in coalition with parties on the Left. Social democrats have managed to punch above their weight through coalition governments of various complexions and through trade unionism. Since their earliest days, the SDP and the Confederation of Labour have campaigned hard for various human rights and improvements in wages and working conditions. The Workers' Dwellings Act is hailed as a major legislative milestone of the twentieth century. Passed in 1929 after being introduced by the SDP MP and Dagsbrún Union chairman Héðinn Valdimarsson, the Act marked a sea change in the history of public housing in Reykjavík. The first workers' dwellings were constructed in the wake of the law's passing, to be followed by many more over the next few decades, ensuring housing access and security for working people at generally affordable prices.

The SDP's first taste of government came in 1934 in a coalition formed with the Progressive Party. Called the "Government of the Working Classes", it achieved many important goals, such as the enactment of the Social Security Act and the repeal of the notorious poor laws. The coalition partners initially worked well together, delivering major legislative reforms that benefitted the general populace in many ways. Their policies differed mainly over aspects of nationalisation and public sector activities, with the Progressive Party particularly opposed to the idea of municipal and state-operated trawlers, instead preferring to strengthen cooperative societies' operation of small fishing vessels.

The Social Security Act was one of the SDP's key policies in its first few years of existence. Passed by the Althingi on 1 April 1936, it delivered a range of breakthroughs for working people's legal rights and was a major landmark on the road to a modern welfare society in Iceland, which was lagging far behind its Nordic neighbours in this area. At the heart of this legislation – one of the most momentous passed in the years after regaining sovereignty – were three strands: accident insurance, old-age and disability insurance and unemployment insurance. Over the following decades, the Social Security Act underwent various improving amendments. It remains without doubt one of the SDP's biggest political achievements and transformed the general public's legal rights in Iceland. To ensure that all social security affairs were under a single governing body, the Social Security Administration was established in the wake of the legislation. SDP members wielded considerable control within the Administration, all of whose Directors General came from the party's ranks until 2007.

Besides being the authors and architects of social insurance schemes and services, the SDP has been instrumental in developing Iceland's education system. During his tenure as Minister of Education, Gylfi Þ. Gíslason can be said to have revolutionised the education system from the compulsory to the tertiary level. The first Act on Financial Support for Music Schools, which was passed during his tenure, transfigured the situation for music education, including access to it. To ensure equal access to education for all sections of society, the Icelandic Student Loan Fund was established in 1961, with legislation on the Fund spearheaded by Gíslason and the SDP as partners in the "Viðey government". The number of upper-secondary schools was increased significantly, as was the number of available programmes of study within the University of Iceland. The University's scientific activities were also strengthened greatly. Gíslason later wrote: "A society must be based not only on increasing prosperity in parallel with rising income security ... It must also aim for a more civilised way of life. This is why culture must be a cornerstone of a good and just society."

SPLITS, CONFLICTS AND FOREIGN MODELS OF SOCIAL DEMOCRACY

Fragmentation and conflict within the SDP began as early as the late 1930s and were to have a substantial impact on the party's development and prospects. In the 1937 Althingi elections, the party lost a substantial number of votes to the Communist Party, which had been gaining ground since its founding in 1930. This dealt a shock to the SDP and was the first sign of the fractured political landscape on the Left that was to persist throughout the century. A party positioning itself left of the SDP was now a fact of life, and to this day these parties, or their successors, have been vying for the left-of-centre vote, which has averaged around 40 per cent of all votes cast.

This situation was further exacerbated by the SDP's first split in 1938, when Héðinn Valdimarsson, one of its most prominent figures and chairman of the Dagsbrún Union, joined the communists to form the People's Unity Party – Socialist Party. Valdimarsson was not to remain long in the

Socialist Party, as he was soon drawn into a fierce debate with the communists on what position to adopt on the Soviet Union. When the Winter War began in 1939 with a Soviet invasion of Finland, Valdimarsson resigned from the party. The 1938 split of the SDP dealt a blow to unity around a single labour party in Iceland. Now two parties were pinning their colours to the labour movement's mast, which led to the Independence Party's dominance of Icelandic politics. This shifted the emphasis away from welfare and equality compared with the other Nordic countries, as the influence of social democrats and socialists was hampered by fragmentation and discord.

The SDP and the Confederation of Labour based themselves on the Nordic model and the Labour Party in the United Kingdom, whose working-class population was united in one party functioning as the political arm of the labour movement. But the rise of the Communists in Iceland came as a surprise, and they gained a far stronger foothold in Iceland than in the other Nordic countries as a result of the SDP's fragmentation.

The Communists modelled themselves on the Comintern and the Soviet Communist Party. These international relations, and the SDP's with its Nordic counterparts, were to be a decisive factor in obstructing the reunification of the labour movement parties. The Russian Revolution and Lenin's political evangelism also greatly aided the rise of the Communists in Iceland and poured petrol on the fires burning within the labour movement and the left wing of the SDP. The coming conflict between the Social Democrats and the Communists was counterproductive for Icelandic working people, whose party-political representation remained fractured for the rest of the twentieth century.

Iceland's NATO membership further aggravated the fragmentation and conflict on the left of the political spectrum. This bone of fierce contention further deepened the rift between the parties, which was nearly unbridgeable for decades to come. The SDP supported Iceland's NATO membership from the outset, whereas the Communists and later Socialists were bitterly opposed. NATO membership, attitudes to the United States' Iceland Defence Force at Keflavík Airport and the controversy around the US military presence became a symbolic expression of the difference between the two labour-based parties well into the 1970s, making a merger or an electoral alliance between them nigh-on unthinkable.

BIRTH OF THE REPUBLIC AND DIVORCE FROM DENMARK

Different views on the founding of the Republic of Iceland proved a knotty issue for the SDP, whose approach to how and when to found the Republic was opposed by the majority of the populace and all the other parties. The debate was not about whether, but how and when to found a Republic, given that Denmark was under German occupation. When Denmark was occupied by German forces in April 1940, Iceland took its foreign affairs into its own hands, effectively dissolving the Union with Denmark. Because occupied Denmark was unable to meet its obligations, a movement arose in Iceland for unilateral repeal of the Act of Union and for the founding of a Republic. Others were in favour of complying with the termination provisions of the 1918 Act of Union, under which the Act could be repealed in 1943. The choice between a speedy separation from Denmark or one abiding by the Act's provisions polarised Icelandic opinion in the run-up to the Republic's establishment.

The Socialists were the most ardent supporters of a speedy separation, and their view was shared by the majority of Independence Party and Progressive Party members. This was not the case for the SDP, however, whose members generally favoured a separation along the lines prescribed by the Union Act. That meant waiting to resolve the matter only when Denmark was free from Nazi occupation, it being improper to dissolve the Union in such grave circumstances. Probably, their strong ties with the Danish Social Democrats affected their outlook on the Union and how best to found a Republic, after gaining sovereignty just over two decades earlier. Britain, whose forces occupied Iceland in May 1940, opposed a speedy divorce, which was the most important factor in preventing such an outcome.

The SDP was a partner in the wartime national unity government, which did not include the Socialists. A draft parliamentary resolution put forward by the government was passed by the Althingi, which thereby declared the full right to dissolve the Union with Denmark and found a republic. No time limits were specified, except that the republic was to be established no later than at the end of the war. The SDP and its MPs supported the resolution following intense debate and upheaval within the party.

Still, many found it dishonourable to dissolve the Union and found a Republic during Denmark's German occupation. This view produced a movement of "Legal Separatists", who debated fiercely with the opposite camp, called the "Quick Separatists". The view that Iceland should bide its time until Denmark was free from the yoke of military occupation so that Iceland could negotiate the matter as a free country was widely accepted within the SDP. One of the Legal Separatists' main leaders was Hannibal Valdimarsson, editor of *Skutull* in the town of Ísafjörður in the Western Fjords and later an SDP MP and leader. Valdimarsson was the most ardent advocate of a "legal separation", his message being that a republic should indeed be constituted, "but neither in a hasty nor disrespectful manner towards our King, who is now a prisoner".

At a meeting of the SDP's Executive Committee in June 1943, the Legal Separatists' views won the day and became the party's formal position. It was agreed that the Althingi should prepare the founding of a republic and a new constitution should take effect when the war ended. The republic's founding should be suspended until the Union member countries could speak to each other as free nations, instead of Iceland unilaterally dissolving the Union during military occupation. In contrast, the Socialists, Independence Party and Progressive Party formed an alliance for the Republic to be established on 17 June 1944. Many in the SDP's ranks sought a compromise by various means, but in vain. The party was swimming against the tide, with the overwhelming majority of Icelanders in support of founding the republic at the ancient parliamentary site of Þingvellir on 17 June 1944, which is what happened.

THE SDP'S GOLDEN AGE

The party's second decade in existence (1926–1936) is often called its "Golden Age". The majority of workers were by now organised in the trade union centre. The SDP's base was growing and the party joined its first government, which made several crucial changes, as outlined above. The overall movement had gained considerable strength and was substantially improving the rights of workers and trade union members.[6] Already at this time, there was debate about a possible alliance of the SDP and the Communists, later Socialists. This debate was not settled, it could be said, until 60 years later when the Social Democratic Alliance first ran as an electoral bloc of the SDP, the People's Alliance, the Women's List and the "National Awakening". In four subsequent parliamentary elections, the Social Democratic Alliance won a 27–30 per cent share of the vote, by far the highest countrywide share of the poll ever achieved by any left-wing party in Iceland.[7] Already in its first elections, the Alliance recovered the Left's former polling strength in many municipalities, winning a clear majority in the town of Hafnarfjörður and a strong position in most of the largest municipalities, including the capital, Reykjavík, where it has held a majority more or less since 1994.

In the decades following the Republic's founding in 1944, Iceland's politics settled into a four-party system, with all four main parties maintaining a fairly stable share of the vote. The SDP suffered the consequences of its splits and the rise of the Socialists, but nonetheless preserved a stable vote share, which was sufficient take it into various coalition governments.[8] The "Innovation government" of 1944–1947, a coalition with the Independence Party and the Socialist Party – the party's arch-opponents on its right and left – took many initiatives and invested in social infrastructure after the economic boom of the war years. This included the purchase of a whole fleet of trawlers and preparations for the construction of hydroelectric power stations.

When this coalition came to an end, the country's first SDP-led government was formed, with the party's leader, Stefán Jóhann Stefánsson, serving as its first and only prime minister until Emil Jónsson held the same role in a minority government for just under a year in 1958–1959. The biggest task of Stefánsson's government – dubbed "Stefanía" – was to negotiate Iceland's membership of the fledgling NATO alliance. This issue, and the coalition partnership with the centrist Progressive Party and conservative Independence Party, became a source of discord within the SDP. Young MPs on its left flank criticised the party leadership for lurching too far rightwards. After a tough struggle, the left wing of the party seized the opportunity at the 1952 party conference and elected their torchbearer, Hannibal Valdimarsson, as leader of the party, supplanting Stefánsson. This turn of events led to on-going intra-party conflict, which eventually resulted in Valdimarsson leaving the party, having been ousted as leader after two years at the helm. This split the SDP for the second time.

The year 1956 saw the formation of Iceland's first "Left government", a coalition of the Progressive Party, the SDP and the People's Alliance, the latter being an electoral bloc between the Socialist Party and Valdimarsson's breakaway from the SDP. This government achieved many milestones. One of these was to expand the limits of Iceland's territorial waters to 12 nautical miles, much to the dismay of the United Kingdom, which immediately sent warships to the Icelandic waters to protect British trawlers violating the new fishing limit. The First Cod War had broken out. Following disagreement on economic issues, the Left Government departed from power after two years and was replaced by an SDP-led minority government under the prime ministership of party leader Emil Jónsson. This government, in cooperation with the People's Alliance and the Independence Party, reached an agreement on constituency reform to make each vote of more equal value. The existing system had given very disproportionate weight to rural votes, thus favouring the Progressive Party, whereas the SDP was allocated far fewer seats than its share of the vote would warrant. After the constituency reform, with counties and boroughs merging into eight constituencies, a parliamentary election was held in 1959.

Thus, from the mid-1920s onwards, it befell the SDP to cooperate with all the other parties under various coalition guises. This enabled the SDP to drive its policies forward far beyond its share of the vote, which contracted after the 1938 and 1954 splits. Social democrats exercised a major and fairly continuous influence in shaping Icelandic society during the Republic's first few decades. From Jón Baldvinsson's introduction of the bill on mandatory rest periods for seamen to the formation of the Viðey government in 1959, the SDP brought most, if not all, of its major policies to fruition in one form or another, although compromises were obviously necessary in Iceland's coalition politics.

In 1959, the party embarked on its longest continuous spell in power, which enabled it to have a decisive influence on the Republic's development. This time it formed a two-party coalition with the Independence Party in the "Reconstruction government" (1959–1971), which achieved several landmark accomplishments for Icelandic society. The SDP used this opportunity to exert a strong and lasting influence, not least on education policy and freedom of trade, domestically and internationally.

A CENTURY OF SOCIAL DEMOCRACY

Iceland's social democrats have a proud history reaching back to the SDP's establishment over a century ago. Their influence has been varied and profound, and it is safe to say that they have shaped many aspects of Icelandic society in the spirit of classical social democracy. Undeniably, frequent splits and conflict within the social democratic and socialist parties have impeded their power and influence. Nonetheless, the values of social democracy have played a key role in moulding Iceland's social model, mainly in the image of a Nordic-type welfare society.

This is illustrated by the several examples given above, ranging from the legislation on fishing vessels' working hours, social insurance and workers' dwellings to the breakthroughs in education and cultural affairs achieved during the SDP's time in office. Right from the party's inception, it has championed freedom of trade within and beyond Iceland's borders and fought for Iceland's membership of the EU single market and NATO.

The future will tell whether Iceland's social democrats will be able to rally their combined forces again and strengthen the party formed around their 1999 unification. The unforeseen events of the 2007–2008 international financial crisis and the deep mistrust of politics that followed dealt a substantial blow to social democrats' standing in Iceland, but there are many hopeful signs that they are regaining considerable confidence and support.

SUMMARY

Social democrats in Iceland founded the Social Democratic Party (SDP) and the Icelandic Confederation of Labour in 1916, both of which remained under one rule for four decades. Following the SDP's founding, significant strides were made in spreading and increasing the influence of social democracy and trade unionism.

Frequent splits and conflict within the SDP would later hamper its efforts to retain political power, but it still exerted a major influence in shaping Icelandic society, including the enactment of legislation on fishing vessels' working hours, social security and workers' dwellings in the party's earliest years and during the first years after Iceland regained sovereignty. The SDP formed various coalitions with other parties, thereby implementing a range of social democratic policies.

The party split five times, first of all in 1938 when one of its most prominent members joined the Communists. From that time onwards, there was always a powerful party to the left of the SDP, fragmenting the left wing of Icelandic politics until the parties reunited as the Social Democratic Alliance at the end of the twentieth century. The labour-based parties' combined share of the vote, excluding the Progressive Party, ranged between 35 and 40 per cent, compared with the SDP's average share of 15 per cent until the formation of the Alliance.

The biggest milestone on Iceland's journey towards sovereignty and independence was achieved in 1918 when the Act of Union with Denmark was passed. Up to that point, Iceland had been part of the Kingdom of Denmark. Through the Act of Union, Denmark officially relinquished its claim to Iceland and declared it a free and sovereign state in a personal union with the Danish king. Although this formally ended foreign control over Iceland, the last step remained, namely the founding of a republic completely independent of Denmark and with an Icelandic president as head of state.

During the First World War, a new, class-based party system emerged in Iceland. All the parties avoided making electoral promises on the relationship with Denmark, and Iceland's first coalition government, formed in 1917, can be said to have settled the issue without party-political conflict. The resolution of the sovereignty issue was thus not a party-political issue for the new class-based parties.

The SDP and Icelandic social democrats in general had a substantial influence on the conclusion of the Act of Union and the sovereignty agreement with Denmark, however. The contributions made by representatives of the fledgling social democratic movement were even critical to reaching an agreement with the Danish negotiation team. The greatest of these contributions was made by the SDP member Ólafur Friðriksson, who travelled to Denmark to win support from members of the Social Democracy party.

Different views on the founding of the Republic of Iceland during the Second World War were to prove problematic for the SDP, whose approach to how and when to found the republic was opposed by the majority of Icelanders and all the other parties. The debate was not about whether to found a republic, but how and when, with Denmark under German occupation. At the centre of the debate was the choice between a rapid separation between the two countries or a divorce along legal lines based on the 1918 Union agreement, with the SDP favouring the latter option.

The Social Democrats in Iceland have a proud and colourful history reaching back to the SDP's founding over a century ago. They have had a profound influence on many aspects of Iceland's social model, shaping it in the form of classical social democracy despite becoming fragmented into two to three parties for over six decades.

1 Guðjón Friðriksson, Úr fjötrum, 31.
2 Helgi Skúli Kjartansson, Vangaveltur um fullveldi Íslands, 104.
3 Bergsteinn Jónsson. Alþýðuflokkurinn og íslenzkir jafnaðarmenn gagnvart Sambandslagasamningunum árið 1918, 183–86.
4 Bergsteinn Jónsson, 187.
5 Gylfi Þ. Gíslason, Alþýðublaðið.
6 Helgi Skúli Kjartansson, Alþýðuflokkurinn 75 ára, 7.
7 Kosningasaga.wordpress.com
8 Helgi Skúli Kjartansson, 8.

References

Bjarnason, Ágúst H. (1929): Fullveldisins minnzt: 1. des. 1928, *Vaka*.

Bergsteinn Jónsson (1976): Alþýðuflokkurinn og íslenzkir jafnaðarmenn gagnvart Sambandslagasamningunum árið 1918, *Saga*, 1 (January).

Jónsson frá Vogi, Bjarni (1923): Ísland og fullveldi þess, *Andvari*.

Friðriksson, Guðjón (2016): *Úr fjötrum: saga Alþýðuflokksins*. Forlagið.

Gíslason, Gylfi Þ. (1991): Alþýðuflokkurinn 75 ára, supplement to *Alþýðublaðið*, 12 March 1991.

Gíslason, Gylfi Þ. (1993): *Viðreisnarárin*. Almenna bókafélagið.

Skúli Kjartansson, Helgi (1991): Alþýðuflokkurinn 75 ára, supplement to *Alþýðublaðið*, 12 March 1991. *Alþýðublaðið* 1991.

Skúli Kjartansson, Helgi (1991): Vangaveltur um fullveldi Íslands, *Andvari*.

Valdimarsson, Hannibal (1944): Hversvegna ég greiði atkvæði með sambandsslitum en á móti stjórnarskránni, *Skutull*, 12 May.

Halldórsson, Jón Ormur (1985): *Löglegt en siðlaust: stjórnmálasaga Vilmundar Gylfasonar*. Bókhlaðan.

Websites

Kosningasaga.wordpress.com

Althingi.is

Stjornarradid.is

AUTHORS

PÉTER CSUNDERLINK

A historian, he received his PhD in 2016. In 2017 he started work at the Social and Economic History Department of Eötvös Loránd University (ELTE) in Budapest. He lectures on the history of Austro-Hungarian Monarchy, the intellectual life of the "fin de siècle" and historiography. He is interested in the history of left-wing radical movements, the Hungarian Soviet Republic, the theory of history and the social history of the nineteenth and twentieth centuries in general.

YAROSLAV HRYTSAK

Doctor of Historical Sciences and professor at the Ukrainian Catholic University in Lviv. He gained his PhD (habilitation) in 1987 at the University of Lviv and a PhD in history at the Institute of Archeography, Ukrainian Academy of Sciences in 1996. He has been the director of the Institute for Historical Research, Ivan Franko National University of Lviv since 1992 and an associate professor and chair of the history of Slavic countries at the Department of History, Lviv State University since 1994. His research interests include: history of Austrian Galicia, modern history of Ukraine, nationalism in Eastern Europe and modern eastern European historiography.

IVARS ĪJABS

Latvian political scientist and commentator, associate professor at the University of Latvia. His research interests include the history of political ideas and nationalism, as well as interethnic relations in central and eastern Europe. He is the author of several books on political theory and Latvian politics, as well as many scholarly articles. He studied philosophy and political science in Latvia, Germany and Iceland. He is one of the best known political and cultural commentators in Latvia.

TÕNU INTS

Studied history at the University of Tartu 1987–1990. Since 2000 he has been head of the Johannes Mihkelson Centre in Tartu. In 1990 he was one of the founders of the Social Democratic Party of Estonia (SDE) and is still a member of the party executive. In 2005–2017 he was a member and chair of the Social Democratic group in Tartu city council. He has also researched and published on the history of the SDE.

DR TVRTKO JAKOVINA

Professor of twentieth-century world history, Department of History, Faculty of Humanities and Social Sciences, University of Zagreb.

LEVAN LORTKIPANIDZE

Political scientist, researching political parties. PhD student in political science at Ivane Javakhishvili Tbilisi State University (TSU). Invited lecturer at TSU and the Georgian-American University (GAU) in the sociology of political parties. Member of several Georgian social democratic and left-wing civil society groups.

MIKKO MAJANDER

Adjunct professor of political history at the University of Helsinki and research fellow at the Helsinki-based think tank Magma. He specialises in the history of labour movements and Cold War history, as well as Finnish politics and international relations.

GINTARAS MITRULEVIČIUS

Historian and lecturer in history and political science. He has done research on the history of left-wing ideologies and left movements in Lithuania and Europe. He has written a monograph on the ideological-political development of Lithuanian social democracy 1914–1919 and is the author of numerous other scholarly and popular publications.

TOBIAS MÖRSCHEL

Born 1970, Dr. Phil. Head of the Friedrich-Ebert-Stiftung bureau in the Baltic states (2016–2019), with offices in Estonia, Latvia and Lithuania. Since spring 2019 Director of FES Italy. Many publications on the theory and practice of (social) democracy.

ZUZANA POLÁČKOV

Dr Zuzana Poláčková, CSc, Historical Institute of the Slovak Academy of Sciences, Department of Contemporary History. Her research interests include the development of minority and human rights in the second half of the twentieth century.

MARTIN POLÁŠEK

PhD. Political scientist and historian, research fellow at the Charles University in Prague, Faculty of Arts. He is interested in issues of party politics, the social democratic movement and policy-making processes. He has been working in public administration since 2014.

ANA RAJKOVIĆ

Doctoral candidate, Programme in Modern and Contemporary Croatian History, Faculty of Humanities and Social Sciences, University of Zagreb.

OLIVER RATHKOLB

Dr. jur. (1978) Dr. phil. (1982), Professor of Contemporary History at the University of Vienna. Since 2016 director of the Institute of Contemporary History, managing editor of the journal *Zeitgeschichte* (Contemporary History), as well as board member of the Austrian Society of Contemporary History. His main areas of research include European history in the twentieth century, Austrian and European contemporary history and current events in the area of political history and the history of the Austrian republic in the European context, historical research on dictatorships and transformation, and the history of international relations, the history of perceptions of the Nazis, cultural and media history, economic history (industry and banking), national socialism and history of law.

KRISTJAN SAHAROV

Studied modern history at the University of Tartu. His research interests include the stance of the Estonian Socialist Revolutionary Party on the question of state independence 1914–1918, as well as the attitude of the foreign wing of the Estonian Socialist Party towards the Soviet Union after the Second World War. Saharov is currently working as Collections Manager at the Vabamu Museum of Occupations and Freedom in Tallinn.

ANATOL SIDAREVIČ

Born in 1948. He graduated from the Philosophy Faculty of the Belarusian State University (Minsk). He has taught in secondary and higher education institutions, as well as working in the media. He studies the history of the Belarusian national movement, as well as Anton Luckevič's biography and activities. He has prepared three volumes of Anton Luckevič's works for publication and a book of memoirs about Ivan Luckevič. One of the founders of the Belarusian Social Democratic Party (Hramada) and one of the authors of its manifestos and policies.

BJÖRGVIN G. SIGURÐSSON

Former member of parliament for the Social Democratic Alliance and former minister of trade and commerce. He has a degree in history and philosophy and a Master's degree in political philosophy. He is now working as a freelance writer and as an editor of a regional newspaper.

MICHAŁ SYSKA

Director of the Ferdinand Lassalle Centre of Social Thought (Wroclaw, Poland). Lawyer, graduate of the University of Wrocław and carried out postgraduate studies at the Polish Academy of Sciences. Working on a PhD in political science. Author of scholarly articles on right-wing populism, social democracy and the radical left. Co-author and editor of books devoted to social policy, crisis of democracy and historical politics of the left.